ENCYCLOPEDIA
of Classic
Quilt Patterns

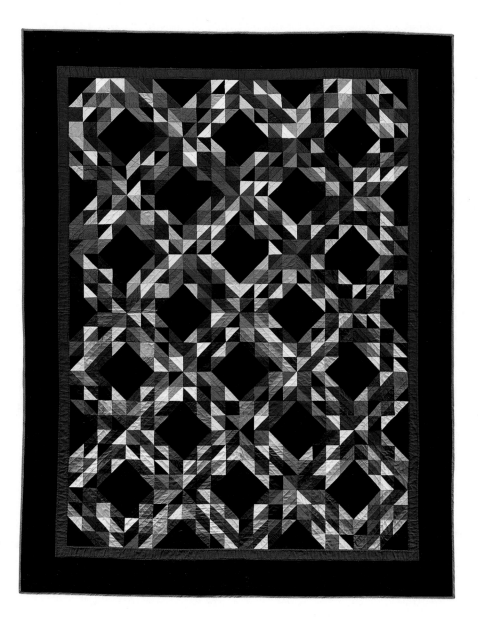

Encyclopedia of Classic Quilt Patterns

©2001 by Oxmoor House, Inc.
Book Division of Southern Progress Corporation
P.O. Box 2463, Birmingham, Alabama 35201

Published by Oxmoor House, Inc., and Leisure Arts, Inc.

Library of Congress Control Number: 2001-135242
ISBN: 0-8487-2474-7
Printed in the United States of America
Fifth Printing 2002

Editor-in-Chief: Nancy Fitzpatrick Wyatt
Senior Crafts Editor: Susan Ramey Cleveland
Senior Editor, Copy and Homes: Olivia Kindig Wells
Art Director: Cynthia R. Cooper

Encyclopedia of Classic Quilt Patterns

Editor: Patricia Wilens
Contributing Copy Editor: Susan S. Cheatham
Editorial Assistant: Jane Lorberau Gentry
Designer/Illustrator: Kelly Davis
Senior Photographer: John O'Hagan
Photo Stylist: Katie Stoddard
Director, Production and Distribution: Phillip Lee
Books Production Manager: Theresa L. Beste
Production Assistant: Faye Porter Bonner

To order additional publications, call 800-633-4910.

For more books to enrich your life, visit
oxmoorhouse.com

Introduction

Americans didn't invent patchwork and quilting, which are nearly as old as history. But when the Pilgrims came to the New World, **patchwork found a place to flower.**

Quiltmaking is now considered a particularly American craft, though societies from ancient Egypt to Renaissance Italy have left their mark. And quilts are now being made all over the world. But it was in early America that the same spirit that forged a new nation latched onto the *idea* of patchwork and added a touch of Yankee **ingenuity and independence**. The result is a lexicon of new and original patterns for the ages.

Since those first settlers, American women have made quilts in colonial villages, covered wagons, prairie towns, and bustling cities. They've shared patterns and improvised their own until known and published patterns number in the thousands.

Of course, there are **perennial favorites** among them. We like to think of them as classics—designs that are familiar, friendly, and yet always open to interesting new interpretations.

This book is an A-to-Z sampler of 101 classic quilts for you to make. If you're new to quilting, the Workshop (page 8) will introduce you to the **basic techniques** you need. If you're an experienced quiltmaker, jump right in—you'll find a assortment of styles and degrees of difficulty.

Our pioneer forebears would envy today's quilter, for we are making quilts at a time of unparalleled fabrics, tools, and equipment. The quality and quantity of cotton fabrics for quiltmaking are superb, as are many of the "smart" new sewing machines. And there's no shortage of nifty gadgets for every step of the process. All the better to **make more quilts**—for love, for pleasure, for comfort, and a continuing **tradition** of classic quilts.

Table of Contents

Table of Contents (continued)

Quiltmaker's Workshop

Selecting Fabrics

The best fabric for quilts is 100% cotton. Yardage requirements in this book are based on 44"-wide fabric and allow for shrinkage. All fabrics, including backing, should be machine-washed, dried, and pressed before cutting. Use warm water and detergent but do not use fabric softener.

NECESSARY NOTIONS
- Scissors
- Rotary cutter and mat
- Acrylic rulers
- Template plastic, pencils
- Sewing needles, sewing thread
- Sewing machine
- Seam ripper
- Pins
- Iron and ironing board
- Quilting needles
- Thimble
- Hand-quilting thread
- Machine-quilting thread (optional)

Using Templates

A template is a duplication of a printed pattern, made from a sturdy material, which is traced onto fabric. Regular shapes, such as squares and triangles, can be marked directly on fabric with a ruler, or cut without a template at all (see Rotary Cutting). But you need templates for other shapes. Some quiltmakers use templates for all shapes.

Trace patterns directly onto template plastic. When a large pattern is given in two pieces, make one template for the complete piece.

Cut out the template on the drawn line. If desired, punch out corner dots with a ⅛" diameter hole punch (**Diagram 1**).

Mark each template with its letter and the fabric grain line. Verify the template's accuracy by placing it over the printed

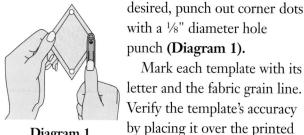

Diagram 1

pattern. A template must be traced, marked, and cut accurately—any discrepancy, however small, is multiplied many times as the quilt is assembled. Another way to check the accuracy of templates is to make a test block before cutting more pieces.

Tracing Templates on Fabric

For hand piecing, templates are cut to the finished size of the piece so seam lines can be marked on the fabric. Place the template *facedown* on the *wrong* side of the fabric, aligning the template grain line with the grain of the fabric. Hold the template firmly and trace around it. Repeat as needed, leaving ½" between tracings (**Diagram 2**).

For machine piecing, templates include seam allowances, so you can mark the fabric using common lines for efficient cutting (**Diagram 3**). Mark corners on fabric through holes in the template.

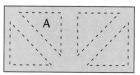

Diagram 2

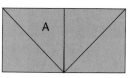

Diagram 3

For hand or machine piecing, use **window templates** to enhance accuracy by drawing and cutting out both cutting and sewing lines. A drawn seam line is useful for sewing set-in seams, when pivoting at a precise point is critical. Used on the right side of the fabric, window templates help you cut specific motifs with accuracy (**Diagram 4**).

For hand appliqué, make templates the finished size of the appliqué piece. Place templates *faceup* on the *right* side of the fabric. Position tracings at least ½" apart (**Diagram 5**). Add a ¼" seam allowance around pieces when cutting.

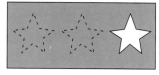

Diagram 5

Cutting

Woven threads form the fabric's grain. Lengthwise grain, parallel to the selvages, has the least stretch; crosswise grain has a little more give. Long strips, such as borders, should be cut lengthwise whenever possible; also cut them first to ensure that you have the necessary length. Most other pieces can be cut aligned with either grain.

Bias is the 45° diagonal line between the two grain directions. Bias has the most stretch and is used for curving vines and flower stems.

Never use the selvage (finished edge). Selvage does not react to washing, drying, and pressing like the rest of the fabric and may pucker when the finished quilt is laundered.

Rotary Cutting

A rotary cutter, used with a self-healing mat and a ruler, is very efficient for cutting strips, squares, and triangles. These tools make quick work of cutting because you can measure and cut multiple layers with a single stroke, without making templates or marking patterns. Using a rotary cutter is also more accurate than cutting with scissors because fabrics remain flat and do not move during cutting. A good mat for cutting strips is at least 23" wide.

Because the blade is very sharp, keep the safety guard in place at all times, except when making a cut. *Keep the rotary cutter out of the reach of children.*

1. Squaring the fabric is the first step in accurate cutting. Fold the fabric with the selvages aligned. With the yardage to your right, align a square ruler with the fold near the edge. Butt a long ruler up against the left side of the square

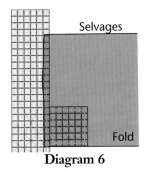

Diagram 6

(Diagram 6). Remove the square, keeping the long ruler in place. Hold the ruler in place with your left hand as you cut, rolling the cutter away from you along the ruler's edge with a steady motion. You can move your left hand up as you cut but the ruler must not move. *Keep your fingers away from the ruler's edge when cutting.*

2. Open the fabric. If the cut is not accurately perpendicular to the fold, the edge will be V-shaped instead of straight **(Diagram 7).**

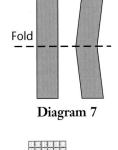

Diagram 7

3. With a transparent ruler, you can measure and cut at the same time. Fold the fabric in half again, aligning the selvages with the fold, making four layers that line up perfectly along the cut edge. Project instructions designate the strip width needed. Position the ruler to the desired measurement from the edge **(Diagram 8)** and cut.

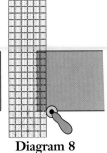

Diagram 8

The blade will easily cut through all four layers. Check each strip to be sure the cut is straight. Each strip length is the width of the fabric, approximately 43" to 44". Using the ruler again, trim the selvages, cutting about ⅜" from each end.

4. To cut squares and rectangles from a strip, align the desired measurement on the ruler with the strip end and cut across the strip **(Diagram 9).**

Diagram 9

5. Cut triangles from squares or rectangles. Cutting instructions often direct you to cut a square in half or in quarters diagonally to make right triangles, and this technique can apply to rectangles, too **(Diagram 10).** The outside edges of the square or rectangle are on the straight of the grain, so triangle sides cut on the diagonal are bias.

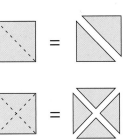

Diagram 10

6. Some projects use a time-saving technique called strip piecing. With this method, you cut across the seams of a pieced band to get preassembled units **(Diagram 11).**

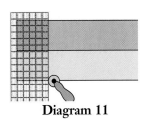

Diagram 11

Hand Piecing

Make a running stitch of 8 to 10 stitches per inch along the marked seam line on the wrong side of the fabric. Don't pull the fabric as you sew. Sew from seam line to seam line, not from edge to edge as in machine piecing.

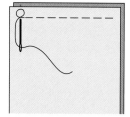

Diagram 12

1. When ending a line of stitching, backstitch over the last stitch and make a loop knot (**Diagram 12**).

2. Match seams and points accurately, pinning patches together before piecing. Align match points as described in Step 4 under Machine Piecing.

3. When joining units where seams meet, do not sew over seam allowances; sew through them at the match point (**Diagram 13**). When four or more seams meet, press the seam allowances in the same direction to reduce bulk (**Diagram 14**).

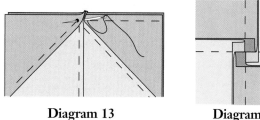

Diagram 13   **Diagram 14**

Machine Piecing

Your sewing machine does not have to be a new, computerized model. A good straight stitch is all that's necessary, but it is helpful to have a satin stitch for appliqué. Clean and oil your machine regularly, use good thread, and replace needles frequently.

1. Patches for machine piecing are cut with the seam allowance included, but the sewing line is not usually marked. So, a way to make a consistent ¼" seam is essential. Some presser feet have a right toe that is ¼" from the needle. Other machines have an adjustable needle that can be set for a ¼" seam. If your machine has neither feature, experiment to find how the fabric must be placed to make a ¼" seam. Mark this position on the foot or throat plate.

2. Use a stitch length that makes a strong seam but is not too difficult to remove with a seam ripper. The best setting is usually 10–12 stitches per inch.

3. Pin only when really necessary. If a straight seam is less than 4" and does not have to match an adjoining seam, pinning is usually not necessary.

4. When intersecting seams must align (**Diagram 15**), match the units with right sides facing and push a pin through both seams at the seam line. Turn the pinned unit to the right side to check the alignment; then pin securely. As you sew, remove each pin just before the needle reaches it.

5. Block Assembly diagrams are used in this book to show how pieces should be joined. Make small units first; then join them in rows and continue joining rows to finish the block (**Diagram 16**).

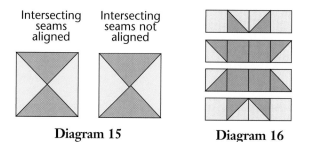

Intersecting seams aligned   Intersecting seams not aligned

Diagram 15   **Diagram 16**

Chain Piecing

Chain piecing saves time. Stack pieces to be sewn in pairs, with right sides facing. Join the first pair as usual. At the end of the seam, do not backstitch, cut the thread, or lift the foot. Just feed in the next pair of pieces—the machine will make a few stitches between pieces before the needle strikes the second piece of fabric. Continue sewing in this way until all pairs are joined. Stack the chain of pieces until you are ready to clip them apart (**Diagram 17**).

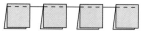

Diagram 17

Sewing a Set-In Seam

Most seams are sewn straight across, from raw edge to raw edge. Since they will be crossed by other seams, backstitching is not needed to secure them.

When sewing with diamonds or other angled pieces, you may need to sew a Y-shaped seam, setting a square or a triangle into the opening between two diamonds. For set-in seams, always mark the corner dots (shown on all patterns) on the fabric

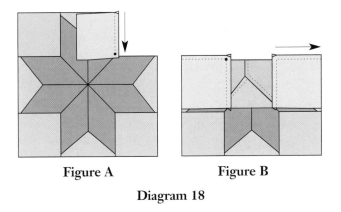

Figure A   **Figure B**

Diagram 18

pieces. Stitch one side of the seam, starting at the outside edge and being careful not to sew beyond the dot into the seam allowance **(Diagram 18, Figure A)**. Backstitch. Align the other side of the piece as needed, with right sides facing. Sew from the dot to the outside edge **(Figure B)**.

Sewing a Curved Seam

Sewing curved seams requires extra care. For each seam, first mark the centers of both the convex (outward) and concave (inward) curves **(Diagram 19)**.

1. Clip the curved edge of the concave piece to the seam line **(Figure A)**.

2. With right sides facing and raw edges aligned, pin the two patches together at the center and at the left edge **(Figure B)**. Place one or two pins between center and edge. Sew from edge to

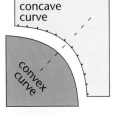

Figure A

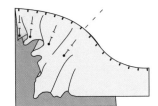

Figure B

Figure C

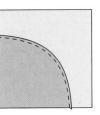

Figure D

Diagram 19

center, stopping frequently to check that the raw edges are aligned. Stop at the center with the needle down. Raise the presser foot and pin the pieces together from the center to the right edge. Lower the foot and continue to sew **(Figure C)**.

3. Press seam allowances toward the concave curve **(Figure D)**.

Pressing

Careful pressing is necessary for precise piecing. Press each seam as you go. Sliding the iron back and forth may push the seam out of shape. Use an up-and-down motion, lifting the iron from spot to spot. Press the seam flat on the wrong side. Open the piece and, on the right side, press both seam allowances to one side (usually toward the darker fabric). Pressing the seam open leaves tiny gaps through which batting may pill or beard.

Quick-Piecing Techniques

Several time-saving techniques used in this book are designed to be used with rotary cutting and machine stitching. You can always piece traditionally, if you prefer, but these methods cut your work time significantly, so they're worth trying.

Making Quick-Pieced Triangle-Squares

When two same-size right triangles are joined along diagonal edges to form a square, it is called a triangle-square. Each triangle equals half the square.

1. Project instructions illustrate and describe the grid, stating the number and size of the squares needed. These squares are ⅞" larger on each side than the leg (short side) of the desired finished triangle. Draw diagonal lines through the grid as illustrated **(Diagram 20)**.

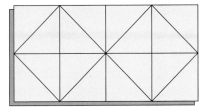

Diagram 20

2. Match the marked fabric to its companion fabric, with right sides facing. Pin the layers together along horizontal and vertical lines, avoiding diagonal lines so the pins will not interfere with stitching.

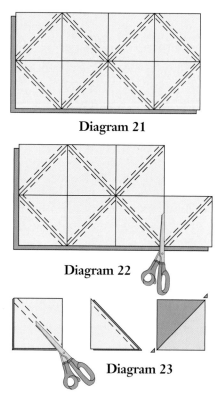

Diagram 21

Diagram 22

Diagram 23

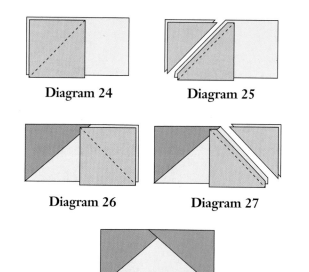

Diagram 24   **Diagram 25**

Diagram 26   **Diagram 27**

Diagram 28

3. Machine-stitch ¼" from *both* sides of all diagonal lines **(Diagram 21)**. At corners, pivot fabric without lifting the needle. When stitching is done, press fabric to set stitches.

4. Trim the excess fabric around the grid; then cut on all horizontal and vertical lines, cutting the fabric into squares **(Diagram 22)**. Next, cut on diagonal lines between stitching **(Diagram 23)**.

5. Press seam allowances toward the darker fabric. Cut points off the seam allowances, making a neat square. Be careful not to pull on the seam, as this will stretch the bias and distort the square.

Diagonal-Corners Method for Flying Geese

This method for making Flying Geese units eliminates cutting of triangles —for each Flying Geese unit, you will cut 2 squares for the corners and 1 rectangle (sizes given with project instructions).

1. Fold each square in half diagonally and crease or press the fold. Or lightly draw a diagonal line from one corner to the other corner.

2. With right sides facing, place a square on top of one rectangle **(Diagram 24)**. Using the creased or drawn line as a sewing line, stitch through both layers from corner to corner as shown. It is crucial that you stitch a straight line from point to point.

3. Use your rotary cutter and a ruler to trim excess fabric from corner, leaving ¼" seam allowance **(Diagram 25)**. Press seam allowance toward triangle corner.

4. Place another square (with diagonal line drawn or creased) on top of this unit **(Diagram 26)**. Stitch across it diagonally.

5. Trim corner, leaving ¼" seam allowance **(Diagram 27)**. Press seam allowance toward corner. **Diagram 28** shows finished unit, with crossed seam allowances at top of unit.

Appliqué
Traditional Hand Appliqué

Hand appliqué requires that you turn under a seam allowance around the edges of each shape to secure the piece and to prevent fraying.

1. Trace around the template onto right side of the fabric. This is the seam allowance turn line. Cut each piece approximately ¼" outside the line.

2. For simple shapes, turn the edges by pressing the seam allowance to the back; complex shapes may require basting the seam allowance. Sharp points and strong curves are best appliquéd with freezer paper (see next section). Clip curves to make a smooth edge. With practice, you can work without pressing seam allowances, turning edges under with the needle as you sew.

3. Do not turn under any seam allowance that will be covered by another piece.

4. Use one strand of sewing thread in a color that matches the appliqué. Use a slipstitch, but keep the stitch very small on the surface. Working from right to left, pull the needle through the base fabric and catch only a few threads on the fold of the appliqué. Reinsert the needle into the base fabric, under the top thread on the appliqué edge to keep the thread from tangling **(Diagram 29)**.

5. An alternative to slipstitching is a decorative buttonhole stitch around each figure **(Diagram 30)**.

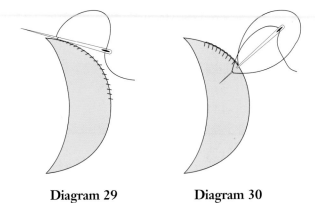

Diagram 29   **Diagram 30**

Freezer-Paper Hand Appliqué

Supermarket freezer paper saves time because it eliminates the need to baste seam allowances.

1. Trace the template onto the *dull* side of the freezer paper and cut the paper on the marked line. *Note:* If a design is not symmetrical, turn the template over and trace a mirror image so the fabric piece won't be reversed when you cut it out.

2. Pin the freezer-paper shape to the *wrong* side of the fabric, *shiny side* up. Following the paper shape and adding a scant ¼" seam allowance, cut out the fabric piece. Do not remove pins.

3. Using just the tip of a dry iron, press the seam allowance to the shiny side of the paper. Be careful not to touch the freezer paper with the iron.

4. Sew the piece to the background as in traditional appliqué. Trim the fabric from behind the shape, leaving ¼" seam allowances. Lift the freezer paper from the fabric and gently pull it off. If you prefer not to trim the background fabric, pull out the paper before you finish stitching.

5. Sharp points require special attention. Turn the point down and press **(Diagram 31, Figure A)**. Fold the seam allowance on one side over the point

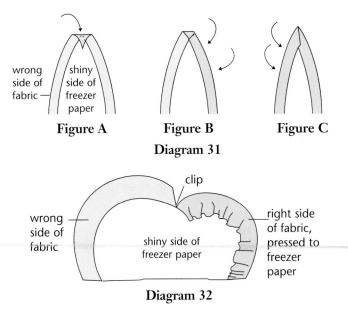

Figure A   **Figure B**   **Figure C**

Diagram 31

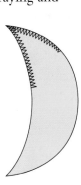

Diagram 32

and press **(Figure B)**; then fold the other seam allowance over the point and press **(Figure C)**.

6. When pressing curved edges, clip sharp inward curves **(Diagram 32)**. If the shape doesn't curve smoothly, separate the paper from the fabric with your fingernail and try again.

7. Remove the pins when all seam allowances have been pressed to the freezer paper. Position the prepared appliqué right side up on the background fabric. Press to adhere it to the background fabric.

Machine Appliqué

A machine-sewn satin stitch makes a neat edging for appliqué, For machine appliqué, cut appliqué pieces without adding seam allowances.

Using fusible web to adhere pieces to the background adds a stiff extra layer to the appliqué and is not appropriate for some quilts. It is best used on wall hangings and accessories in which added stiffness is acceptable. The web prevents fraying and shifting during appliqué.

Place tear-away stabilizer under the background fabric behind the appliqué. Machine-stitch the appliqué edges with a satin stitch or close-spaced zigzag **(Diagram 33)**. Test the stitch length and width on a sample first. Use an open-toed presser foot. Remove the stabilizer when appliqué is complete.

Diagram 33

Measuring Borders

Because seams may vary and fabrics may stretch a bit, opposite sides of your assembled quilt top may not be the same measurement. You can (and should) correct this when you add borders.

Measure the length of the quilt vertically through the *middle* of the quilt, not at the sides. Trim side border strips to this size and join, easing to fit as described below. Measure the quilt's width horizontally through the middle, including side borders. Trim top and bottom borders to this size and join.

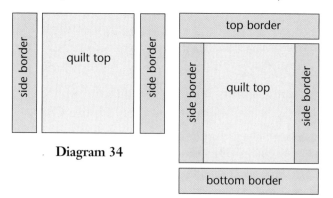

Diagram 34

Straight Borders

Side borders are usually added first **(Diagram 34)**. With right sides facing and raw edges aligned, pin the center of one border strip to the center of one side of the quilt top. Pin the border to the quilt at each end and then along the side. Machine-stitch with the border strip on top, easing quilt to fit border. Press seam allowance toward the border. In the same manner, add the border to the opposite side and then to the top and the bottom **(Diagram 35)**.

Mitered Borders

1. Mark the center of each quilt edge with a pin.

2. Measure the quilt's sides. Trim side border strips to fit the shorter of the two sides *plus* the width of the border *plus* 2". Mark the center of the border strip with a pin. Measuring outward from the center pin, measure the length of the quilt edge on the border strip and mark both ends with a pin.

3. With right sides facing and raw edges aligned, match pins on border strip to center and corners of the longer quilt side. Working from the center out, pin border to quilt. (Border fabric will extend beyond corners.) Repeat on opposite side.

4. Measure top and bottom edges of quilt. Trim remaining borders and pin to quilt in same manner as for side borders.

5. On any side of the quilt, start machine-stitching at the top pin, backstitching to lock the stitches. Continue to sew, easing the fabric between the pins. Stop at the last pin; backstitch. Join the remaining borders in the same manner. Press seam allowances toward the borders.

6. With right sides facing, fold the quilt diagonally, aligning the raw edges of adjacent borders. Pin securely **(Diagram 36)**.

7. Align a yardstick or a quilter's ruler along the diagonal fold **(Diagram 37)**. Holding the ruler firmly, mark a line from the end of the border seam to the raw edge.

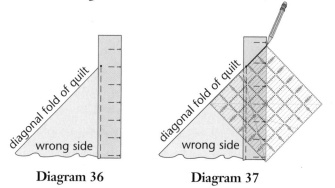

Diagram 36   **Diagram 37**

8. Start machine-stitching at the beginning of the marked line, backstitch, and then stitch on the line out to the raw edge. Unfold the quilt to be sure the corner lies flat. Correct stitching if necessary. Trim seam allowance to ¼". Press corner seam open.

9. Miter remaining corners in the same manner.

Quilting Without Marking

If you choose to quilt your project, consider stitching in-the-ditch (right along the seam line), outline-quilting (¼" from the seam line), or echo-quilting (lines of quilting rippling outward from the design like waves on a pond). These methods can be used without marking the quilt top. If you are machine quilting, use the presser foot edge and the seam line as guides. If you are hand quilting, by the time you have pieced a top, your eye should be practiced enough for you to make straight, even lines of quilting without the guidance of marked lines.

Marking Quilting Designs

If you choose quilting designs that need to be marked, here are some tips. The most common tool for marking is a sharp **pencil**. However, most pencils are made with an oil-based graphite lead, which often will not wash out completely. Look for a high-quality artist's pencil marked "2H" or higher (the higher the number, the harder the lead and the lighter the line it will make). Sharpen the pencil frequently to keep the line on the fabric thin and light. Or try a mechanical pencil with a 0.5-mm lead; it will maintain a fine line without sharpening.

While you are in the art-supply store, get a **white plastic eraser** (brand name Magic Rub). This eraser, used by professional drafters and artists, cleanly removes carbon smudges left by pencil lead without fraying the fabric or leaving eraser crumbs.

Water- and **air-soluble marking pens** are convenient, but controversial, marking tools. Some quilters find that the marks reappear, often up to several years later, while others experience no problems with them.

Test these pens on each fabric you mark and *follow package directions precisely*. Because the inks can be permanently set by heat, be very careful with a marked quilt. Do not leave it in your car on a hot day and never touch it with an iron until the marking is removed. Plan to complete the quilting within a year after marking it with a water-soluble pen.

Air-soluble pens are best for marking small sections at a time. The marks disappear within 24 to 48 hours, but the ink remains in the fabric until it is washed. After the quilt is completed and before it is ironed, rinse it twice in clear, cool water, using no soap, detergent, or bleach. Let the quilt air-dry.

For dark fabrics, the cleanest marker you can use is a thin sliver of pure **white soap**. Choose a soap that contains no creams, deodorants, dyes, or perfumes; these added ingredients may leave a residue on the fabric.

Other marking tools include **colored pencils** made specifically for marking fabric and **tailor's chalk** (available in powdered, stick, and traditional cake form). When using chalk, mark small sections at one time because the chalk rubs off easily.

Quilting Stencils

Quilting patterns can be purchased as precut stencils. Simply lay a stencil on your quilt top and mark the design through the cutout areas.

To make your own stencil of a printed pattern, trace the design onto a blank sheet of template plastic. Then cut out the design with a craft knife.

Making a Quilt Backing

Some stores sell 90" and 108" widths of 100%-cotton fabric for quilt backing. Use these whenever possible. Instructions in this book also give backing yardages based on 44"-wide fabric.

When using 44"-wide fabric, all quilts wider than 41" will require a pieced backing. For quilts 41" to 80" wide, you need an amount of fabric equal to two times the desired length of the unfinished backing. (The unfinished backing should be at least 3" larger on all sides than the quilt top.)

The simplest way to make a backing is to cut the fabric in half widthwise **(Diagram 38)** and then to sew the two panels together lengthwise. This results in a backing with a vertical center seam. Press the seam allowances to one side.

Selvages   Cut.

Diagram 38

Another method of seaming a backing results in two vertical seams. (This method is often preferred by quilt show judges.) Begin with two equal lengths of fabric. Cut one length in half lengthwise. Sew a narrow panel to each side of wide panel **(Diagram 39)**. Press seam allowances to one side.

If the quilt is wider than 80", cut three lengths of fabric that equal the desired width of the backing. Join the three lengths with the

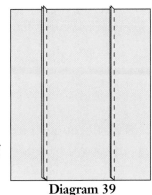

Diagram 39

seams horizontal to the quilt, rather than vertical. For this method, you need yardage equal to three times the width of the unfinished backing.

Layering and Basting

After the quilt top and backing are made, the next steps are layering and basting to prepare for quilting or tying. Prepare a work surface to spread out the quilt—the floor, a large table, or two tables pushed together. Lay the backing on the surface, *wrong* side up. Unfold the batting and place it on top of the backing, smoothing away wrinkles or lumps.

Lay the quilt top right side up on top of the batting. Make sure the edges of the backing and the quilt top are parallel.

Basting keeps layers from shifting during quilting. Baste with a long needle and white thread (colored thread can leave a residue on light fabrics).

Start in the center and baste a line of stitches to each corner, making a large X. Then baste parallel lines about 6" apart. Finish with a line of basting stitches ¼" from the edge.

Some quilters use nickel-plated safety pins for basting. Pin every 2" to 3". Don't close the pins as you go, as this can pucker the backing. When all pins are in place, gently tug the backing as you close each pin so that pleats don't form underneath.

Another popular method is to use a basting gun, which shoots plastic tabs through the quilt layers. Use paper-cutting scissors to trim the tabs after the quilting is finished.

Hand Quilting

Hand-quilted running stitches should be evenly spaced, with the spaces between the stitches about the same length as the stitches themselves. The *number* of stitches per inch is less important than the *uniformity* of the stitching. Don't worry if you take only five or six stitches per inch; just be consistent throughout the project.

Tying a Quilt

Instead of quilting, you can secure the layers of a quilt by tying. Tying is a fast way to secure the quilt layers and the only way to work with thick batting often used for comforters.

Ties can be of pearl cotton, yarn, floss, or narrow ribbon. The material used must be strong enough to be tied tightly and stay tied. Ties may be double knots, bows, or knots that hold buttons, charms, or beads. *Never use buttons or other small objects on quilts intended for babies or small children.*

Use a sharp embroidery needle with an eye large enough to accommodate the material. Thread the needle but do not knot the end. Starting in the center of the basted quilt top, take a ⅛" to ¼" stitch through all three layers. Clip the thread, leaving a tail several inches long on each side of the stitch **(Diagram 40)**. Tie the tails in a tight knot **(Diagram 41)**. Trim tails of all knots to the same length.

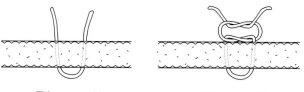

Diagram 40   Diagram 41

Machine Quilting

For machine quilting, the backing and the batting should be 3" larger all around than the quilt top, because the quilting process pushes the quilt top fabric outward. After quilting, trim the backing and the batting to the same size as the quilt top.

Thread your bobbin with good-quality sewing thread (not quilting thread) in a color to match the backing. Use a top thread color to match the quilt top or use invisible nylon thread.

An even-feed or walking foot feeds all the quilt's layers through the machine at the same speed. It is possible to machine-quilt without one (by experimenting with tension and presser foot pressure), but it is much easier with it. If you do not have a walking foot, get one from your sewing machine dealer.

Straight-Grain Binding

Binding can be made with either bias or straight-grain strips. Use bias to bind a scalloped edge or rounded corners, but either kind will do for most quilts. Straight-grain binding is often deemed less durable than bias because the threads run parallel to the edge of the quilt and are more likely to break than bias grain, which is diagonal to the edge.

1. Cut straight-grain strips 2½" to 3" wide.

2. Join strips end-to-end to make a continuous

strip long enough to bind the quilt. You can make the joining seams straight or diagonal, as you prefer.

3. Fold the fabric strip in half lengthwise, right sides out, and press. See Applying Binding.

Continuous Bias Binding

This technique can be used to make continuous bias for appliqué as well as for binding.

1. Cut a square of fabric in half diagonally to make two triangles. With right sides facing, join the triangles **(Diagram 42)**. Press the seam allowance open.

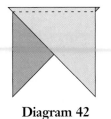

Diagram 42

2. Starting at one long edge, mark parallel lines equal to the desired width of the binding (usually 2½" to 3" wide), taking care not to stretch the bias **(Diagram 43)**. With right sides facing, align the raw edges (indicated as Seam 2). As you align the edges, offset one Seam 2 point past its natural matching point by one line. Stitch the seam; then press the seam allowance open.

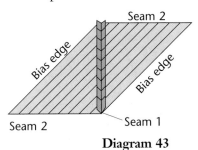

Diagram 43

3. Cut the binding in a continuous strip, starting with the protruding point and following marked lines around the tube **(Diagram 44)**. Press the strip in half lengthwise, right side out.

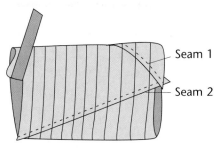

Diagram 44

Applying Binding

In this double-fold technique, binding is applied to the front of the quilt first and then hand-stitched onto the backing. You may begin anywhere on the edge of the quilt except at a corner.

1. Matching raw edges, lay the binding on the quilt. Fold down the top corner of the binding at a

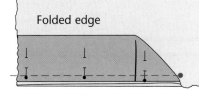

Diagram 45

45° angle, align raw edges, and pin **(Diagram 45)**. Beginning at the folded end, machine-stitch the binding to the quilt.

2. Stop stitching ¼" from the corner and backstitch. Fold the binding strip diagonally away from the quilt, making a 45° angle **(Diagram 46)**.

3. Fold the binding strip straight down along the next side to be stitched, creating a pleat in the corner. Position the needle at the ¼" seam line of the new side **(Diagram 47)**. Make a few stitches, backstitch, and then stitch the seam. Continue until all the corners and the sides are done. Overlap the end of the binding strip over the beginning fold and stitch about 2" beyond it. Trim any excess binding.

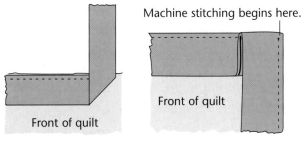

Diagram 46   **Diagram 47**

4. Turn the binding over the raw edge of the quilt. Slipstitch it in place on the back, using thread that matches the binding. The fold at the beginning of the binding strip creates a neat, angled edge when it is folded to the back.

5. At each corner, fold the binding to form a miter **(Diagram 48)**. Handstitch the miters closed if desired.

Diagram 48

Amethyst

The cool beauty of February's birthstone is reflected in the colors of this charming patchwork pattern, also known as Diamond Star, Windmill, and Golden Wedding.

Quilt designed by Susan Ramey Cleveland, Leeds, Alabama
Made by Mary Ramey, Leeds, Alabama

Finished Quilt Size
73" x 91"

Number of Blocks and Finished Size
12 blocks   18" x 18"

Fabric Requirements
Pink/blue print	5 yards*
Blue print	1⅞ yards
Cranberry	¾ yard
Muslin	2¼ yards
Backing	5½ yards

*Includes fabric for binding.

Cutting
Make templates of patterns A, B, and C on page 20.

From pink/blue print fabric
- 2 (6½" x 76") and 2 (6½" x 94") lengthwise strips for outer border.
- 192 of Template C.

From blue print fabric
- 192 of Template B.

From cranberry fabric
- 48 of Template A.

From muslin
- 2 (4" x 81") and 2 (4" x 63") lengthwise strips for inner border.

Quilt Top Assembly
1. Join 1 B to each side of A piece **(Piecing Diagram)**. Set 1 C into openings between Bs to make a pieced square (see page 10 for tips on sewing a set-in seam). Join 4 pieced squares to complete a block **(Block Assembly Diagram)**. Make 12 blocks.

2. Join blocks in 4 horizontal rows of 3 blocks each **(Setting Diagram)**. Join rows.

3. Mark centers on edges of each muslin and print border strip. Matching centers, join 1 muslin border strip to each print border strip along 1 long edge.

4. Mark center on each edge of quilt. Matching centers of borders and quilt top, join shorter borders to top and bottom edges. Join long borders to quilt sides. See page 14 for tips on mitering border corners.

Quilting and Finishing
1. Outline-quilt blocks. Quilt borders as desired.

2. See pages 16 and 17 for instructions on making binding. Make 9¼ yards of 2½"-wide bias or straight-grain binding from remaining pink/blue fabric. Apply binding to quilt edges.

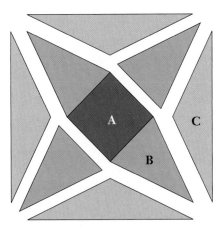

Piecing Diagram

Block Assembly Diagram

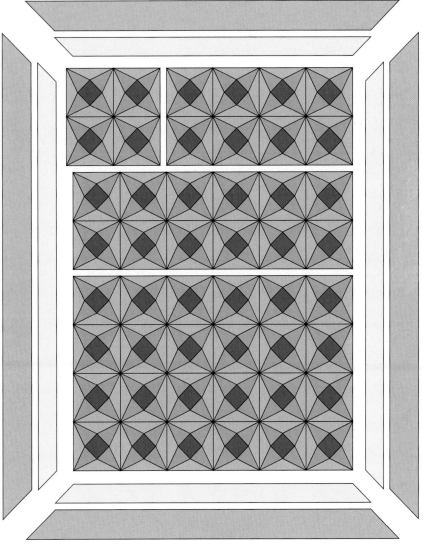

Setting Diagram

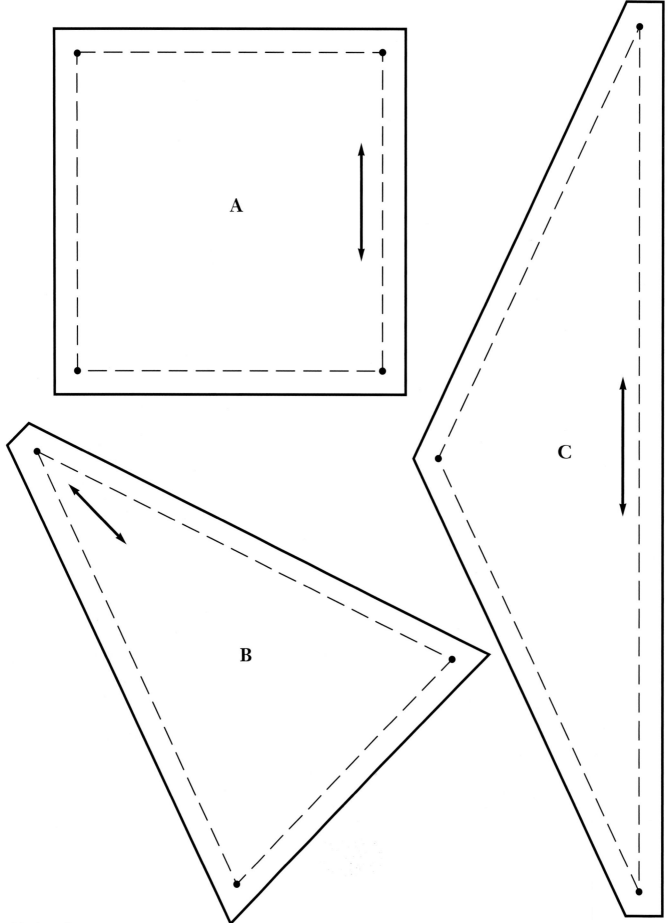

Amish Medallion

Sixteen basket blocks border four slightly different blocks that create a diamond medallion in the center of this elegant quilt, inspired by antique Amish quilts. A rose-colored flange accents the border like the mat of a framed picture.

Quilt by Mary Lou Thayer
South Easton, Massachusetts

Finished Quilt Size
69" x 83¼"

Number of Blocks and Finished Size
16 basket blocks   10" x 10"
4 medallion blocks   10" x 10"

Fabric Requirements
White   2¾ yards
Navy   2⅝ yards*
Blue print   1½ yards
Rose   ½ yard
Rose print   ⅜ yard
Cranberry   1 fat quarter**
Backing   5 yards
*Includes fabric for binding.
**Fat quarter = 18" x 22"

Cutting
Cut all strips cross-grain unless specified otherwise. Cut pieces in order listed to get best use of yardage.

From white fabric
- 2 (13"-wide) strips. From these, cut 7 (7" x 13") pieces for B quick-pieced triangles, 1 (11" x 21") piece for blue print/white C triangle-squares, and 1 (6" x 11") piece for navy/white C triangle-squares.
- 3 (2⅞"-wide) strips. From these, cut 40 (2⅞") squares. Cut each square in half diagonally to get 80 B triangles.
- 1 (4⅞"-wide) strip. From this, cut 8 (4⅞") squares. Cut each square in half diagonally to get 16 C triangles.
- 7 (2½"-wide) strips. From these, cut 32 (2½" x 6½") D pieces and 24 (2½") A squares.
- 3 (10½"-wide) strips. From these, cut 12 (10½") X squares.

From navy fabric
- 2 (6¾" x 88") and 2 (6¾" x 74") lengthwise strips for border.
- 2 (7" x 13") pieces for B quick-pieced triangles.
- 1 (6" x 11") piece for C triangle-squares.
- 5 (2½" x 75") lengthwise strips for straight-grain binding.

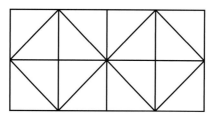

Diagram 1

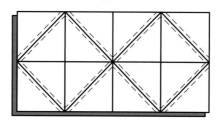

Diagram 2

From blue print fabric
- 5 (2⅞"-wide) strips. From these, cut 76 (2⅞") squares. (You'll probably need to cut last square from a scrap.) Cut each square in half diagonally to get 152 B triangles.
- 4 (15½") squares. Cut each square in quarters diagonally to get 14 Y setting triangles (and 2 extra).
- 1 (11" x 21") piece for C triangle-squares.
- 2 (8") squares. Cut each square in half diagonally to get 4 Z corner triangles.

From rose fabric
- 8 (1" x 44") strips for flange.
- 1 (7" x 13") piece for B quick-pieced triangles.

From rose print fabric
- 4 (7" x 13") pieces for B quick-pieced triangles. (In quilt shown, 2 basket blocks have rose fabric in place of rose print; for ease of assembly, these instructions are for all basket blocks to be the same.)

From cranberry fabric
- 3 (4⅞" x 22") strips. From these, cut 10 (4⅞") squares. Cut each square in half diagonally to get 20 C triangles.

Quick Piecing
See page 11 for tips on sewing quick-pieced triangle-squares.

1. On wrong side of each 7" x 13" white piece, mark a 2- x 4-square grid of 2⅞" squares (Diagram 1). Draw diagonal lines through squares as shown.

2. Match 1 white piece to a navy piece, right sides facing. Machine-stitch ¼" from each side of all *diagonal* lines (Diagram 2). Cut on *all* grid lines to get 16 B triangle-squares. Press seam allowances toward navy.

3. Repeat procedure to get a total of 32 navy/white B triangle-squares, 16 rose/white B triangle-squares, and 64 rose print/white B triangle-squares.

4. Using 11" x 21" pieces of white and blue print, draw same grid, this time with 4⅞" squares. Stitch and cut 16 C triangle-squares.

5. On wrong side of 6" x 11" white piece, draw 2 (4⅞") squares. Draw a diagonal line through each square. Match white piece with navy piece and machine-stitch along diagonal lines as before. Cut out 4 C triangle-squares for medallion blocks. Press seam allowance toward navy.

Quilt Top Assembly
1. For 1 medallion block, select 6 blue print B triangles and 2 white Bs. Sew 2 blue print Bs to opposite sides of white triangles (**Medallion Block Assembly Diagram**). Add

Medallion Block Assembly Diagram

remaining blue print triangles to bottom of units as shown. Press seam allowance toward blue print.

2. Sew blue print/white triangle units to sides of navy/white C triangle-squares as shown.

3. Join 2 rose/white B triangle-squares in a row; sew row to 1 side of cranberry C triangle. Join 2 more rose/white B triangle-squares; add an A square to end of row as shown. Sew row to adjacent side of C triangle. Add white B triangles to row ends as shown. Sew this unit to blue B/C unit. Press.

4. Join 2 rows of navy/white B triangle-squares, with 4 squares in each row. Sew 1 row to 1 side of block. Add an A square to end of remaining row as shown; sew row to adjacent edge to complete block.

5. Make 4 medallion blocks.

6. For each basket block, join 6 blue print B triangles and 2 white B triangles in 2 units as before **(Basket Block Assembly Diagram)**. Sew units to sides of blue print/white C triangle-square.

7. Sew blue print B triangles to ends of 2 D pieces. Sew D pieces to sides of B/C unit. Sew white C triangle to bottom of unit.

8. Assemble rose print B triangle-squares, A square, C triangle, and B triangles as shown. Sew completed unit to bottom unit to complete block.

9. Lay out basket blocks and X setting squares in diagonal rows, turning blocks on point as shown **(Setting Diagram)**. Add Y and Z triangles to row ends as shown. Join units in each diagonal row; then join rows.

10. For flange, join 2 (1" x 44") rose strips end-to-end for each side of quilt. With wrong sides facing, fold each strip in half lengthwise and press. Matching raw edges, pin a flange strip to each side of quilt, letting ends extend past corners.

11. Matching centers of borders and quilt, sew navy border strips to quilt sides, catching flange in seam. Miter border corners.

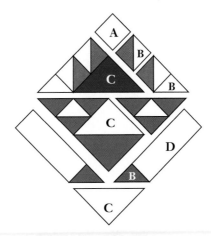

Block Assembly Diagram

Quilting and Finishing

1. Quilt shown has fancy feather quilting in setting squares and border. Make or buy appropriate quilting stencils and mark quilting design as desired. Outline-quilt blocks; then quilt marked designs.

2. See page 16 for instructions on making binding. Make $8\frac{5}{8}$ yards of $2\frac{1}{2}$"-wide continuous straight-grain binding from reserved navy strips. Apply binding to quilt edges.

Setting Diagram

Amish Stripes

Bold colors highlight this queen-size quilt. Black half-square triangles form the background, giving the quilt a decidedly Amish flavor. The striped triangles are cut from multi-colored strip-pieced units.

Quilt by Monica J. Starrett
Statesville, North Carolina

Finished Quilt Size
103" x 113"

Number of Blocks and Finished Size
90 Blocks   10" x 10"

Fabric Requirements
Black solid   7¼ yards*
10 assorted solids   ¾ yard each
Blue solid   ¾ yard
Backing   10 yards
*Includes fabric for binding.

Cutting
From black
- 4 (5½" x 116") strips for outer border.
- 45 (10⅞") squares from black. Cut squares in half diagonally to get 90 half-square triangles. (*Note:* For more on cutting triangles from squares, see page 9.)
- 1 (36") square for binding.

From each assorted solid
- 2 (22" x 27") pieces. From 1 piece, cut 13 (2" x 22") cross-grain strips. From second piece, cut 13 (2"-wide) bias strips. (Bias strips will be of varying lengths.)

From blue solid
- 4 (2"-wide) cross-grain strips for inner border.

Quilt Top Assembly
1. Join 5 strips, mixing straight-grain and bias strips. (This prevents distortion of bias when handling blocks.) Make 52 (5-strip) units, varying color sequence. Press seam allowances in same direction.

2. Make a triangle template by cutting a 10⅞" square in half diagonally. Use template to cut 90 triangles from strip-pieced units **(Cutting Diagram).**

3. Join 1 black triangle to each strip-pieced triangle **(Block Diagram).** Make 90 blocks.

4. Join blocks in 10 horizontal rows of 9 blocks each, arranging blocks as shown **(Setting Diagram).** Join rows.

5. Piece blue border strips end-to-end to fit quilt sides. Sew

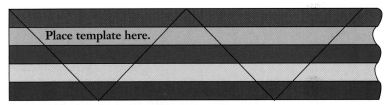

Cutting Diagram

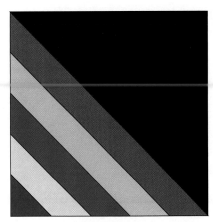

Block Diagram

borders to quilt sides; press seam allowances toward borders. Piece remaining blue strips to fit top and bottom edges; sew borders to quilt. Join black outer borders to quilt in same manner.

Quilting and Finishing
1. Outline-quilt colored strips with black quilting thread. Quilt black triangles as desired.

2. See pages 16 and 17 for instructions on making binding. Make 12 yards of 2½"-wide bias or straight-grain binding. Apply binding to quilt edges.

Setting Diagram

Amish Wedding Ring

Linda Carlson designed and made this quilt as a gift for Ellen and Bruce Horowitz. It affirms their special friendship. "We planned our wedding for a Saturday afternoon, forgetting that it was the Jewish Sabbath and therefore that Bruce and Ellen couldn't come by car," Linda says. "They walked three miles in the rain to be there for us."

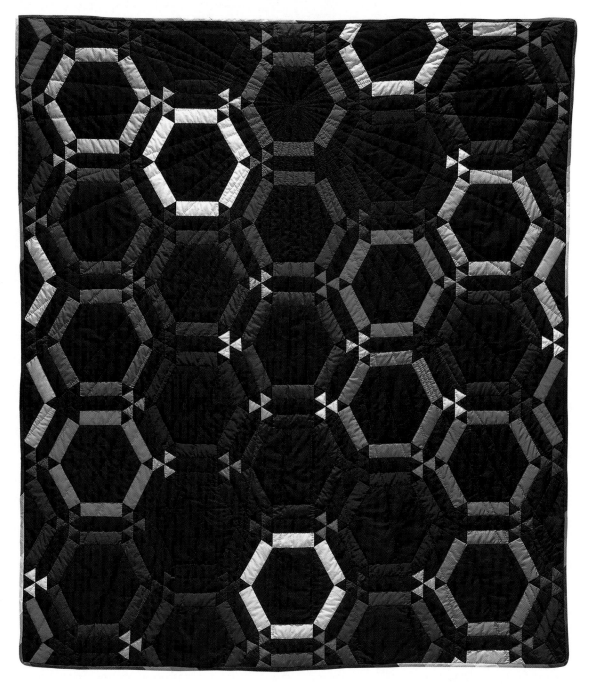

Quilt by Linda Carlson
Mexico, Missouri

Finished Quilt Size
56" x 64"

Fabric Requirements
Black   3¾ yards
11 solid fabrics   1 fat quarter each*
Backing   4 yards
*Fat quarter = 18" x 22"

Cutting
Cut all strips cross-grain unless specified otherwise. Cut pieces in order listed to get best use of yardage. Make templates of patterns A–D on pages 28 and 29.

From black
- 13 (2"-wide) strips. From these, cut 100 of Template B.
- 396 of Template C.
- 27 of Template A.
- 12 of Template D.

From each solid fabric
- 5 (2" x 22") strips. From these, cut 18 of Template B (3 sets of 6 Bs from each color, 198 total); then cut 2 more to get 200 Bs.
- 18 of Template C (6 sets of 3 C from each color, 198 total).
- Set aside scraps for binding.

Quilt Top Assembly
See page 10 for tips on sewing a set-in seam.

1. Join 6 black Cs and 3 solid Cs of same color to make 1 triangle unit (**Diagram 1**). Make 66 units.

2. Lay out As, triangle units, and Bs in vertical rows as shown (**Setting Diagram**). Arrange Bs to form rings of same color around As.

3. Join 1 black B and 2 colored Bs to make 1 bar unit (**Diagram 2**). Press seam allowances toward black. *Note:* To make sure colors work in quilt layout, replace bar units in layout rows as you complete them. Make 100 bar units.

4. When satisfied with layout and color placement, join units in each row as shown. Press all joining seam allowances toward bar units. *continued*

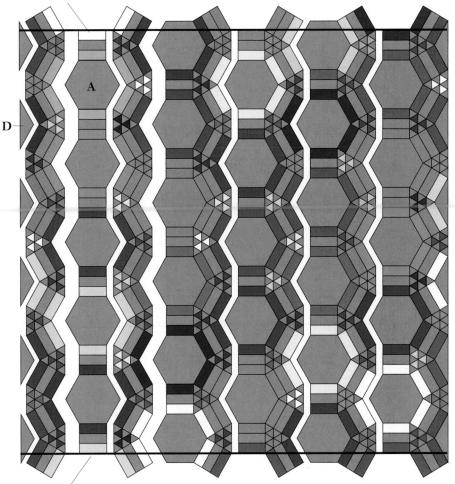

Trim along this line.

Trim along this line.

Setting Diagram

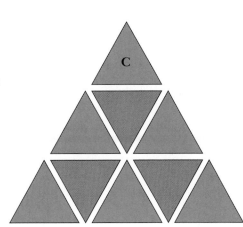

Diagram 1

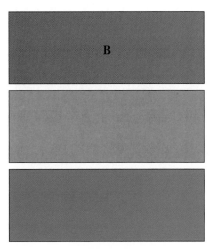

Diagram 2

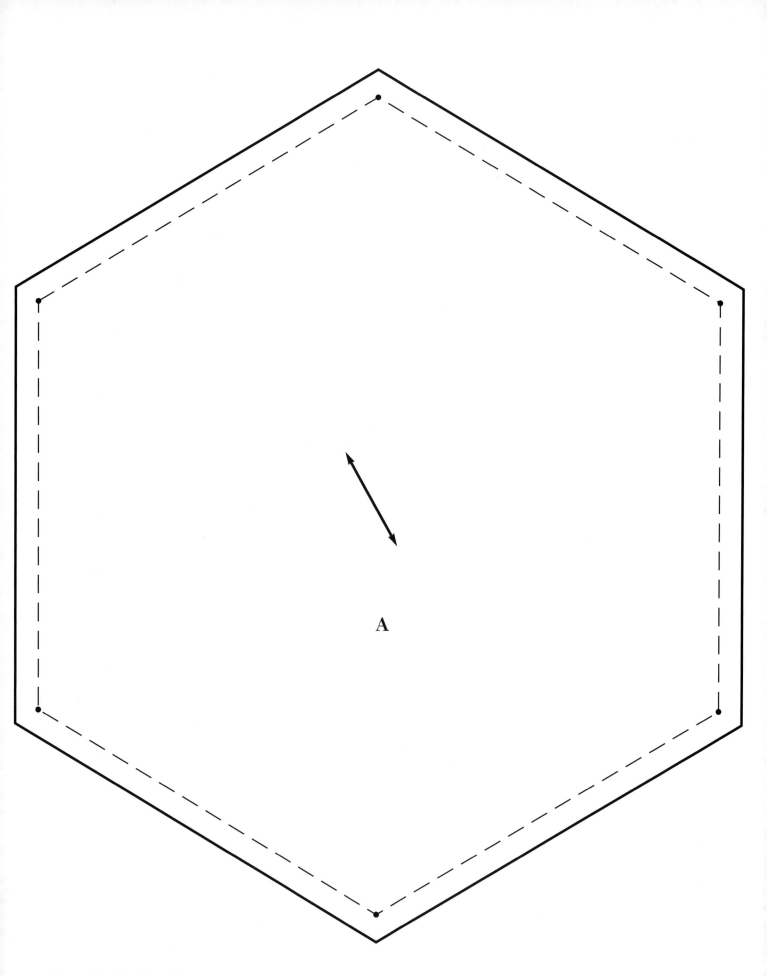

A

5. Starting at 1 side, join adjacent rows, sewing set-in seams.

6. Set in D pieces at sides.

7. Trim rows along lines at top and bottom as shown.

Quilting and Finishing

1. Quilt in-the-ditch or as desired.

2. From solid scraps, cut 2"-wide strips of varying lengths. Join pieces end-to-end to get 7¼ yards of straight-grain binding (see page 16). Apply binding to quilt edges.

C

D

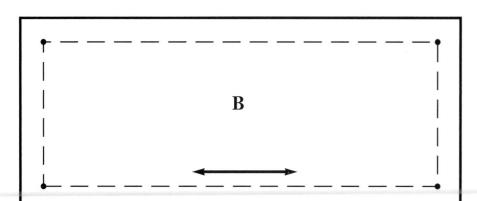

Make Your Own Quilt Label
See page 366 for instructions.

B

Arkansas Crossroads

Looking for a pattern that would use some of her fabric scraps, Corrie Corkern found this block in a book of scrap quilt patterns and knew immediately that it was the one she wanted to make. *Arkansas Crossroads* won a blue ribbon at the 1993 Washington Parish Fair.

Quilt by Corrie B. Corkern
Franklinton, Louisiana

Finished Quilt Size
80" x 96"

Number of Blocks and Finished Size
80 blocks   8" x 8"

Fabric Requirements

Light prints	scraps or 21 fat eighths*
Medium prints	scraps or 21 fat eighths*
Dark prints	scraps or 14 fat eighths*
Red print	2½ yards**
Yellow print	2⅜ yards
Backing	5¾ yards

* Fat eighth = 9" x 22"
** Includes 1 yard for straight-grain binding.

Cutting

Cutting instructions are for rotary cutting. Cut all strips cross-grain unless specified otherwise. Cut pieces in order listed to get best use of yardage.

From light prints
- 320 (2½") A squares.
- 160 (2⅞") squares. Cut each square in half diagonally to get 320 B triangles.

From medium prints
- 320 (2½") A squares.
- 160 (2⅞") squares. Cut each square in half diagonally to get 320 B triangles.

From dark prints
- 320 (2½") A squares.

From yellow print
- 2 (2½" x 85") and 2 (2½" x 75") lengthwise strips for inner border.

From red print
- 2 (6½" x 90") and 2 (6½" x 86") lengthwise strips for inner border.
- 4 (2½" x 90") lengthwise strips for straight-grain binding.

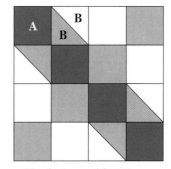

Block Assembly Diagram

Quilt Top Assembly

1. For each block, lay out 4 light print As, 4 medium print As, 4 dark print As, 4 light print Bs, and 4 medium print Bs as shown (**Block Assembly Diagram**).

2. Join light and medium Bs in pairs to make 4 squares. Press seam allowances toward medium Bs.

3. Join units in rows; join rows to complete block. Make 80 blocks.

4. Lay out blocks in 10 horizontal rows, with 8 blocks in each row (**Setting Diagram**). Turn blocks to alternate direction of diagonal stripes as shown. Join blocks in each row; then join rows.

5. Sew longer yellow borders to quilt sides. Sew shorter yellow borders to top and bottom edges. Join red print borders in same manner.

Quilting and Finishing

1. Quilt in-the-ditch around each star or quilt as desired.

2. See page 16 for instructions on making binding. Make 10 yards of 2½"-wide striaght-grain binding from red print. Apply binding to quilt edges.

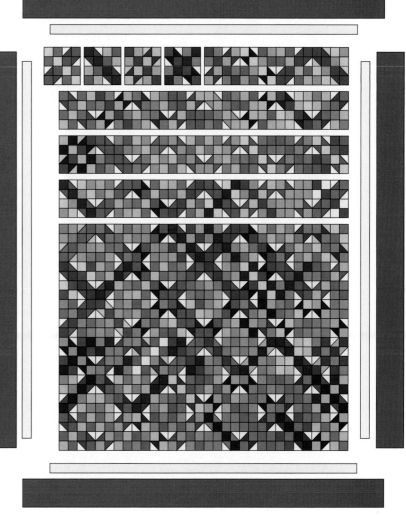

Setting Diagram

Attic Windows

This design is an excellent choice for a scrap-quilt project. For best results, choose a dark solid for the square. Try more than one dark solid if you're adventurous. Then divide your print scraps into two categories: dark and light.

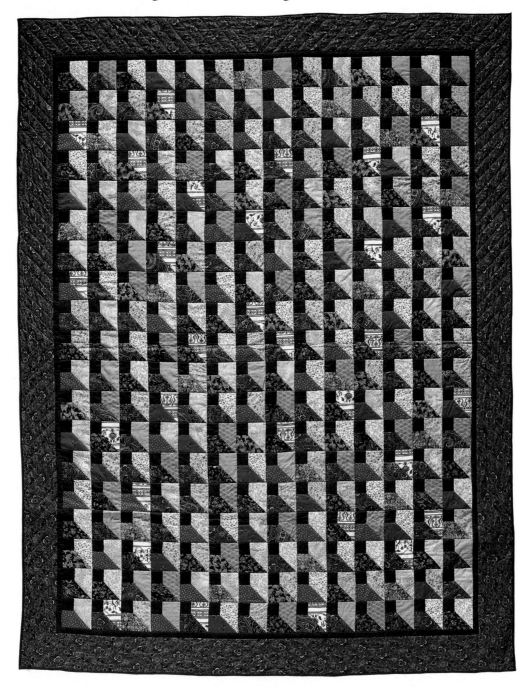

Quilt by Judy Cantwell
Birmingham, Alabama

Finished Quilt Size
84" x 109"

Number of Blocks and Finished Size
266 blocks   5" x 5"

Fabric Requirements
Dark solid   3 yards*
7 dark prints   1 fat quarter each**
7 light prints   1 fat quarter each**
Outer border fabric   1¾ yards
Backing   6¼ yards
*Includes fabric for binding.
**Fat quarter = 18" x 22"

Cutting
From dark solid
- 17 (2½"-wide) cross-grain strips. From these, cut 266 (2½") squares.
- 9 (1½"-wide) cross-grain strips for inner border.

From each fat quarter
- 6 (3½" x 18") strips. (*Note:* If you are using scraps, the length of strips you can cut may vary. Cut as many strips as you need to get 266 dark trapezoids and 266 light trapezoids, following instructions in Step 1 below.)

Quilt Top Assembly
1. Lay 1 light print strip on top of 1 dark print strip with right sides facing and raw edges aligned. Measure 5⅞" from 1 end on *bottom* of strip and mark (**Trapezoid Diagram, Figure 1**). Place edge of ruler at mark and 45-degree angle line of ruler along *bottom* edge of strip (**Figure 2**). Cut angle as indicated through both layers of fabric to get 1 mirror-image set of trapezoids (**Figure 3**). Measure 5⅞" from cut end on *top* of remaining strip (**Figure 4**). Cut next set of trapezoids as indicated. Repeat procedure to cut 266 mirror-image sets of trapezoids (you should get at least 3 trapezoids from each set of strips).
2. Sew 1 side of square to short side of 1 light trapezoid, starting and stopping seam at ¼" seam line

(**Diagram 1**). Press seam allowance toward square.
3. Sew short side of dark trapezoid to square, starting at outside edge and stopping where previous seam begins (**Diagram 2**).
4. With right sides facing and raw edges aligned, join trapezoids along diagonal edges, sewing from outside edge to seam at square (**Diagram 3**).
5. Make 266 blocks (**Diagram 4**).
6. Referring to photograph, join blocks in 19 horizontal rows with 14 blocks in each row. Join rows.
7. Measure length of quilt top through middle of pieced section. Piece inner border strips end-to-end as needed to make 2 borders to match length. Sew borders to quilt sides, easing to fit as needed. Press seam allowances toward borders.
8. Measure width of quilt top through middle, including side borders. Piece borders to match width. Sew borders to top and bottom edges of quilt, easing to fit as needed. Press seam allowances toward borders.
9. For outer borders, cut 9 (6½"-wide) cross-grain strips. Piece borders as for inner border strips; sew borders to quilt.

Quilting and Finishing
1. Quilt blocks in-the-ditch. Quilt borders as desired.
2. See pages 16 and 17 for instructions on making binding. Make 11 yards of 2½"-wide bias or striaght-grain binding from dark solid. Apply binding to quilt edges.

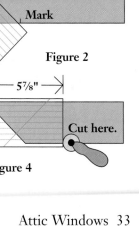

Diagram 1

Diagram 2

Diagram 3

Diagram 4

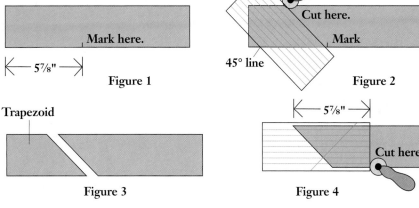

Mark here.

|← 5⅞" →|

Figure 1

Trapezoid

Figure 3

Cut here.

Mark

45° line

Figure 2

|← 5⅞" →|

Cut here.

Figure 4

Trapezoid Diagram

Autumn Leaves

Anna Hartzell was quilting *Autumn Leaves* on the day a young girl named Milly Splitstone came to visit. The day's impressions inspired Milly to become a quiltmaker herself, and she was able to buy the quilt after Anna's death. The *Autumn Leaves* pattern was available in the 1930s and '40s. Its popularity soared when it was seen at the 1933 Chicago World's Fair at a quilt contest sponsored by Sears.

Quilt by Anna Hartzell, Fremont, Michigan
Owned by Milly Splitstone

Finished Quilt Size
83" x 90"

Fabric Requirements
Prints   scraps or 20 fat eighths*
Muslin   4¾ yards
Pink   2 yards**
Green   1 yard
Backing   2½ yards, 90" wide
* Fat eighth = 9" x 22"
** Includes fabric for straight-grain binding.

Cutting
Make a template of Leaf Pattern.
Cut pieces in order listed to get
best use of yardage.
From print fabrics
• 634 of Leaf Template.

From muslin
• 8 (11¼"-wide) cross-grain strips
for outer appliqué section.
• 1 (25½" x 32½") center rectangle.
• 4 (10½"-wide) cross-grain strips
and 2 (10½" x 12") strips for middle appliqué section.

From pink
• 4 (4½" x 64") lengthwise strips
for second border.
• 4 (4½" x 35") lengthwise strips
for first border.

Setting Diagram

Quilt Top Assembly
1. See page 17 for instructions
on making continuous bias. From
green fabric, cut 40 yards (1,440")
of ¾"-wide continuous bias.

2. Cut vines and stems of desired
length and pin in place on muslin
rectangle **(Setting Diagram)**. Add
leaves as shown. Appliqué.

3. Sew 35"-long pink strips to
sides of rectangle; then sew 2 more
strips to top and bottom edges.

4. Sew 10½"-wide muslin strips
to side edges. Join remaining
10½"-wide strips to get 2 strips
54" long; sew these to top and bottom edges. Pin vine on muslin in
gentle curves; add stems and leaves
as shown. Appliqué.

5. Sew 2 (64"-long) pink strips to
quilt sides; then sew 2 more strips
to top and bottom edges.

6. Join 2 (11¼"-wide) muslin
strips for each outer border. Sew
strips to quilt sides; trim as needed.
Sew 2 remaining strips to top and
bottom edges of quilt. Pin vine,
stems, and leaves on muslin as
shown, and appliqué.

Leaf Pattern
*Pattern is finished size.
Add ¼" seam allowance
for hand appliqué or cut as
is for machine appliqué.*

Quilting and Finishing
1. Quilt as desired.
2. See page 16 for instructions
on making binding. Make 10 yards
of 2½"-wide straight-grain binding
from remaining pink fabric. Apply
binding to quilt edges.

Baskets & Bears

To make this prize-winning quilt, Kathy Munkelwitz mixed an original appliquéd basket design with traditional Bear's Paw blocks. Burgundy hearts and bows spice up the rich browns and tans of the patchwork.

Quilt by Kathy Munkelwitz,
Isle, Minnesota

Finished Quilt Size

81" x 106"

Number of Blocks and Finished Size

| 15 basket blocks | 12" x 12" |
| 8 Bear's Paw blocks | 12" x 12" |

Fabric Requirements

Tan or muslin	5¼ yards
Brown	4⅜ yards
Dark brown	1¾ yards
Burgundy	1½ yards
Pink	1 yard
Binding	1 yard
Backing	6⅜ yards

Cutting

Cut all strips cross-grain unless specified otherwise. Cut pieces in order listed for best use of yardage. Make templates of appliqué patterns A–M on pages 39 and 40.

From tan fabric

- 2 (9½" x 98") and 1 (9½" x 79") lengthwise strips for border.
- 5 (12½"-wide) strips. From these, cut 15 (12½") S squares.
- 3 (7"-wide) strips. From these, cut 15 (7" x 12") pieces for quick-pieced Q triangle-squares.
- 8 (2") T squares.
- 8 (2⅜") squares. Cut each square in half diagonally to get 16 R triangles.

From brown fabric

- 6 (3½" x 110"), 2 (3½" x 85"), and 1 (6½" x 54") lengthwise strips for borders. Use leftover pieces from this for next 4 cuts.
- 15 of Template B and 15 of Template B reversed.
- 15 of Template D.
- 15 of Template E.
- 44 (2¼") X squares.
- 9 (2"-wide) strips. From these, cut 60 (2" x 5¾") V pieces.
- 3 (7"-wide) strips. From these, cut 15 (7" x 12") pieces for quick-pieced Q triangle-squares. From remaining fabric, cut 16 (2⅜") squares. Cut each square in half diagonally to get 32 individual Q triangles for half-blocks and quarter-blocks.

From dark brown

- 5 (5"-wide) strips. From these, cut 15 of Template A.
- 4 (4⅜"-wide) strips. From these, cut 16 (4⅜") squares. Cut each square in half diagonally to get 32 P triangles.
- 4 (4"-wide) strips. From these and scrap, cut 44 (4") N squares.

From burgundy

- 45 of Template C.
- 31 of Template F and 31 of Template F reversed.
- 31 of Template H.
- 15 of Template J.
- 16 of Template K.
- 13 of Template L reversed.
- 2 of Template M.

From pink

- 31 of Template G and 31 of Template G reversed.
- 15 of Template I.
- 16 of Template K reversed.
- 13 of Template L.
- 2 of Template M.

Quilt Top Assembly

1. Fold each tan S square in half diagonally and crease fold line for center placement guide.

2. For each basket block, select 3 Cs and 1 each of A, B, B reversed, D, E, F, F reversed, G, G reversed, H, I, and J **(Basket Block Assembly Diagram)**. Turn under seam allowances on appliqué pieces. (It is not necessary to turn under edges that will be covered by another piece, such as top and bottom edges of A piece.)

3. Matching center lines, pin A on S square 4" from bottom corner as shown. Pin remaining pieces in place. When satisfied with placement, appliqué pieces A, B, C, D, and E in alphabetical order. For bow pieces, appliqué G and I pieces; then stitch down F and J pieces. Appliqué piece H last.

4. See page 11 for instructions and diagram for making quick-pieced triangle squares. Using 7" x 12" pieces of tan and brown fabrics, draw a 2 x 4-square grid of 2⅝" squares. Stitch and cut 16 triangle-squares from each of 15 grids to get 240 Q triangle-squares for Bear's Paw blocks.

continued

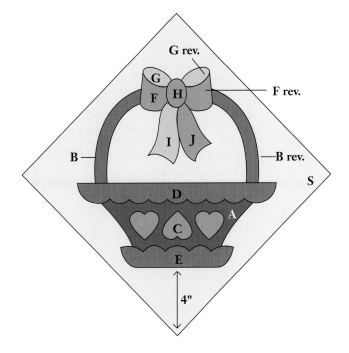

Basket Block Assembly Diagram

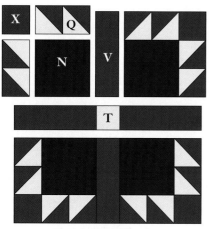

Bear's Paw Block Assembly Diagram

Half-Block Assembly Diagram

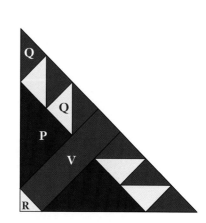

Quarter-Block Assembly Diagram

5. For each Bear's Paw block, select 16 Q triangle-squares, 1 T square, 4 V pieces, 4 N squares, and 4 X squares. Join Q triangle-squares in pairs **(Bear's Paw Block Assembly Diagram).** Sew an X square to end of 1 pair; then sew both rows to adjacent sides of N square. In this manner, make 4 Paw units. Sew 2 units to opposite sides of 2 V pieces. Press seam allowances toward Vs. Sew both remaining Vs to opposite sides of T square; press seam allowances toward Vs. Join rows to complete block. Make 8 Bear's Paw blocks.

6. Make 12 Bear's Paw half-blocks **(Half-Block Assembly Diagram).** Then make 4 Bear's Paw quarter-blocks, trimming R triangles to fit **(Quarter-Block Assembly Diagram).**

7. Lay out basket blocks and Bear's Paw blocks in diagonal rows **(Setting Diagram).** Add half-blocks and quarter-blocks at row ends as shown. Join blocks in each row; then join rows.

8. Sew 6½" x 54" brown strip to top edge of quilt. Press seam allowance toward border. Sew 3½" x 85" brown strip to bottom edge and 3½" x 110" brown strips to side edges. Miter bottom corners.

9. For middle borders, sew 98"-long tan strips to quilt sides. Trim borders even with quilt. Sew 79"-long strip to bottom edge. Press.

Setting Diagram

10. Sew 110"-long brown strips to quilt sides and 85"-long brown strip to quilt bottom. Miter bottom corners.

11. Position 6 bows (pieces F–H) and swags (K and L) on each tan side border; then place 4 bows and swags on tan bottom border, placing Ms at corners as shown. When satisfied with placement, appliqué pieces on tan border.

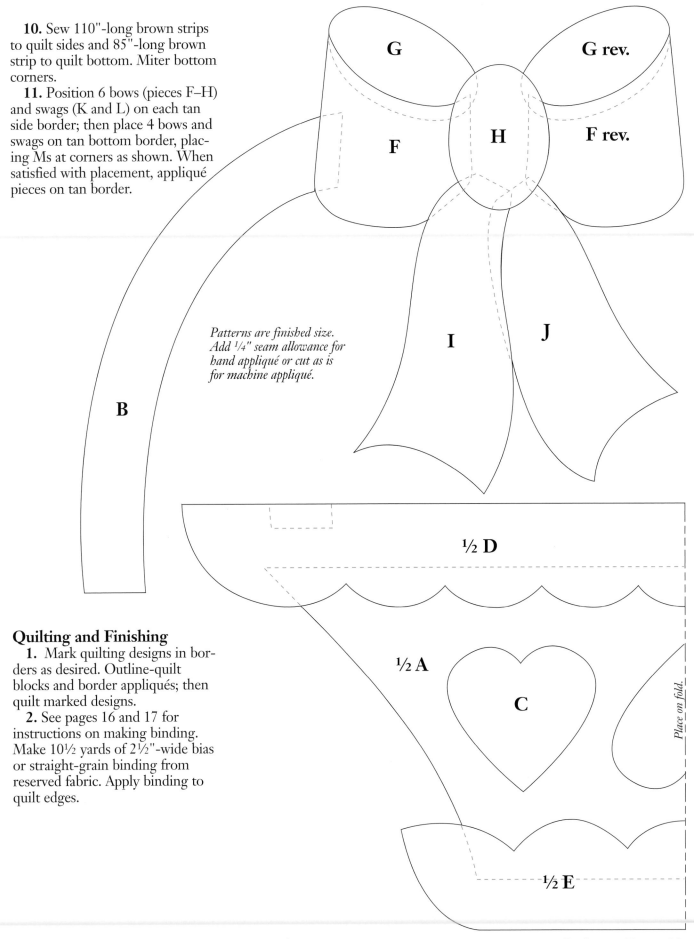

Patterns are finished size. Add ¹⁄₄" seam allowance for hand appliqué or cut as is for machine appliqué.

Quilting and Finishing

1. Mark quilting designs in borders as desired. Outline-quilt blocks and border appliqués; then quilt marked designs.

2. See pages 16 and 17 for instructions on making binding. Make 10½ yards of 2½"-wide bias or straight-grain binding from reserved fabric. Apply binding to quilt edges.

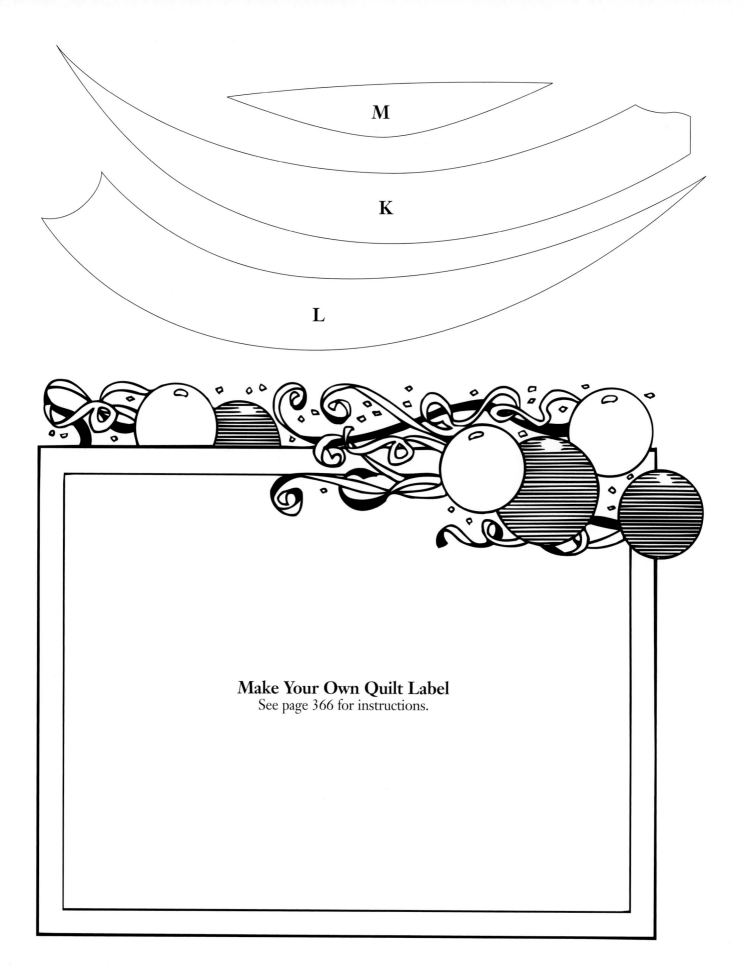

M

K

L

Make Your Own Quilt Label
See page 366 for instructions.

Birds in the Air

The traditional Birds in the Air block uses
two sizes of right-angle triangles. Mary Ann
Keathley added charm and a feeling of
movement with the addition of appliquéd birds.

Quilt by Mary Ann Keathley
Jacksonville, Arkansas

Finished Quilt Size
72½" x 87½"

Number of Blocks and Finished Size
99 blocks   7½" x 7½"

Fabric Requirements
Assorted prints   25 fat eighths*
Muslin   5 yards
Aqua   ¼ yard
Brown print   2⅜ yards**
Backing   5½ yards

*Fat eighth = 9" x 22"

**Includes fabric for straight-grain binding.

Other Materials
10 (⅛") flat buttons (optional)

Cutting
Make a template of Bird Pattern, opposite. Cut all strips cross-grain unless specified otherwise. Cut pieces in order listed to get best use of yardage.

From each *print fat eighth*
- 12 (3⅜") squares. Cut each square in half diagonally to get 24 A triangles, 6 for each of 4 blocks. (You'll have 1 extra set.)

From muslin
- 25 (3⅜"-wide) strips. From these, cut 149 (3⅜") squares. Cut each square in half diagonally to get 297 A triangles (and 1 extra).
- 10 (8⅜"-wide) strips. From these, cut 50 (8⅜") squares. Cut each square in half diagonally to get 99 B triangles (and 1 extra).

From aqua
- 8 (1"-wide) strips for inner border.

From brown print
- 2 (2½" x 85") and 2 (2½" x 74") lengthwise strips for outer border.
- 1 (30") square for binding.
- 10 of Bird Template.

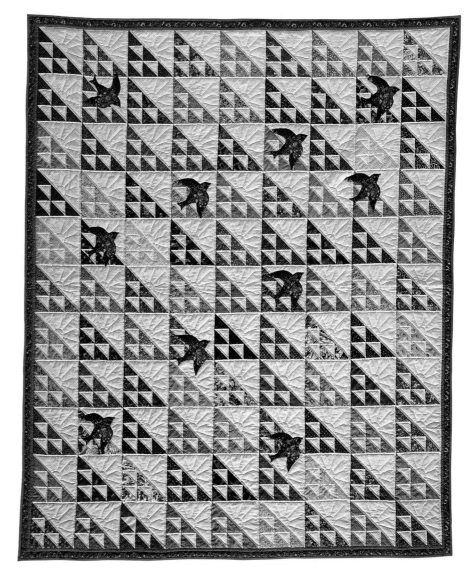

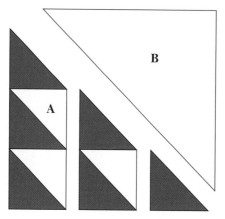

Block Assembly Diagram

Quilt Top Assembly
1. For each block, select 6 A triangles of the same print fabric, 3 muslin A triangles, and 1 muslin B.

2. Join 9 A triangles in rows as shown **(Block Assembly Diagram)**; press seam allowances toward print triangles. Then join rows to make a pieced triangle.

3. Join pieced triangle to B to complete 1 block.

4. Make 99 blocks.

5. Lay out blocks in 9 horizontal rows with 11 blocks in each row. Arrange blocks to get a pleasing balance of color and pattern. When satisfied with placement, join blocks in each row. Join rows.

Placement for button ✳

Bird Pattern

6. Prepare birds for appliqué. Referring to photograph for placement, appliqué birds to quilt top.

7. Join 2 aqua strips end to end to get a border for each quilt edge. Matching centers, stitch an aqua border to each brown border strip along long edges. Sew borders to edges of quilt, mitering corners.

Quilting and Finishing

1. Quilt as desired.

2. If desired, sew a button in place for each bird's eye as indicated on bird pattern.

3. See page 16 for instructions on making binding. Make 9¼ yards of 2½"-wide straight-grain binding from remaining brown fabric. Apply binding to quilt edges.

Make Your Own Quilt Label
See page 366 for instructions.

Broken Star

Zelda Fasciano was 17 when she first saw a picture of a Broken Star quilt. It was the Depression and she had just begun her first job. Without the aid of a rotary cutter or strip piecing, Zelda drafted a pattern and began to sew. It took Zelda five years to complete her masterpiece, which has been winning blue ribbons for more than 50 years. We provide instructions for both strip piecing and traditional piecing.

Quilt by Zelda Wheeler Fasciano
Greenville, North Carolina

Finished Quilt Size
72" x 83"

Number of Diamonds and Finished Size
32 pieced diamonds   10½" on each side

Fabric Requirements
Yellow	⅞ yard
Pink	¾ yard
Blue	¾ yard
Orange	¾ yard
Red	¾ yard
Green	¾ yard
Muslin	3 yards
Binding fabric	⅞ yard
Backing	5 yards

Cutting
For traditional piecing, make a template of Diamond Pattern on page 47. Cut all strips cross-grain.
From yellow
- 18 (1½"-wide) strips. For traditional piecing only, cut 288 diamonds from this strip.

From pink, blue, orange, red, and green
- 16 (1½"-wide) strips of each color. For traditional piecing only, cut 256 diamonds of each color from these strips.

Quilt Top Assembly
1. For traditional piecing, join diamonds in rows **(Diamond Piecing Diagram)**, sewing 7 diamonds in each row. Make 7 rows for each pieced diamond. Press seam allowances in odd-numbered rows toward top of row and those in even-numbered sets toward bottom of row.

2. For strip piecing, join strips in sets as shown **(Strip Set Diagrams).** Each set has a slightly different order, so follow color placement carefully. Piece 4 of Strip Set 1; piece 2 each of strip sets 2, 3, 4, 5, and 6. Press all seam allowances in odd-numbered sets toward top row and those in even-numbered sets toward bottom row.

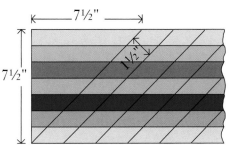

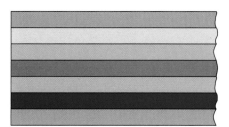

Strip Set 1—Make 4.   Strip Set 2—Make 2.

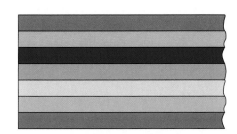

Strip Set 3—Make 2.   Strip Set 4—Make 2.

Strip Set 5—Make 2.   Strip Set 6—Make 2.

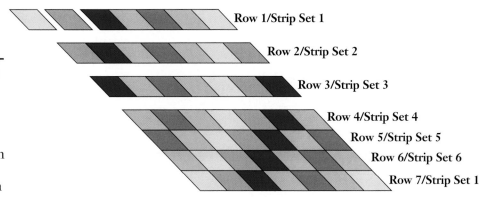

Row 1/Strip Set 1
Row 2/Strip Set 2
Row 3/Strip Set 3
Row 4/Strip Set 4
Row 5/Strip Set 5
Row 6/Strip Set 6
Row 7/Strip Set 1

Diamond Piecing Diagram

3. On each strip set, trim a 7½" triangle from 1 corner as shown **(Strip Set 1 Diagram).** (If desired, you can use these triangles later to make pieced binding.) Measuring from cut edge, rotary-cut 16 (1½"-wide) segments from each strip set.

4. Select 7 rows or strip-set segments for each pieced diamond. Matching seam lines in adjacent rows, join strips to make a large pieced diamond **(Diamond Piecing Diagram)**. Make 32 pieced diamonds. *continued*

5. Join 2 pieced diamonds, matching colors and seam lines **(Star Piecing Diagram).** Sew from center out. Do not sew from edge to edge, but begin and end each seam at seam line. Make 4 quarter units. Each joined pair of diamonds forms a 90° angle.

6. Join 2 quarters to make half star. Sewing from center out, join 2 halves, matching seam lines.

7. Measure straight edge of each pieced diamond. Add ½" to this measurement for seam allowances, and cut 8 squares from muslin.

8. To set a square in each corner of star **(Diagram A)**, match a square to leg of 1 diamond, right sides together, and stitch from seam line of outside edge to seam line of inside edge. Align remaining side with leg of opposite diamond and stitch from inside seam line to seam line of outside edge. Join all 8 squares as shown.

9. Join remaining pieced diamonds into 8 groups of 3 **(Diagram B).** Set 1 diamond unit to adjacent muslin squares in same manner as set-in squares in Step 8 **(Diagram C).** Set in all 8 diamond units; then join sides of diamonds in mitered seams.

10. Measure straight edge of pieced diamonds; add ⅞" to measurement and cut 4 muslin squares. Fold squares diagonally and crease. Unfold and staystitch ¼" from each side of crease. Cut squares on diagonal to get 8 side triangles.

11. Set triangles into sides, top, and bottom of star in same manner as set-in squares in Step 8 **(Diagram D).**

12. Measure straight edge of pieced diamonds. As in Step 8, add ½" for seam allowances and cut 12 muslin squares. Join squares in groups of 3. Set squares into corners **(Diagram D).**

13. Cut 4 (6" x 42") muslin border strips. Join 2 strips end-to-end for each border. Matching center seams, stitch borders to top and bottom of quilt. Trim excess border fabric.

90°

Star Piecing Diagram

Diagram A

Diagram B

Diagram C

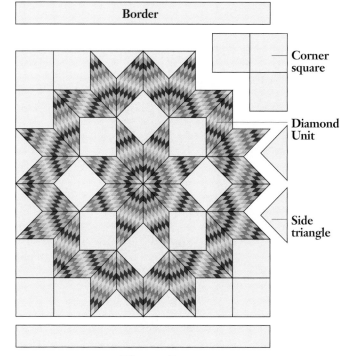

Border

Corner square

Diamond Unit

Side triangle

Diagram D

Quilting and Finishing

1. Outline-quilt ¼" inside all seam lines. Quilt shown also has a feathered wreath quilted in each muslin square. Quilt remainder of quilt in 1" cross-hatching.

2. See pages 16 and 17 for instructions on making binding. Make 8¾ yards of 2½"-wide bias or straight-grain binding from reserved fabric. If you want to use strip-set scraps, cut 2½"-wide bias strips from leftover triangles and scraps. Join pieces end-to-end to get 8¾ yards of bias binding. Apply binding to quilt edges.

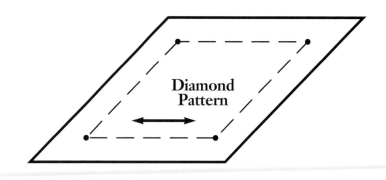

Diamond Pattern

Buckeye Beauty

Strip-pieced four-patch blocks combine with quick-pieced triangle-squares to make this blue-and-rose beauty. Careful placement of light and dark fabrics make the four-patches appear to float on a series of diagonal stripes.

Quilt by Arleen Boyd
Rochester, New York

Finished Quilt Size
72" x 87"

Number of Blocks and Finished Size
45 Block As	5" x 5"
45 Block Bs	5" x 5"
90 Block Cs	5" x 5"

Fabric Requirements
Dark rose print	¾ yard
Medium rose print	¾ yard
Medium blue print	¾ yard
Light print	¾ yard
Dark blue print	1½ yards
Light rose print	1½ yards
Inner border fabric	2½ yards
Outer border fabric	3⅜ yards*
Backing	5¼ yards

*Includes 30" square for binding.

Cutting
From dark rose print
• 7 (3"-wide) strips.

From medium rose print
• 7 (3"-wide) strips.

From medium blue print
• 7 (3"-wide) strips.

From light print
• 7 (3"-wide) strips.

From dark blue print
• 6 (14" x 26") pieces for Block C (triangle-squares).

From light rose print
• 6 (14" x 26") pieces for Block C (triangle-squares).

Quilt Top Assembly
1. With right sides facing and raw edges aligned, join each medium blue strip to a light print strip along 1 long edge. Press seam allowances toward darker strip.

2. From these strip sets, cut 90 (3"-wide) segments **(Diagram 1).**

3. Join 2 segments to make a block as shown **(Block A Diagram).** Join 2-color units in chain-piecing fashion to make 45 Block A four-patches. *Note:* For tips on chain-piecing, see page 10.

4. Use strips of dark rose print and medium rose print to make 45 of Block B in same manner.

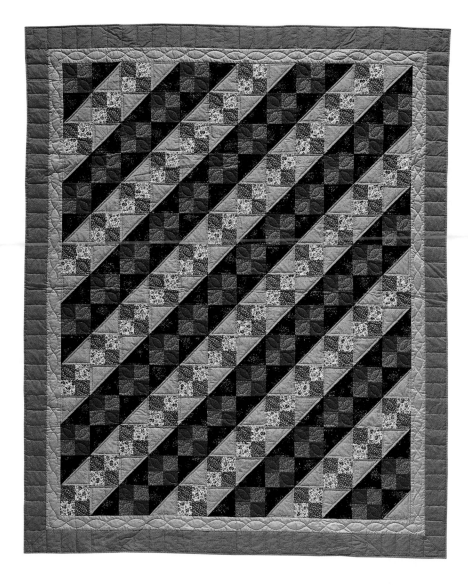

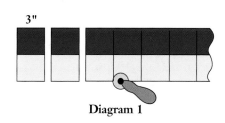

Block A Diagram

Block B Diagram

3"

Diagram 1

continued

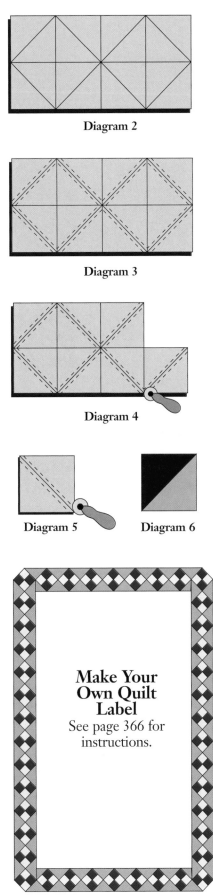

Diagram 2

Diagram 3

Diagram 4

Diagram 5   Diagram 6

Setting Diagram

Make Your Own Quilt Label
See page 366 for instructions.

Quilt Label

5. On wrong side of each light rose print piece, draw a 2 x 4-square grid of 8 (5⅞") squares **(Diagram 2).** Leave a margin of at least ¼" around outside of grid.

6. With right sides facing and raw edges aligned, lay each light rose print piece on top of a dark blue print piece. Machine-stitch ¼" on either side of drawn diagonal lines **(Diagram 3).**

7. Cut squares apart on drawn horizontal and vertical lines **(Diagram 4).** Cut on drawn diagonal lines between stitching **(Diagram 5).** Unfold triangles; press seam allowances toward darker fabric **(Diagram 6).** Repeat to make 90 Block C triangle-squares.

8. Lay out blocks in 15 horizontal rows of 12 blocks each **(Setting Diagram).** When satisfied with placement, join units in each row. Then join rows.

9. Cut 4 (3" x 90") lengthwise borders from light blue solid and 4 (4" x 90") borders from rose solid. Join borders in pairs. Sew borders to quilt, mitering corners.

Quilting and Finishing
1. Quilt as desired.
2. See pages 16 and 17 for instructions on making binding. Make 9 yards of 2½"-wide bias or straight-grain binding from remaining rose solid. Apply binding to quilt edges.

Butterflies

June Wolpert discovered this pattern in 1962 when Dover Publications reprinted *101 Patchwork Patterns*, a collection of patterns created by McKim Studios of Independence, Missouri. Ruby S. McKim, owner of McKim Studios, syndicated a newspaper column of quilt patterns during the 1920s and 1930s.

Quilt by June Wolpert
Nashville, Indiana

Finished Quilt Size
64" x 84"

Number of Blocks and Finished Size
18 butterfly blocks   10" x 10"

Fabric Requirements
Prints	18 (12" x 12") scraps
Solids	18 (12" x 12") scraps
Muslin	¾ yard
Black	⅛ yard
Beige	1¾ yards
Burgundy/white print	2¼ yards
Burgundy	3¼ yards*
Burgundy stripe	2½ yards
Backing	5 yards

*Includes fabric for binding.

Other Materials
Black embroidery floss

Cutting
Make templates of patterns A–H on pages 53 and 54.

From each *print scrap*
• 2 of Template C.
• 1 each of templates B and B reversed.

From each *solid scrap*
• 2 of Template E.
• 1 each of templates F, F reversed, H and H reversed.

From muslin
• 18 *each* of templates A and G.
• 36 of Template D.

From black
• 18 (1¾" x 4¾") for butterfly body.

Quilt Top Assembly
1. For each block, select 1 B/C set and 1 E/F/H set.

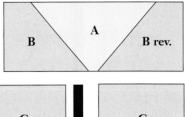

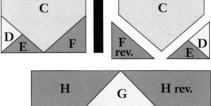

Block Assembly Diagram

2. For top unit, sew B and B rev. to A **(Block Assembly Diagram)**.

3. Make 2 D/E units. Sew D/E and F (or F reversed) to each C as shown. Sew these units to opposite sides of black body piece to complete middle unit.

3. Join 1 H and 1 H rev. to G to make bottom unit.

4. Join top, middle, and bottom units to complete block. Make 18 butterfly blocks.

5. Using 3 strands of floss, make small running stitches to work antennae.

6. Cut 17 (10½") beige squares. Lay out squares and butterfly blocks in 7 horizontal rows as shown **(Setting Diagram)**. Join blocks and squares in each row; then join rows.

7. From burgundy/white print, cut 2 (2½" x 56") and 2 (2½" x 76") lengthwise strips for inner border. From burgundy, cut 2 (1½" x 58") and 2 (1½" x 78") strips for middle border. From stripe, cut 2 (4½" x 66") and 2 (4½" x 86") strips for outer border.

8. Mark centers on edges of each border strip. Join strips in sets of 3 as shown to make 1 border unit for each quilt side **(Setting Diagram)**.

9. Matching centers of borders and quilt edges, sew borders to all edges. See page 14 for instructions on mitering border corners.

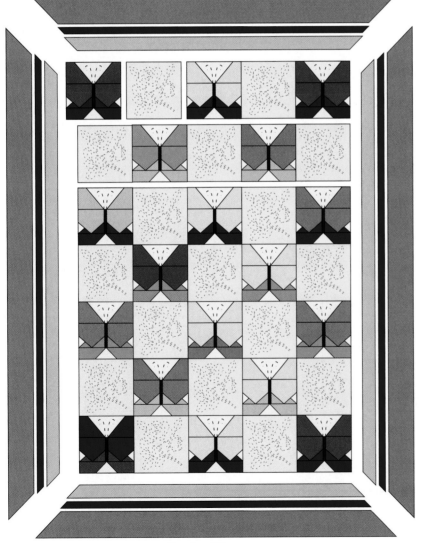

Setting Diagram

Quilting and Finishing

1. Outline-quilt butterflies. Quilt rose pattern (page 54) in beige squares.

2. See pages 16 and 17 for instructions on making binding. Make 9 yards of 2½"-wide bias or straight-grain binding from remaining burgundy fabric. Apply binding to quilt edges.

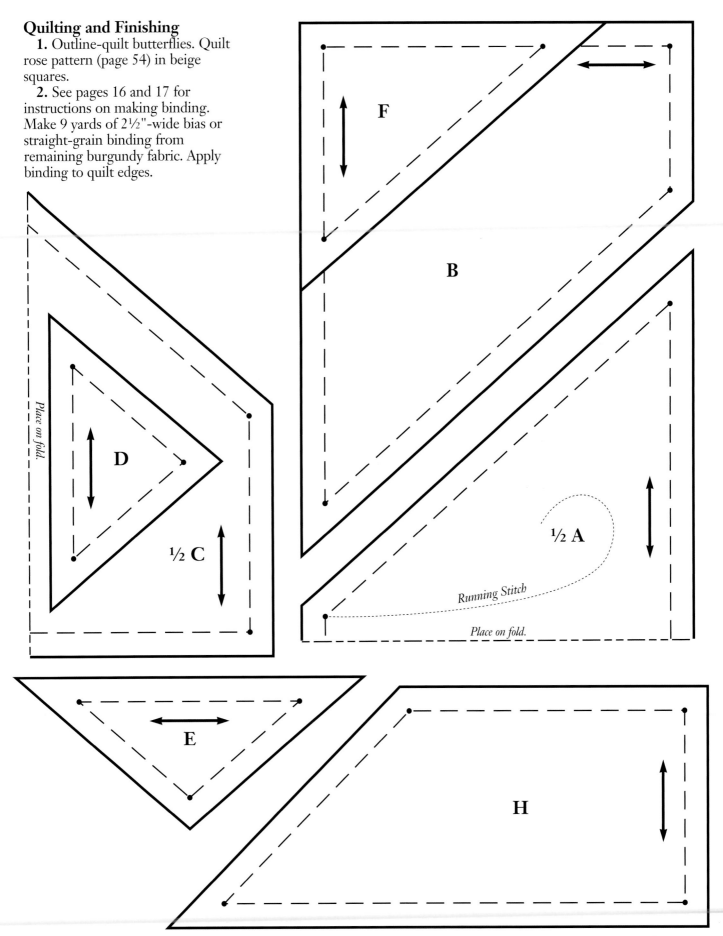

F

B

½ A

Running Stitch

Place on fold.

Place on fold.

D

½ C

E

H

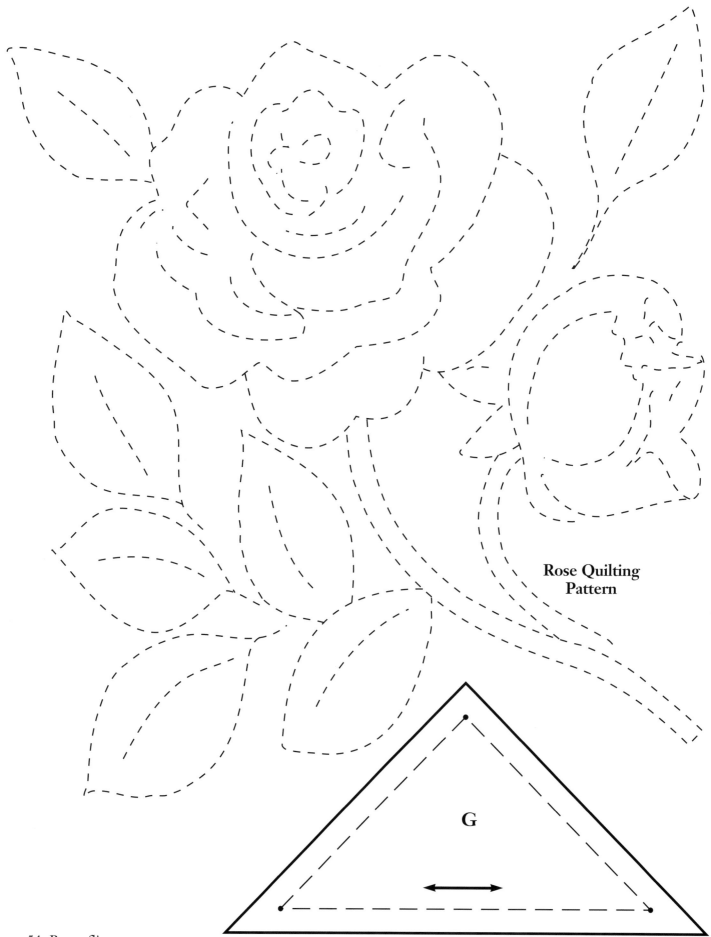

Rose Quilting Pattern

G

Caesar's Crown

In 1936, a teenager named Betty Jane bought the pattern and fabric for this quilt for a total of $6.38. Her inexperienced hands soon frustrated her, however, and Betty Jane put the quilt away. Decades later, she took it out again. She presented the finished quilt to her granddaughter in 1988, more than 50 years after she first began *Caesar's Crown*.

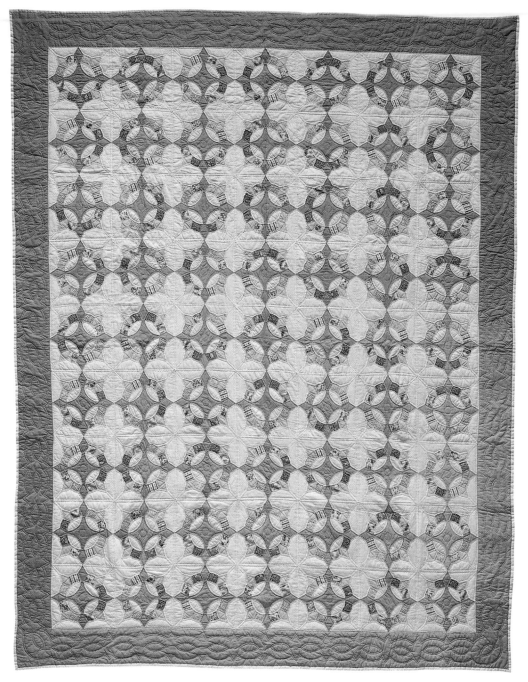

Quilt by Betty Jane Dollriehs
Cincinnati, Ohio

Finished Quilt Size
83¼" x 103¾"

Number of Blocks and Finished Size
63 blocks   10¼" x 10¼"

Fabric Requirements
Lavender	4⅜ yards
Muslin	7 yards
Peach	1¼ yards
Assorted prints	7 fat quarters*
Binding fabric	⅞ yard
Backing	6¼ yards

*Fat quarter = 18" x 22".

Cutting
Make templates of patterns A– E. Cut strips cross-grain unless specified otherwise. Cut pieces in order listed to get best use of yardage.

From lavender
- 9 (6"-wide) strips. From these, cut 63 of Template D.
- 2 (6" x 86") and 2 (6" x 97") lengthwise border strips.
- 42 (2" x 19") strips. From these, cut 252 of Template A.

From muslin
- 252 *each* of templates C, E, and E reversed.

From peach
- 252 of Template A.

From each fat quarter
- 72 of Template B.

Quilt Top Assembly
1. Sew 2 Bs to 1 peach A **(Diagram 1).** Join unit to C. (See page 11 for tips on sewing a curved seam.) Make 4 A/B/C units for each block. Join these units to D.

2. Set in 4 lavender As **(Diagram 2).**

3. Set in 4 Es and 4 Es reversed to complete block **(Diagram 3).** Make 63 blocks.

4. Lay out blocks in 9 horizontal rows with 7 blocks in each row. Join blocks in each row. Join rows.

5. Sew longer borders to quilt sides. Sew remaining border strips to top and bottom edges.

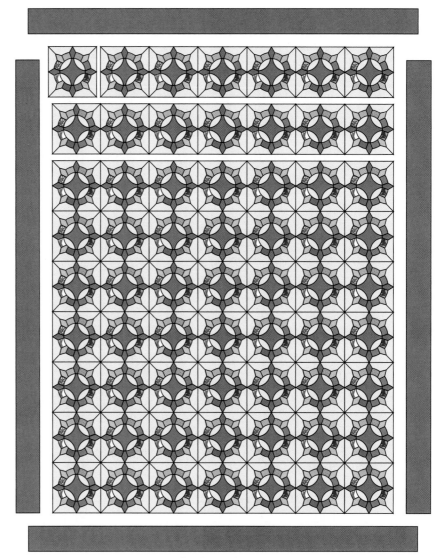

Setting Diagram

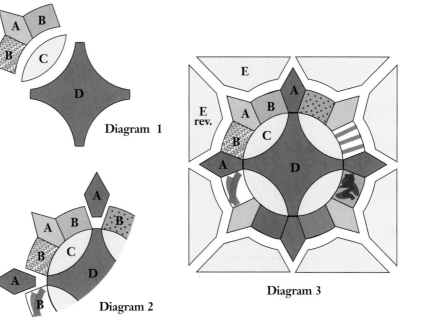

Diagram 1

Diagram 2

Diagram 3

Quilting and Finishing

1. Outline-quilt block pieces. Add other quilting as desired.

2. See pages 16 and 17 for instructions on making binding. Make 10¾ yards of 2½"-wide bias or straight-grain binding. Apply binding to quilt edges.

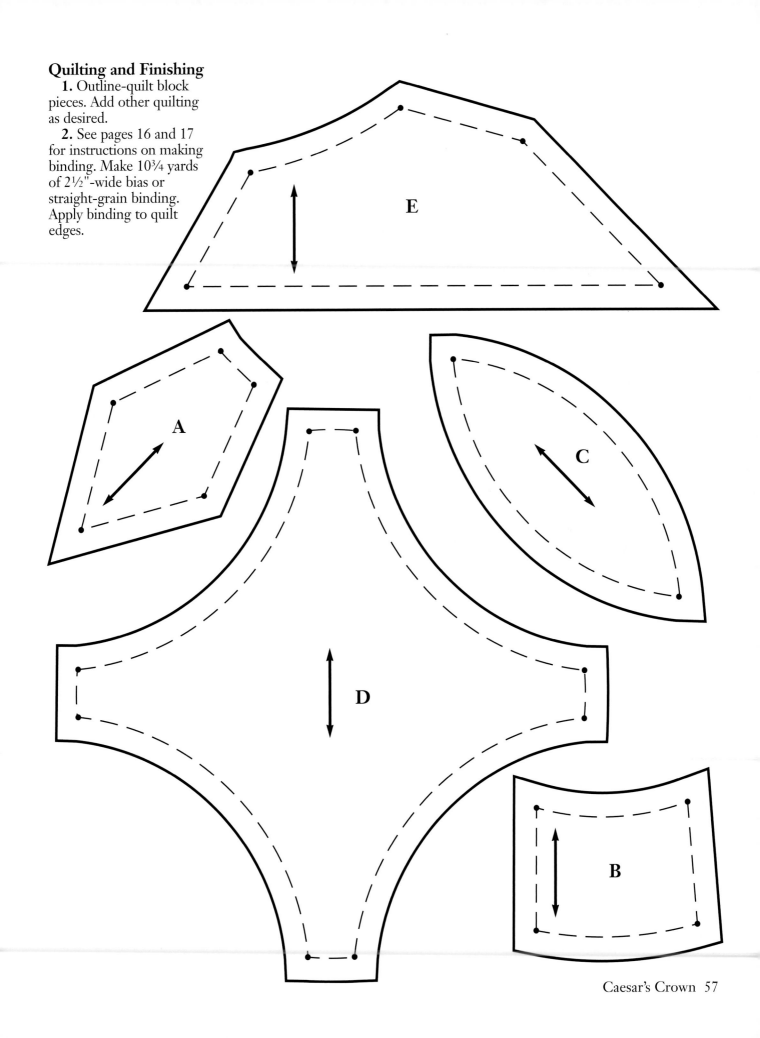

Cathedral Windows

Made without batting or quilting, this quilt is ideal for lovers of handwork. The three-dimensional effect of the design is achieved by inserting scrap squares into folded squares of background fabric. The layers of folded fabric eliminate the need for quilting.

Quilt by Eugenia L. Hardin
Appling, Georgia

Finished Quilt Size

Twin-size	66" x 78"
Full-size	72" x 84"
Queen-size	84" x 84"
King-size	96" x 108"

Number of Blocks and Finished Size

Twin-size: 143 Blocks	6" x 6"
Full-size: 168 Blocks	6" x 6"
Queen-size: 196 Blocks	6" x 6"
King-size: 288 Blocks	6" x 6"

Fabric Requirements

Muslin

Twin-size	19 yards
Full-size	22 yards
Queen-size	26 yards
King-size	38 yards

Scraps of solids and prints

Twin-size	13 fat quarters* or 3 yards
Full-size	15 fat quarters* or 3¾ yards
Queen-size	17 fat quarters* or 4 yards
King-size	25 fat quarters* or 6 yards

*Fat quarter = 18" x 22".

See page 61 for an alternate color scheme, using just two contrasting fabrics.

Cutting

From muslin
> Twin-size: 572 (7") squares.
> Full-size: 672 (7") squares.
> Queen-size: 784 (7") squares.
> King-size: 1,152 (7") squares.

From assorted scraps
> Twin-size: 1,100 (2") squares.
> Full-size: 1,292 (2") squares.
> Queen-size: 1,512 (2") squares.
> King-size: 2,215 (2") squares.

Quilt Top Assembly

1. Press under ¼" on all 4 sides of 1 muslin square (**Diagram 1**).

2. With right sides facing, fold square in half (**Diagram 2**). Whipstitch ends together, catching just folds of fabric in stitches.

3. Turn stitched piece right side out. Refold it into a square with seams meeting at center (**Diagram 3**). Stitching through top layer of fabric only, whipstitch open edges together as shown.

4. Fold corners of square so that points meet at center where seams cross (**Diagram 4**). Tack corners together at center, stitching through all layers of fabric, to complete 1 folded square. Folded square should measure 3". Make 4 folded squares for each block.

continued

Diagram 1

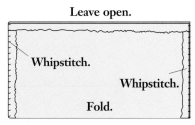

Leave open.
Whipstitch. Whipstitch. Fold.

Diagram 2

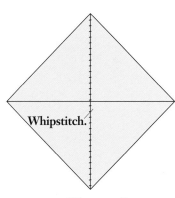

Whipstitch.

Diagram 3

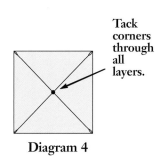

Tack corners through all layers.

Diagram 4

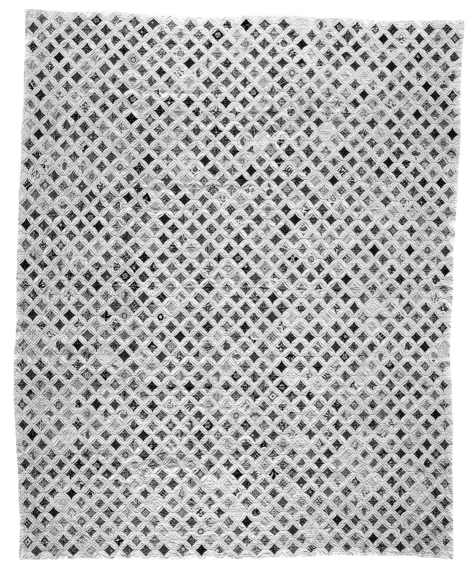

5. With right sides (sides with tacked corners) facing, whipstitch 2 folded squares together along 1 side, catching just folds of fabric in stitches. Join 2 more squares in same manner. With right sides facing, join both two-square units to make 1 four-square block (**Diagram 5**).

6. Center 1 (2") scrap square over diamond shape formed by 2 adjacent squares (**Diagram 5**), and pin. Turn 1 folded edge of diamond in a curve over edge of scrap square (**Diagram 6**), and slipstitch curve in place. Fold remaining 3 edges over scrap square in same manner and slipstitch in place.

7. Add 3 more scrap squares to complete block (**Diagram 6**).

8. Make 143 blocks for a twin-size quilt, 168 blocks for full-size, 196 blocks for queen-size, or 288 blocks for king-size.

9. To form a row, join 11 blocks for twin-size, 12 blocks for full-size, 14 blocks for queen-size, or 16 blocks for king-size. Make 13 rows for twin-size, 14 rows for full-size and queen-size, or 18 rows for king-size.

10. Sew colored squares into diamonds formed by adjacent blocks.

11. Join rows. Sew colored squares into diamonds formed by adjacent rows.

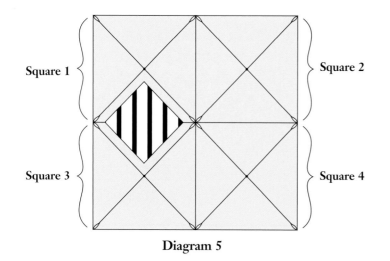

Square 1 Square 2

Square 3 Square 4

Diagram 5

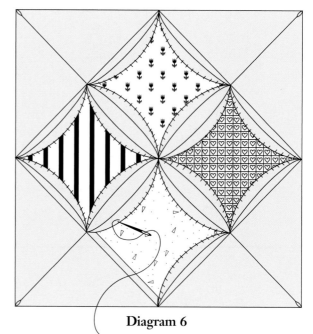

Diagram 6

Elizabeth R. Lawrence of Athens, Georgia, chose to use
a single fabric for the insets rather than assorted scraps.

Cherry

Cherries, symbols of sweet character and good works, were popular motifs among quilters throughout the United States, especially during the original era of Baltimore Album quilts. Cherries embellished floral wreaths, cornucopias, baskets, and other designs. Here clusters of them stand alone in a radiant splash of color and symmetry. Helen Louise Lindsey's aptitude for fine needlework shows in every cherry. Each is round, of equal size, lies flat, and is evenly spaced in relation to the next. Rows of cross-hatched quilting over this large quilt make it a noteworthy quilting feat.

Quilt by Helen Louise Lindsey
Owned by David Sanders
Mobile, Alabama

Finished Quilt Size
96" x 113"

Number of Blocks and Finished Size
20 blocks   17" x 17"

Fabric Requirements
Muslin   10¾ yards*
Red   2 yards
Green   2½ yards
Backing   9¾ yards
*Includes fabric for binding.

Cutting
Make templates of appliqué patterns A, B, and C below.

From muslin
- 20 (17½") squares.
- 18 (14½" x 17½") rectangles.
- 4 (14½") corner squares.

From red fabric
- 840 of Template A.

From green fabric
- 240 *each* of templates C, B, and B reversed.

Quilt Top Assembly
1. Place A cherries and B leaves on 17½" muslin squares **(Placement Diagram)**; appliqué. Note that cherry placement leaves a space 5" square in center of block. Appliqué C stems as shown.

2. For side rectangles and corner squares, appliqué cherries, leaves, and stems **(Placement Diagram)**.

3. Join blocks in 5 rows with 4 blocks in each row. Add side rectangles at row ends. Join rows.

4. Join 4 appliquéd rectangles each to make top and bottom borders. Join an appliquéd corner square to each end. Join borders to top and bottom edges of quilt.

Quilting and Finishing
1. Quilt background with 1" diagonal cross-hatching pattern.

2. See pages 16 and 17 for instructions on making binding. Make 12 yards of 2½"-wide bias or straight-grain binding from remaining muslin. Apply binding to quilt edges.

Perfect Cherries
To make perfectly circular, ready-to-appliqué cherries, use a pressing template and a few gathering stitches.

From cardboard or other heat-resistant material, cut a circular template using pattern A *without* seam allowances.

Using a long running stitch, stitch by hand around the edges of one fabric cherry (A), about ⅛" to ¼" from the raw edge. Center the cardboard template on the wrong side of the cherry and pull the thread to gather the stitches. Press. Loosen the gathering stitches enough to remove the template, and press again to flatten.

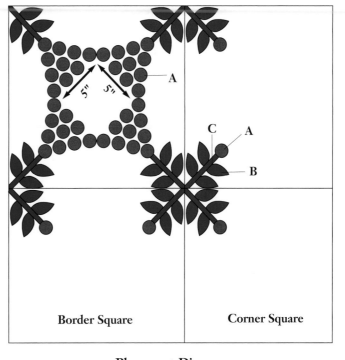

Placement Diagram

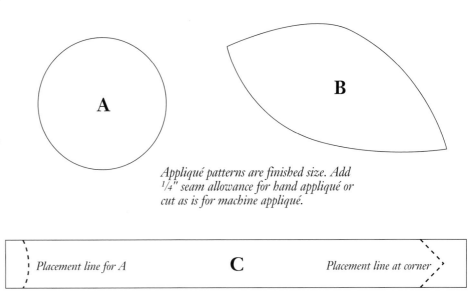

Appliqué patterns are finished size. Add ¼" seam allowance for hand appliqué or cut as is for machine appliqué.

Cherry Rose

Margie Karavitis learned to quilt by trial and error. "Mostly error," she jokes. "It wasn't until I joined a quilt group that I had access to classes, books, and other quilters." *Cherry Rose* was Margie's first appliquéd quilt. The corded quilting makes this an impressive work. *Cherry Rose* is now part of a permanent collection at the Museum of the American Quilters Society in Paducah, Kentucky.

Quilt by Margie Turner Karavitis
Spokane, Washington

Finished Quilt Size
94⅜" x 94⅜"

Number of Blocks and Finished Size
16 blocks   18" x 18"

Fabric Requirements
Muslin   8¼ yards*
Green   3⅛ yards
Red   2¼ yards
Backing   8⅛ yards
*Includes fabric for binding.

Cutting
Make templates of patterns A–G on page 66.
From muslin
- 4 (11" x 97") lengthwise strips for border.
- 1 (32") square for bias binding.
- 16 (18½") squares.
- 200 of Template F.

From green
- 1 (30") square for border vine.
- 64 of Template B.
- 64 of Template C.
- 464 of Template E.
- 40 of Template G.

From red
- 80 of Template A.
- 952 of Template D.
- 200 of Template F.

Quilt Top Assembly
1. Fold 1 muslin square in half vertically, horizontally, and diagonally, finger-pressing folds to make placement guidelines.

2. Arrange pieces on muslin square as shown **(Appliqué Placement Diagram).** Appliqué pieces in place in alphabetical order. (See page 63 for tips on making perfect cherries.) Make 16 blocks.

3. Arrange blocks in 4 horizontal rows with 4 blocks in each row. Join blocks in rows; then join rows.
continued

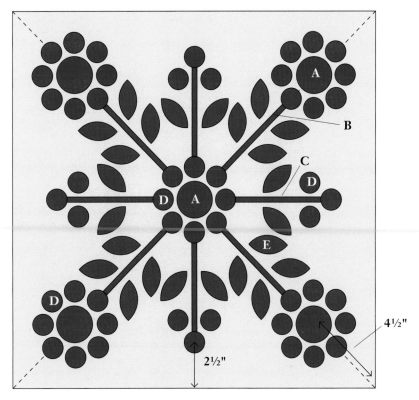

Appliqué Placement Diagram

Color Variations
These are some suggestions for other color schemes.

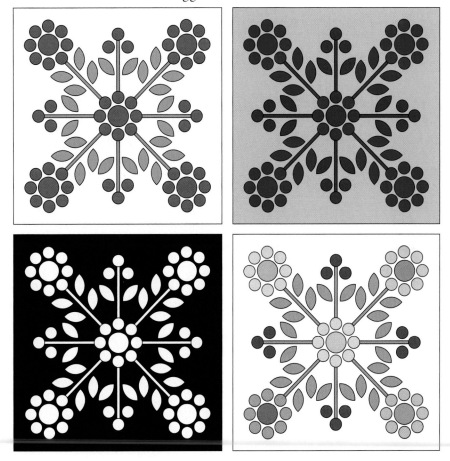

Cherry Rose 65

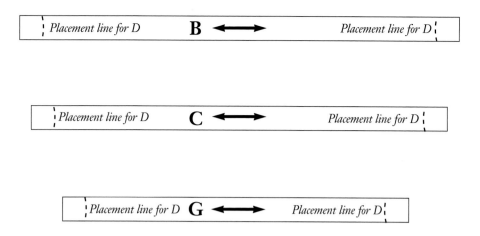

B ⟷

Placement line for D   Placement line for D

C ⟷

Placement line for D   Placement line for D

G ⟷

Placement line for D   Placement line for D

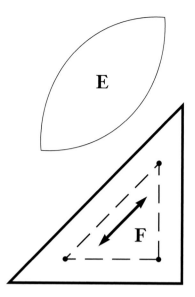

E

F

Appliqué patterns are finished size. Add ¼" seam allowance for hand appliqué or cut as is for machine appliqué.

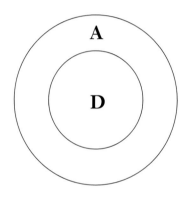

A

D

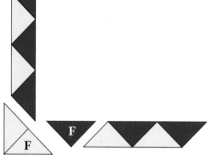

F   F   F

Triangle Strip Diagram

4. For each sawtooth border, select 50 red Fs and 48 muslin Fs. Join triangles in a strip, alternating colors as shown, beginning and ending with red Fs (**Triangle Strip Diagram**). Make 4 border strips. Matching red triangles with quilt edge, sew 1 strip to each side of quilt, easing to fit as needed. Join 2 muslin Fs and stitch to each corner as shown.

5. Mark centers on each edge of quilt and on edges of each border strip. Matching centers, sew border strips to all quilt sides; miter border corners.

6. Divide each border into 10 segments and mark placement lines

for cherry clusters (**Border Placement Diagram**). Arrange Gs, Ds, and Es on border and appliqué. Center 1 cherry cluster in each corner over miter.

7. See page 17 for instructions on making continuous bias. From reserved green square, cut approximately 17 yards (600") of ¾"-wide continuous bias.

8. Fold under ¼" on both long edges of bias strip; press. Referring to photograph on page 64, weave bias-strip vine around clusters and appliqué in place.

Quilting and Finishing

1. Outline-quilt around all appliquéd pieces and inside seam lines of all muslin triangles. Echo-quilt 2 lines outside vine and border cherry clusters at ¼" intervals. Quilt remainder of quilt with 1" double cross-hatching grid.

2. See page 17 for instructions on making binding. Make 10¾ yards of 2½"-wide bias binding. Apply binding to quilt edges.

Border Placement Diagram

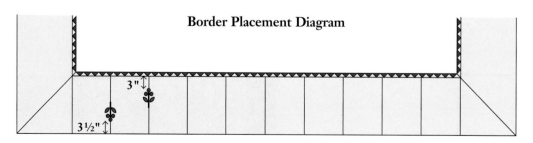

3"

3½"

66 Cherry Rose

Christmas Beauty

Classic geometry and holiday fabrics make this a quilt for all seasons. A variation of a traditional Irish Chain, the checkerboard units are strip-pieced, while patterns are given for the center triangles and the Flying Geese border.

Quilt by Dorothy Repass Umberger
Ceres, Virginia

Finished Quilt Size
77¾" x 92¾"

Number of Blocks and Finished Size
20 blocks   16" x 16"

Fabric Requirements
Red paisley print   1½ yards
Green paisley print   1½ yards
Muslin   4 yards
Red   1½ yards
Green   1¾ yards*
Backing   5½ yards
*Includes fabric for binding.

Cutting
Instructions are for rotary cutting. If you prefer traditional methods, make templates of patterns A, B, and C, opposite. Cut all strips cross-grain unless specified otherwise. Cut pieces in order listed to get best use of yardage.

From red paisley print
- 5 (4⅞"-wide) strips. From these, cut 40 (4⅞") squares. Cut each square in half diagonally to get 80 A triangles.
- 3 (6¼"-wide) strips. From these, cut 17 (6¼") squares. Cut each square in quarters diagonally to get 67 B triangles (and 1 extra).

From green paisley print
- 5 (4⅞"-wide) strips. From these, cut 40 (4⅞") squares. Cut each square in half diagonally to get 80 A triangles.
- 3 (6¼"-wide) strips. From these, cut 17 (6¼") squares. Cut each square in quarters diagonally to get 67 B triangles (and 1 extra).

From muslin
- 20 (2½"-wide) strips.
- 10 (3⅜"-wide) strips. From these, cut 118 (3⅜") squares. Cut each square in half diagonally to get 236 C triangles.
- 10 (4⅞"-wide) strips. From these, cut 40 (4⅞") squares. Cut each square in half diagonally to get 160 A triangles.

From red
- 10 (2½"-wide) strips.
- 4 (1¾"-wide) strips and 4 (2¼"-wide) strips for inner border.

From green
- 10 (2½"-wide) strips.

Quilt Top Assembly
1. Sew 1 muslin strip to each colored strip to make 20 strip sets **(Diagram 1)**. Press seam allowances toward darker fabric. Cut each strip set into 16 (2½"-wide) segments as shown to get 160 segments of each color combination.
2. Join 2 segments to make each four-patch unit **(Diagram 2)**. Make 80 green/muslin units and 80 red/muslin units.

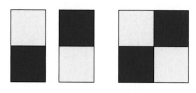

Diagram 1

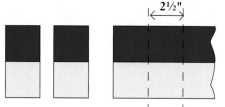

Diagram 2

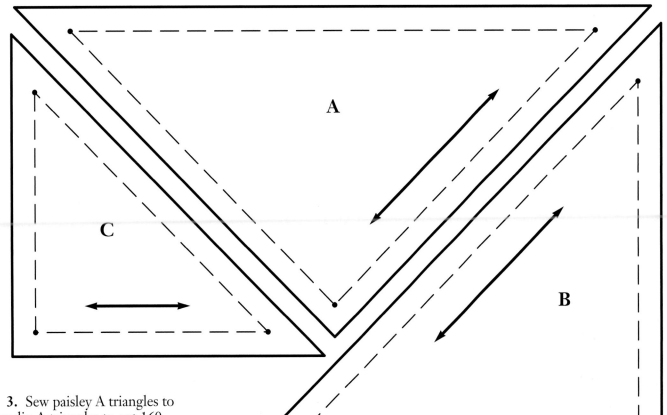

3. Sew paisley A triangles to muslin A triangles to get 160 pieced squares. Press seam allowances toward paisleys.

4. Lay out assembled units in 4 horizontal rows **(Block Assembly Diagram).** Join units in each row; then join rows to complete 1 block.

5. Make 20 blocks.

6. Referring to photograph, lay out blocks in 5 horizontal rows with 4 blocks in each row. Join blocks in each row. Join rows.

7. Join pairs of 2¼"-wide red strips end-to-end. Stitch borders to quilt sides. Join pairs of 1¾"-wide

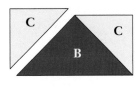

Diagram 3

red strips; sew these to top and bottom edges of quilt.

8. Join Cs to sides of each B to make 1 Flying Geese unit **(Diagram 3).** Make 118 units.

9. Join 17 green units and 16 red units to make right side border, alternating colors as shown in photo. For left side border, alternate 16 green units and 17 red units. Join pieced borders to quilt sides, easing to fit as needed.

10. Beginning with a red unit, join 13 red units and 13 green units for top border, alternating colors. Repeat for bottom border, starting with a green unit.

11. Join remaining Bs in pairs **(Diagram 4),** always sewing red to green. Join pairs to make 4 corner squares. Sew corner squares to ends

of top and bottom borders, positioning squares to maintain alternating colors. Join borders to top and bottom edges of quilt.

Quilting and Finishing

1. Outline-quilt patchwork. Add other quilting as desired. Quilt shown has stipple quilting in each muslin triangle that outlines a hand-drawn paisley.

2. See pages 16 and 17 for instructions on making binding. Make 10 yards of 2½"-wide bias or straight-grain binding from green fabric. Apply binding to quilt edges.

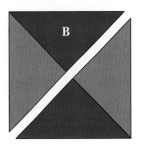

Diagram 4

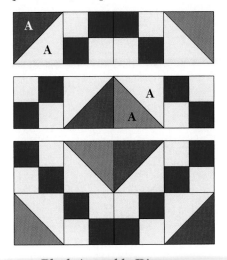

Block Assembly Diagram

Crown of Thorns

This block is sometimes known as Wedding Ring, Rolling Stone, or Georgetown Circle, but we like the biblical reference: "And the soldiers plaited a crown of thorns, and put it on his head, and they put on him a purple robe." *John 19:2*

Quilt by Janice Dietz
Ingleside, Illinois

Finished Quilt Size
92½" x 112"

Number of Blocks and Finished Size
28 blocks   10" x 10"

Fabric Requirements
Brown-and-red print   6½ yards*
Tan   4⅛ yards
Red   ⅝ yard
Backing   3⅜ yards 104" wide
*Includes 1 yard for binding.

Cutting
Instructions are for rotary cutting. Cut all strips cross-grain unless specified otherwise. Cut pieces in order listed to get best use of yardage.

From brown-and-red print
- 7 (2½"-wide) strips. From these, cut 112 (2½") A squares.
- 15 (2⅞"-wide) strips. From these, cut 224 (2⅞") squares. Cut each square in half diagonally to get 448 B triangles.
- 2 (10½" x 96") and 2 (10½" x 86") lengthwise border strips.
- 1 (34" x 59") piece. From this, cut 2 (3" x 59") strips for top border, 1 (34") square for binding, and 2 (16⅝" x 25") rectangles for pillow tuck.

From tan
- 9 (2½"-wide) strips. From these, cut 140 (2½") A squares.
- 15 (2⅞"-wide) strips. From these, cut 224 (2⅞") squares. Cut each square in half diagonally to get 448 B triangles.
- 4 (10½"-wide) strips. From these, cut 16 (10½") setting squares.
- 5 (15⅜") squares. Cut each square in quarters diagonally to get 20 side triangles.
- 4 (7⅛") squares. Cut each square in half diagonally to get 8 corner triangles.

From red
- 10 (1½"-wide) strips.

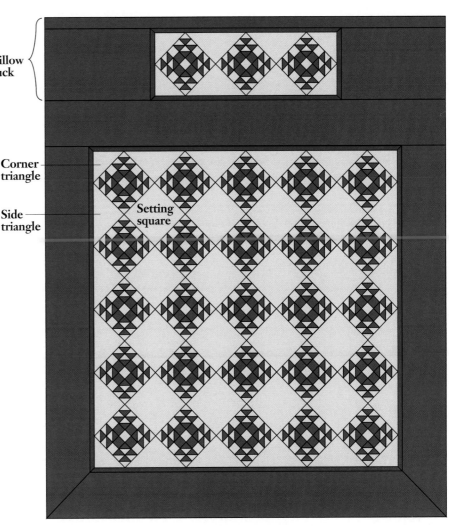

Setting Diagram

Quilt Top Assembly
1. Sew each print B triangle to a tan B to make 448 triangle-squares. Press seam allowances toward print.

2. Lay out 4 print As, 5 tan As, and 16 B triangle-squares **(Block Assembly Diagram).** Join triangle-squares in groups of 4 as shown.

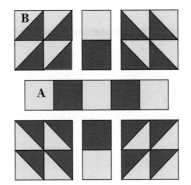

Block Assembly Diagram

Join remaining units to make 3 horizontal rows; then join 1 row to complete 1 block. Make 28 blocks.

3. Lay out 25 blocks, 16 setting squares, 16 side triangles, and 4 corner triangles in diagonal rows **(Setting Diagram).** When satisfied with layout, join blocks in each row. Press seam allowances toward setting squares. Then join rows.

4. Join 2 red strips end-to-end to make a border for each quilt edge. Sew borders to quilt; miter corners.

5. Sew 10½" x 86" print strips to quilt sides and 1 (10½" x 96") print strip to bottom edge; miter corners. Sew 1 (10½" x 92½") print strip to top of quilt, making square corners as shown.   *continued*

½ Celtic Cross Quilting Pattern

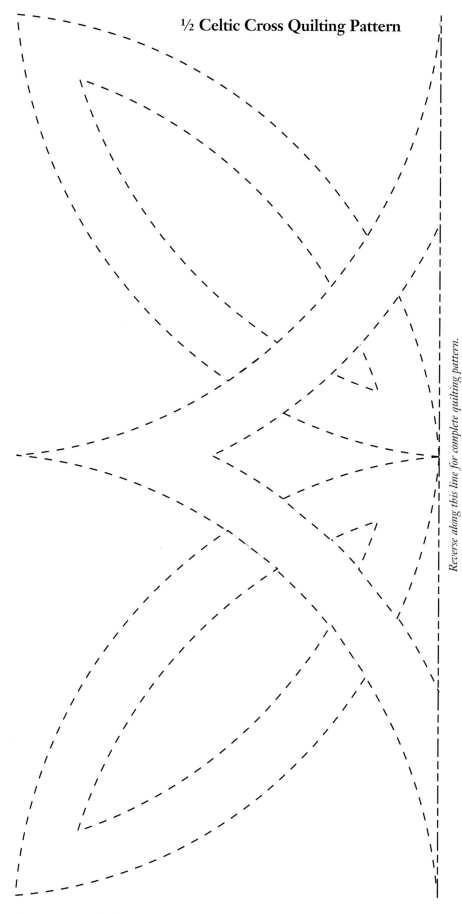

Reverse along this line for complete quilting pattern.

6. For pillow tuck, join remaining blocks and triangles as shown **(Setting Diagram).**

7. Cut 4 (23"-long) and 2 (17"-long) red strips. Join strips to edges of pillow tuck and miter corners.

8. Join 16⅝" x 25" print rectangles to ends of pillow tuck. Join 3" x 59" print strips end-to-end; sew strip to top of pillow tuck as shown. Join pillow tuck to quilt.

Quilting and Finishing

1. Make a stencil of Celtic Cross Quilting Pattern and mark partial pattern in side and corner triangles and full pattern in setting squares.

2. Outline-quilt piecing. Quilt remainder of quilt as desired.

3. See pages 16 and 17 for instructions on making binding. Make 11½ yards of 2½"-wide bias or straight-grain binding from reserved print fabric. Apply binding to quilt edges.

Darting Minnows

Beverley Cosby calls this quilt *Frank's Star* in her
father's honor. "He loved the holidays," she says, "and
the red, green, and white fabrics remind me of
Christmas and of him." Unlike most quilts, this design
is made with rows of pieced sashing rather than blocks.

Quilt by Beverley Cosby
Mechanicsville, Virginia

Finished Quilt Size
88" x 103½"

Fabric Requirements
Muslin   6¾ yards
Red   4¼ yards*
Floral print   1¼ yards**
Backing   3⅛ yards 104" wide

*Includes fabric for binding.

**Yardage is for cross-grain strips, pieced to
  length needed for borders. To cut lengthwise borders, you need 3¼ yards.

Cutting
Make templates of patterns C and
D, opposite. Cut all strips cross-
grain unless specified otherwise.
Cut pieces in order listed to get
best use of yardage.

From muslin
- 1 (105") length. From this, cut
  2 (8" x 105") lengthwise strips and
  2 (8" x 90") lengthwise strips for
  borders. From 11"-wide remainder of this length, cut 12 (8¾" x
  11") strips. From these, cut 36 of
  Template D.
- 8 (8¾"-wide) strips. From these,
  cut 32 (8¾") E squares and 44
  additional D pieces.
- 5 (2¼"-wide) strips. From these
  and scraps from previous cuts,
  cut 98 (2¼") squares. Cut each
  square in half diagonally to get
  196 B triangles.
- 2 (16¾"-wide) strips. From
  these, cut 4 (16¾") squares. Cut
  each square in quarters diagonally to get 14 G setting triangles
  (and 2 extra).
- 1 (14¾"-wide) strip. From this,
  cut 2 (14¾") squares. Cut these
  squares in half diagonally to get 4
  F corner triangles.

From red
- 4 (1" x 74"), 4 (1" x 88"), 2 (1" x
  92"), and 2 (1" x 106") lengthwise
  strips for borders.
- 22 (4⅝" x 31") strips. From these,
  cut 160 of Template C and 160 of
  Template C reversed.
- 1 (36") square for binding.

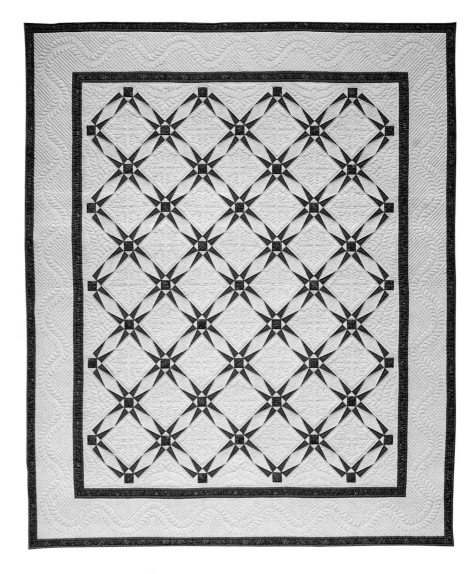

From floral print
- 20 (1½"-wide) strips for borders.
  (For lengthwise borders, cut 8
  [1½" x 108"] lengthwise strips.)
- 49 (2½") A squares.

Unit 1 Diagram

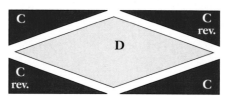

Unit 2 Diagram

Quilt Top Assembly
1. For Unit 1, sew 4 B triangles
to each A square **(Unit 1 Diagram)**. Press seam allowances
toward A. Make 49 of Unit 1.

2. For Unit 2, sew 4 C triangles
to each D diamond **(Unit 2 Diagram)**. Press seam allowances
toward Ds. Make 80 of Unit 2.

3. Lay out units 1 and 2 and E
squares in diagonal rows as shown
(Setting Diagram). Do not add
setting triangles yet. When satisfied with layout, join E squares and
Unit 2s in rows; then join units 1
and 2 in alternating rows. Return
each completed row to layout to
verify correct position of each unit.

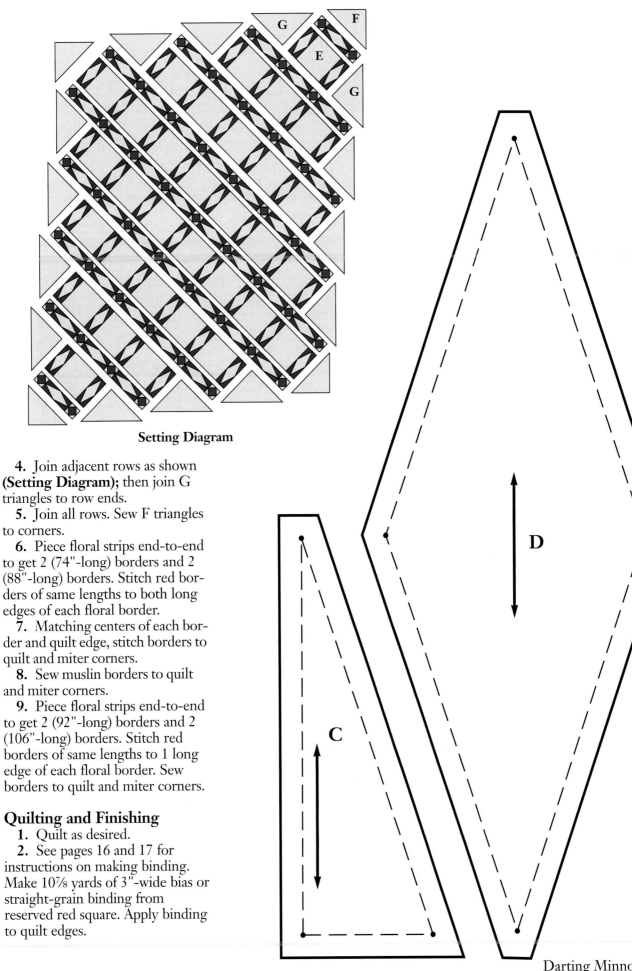

Setting Diagram

4. Join adjacent rows as shown (**Setting Diagram**); then join G triangles to row ends.

5. Join all rows. Sew F triangles to corners.

6. Piece floral strips end-to-end to get 2 (74"-long) borders and 2 (88"-long) borders. Stitch red borders of same lengths to both long edges of each floral border.

7. Matching centers of each border and quilt edge, stitch borders to quilt and miter corners.

8. Sew muslin borders to quilt and miter corners.

9. Piece floral strips end-to-end to get 2 (92"-long) borders and 2 (106"-long) borders. Stitch red borders of same lengths to 1 long edge of each floral border. Sew borders to quilt and miter corners.

Quilting and Finishing

1. Quilt as desired.

2. See pages 16 and 17 for instructions on making binding. Make 10⅞ yards of 3"-wide bias or straight-grain binding from reserved red square. Apply binding to quilt edges.

Darting Minnows 75

Delectable Mountains Star

This scrap quilt is ideal for rotary cutting. Pauline Warren's imaginative setting creates a patchwork frame around a radiating medallion star. The name of the block is derived from a happy place in the 17th-century allegory *Pilgrim's Progress* by John Bunyan.

Quilt by Pauline Warren
Sidney, Ohio

Finished Quilt Size
77¾" x 77¾"

Number of Blocks and Finished Size
108 blocks   6⅞" x 6⅞"

Fabric Requirements
Dark prints   16 fat quarters*
Tan   4½ yards
Binding fabric   1 yard
Backing   4¾ yards
*Fat quarter = 18" x 22".

Cutting
Instructions are for rotary cutting. Cut all strips cross-grain unless specified otherwise. Cut pieces in order listed to get best use of yardage.

From each fat quarter
- 5 (5") squares. Cut each square in half diagonally to get 10 A triangles.**
- 36 (2¼") squares. Cut each square in half diagonally to get 72 B triangles.**

From tan
- 420 (2¼") squares. Cut each square in half diagonally to get 840 B triangles.
- 140 (1⅞") C squares.
- 54 (7¾") squares. Cut each square in half diagonally to get 108 D triangles.
- 4 (7⅜") E squares.

**These instructions give you a few more As and Bs than you need, which enables you to experiment with color combinations before piecing mountains.

Setting Diagram

Quilt Top Assembly
1. For 1 mountain, choose 1 A and 8 Bs of another print.

2. Sew 6 print B triangles to tan Bs to make 6 triangle-squares.

3. Join triangle-squares in 2 rows of 3 as shown (**Mountain Assembly Diagram**). Join 1 print B to tan end of each row. Join 1 row to 1 side of A as shown. Press seam allowances toward A. Join 1 C to

remaining row; then join row to A to complete mountain. Make 140 mountains.

4. Join 1 D to each mountain to complete block (**Block Assembly Diagram**). Make 108 blocks. (Remaining 32 mountains are used at outside edges of quilt.)

5. Lay out blocks, E squares, and remaining mountains in diagonal rows (**Setting Diagram**). When satisfied with color placement, join units in each row. Then join rows to complete quilt top.

Quilting and Finishing
1. Outline-quilt patchwork. Add other quilting as desired.

2. See pages 16 and 17 for instructions on making binding. Make 9 yards of 2½"-wide bias or straight-grain binding from reserved print fabric. Apply binding to quilt edges.

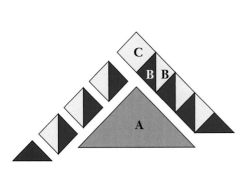

Mountain Assembly Diagram

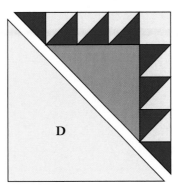

Block Assembly Diagram

Dogwood

The dogwood tree is a welcome harbinger of spring, but its blooming season is short. You can capture its beauty permanently in this stunning medallion quilt.

Vintage quilt from The Antique Quilt Source
Carlisle, Pennsylvania

Finished Quilt Size
76" x 95"

Fabric Requirements
White	5⅝ yards
Rose	1½ yards*
Pink	½ yard
Yellow	⅛ yard
Green	⅝ yard
Brown	¾ yard
Backing	5⅝ yards

*Includes fabric for binding.

Other Materials
Rose embroidery floss
Brown embroidery floss

Cutting
Make templates of appliqué patterns A–G on page 80.

From rose fabric
- 11 of Template A and 11 of Template A reversed.
- 11 of Template B and 11 of Template B reversed.
- 2 of Template F and 2 of Template F reversed.

From pink fabric
- 11 of Template A and 11 of Template A reversed.
- 11 of Template B and 11 of Template B reversed.
- 2 of Template E and 2 of Template E reversed.

From yellow fabric
- 22 of Template C.

From green fabric
- 32 of Template D and 32 of Template D reversed.
- 4 of Template G.

Quilt Top Assembly
1. Referring to backing instructions on page 15, use white fabric to assemble a 3-panel quilt top with 2 vertical seams. Fold quilt top into quarters to make placement guidelines; mark center.

2. Cut a 24" square from brown for stems. See page 17 for instructions on making continuous bias. Cut 11¾ yards (423") of ¾"-wide continuous bias from square. Fold long edges under ¼" and press.

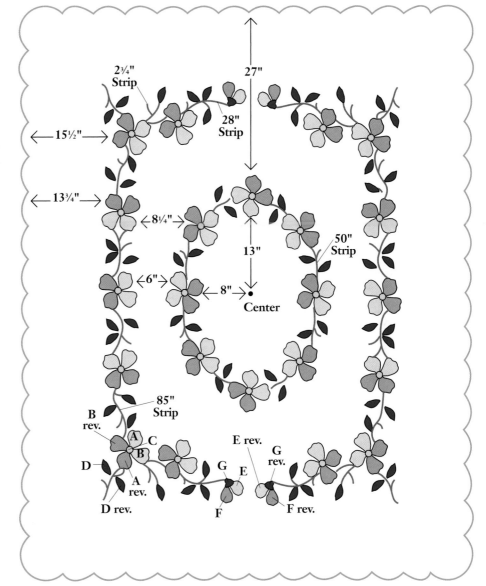

Appliqué Placement Diagram

Cut 1 (50"), 2 (85"), 4 (28"), and 33 (2¾") strips from bias strip.

3. Appliqué 50" bias strip for center medallion in place (**Appliqué Placement Diagram**).

4. For each flower, appliqué 1 A, 1 A rev., 1 B, and 1 B rev to center medallion, using 2 rose and 2 pink petals as desired (**Appliqué Placement Diagram**). Add C to center of each flower. Make 8 flowers on medallion. Appliqué 1 D leaf and 1 D rev. between flowers, adding 4 small stems as shown.

5. Appliqué remaining vines, flowers, leaves, and stems as shown. Appliqué 1 E, 1 F, and 1 G to 1 top center stem end. Repeat for 1 bottom center stem end. Appliqué 1

E rev., 1 F rev., and 1 G rev. to each remaining center stem.

6. Using rose floss, make French knots in flower centers and backstitch petal centers. Using brown floss, backstitch petal tips.

Quilting and Finishing
1. Use a dinner plate as a guide to mark 5⅜"-wide scallops on edge of quilt top. Quilt top as desired.

2. Make 14 yards of 2½"-wide continuous bias from rose. Apply binding on marked lines, easing binding along curves and pivoting at corners. When binding is complete, trim layers to ¼" seam allowance. Fold binding to back; blindstitch in place.

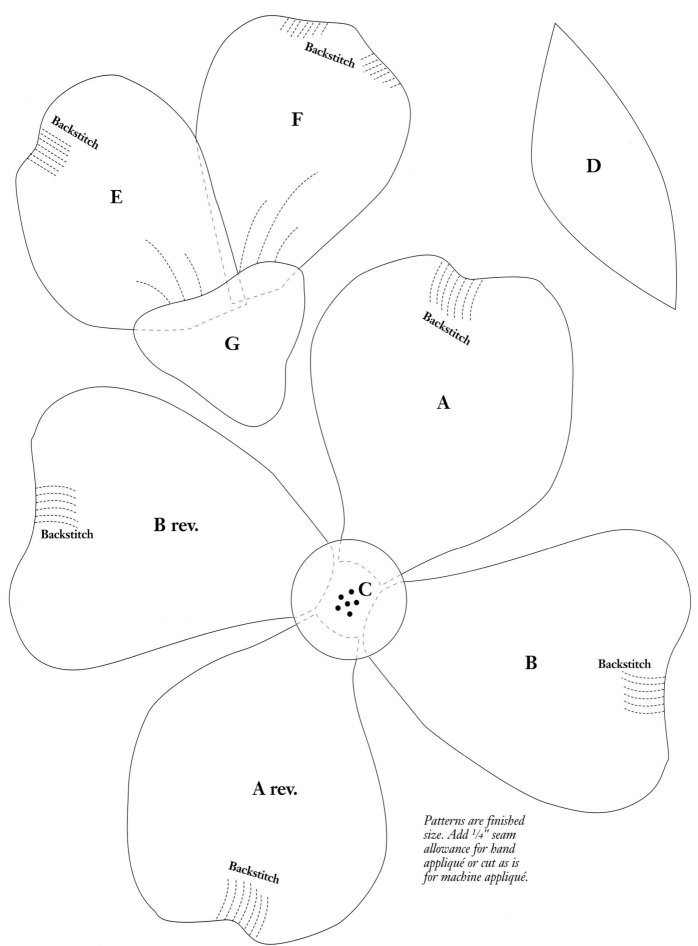

Backstitch

F

Backstitch

E

D

Backstitch

A

G

Backstitch

B rev.

Backstitch

C

B

Backstitch

A rev.

Backstitch

*Patterns are finished
size. Add ¼" seam
allowance for hand
appliqué or cut as is
for machine appliqué.*

Double Irish Chain

The chain effect in this traditional beauty is achieved by the alternate placement of two easy strip-pieced blocks. When the quilt top is finished, individual blocks disappear into the overall design.

Quilt by Judy Cantwell
Birmingham, Alabama

Finished Quilt Size
84" x 104"

Number of Blocks and Finished Size
32 Block As	10" x 10"
31 Block Bs	10" x 10"

Fabric Requirements
Rose print	2⅝ yards*
Blue print	2½ yards
Muslin	3¼ yards
Wide outer border	1½ yards
Backing	6¼ yards

*Includes fabric for binding.

Cutting
Instructions are for rotary cutting. Cut all strips cross-grain unless specified otherwise. Cut pieces in order listed to get best use of yardage.

From rose print
- 18 (2½"-wide) strips.
- 9 (1½"-wide) border strips.

From blue print
- 32 (2½"-wide) strips.
- 9 (6½"-wide) border strips.

From muslin
- 8 (2½"-wide) strips.
- 12 (6½"-wide) strips. From 8 of these, cut 31 (6½" x 10½") rectangles.

Quilt Top Assembly
1. Join rose, muslin, and blue strips in sets 1, 2, and 3 as shown **(Strip Set Diagrams** opposite**)**. In strip sets 1 and 3, press all seam allowances toward center strip. In Strip Set 2, press seam allowances away from center.

2. Cut 2½"-wide segments from each strip set.

3. For Block A, select 5 segments as shown **(Block A Assembly Diagram)**. Join segments to assemble block. Make 32 of Block A.

4. For Strip Set 4, sew blue strips to opposite sides of remaining muslin strips. Press seam allowances toward blue. Cut 2½"-wide segments from Strip Set 4.

Block A

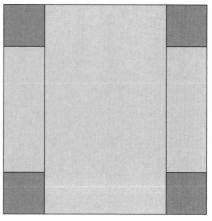

Block B

5. Sew Strip Set 4 segments to sides of each 6½" x 10½" muslin rectangle to make 1 Block B **(Block B Assembly Diagram)**. Make 31 of Block B.

6. Lay out blocks in 9 horizontal rows of 7 blocks each, alternating blocks A and B as shown **(Setting Diagram)**. When satisfied with layout, join blocks in each row. Then join rows.

7. Join rose strips end-to-end to make a border for each quilt edge.

Stitch borders to quilt. Add blue outer borders in same manner.

Quilting and Finishing
1. Quilt piecing in-the-ditch. Quilting pattern for design quilted in B blocks is on facing page.

2. See pages 16 and 17 for instructions on making binding. Make 10⅝ yards of 2½"-wide bias or straight-grain binding from rose fabric. Apply binding to quilt edges.

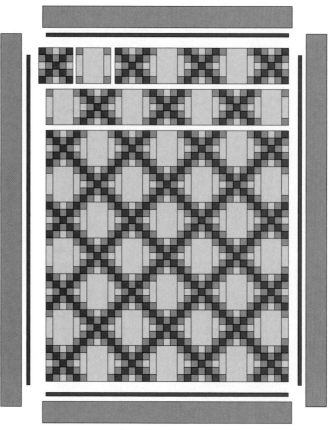

Setting Diagram

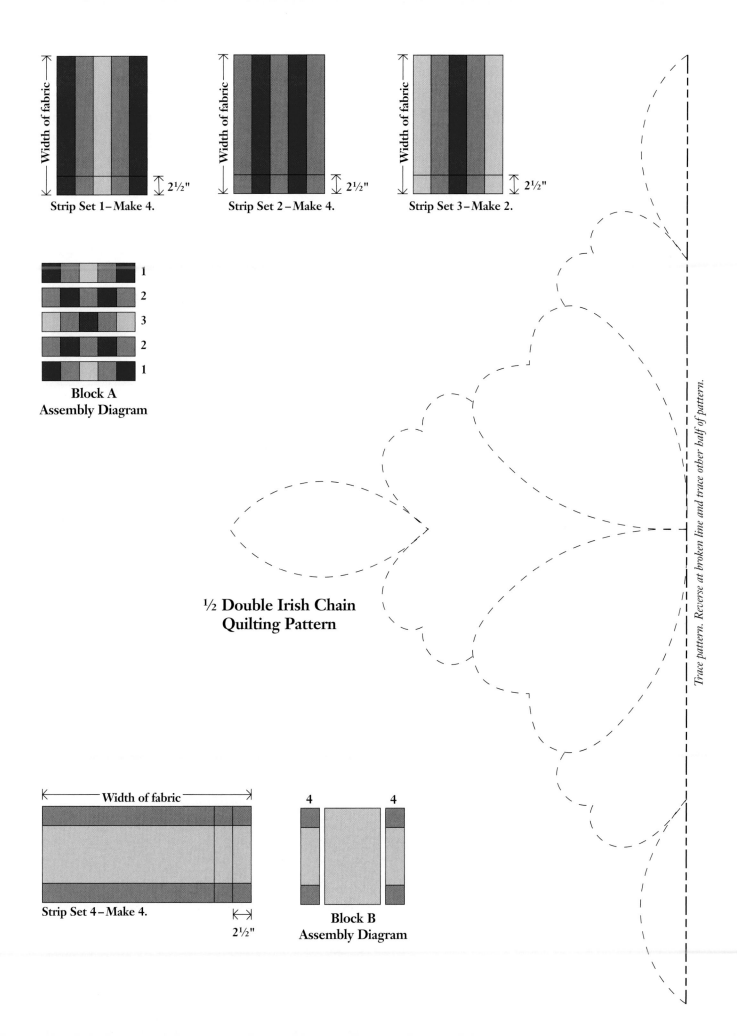

Width of fabric 2½"
Strip Set 1–Make 4.

Width of fabric 2½"
Strip Set 2–Make 4.

Width of fabric 2½"
Strip Set 3–Make 2.

1
2
3
2
1

Block A
Assembly Diagram

½ **Double Irish Chain**
Quilting Pattern

Trace pattern. Reverse at broken line and trace other half of pattern.

Width of fabric
Strip Set 4–Make 4. 2½"

4   4

Block B
Assembly Diagram

Double Wedding Ring

The Double Wedding Ring is one of the most loved of all quilt designs—and one of the most challenging to piece. This adaptation cuts piecing time in half by incorporating the several tiny pieces that usually make up the arc into one large piece.

Quilt by Julie Borg
Cokato, Minnesota

Finished Quilt Size
95½" x 121"

Fabric Requirements
Muslin	8 yards*
Blue print	6¾ yards
Red print	1⅜ yards
Rose print	1⅜ yards
Backing	3⅝ yards 108" wide

*Includes fabric for bias binding.

Cutting
Make templates of patterns A, B, C, and D on page 87. Cut pieces in order listed to get best use of yardage.

From muslin
• 1 (34") square for bias binding.
• 63 of Template A.
• 142 of Template C.

From blue print
• 284 of Template B.

From red and *rose print fabrics*
• 156 (each fabric) of Template D.

Quilt Top Assembly
See pages 10 and 11 for tips on sewing set-in and curved seams.

1. For a whole ring, select 1 A, 8 Bs, 4 Cs, 4 red Ds, and 4 rose Ds.

2. Sew Bs to 1 side of each C piece **(Block Assembly Diagram)**. Stitch 2 Ds of same fabric to ends of each remaining B. Stitch these to C pieces as shown to complete 4 arc units.

3. Stitch arc units to A, placing Ds of same fabric on opposite sides of A as shown **(Diagram 1)**. Make 32 whole rings.

4. Make 6 quarter rings as shown in **Diagram 2** and 8 quarter rings as shown in **Diagram 3**. You will have 17 As remaining after making whole rings and quarter rings.

continued

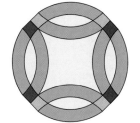

Diagram 1
Whole Ring
Make 32.

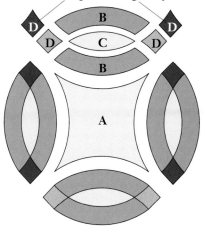

Add to quarter rings only.

Block Assembly Diagram

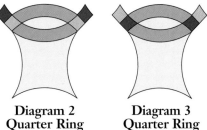

Diagram 2
Quarter Ring
Make 6.

Diagram 3
Quarter Ring
Make 8.

Setting Diagram

5. Referring to **Setting Diagram,** join whole rings, quarter rings, and remaining As. Some people prefer to work in rows and then join rows. Other quilters like to start at center and work out, while others work from 1 corner. Join units in manner that works best for you.

Quilting and Finishing
1. Quilt in-the-ditch around arcs, or quilt as desired.
2. See page 17 for instructions on making continuous bias binding. Make 14 yards of 2"-wide bias binding from reserved muslin square. Apply binding to quilt edges, carefully mitering binding corners at point of each D piece.

Make Your Own Quilt Label
See page 366 for instructions.

D

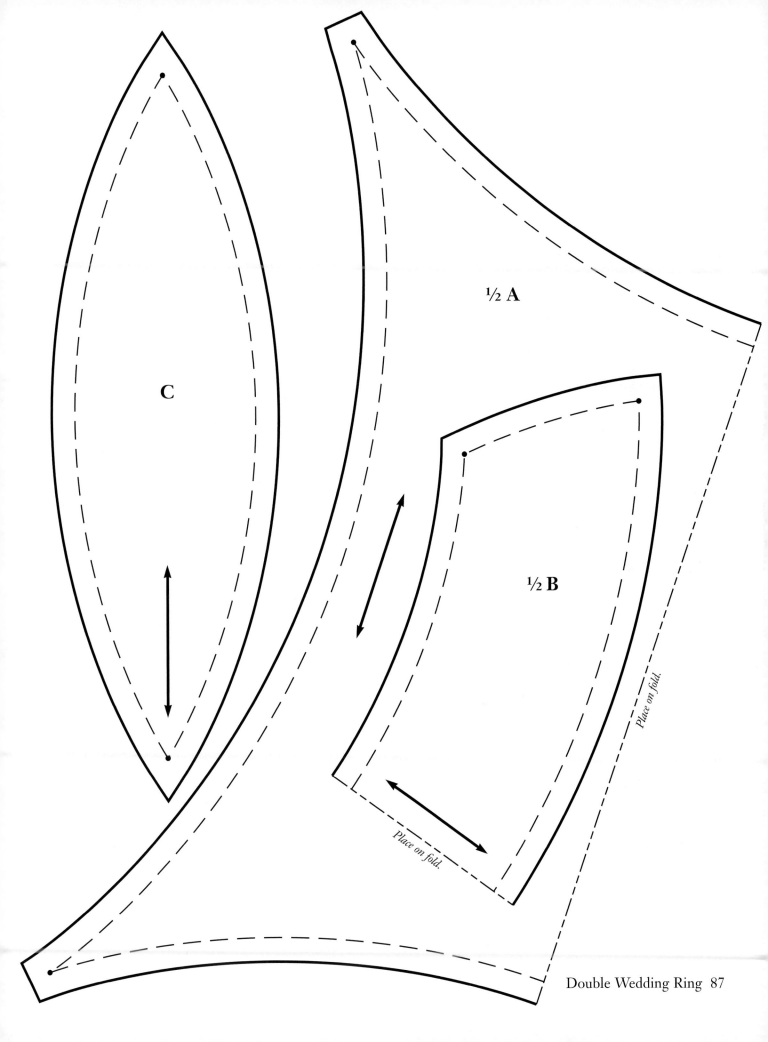

C

½ A

½ B

Place on fold.

Place on fold.

Double Wedding Ring 87

Dove at the Window

"And the dove came in to him in the evening; and lo, in her mouth was an olive leaf plucked off: so Noah knew that the waters were abated from off the earth." *Genesis 8:11*

Quilt by Araminta Jane Marr; owned by Betty J. Simpson
Weatherford, Texas

Finished Quilt Size
80" x 90"

Number of Blocks and Finished Size
36 Dove blocks   10" x 10"
36 setting blocks   10" x 10"

Fabric Requirements
Muslin	4¾ yards
Pink	1¼ yards
Light brown	1¼ yards
Dark brown	1¼ yards
Binding fabric	⅞ yard
Backing	5½ yards

Cutting
Make a template of pattern C (page 90); remaining pieces can be rotary cut. Cut pieces in order listed to get best use of yardage.

From muslin
- 36 (10½") F squares.
- 144 (2⅝") D squares.
- 108 (4⅛") squares. Cut each square in quarters diagonally to get 432 B triangles.

From pink
- 36 (3⅜") A squares.
- 144 (2⅝") squares for diagonal-corner quick-piecing technique [or 72 (3") squares for traditional piecing; cut each 3" square in half diagonally to get 144 E triangles].

From light brown
- 288 of Template C.

From dark brown
- 288 of Template C.

Dove Block Assembly Diagram

Setting Diagram

Quilt Top Assembly
1. For each Dove block, select 1 A, 12 Bs, 8 light brown Cs, 8 dark brown Cs, and 4 Ds.

2. See page 10 for tips on sewing set-in seams. Join light brown and dark brown Cs in pairs **(Dove Block Assembly Diagram)**. Note that color placement is reversed in corner pairs and middle pairs. Press seam allowances open.

3. Lay out diamond pairs as shown. Set B triangles into middle diamonds. Join 2 of these units to opposite sides of A square.

4. Set D squares into corner diamond pairs. Sew corner pairs to opposite sides of remaining middle pairs. Sew these units to opposite sides of center A unit.

5. Set in Bs at edges to complete block. Make 36 Dove blocks.

6. See page 12 for instructions on diagonal-corners quick-piecing technique. Use this method to sew 4 E corners onto each F. For traditional piecing, mark 1⅞" from each corner of an F square. Trim triangles at corners of squares. Sew E triangle to each corner **(Setting Block Assembly Diagram)**. Make 36 setting blocks. *continued*

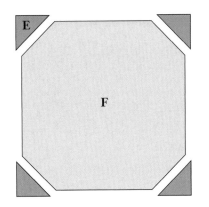

Setting Block Assembly Diagram

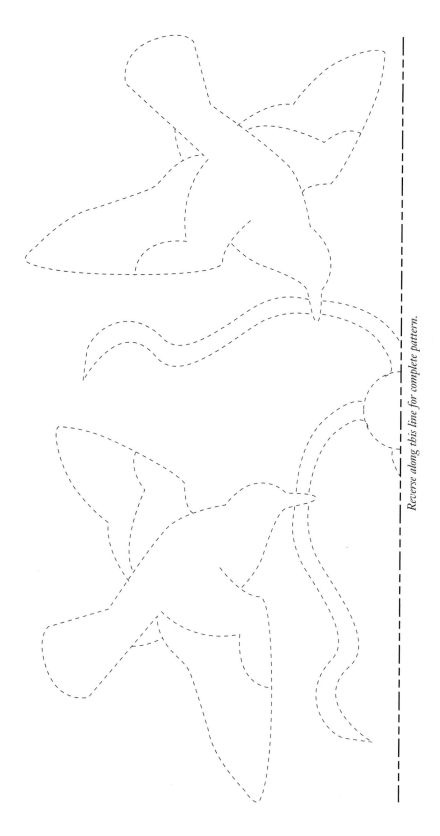

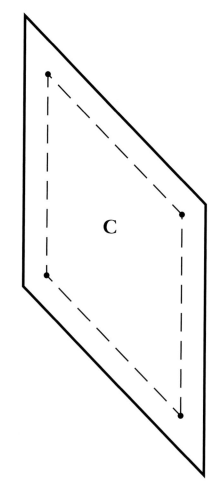

C

Reverse along this line for complete pattern.

½ **Dove Quilting Pattern**

7. Lay out blocks in 9 horizontal rows, with 8 alternating blocks in each row. Odd-numbered rows start with a Dove block and even-numbered rows start with a setting block as shown **(Setting Diagram)**. Join blocks in each row; press seam allowances toward setting blocks.

8. Join rows.

Quilting and Finishing

1. Outline-quilt pieces in each Dove block. Quilt Dove Quilting Pattern in setting blocks.

2. See pages 16 and 17 for instructions on making binding. Make 9¾ yards of 2½"-wide bias or straight-grain binding from rose fabric. Apply binding to quilt edges.

Dresden Plate

This pattern is named for the dainty, ornate porcelain that originated in Dresden, Germany. The design is also referred to as Friendship Ring and sometimes as Grandmother's Sunbonnet.

Quilt by Mable Azbill Webb
Jackson, Tennessee

Finished Quilt Size
71½" x 86½"

Number of Blocks and Finished Size
20 blocks   15" x 15"

Fabric Requirements
Assorted prints   22 fat quarters*
Muslin   4¾ yards
Binding fabric   1 yard
Backing   5 yards
*Fat quarter = 18" x 22",

Other Materials
Yellow embroidery floss (optional)

Cutting
Make templates of patterns A, B, C, and D on pages 93 and 94. Cut pieces in order listed to get best use of yardage.
From muslin
• 20 (15½") squares.
• 90 of Template C.

From assorted prints
• 360 of Template A.
• 94 of Template B.
• 4 of Template D from same print.

Quilt Top Assembly
1. Join 18 assorted As as shown to make 1 plate **(Plate Assembly Diagram)**. Make 20 plates.

2. Center a plate on each muslin square; appliqué in place.

3. If desired, use 2 strands of floss to blanket-stitch around inside and outside of each plate **(Blanket Stitch Diagram)**.

4. Join blocks in 5 horizontal rows with 4 blocks in each row **(Setting Diagram)**. Join rows.

5. For top border, join 21 Bs and 20 muslin Cs in a row as shown. Sew row to top edge of quilt. Repeat for bottom border.

6. For each side border, join 26 Bs and 25 muslin Cs as shown. Join a D piece to ends of each border. Sew borders to quilt sides.

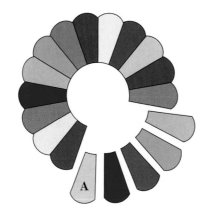

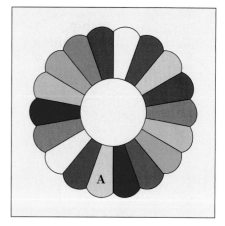

Plate Assembly Diagram   Plate Block Diagram

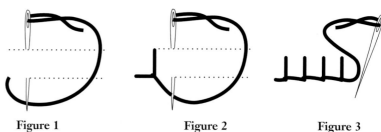

Figure 1   Figure 2   Figure 3

Blanket Stitch Diagram

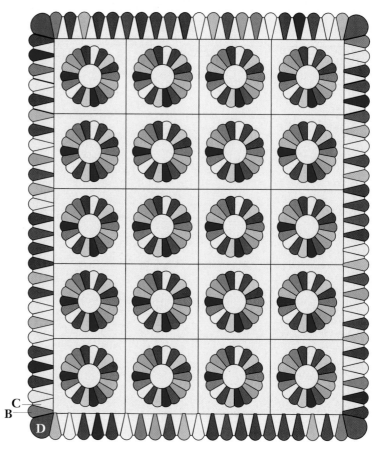

Setting Diagram

Quilting and Finishing

1. Transfer Quilting Pattern 1 to muslin centers of plates and Quilting Pattern 2 to muslin areas between plates.

2. Quilt each plate in-the-ditch. Quilt marked designs. Outline-quilt Bs and Ds in border.

3. See page 17 for instructions on making continuous bias binding. Make 14 yards of 2"-wide bias binding. Apply binding to quilt edges, carefully mitering binding corners between B pieces.

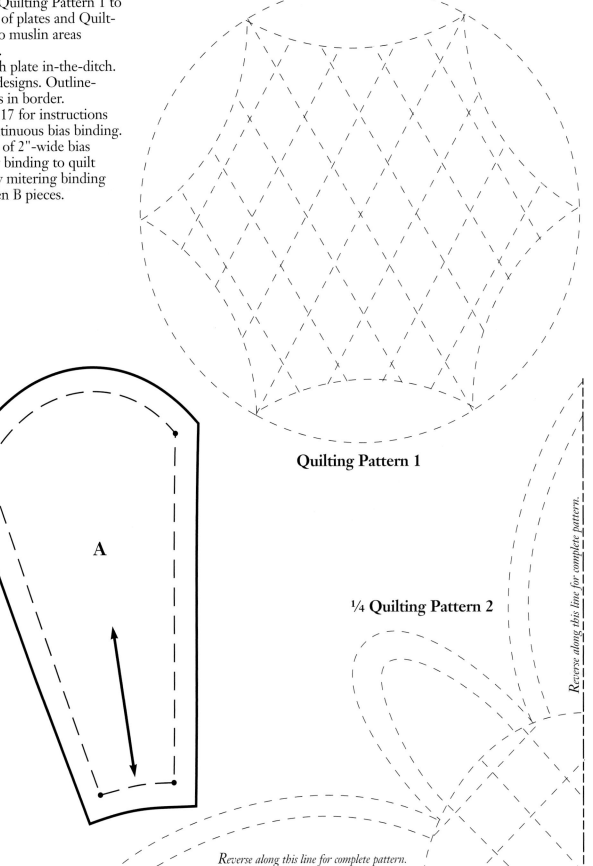

Quilting Pattern 1

A

¼ **Quilting Pattern 2**

Reverse along this line for complete pattern.

Reverse along this line for complete pattern.

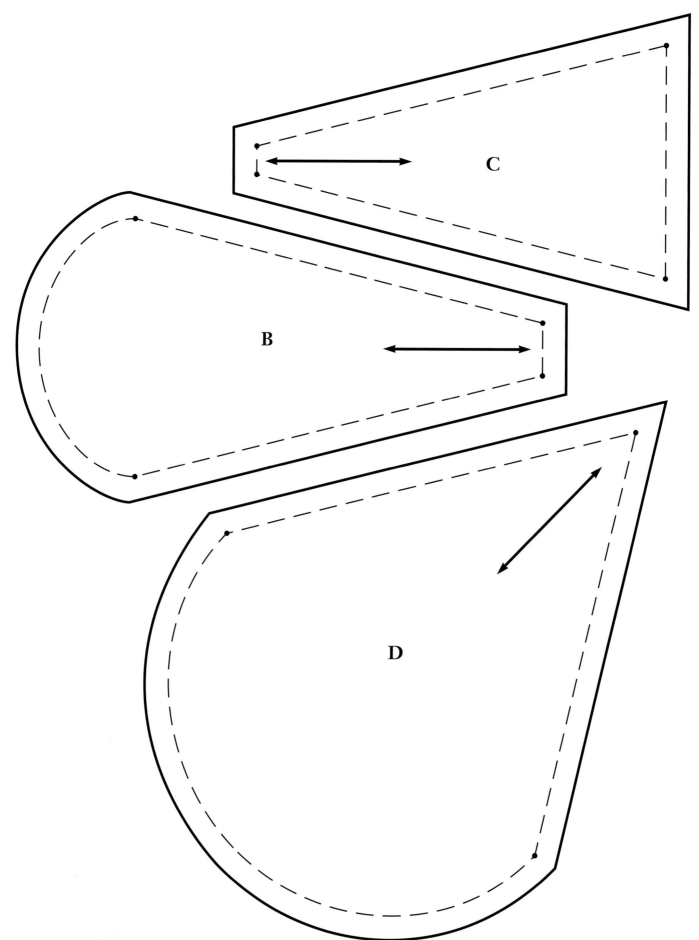

Drunkard's Path

Drunkard's Path is usually pieced with two solid colors, but this *Drunkard's Path* goes one step further. A third fabric and floral prints add interest and visual appeal to the pattern.

Quilt by Shirley Tordo
Guilford, Connecticut

Finished Quilt Size
92" x 108"

Number of Blocks and Finished Size
30 blocks   16" x 16"

Fabric Requirements
White print   6 yards
Blue print   2¾ yards
Dark blue print   4 yards
Binding fabric   1 yard
Backing   3¼ yards 104" wide

Cutting
Make templates of patterns A–H. Cut pieces in order listed to get best use of yardage.

From white print
- 240 *each* of templates A and B.
- 4 *each* of templates D, E, and H.
- 9 (2½"-wide) cross-grain strips for middle borders.

From blue print
- 120 *each* of templates A and B.

From dark blue print
- 2 (3½" x 90"), 2 (3½" x 105"), 2 (1½" x 84") and 2 (1½" x 100") lengthwise strips for borders. Use remainder from border length to cut B pieces.
- 120 *each* of templates A and B.
- 4 *each* of templates C, F, and G.

Quilt Top Assembly
1. See page 11 for tips on sewing a curved seam. Make 4 each of 4 units as shown **(Block Assembly Diagram)**.

2. Lay out units in 4 horizontal rows, rotating units as shown. Join units in rows; then join rows to complete block. Make 30 blocks.

3. Join blocks in 6 rows, with 5 blocks in each row **(Setting Diagram)**. Join rows.

4. Join Cs and Ds, Es and Fs, Gs and Hs to get 4 of each border corner unit.

5. Measure length of quilt top through middle of quilt. Trim 1½" x 100" dark blue border strips to this length. Join C/D corner units to ends of these strips. Sew 1½" x 84" strips to top and bottom edges of quilt and trim; then sew strips with corner units to quilt sides, easing to fit as needed.

6. Measure length of quilt top again. Cut 1 white border strip in half. Join 2½ white print border strips end-to-end to match this length; sew corner E/F corner units to ends of border strips. Join remaining white border strips in pairs; stitch these to top and bottom edges of quilt and trim. Sew strips with corner units to quilt sides, easing to fit as needed.

7. Trim 3½" x 105" dark blue border strips to match length of quilt; stitch G/H corners to ends. Join 3½" x 90" dark blue strips to top and bottom edges of quilt and trim; then sew strips with corner units to quilt sides, easing to fit as needed. Press seam allowances toward borders.

Quilting and Finishing
1. Outline-quilt blue and dark blue pieces. Quilt borders as desired.

2. See pages 16 and 17 for instructions on making binding. Make 11½ yards of 2½"-wide bias or straight-grain binding. Apply binding to quilt edges.

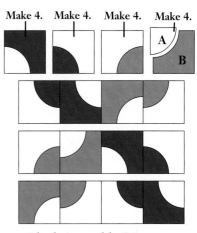

Block Assembly Diagram

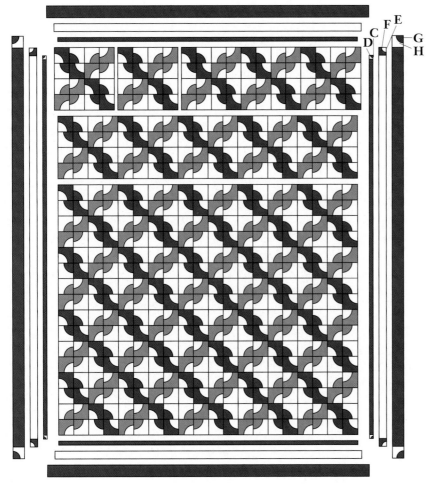

Setting Diagram

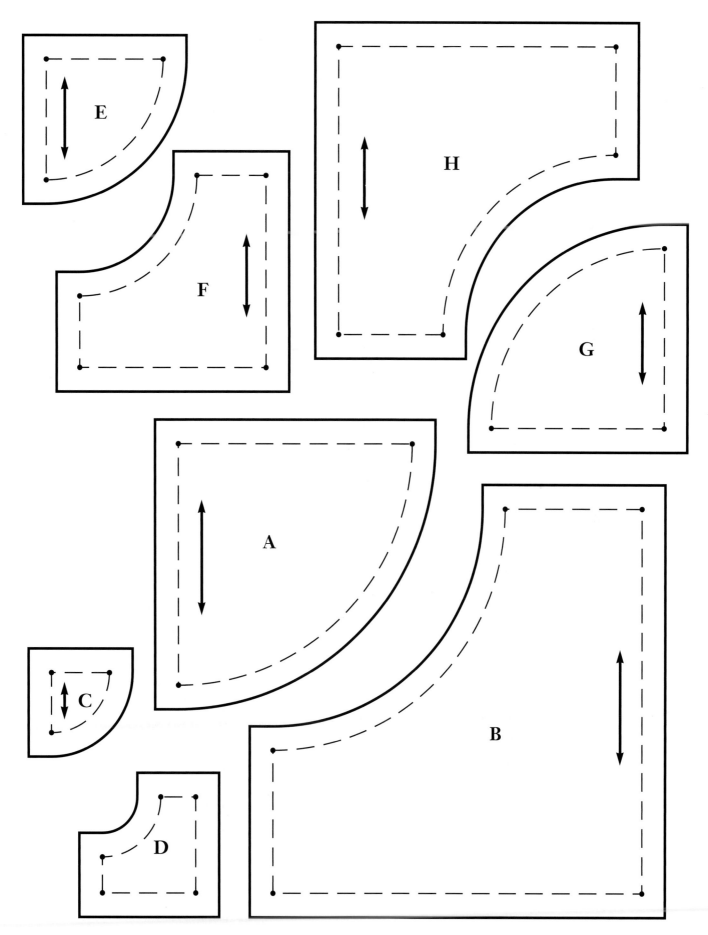

E

F

H

G

A

C

D

B

Evening Star

This quilt represents four generations of quilters. When Jennifer Rozens decided to learn to quilt, she remembered a box of scraps stored in her mom's attic. To Jennifer's delight, the box contained not just scraps, but dozens of blocks made by her great-grandmother, grandmother, and great aunt in the late 1800s. Jennifer hand-pieced the Evening Star blocks into a top and hand-quilted it. "This quilt is my family, and my reason for being proud to be a quilter," Jennifer says.

Quilt by Mary Eleanor Keller, Mary Elizabeth Brading, Nancy Keller, and Jennifer C. Rozens Arrowsmith, Illinois, and St. Clair Shores, Michigan

Finished Quilt Size

56" x 75"

Number of Blocks and Finished Size

120 blocks   4½" x 4½"

Fabric Requirements

Plaids   12 to 13 fat quarters*
Muslin   2¼ yards
Navy border fabric   2¼ yards
Binding fabric   ¾ yard
Backing   4 yards

*Fat quarter = 18" x 22".

Cutting

From plaid fat quarters

• 30 (2¾" x 22") strips. From these, cut 240 (2¾") squares. Cut each square in quarters diagonally to get 960 B triangles.
• 15 (2⅝" x 22") strips. From these, cut 120 (2⅝") A squares.

From muslin

• 8 (2¾" x 44") strips. From these, cut 120 (2¾") squares. Cut each square in quarters diagonally to get 480 B triangles.
• 23 (2" x 44") strips. From these, cut 480 (2") C squares.

From border fabric

• 4 (6" x 78") lengthwise strips.

Quilt Top Assembly

1. For each block, select 1 A square, 8 assorted plaid B triangles, 4 muslin Bs, and 4 C squares.

2. Sew plaid B triangles to 2 adjacent sides of each C square **(Block Piecing Diagram)**. Press seam allowances toward C.

3. Join 2 B/C units to opposite sides of A as shown. Press seam allowances toward A.

4. Sew muslin B triangles to plaid Bs of remaining 2 B/C units as shown. Press seam allowances toward muslin Bs. Then join these units to center A unit to complete 1 block.

5. Make 120 blocks.

6. Lay out blocks in 12 horizontal rows, with 10 blocks in each row **(Setting Diagram)**. Arrange

blocks to achieve a pleasing balance of color and pattern. When satisfied with block layout, join blocks in each row. Then join rows.

7. Sew 2 border strips to side edges of quilt. Press seam allowances toward borders. Join remaining border strips to top and bottom edges of quilt.

Quilting and Finishing

1. Quilt as desired. Quilt shown has 1" cross-hatching quilted in patchwork, and border is quilted with a continuous cable.

2. See pages 16 and 17 for instructions on making binding. Make 7 yards of 2½"-wide bias or straight-grain binding. Apply binding to quilt edges.

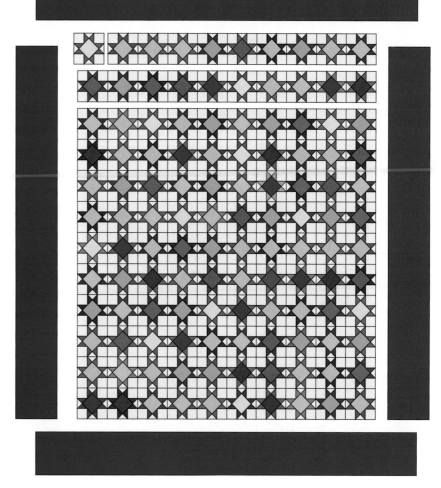

Setting Diagram

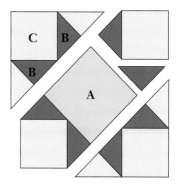

Block Piecing Diagram

Fan & Flowers

Sheri Lalk likes all aspects of quiltmaking, but her favorite innovation is to take a traditional quilt pattern and spin off an original design or setting. In this design, the geometrics of the Jacob's Ladder blocks blend beautifully with the curves of Grandmother's Fan.

Quilt by Sheri Wilkinson Lalk
Electra, Texas

Finished Quilt Size
76" x 100"

Number of Blocks and Finished Size

16 Grandmother's
  Fan blocks   12" x 12"
16 Jacob's Ladder blocks 12" x 12"

Fabric Requirements

White	4 yards
Pink	3 yards
Light pink	¼ yard
Assorted pink prints	6 fat quarters*
Green	1¼ yards
Lavender	1 yard
Dark purple	¼ yard
Striped print or large floral print	1 yard
Binding fabric	⅞ yard
Backing	6 yards

*Fat quarter = 18" x 22".

Cutting

Make templates of patterns A–U on pages 102–105. Cut strips cross-grain except as noted.

From white
- 12 (12½") squares.
- 1 (24½") square.
- 4 (4⅞"-wide) strips. From these and scraps from previous cuts, cut 48 (4⅞") squares. Cut each square in half diagonally to get 96 Q triangles.
- 6 (2½"-wide) strips. From these, cut 96 (2½") P squares.
- 2 (13"-wide) strips. From these, cut 16 of Template T.

From pink
- 2 (2½" x 100") and 2 (2½" x 80") lengthwise strips for borders.
- 1 *each* of templates A, B, D, E, H, and J.
- 16 of Template S.
- 2 of Template U.

From light pink
- 1 *each* of templates C, F, G, I, and K.

From assorted pink prints
- 80 of Template S.

From green
- 1 (26") square for bias stems.
- 6 (2"-wide) strips. From these, cut 74 of Template L and 30 of Template O.

From lavender
- 6 (2½"-wide) strips. From these, cut 96 (2½") P squares.
- 2 (4½"-wide) strips. From these, cut 16 of Template R.
- 30 of Template N.

From dark purple
- 30 of Template M.

From striped print
- 6 (4⅞"-wide) strips. From these, cut 48 (4⅞") squares. Cut each square in half diagonally to get 96 Q triangles.

Quilt Top Assembly

1. Finger-press 24½" square in half diagonally to form guidelines. Lay out pieces A–J on square **(Placement Diagram 1)**. Appliqué pieces in alphabetical order.

2. See page 17 for tips on making continuous bias. From green square, make 11½ yards of ¾"-wide bias for stems. Press bias strip in thirds. Pin stems, flowers (M, N), and leaves (L, O) on square **(Placement Diagram 2)**. Appliqué stems; then appliqué L, M, N, and O in alphabetical order. Appliqué knot (K) last.

3. Join white and lavender Ps in four-patches **(Jacob's Ladder Block Assembly Diagram)**. Join white and striped Q triangles in pairs. Lay out units for each block in rows as shown. Join units in each row; then join rows. Make 16 Jacob's Ladder blocks.

4. Join 6 S blades **(Grandmother's Fan Block Assembly Diagram)**. Include 1 pink S in each fan. *continued*

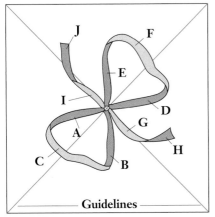

Placement Diagram 1

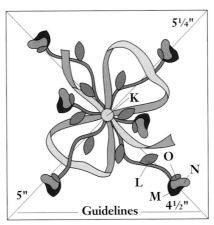

Placement Diagram 2

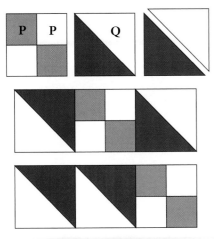

**Jacob's Ladder Block
Assembly Diagram**

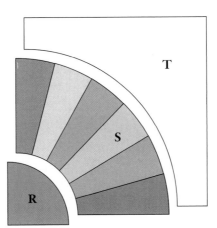

**Grandmother's Fan Block
Assembly Diagram**

Fan & Flowers 101

5. Join fan to pieces R and T to complete block. Make 16 Grandmother's Fan blocks.

6. Join 4 Grandmother's Fan blocks and 4 Jacob's Ladder blocks to 24½" appliquéd square to make center section as shown (**Setting Diagram**).

7. Lay out remaining Grandmother's Fan blocks, Jacob's Ladder blocks, and white squares in 6 rows, with 6 blocks in each row. Join rows to center section as shown.

8. Arrange trailing vines on white squares as shown in quilt photograph on page 100. Appliqué in place. Layer and appliqué leaves, flowers, and U hearts.

9. Join 100"-long pink borders to sides of quilt. Then join 80"-long borders to top and bottom edges of quilt. Press seam allowances toward borders.

Quilting and Finishing

1. Outline-quilt outside seam lines of all appliqué pieces and ¼" inside seam lines of all piecing.

2. See pages 16 and 17 for instructions on making binding. Make 10 yards of 2½"-wide bias or straight-grain binding. Apply binding to quilt edges.

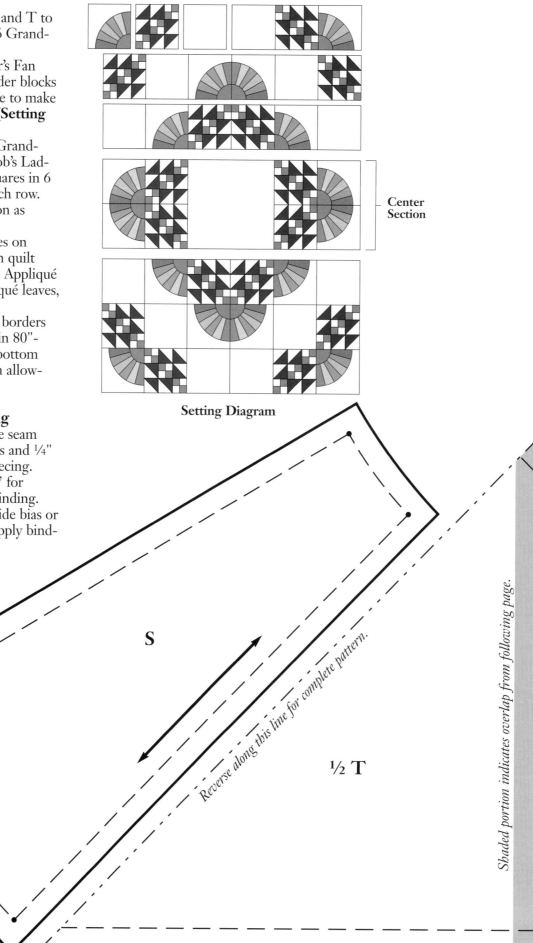

Setting Diagram

Center Section

S

Reverse along this line for complete pattern.

½ T

Shaded portion indicates overlap from following page.

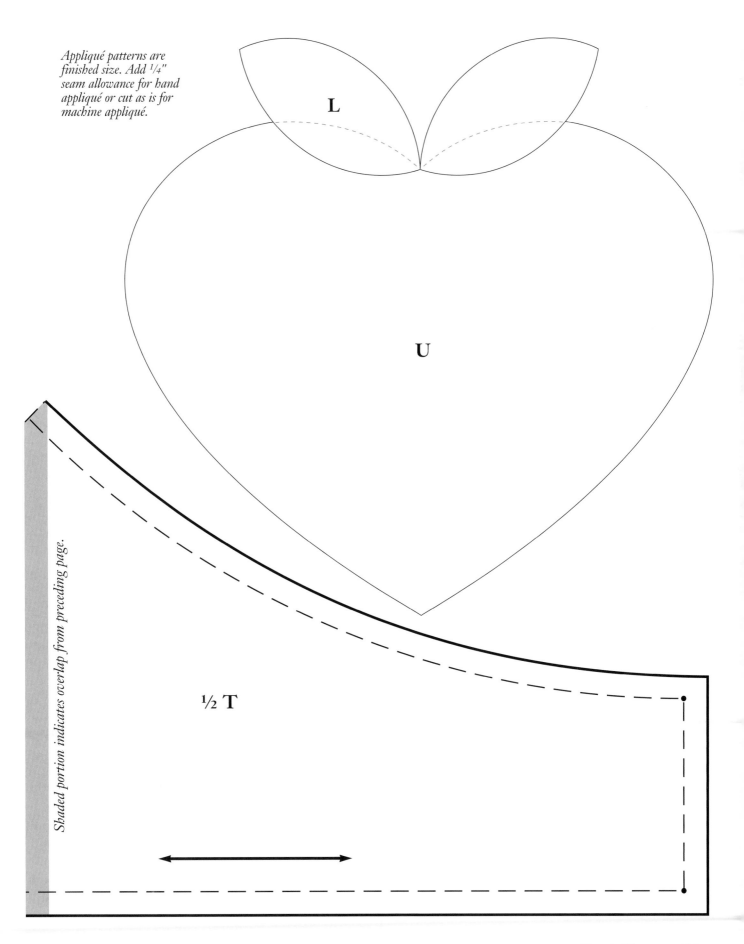

*Appliqué patterns are
finished size. Add ¼"
seam allowance for hand
appliqué or cut as is for
machine appliqué.*

L

U

Shaded portion indicates overlap from preceding page.

½ T

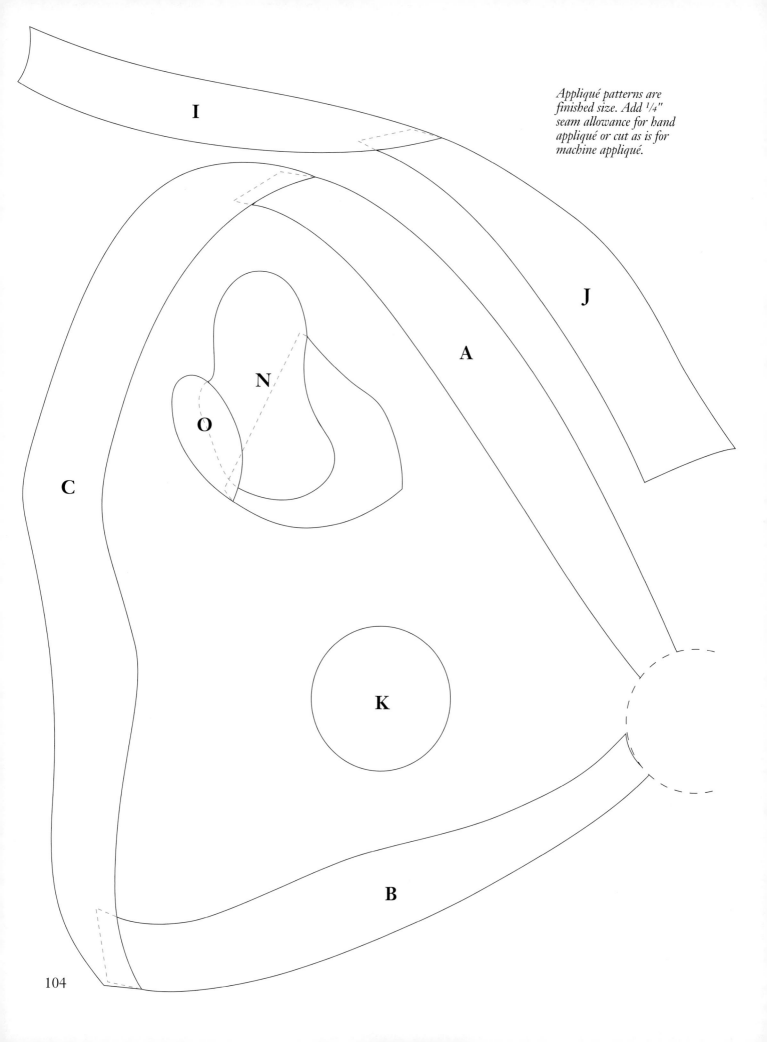

Appliqué patterns are finished size. Add ¼" seam allowance for hand appliqué or cut as is for machine appliqué.

I

J

A

N

O

C

K

B

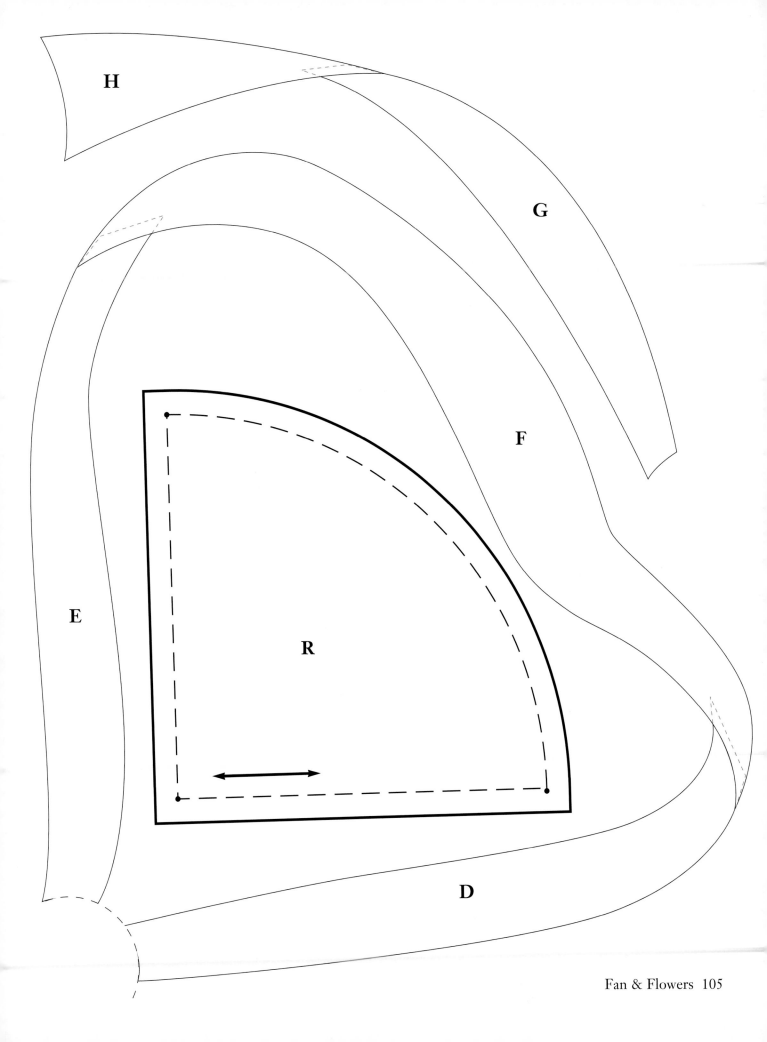

H

G

F

E

R

D

Feathered Star

Fourteen of these Feathered Star blocks are the work of Susan Danielson's quilting pals, who meet monthly to make and exchange blocks. Use fabrics of one color, as Susan did, or go for broke with random fabrics to create a freewheeling quilt of scrappy stars.

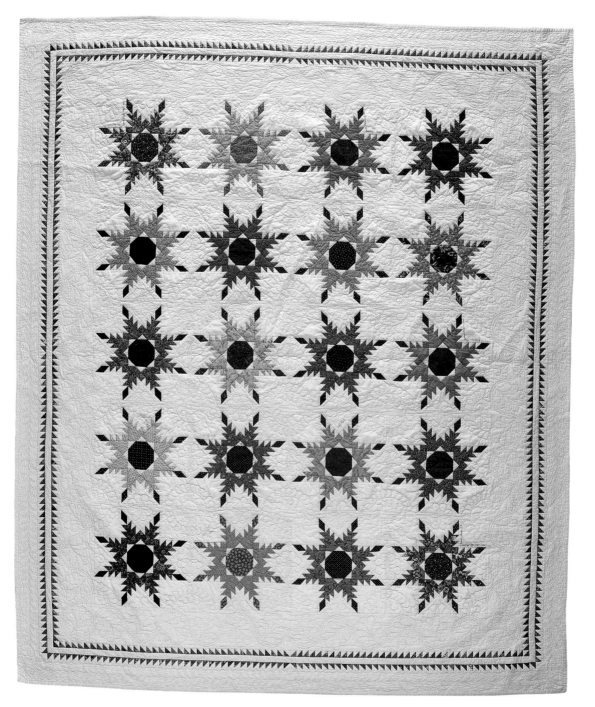

Quilt by Susan Danielson
Golden, Colorado

Finished Quilt Size
89" x 103"

Number of Blocks and Finished Size
20 blocks   15" x 15"

Fabric Requirements
Muslin   10½ yards
20 dark blue prints   6" x 14" each
20 light and medium
   blue prints   ⅜ yard each
Binding fabric   1 yard
Backing   3 yards, 104" wide

Other Materials
6"-square acrylic ruler with bias line

Cutting
Make templates of patterns A–G on page 108. (Pieces B, F, and G are rotary cut.) Cut all strips cross-grain unless specified otherwise.

From muslin
- 4 (2⅛"-wide) strips. From these, cut 80 (2⅛") squares. Cut each square in half diagonally to get 160 B triangles.
- 4 (7⅝"-wide) strips. From these, cut 20 (7⅝") squares. Cut each square in quarters diagonally to get 80 F triangles.
- 21 (1⅞"-wide) strips. From these, cut 480 (1⅞") squares. Cut each square in half to get 960 G triangles.
- 9 (4⅞"-wide) strips. From these, cut 80 (4⅞") H squares
- 14 (1½"-wide) strips. From these, cut 15 (1½" x 15½") strips for sashing and 4 (1½") I squares. Set aside remaining strips for horizontal sashing.
- 7 (18"-wide) strips. From these, cut 20 (14" x 18") pieces for J triangle-squares for border.
- 1 (2¾-yard) length. From this, cut 4 (4" x 99") lengthwise strips for outer border, 4 (1½" x 92") strips for middle borders, 2 (6" x 90") strips and 2 (5" x 70") strips for inner border.

From each dark blue fabric
- 1 of Template A.
- 8 of Template E.

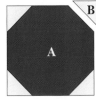

Unit A–Make 1.   **Unit F–Make 4.**   **Unit H–Make 4.**

Unit Piecing Diagrams

From each light/medium blue fabrics
- 1 (14" x 18") piece for J triangle-squares.
- 4 each of templates C and C reversed.
- 8 of Template D.
- 32 of Template G.

Quilt Top Assembly
1. For each block, refer to **Unit Piecing Diagrams** to make 1 Unit A, 4 Unit Fs, and 4 Unit Hs.

2. Join units in rows **(Block Assembly Diagram)**; then join rows to complete block. Make 20 Feathered Star blocks.

3. For each horizontal row, join 4 blocks with 3 (1½" x 15½") sashing strips. Make 5 horizontal rows.

4. Join 1½"-wide strips to make 4 (1½" x 66") horizontal sashing strips. Join rows with sashing strips between rows.

5. Sew 6"-wide border strips to quilt sides. Press seam allowances toward borders. Join 5"-wide strips to top and bottom edges. Press seam allowances toward borders.

6. For sawtooth border, pair each 14" x 18" muslin rectangle with 1 blue rectangle, with right sides facing and raw edges aligned. Using an acrylic ruler to find a 45°-angle, rotary-cut 1½"-wide bias strips across each rectangle **(Diagram 1)**. Keeping muslin and blue strips paired, join each pair along longest edge, using a ¼" seam. Press seam allowances open.

7. Place square ruler on 1 pieced strip so that bias (45°) line aligns with seam **(Diagram 2)**. Rotary-cut 1 (1½") triangle-square as shown. Cut 672 J triangle-squares.

continued

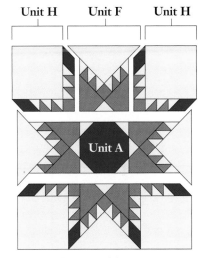

Unit H   Unit F   Unit H

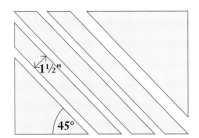

Block Assembly Diagram

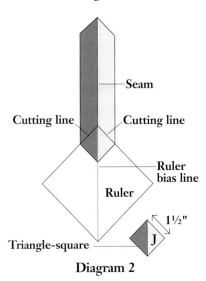

Diagram 1

Diagram 2

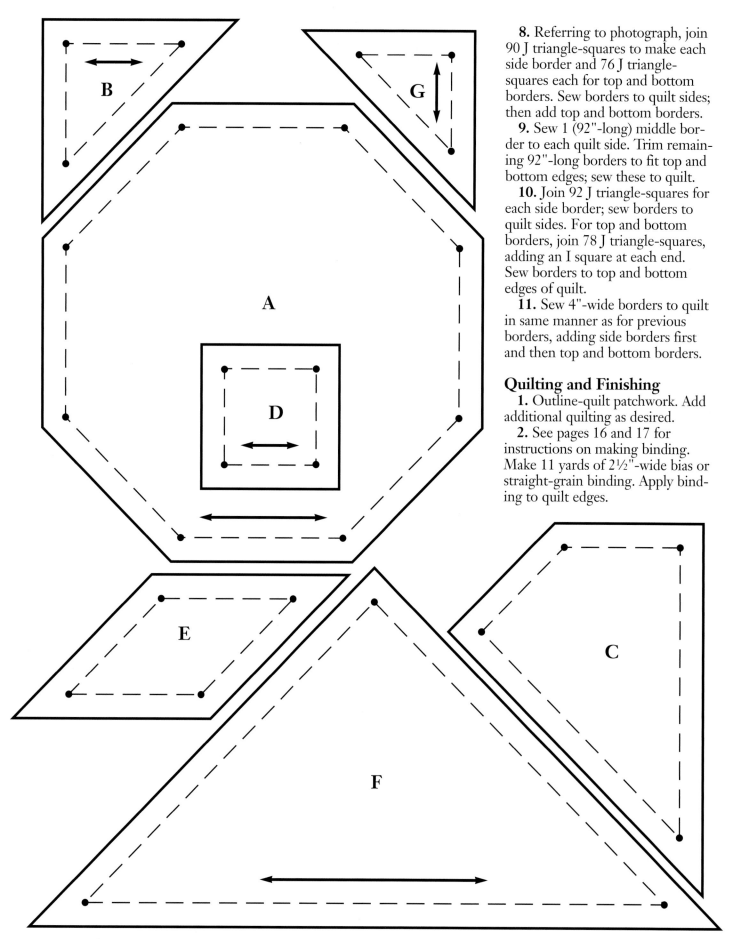

8. Referring to photograph, join 90 J triangle-squares to make each side border and 76 J triangle-squares each for top and bottom borders. Sew borders to quilt sides; then add top and bottom borders.

9. Sew 1 (92"-long) middle border to each quilt side. Trim remaining 92"-long borders to fit top and bottom edges; sew these to quilt.

10. Join 92 J triangle-squares for each side border; sew borders to quilt sides. For top and bottom borders, join 78 J triangle-squares, adding an I square at each end. Sew borders to top and bottom edges of quilt.

11. Sew 4"-wide borders to quilt in same manner as for previous borders, adding side borders first and then top and bottom borders.

Quilting and Finishing

1. Outline-quilt patchwork. Add additional quilting as desired.

2. See pages 16 and 17 for instructions on making binding. Make 11 yards of 2½"-wide bias or straight-grain binding. Apply binding to quilt edges.

Fisherman Fred

Then known only as the Fisher Boy, this cheerful cousin of Sunbonnet Sue made his first appearance in the late 1930s with an empty fishing line. By the mid-1950s, he was headed home, having acquired both a name and a fish on his line.

Quilt by Cynthia Moody Wheeler
Birmingham, Alabama

Finished Quilt Size
73" x 94"

Number of Blocks and Finished Size
20 blocks   12" x 12"

Fabric Requirements
White   2½ yards
Brown   ⅛ yard
Pink   ⅛ yard
Assorted plaids   20 (4" x 6") scraps
Navy   ⅝ yard
Yellow   ⅝ yard
Gray   ⅛ yard
Sashing fabric   1½ yards
Border fabric   2¾ yards*
Backing   5⅝ yards
*Includes fabric for straight-grain binding.

Other Materials
Brown and gray embroidery flosses

Cutting
Make templates of appliqué patterns on page 111.
From white
• 20 (12½") squares.

From brown
• 40 of Template A (shoe).
• 20 of Template I (fish).

From pink
• 20 *each* of templates B and C (hands).

From each plaid
• 1 *each* of templates D (shirt) and E (sleeve).

From navy
• 20 of Template F (pants).

From yellow
• 18 (3½") sashing squares.
• 20 of Template G (hat).

From gray
• 20 of Template H (bucket).

From sashing fabric
• 39 (3½" x 12½") sashing strips.

From border fabric
• 4 (8½" x 99") lengthwise strips.

Fish Quilting Pattern (shown in blue)

Setting Diagram

Quilt Top Assembly
1. Position pieces for 1 fisherman on a white square **(Appliqué Placement Diagram).** Appliqué pieces in alphabetical order. Make 20 blocks.

2. Use 3 strands of floss to embroider pole, line, bucket handle, and pants details. (See page 136 for stitch diagrams.)

3. Join 4 blocks and 3 sashing strips in a row **(Setting Diagram).** Make 5 block rows. Then join 4 sashing strips and 3 yellow squares in a row. Make 6 sashing rows.

4. Join rows as shown.

5. Sew borders to edges of quilt; miter corners.

Quilting and Finishing
1. Outline-quilt blocks. Quilt Fish Quilting Pattern in sashing.

2. See pages 16 and 17 for instructions on making binding. Make 10 yards of 2½"-wide bias or straight-grain binding. Apply binding to quilt edges.

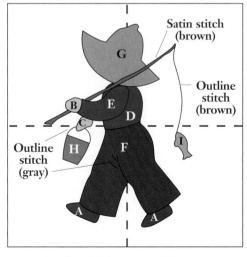

Appliqué Placement Diagram

Satin stitch (brown)

Outline stitch (brown)

Outline stitch (gray)

Patterns are finished size. Add ¼" seam allowance for hand appliqué or cut as is for machine appliqué.

Fisherman Fred 111

Flower Basket

The floral fabric that stands out amidst solid colors in this queen-sized quilt is from a housecoat that Wilma Waxler's mother made for her. Fine quilting and meticulous workmanship are skills that Wilma learned from her mother.

Quilt by Wilma L. Waxler
Malta, Ohio

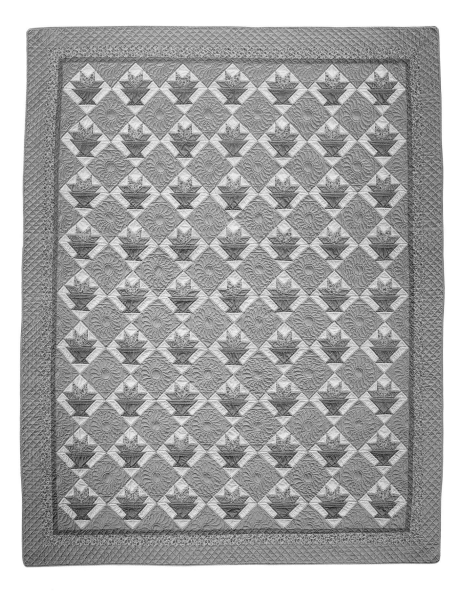

continued

Finished Quilt Size
95" x 117¼"

Number of Blocks and Finished Size
63 blocks   8" x 8"

Fabric Requirements
Green	4¾ yards*
Floral print	3⅛ yards
White	3 yards
Lavender	3 yards
Backing	9 yards

*Includes fabric for binding.

Cutting
Make templates of patterns A and B on page 114.

From green fabric
- 2 (5" x 120") and 2 (5" x 100") lengthwise strips for border.
- 126 of Template A.
- 7 (12½") squares. Cut squares in quarters diagonally to get 28 H triangles.
- 48 (8½") I squares.
- 2 (6½") squares. Cut squares in half diagonally to get 4 J corner triangles.

From floral fabric
- 2 (3" x 112") and 2 (3" x 89") lengthwise strips for border.
- 126 of Template A.

From white fabric
- 63 of Template B.
- 63 of Template B reversed.
- 126 (3¼") squares. Cut squares in half diagonally to get 252 D triangles.
- 32 (3⅞") squares. Cut squares in half diagonally to get 63 E triangles (and 1 extra.)
- 63 (2⅞") G squares.

From lavender fabric
- 2 (1½" x 106") and 2 (1½" x 84") lengthwise strips for border.
- 63 (2⅜") squares. Cut squares in half diagonally to get 126 C triangles.
- 32 (5⅞") squares. Cut squares in half diagonally to get 63 F triangles.

Quilt Top Assembly
1. To make 1 flower unit, join 2 floral As as shown **(Block Assembly Diagram)**; then add 1 green A to opposite sides of unit as shown. Set D triangles and 1 G square into angled openings of flower as shown. (See page 10 for tips on sewing set-in seams.) Complete flower unit by adding D triangles to each side of unit.

2. Assemble basket unit **(Block Assembly Diagram)**; then join flower unit to basket unit. Repeat to make a total of 63 blocks.

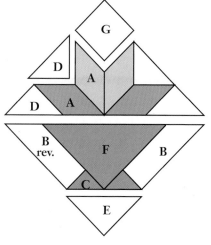

Block Assembly Diagram

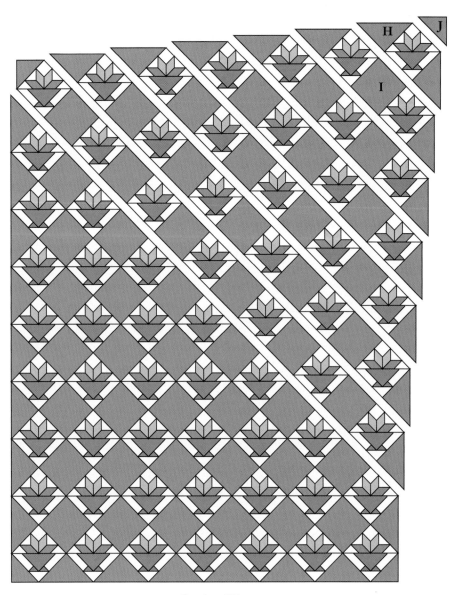

Setting Diagram

3. Arrange blocks and I squares in diagonal rows **(Setting Diagram)**. Join H and J triangles to row ends as shown. Join units in each diagonal row; then join rows.

4. Matching centers, join longer lavender border strips to quilt sides; then join shorter strips to top and bottom edges, mitering corners. Join floral border in same manner; then join green border.

Quilting and Finishing

1. Referring to photograph, select quilting designs for I squares and borders. Mark designs on quilt top before layering and basting. Outline-quilt baskets; then quilt additional designs as desired.

2. See pages 16 and 17 for instructions on making binding. Make 12 yards of 2½"-wide bias or straight-grain binding from green. Apply binding to quilt edges.

Flower of Spring

When this pattern appeared in *The Kansas City Star* in 1936, its alternate name was Two Lips. The liplike shape of the tulip explains the pun.

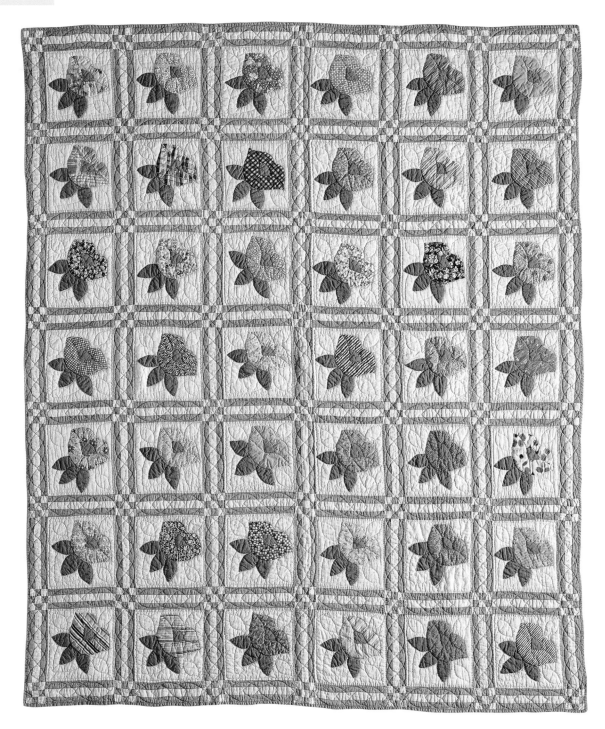

Quilt from The Patchwork Palace
Franklin, Tennessee

Finished Quilt Size
72⅜" x 84"

Number of Blocks and Finished Size
42 blocks   9" x 9"

Fabric Requirements
White   4 yards
Light green   4 yards*
Dark green   1 yard
Assorted prints   42 (7" x 9") scraps
Orange   ¼ yard
Backing   5⅛ yards
*Includes fabric for binding.

Cutting
Cut all strips cross-grain. Cut pieces in order listed to get best use of yardage. Make templates of patterns A–E on page 117.

From white
- 11 (9½"-wide) strips. From these, cut 42 (9½") squares.
- 33 (1½"-wide) strips.

From light green
- 54 (1½"-wide) strips.

From dark green
- 42 of Template A and 42 of Template A reversed.
- 42 of Template B.

From each assorted print
- 1 each of templates C and E.

From orange
- 42 of Template D.

Quilt Top Assembly
1. Fold each 9½" square in quarters diagonally; crease lightly to form placement guidelines.
2. For each block, select 1 each of pieces A, A reversed, B, C, D, and E. Appliqué pieces in place on white square in alphabetical order (**Appliqué Placement Diagram**). Make 42 blocks.

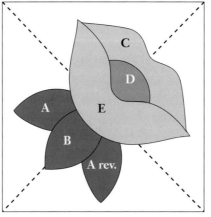

Appliqué Placement Diagram

3. Using 1½"-wide strips of white and light green fabrics, make 25 of Strip Set 1 and 4 of Strip Set 2. Press all seam allowances toward green. From Strip Set 1, cut 97 (9½"-wide) sashing units and 56 (1½"-wide) nine-patch segments. From Strip Set 2, cut 112 (1½"-wide) segments for nine-patches.
4. For each nine-patch, join 2 segments from Strip Set 2 and 1 segment from Strip Set 1 (**Nine-Patch Assembly Diagram**). Make 56 nine-patch units for sashing.

5. Lay out blocks in 7 horizontal rows with 6 blocks in each row (**Row Assembly Diagram**). Place sashing segments between blocks and at row ends as shown. Referring to photograph, lay out 8 rows of sashing units and nine-patches. When satisfied with placement, join units in each row.
6. Join rows.

Quilting and Finishing
1. Outline-quilt each block. Quilt shown also has a cable design quilted in sashing bands.
2. See pages 16 and 17 for instructions on making binding. Make 10 yards of 2½"-wide bias or straight-grain binding from green. Apply binding to quilt edges.

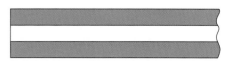

Strip Set 1—Make 25.

Strip Set 2—Make 4.

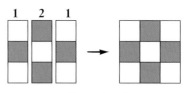

Nine-Patch Assembly Diagram

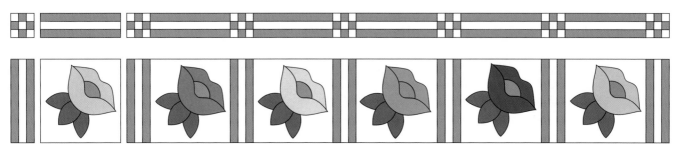

Row Assembly Diagram

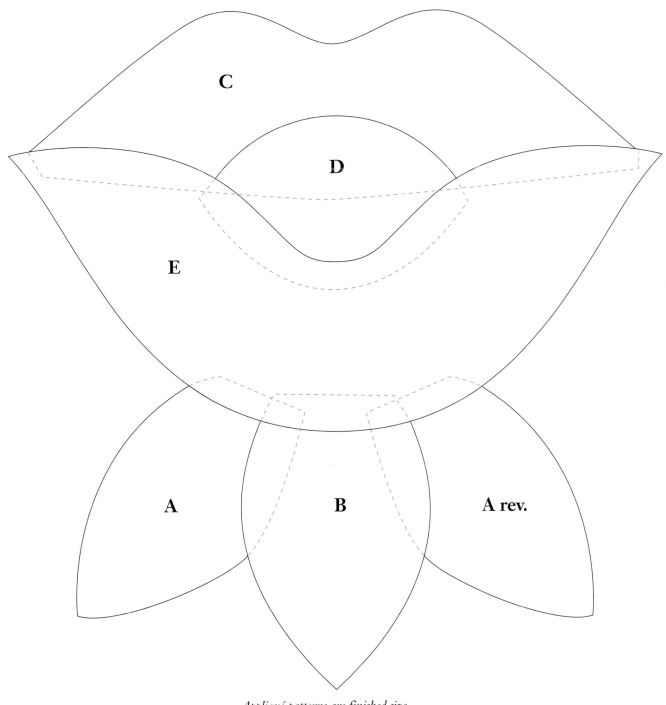

C

D

E

A

B

A rev.

Appliqué patterns are finished size.
Add ¼" seam allowance for hand appliqué or cut as is for machine appliqué.

Flower Reel

You can use reproduction fabrics to make this pretty quilt, based on a 1930s design. Or create an entirely different color scheme. A mix of piecing and appliqué, the setting offers a lot of space to show off fancy quilting.

Quilt by Martha Skelton
Vicksburg, Mississippi

Finished Quilt Size
72" x 87¼"

Number of Blocks and Finished Size
22 blocks   11" x 11"

Fabric Requirements
White   6¼ yards*
Yellow prints   6 fat quarters**
Blue prints   6 fat quarters**
Lavender prints   5 fat quarters**
Pink prints   5 fat quarters**
Green print   ⅝ yard
Yellow solid   ¼ yard
Backing   5¼ yards

*Includes fabric for binding.
**Fat quarter = 18" x 22".

Cutting
Make templates of patterns A–I on pages 121–123. (Pattern C is optional, since triangle can be rotary-cut.)

From white fabric
- 1 (30") square for binding.
- 4 (16¾") squares. Cut each square in quarters diagonally to get 14 Y side triangles (and 2 extra).
- 10 (11½") X setting squares.
- 2 (8¾") squares. Cut each square in half diagonally to get 4 Z corner triangles.
- 4 (6½"-wide) strips. From these, cut 22 of Template A.
- 8 (6⅜"-wide) strips. From these, cut 44 (6⅜") squares. Cut each square in half diagonally to get 88 C triangles.
- 4 (4½"-wide) strips. From these and remaining scraps, cut 62 of Template G.

From yellow prints
- 24 of Template B (4 from each fabric).
- 24 of Template D (4 from each fabric).
- 15 of Template H (2 from each fabric and 3 extra).
- 6 of Template I (1 from each fabric).

From blue prints
- 24 of Template B (4 from each fabric).
- 24 of Template D (4 from each fabric).
- 14 of Template H (2 from each fabric and 2 extra).
- 3 of Template I.

From lavender prints
- 20 of Template B (4 from each fabric).
- 20 of Template D (4 from each fabric).
- 15 of Template H (3 from each fabric).
- 1 of Template I.

From pink prints
- 20 of Template B (4 from each fabric).
- 20 of Template D (4 from each fabric).
- 14 of Template H (3 from each fabric, including 1 extra).
- 2 of Template I.

From green print
- 7 (2½"-wide) strips. From these, cut 176 of Template F.

From yellow solid
- 4 (1½"-wide) strips. From these, cut 88 of Template E.

continued

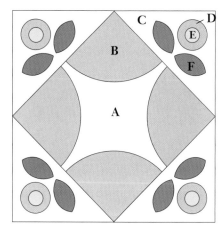

Block Assembly Diagram

Quilt Top Assembly

1. For each block, select 1 A, 4 C triangles, 8 F leaves, 4 Es, and 4 *each* of B and D from same print fabric.

2. See page 11 for tips on sewing a curved seam; then sew Bs to A (**Block Assembly Diagram**). If you prefer, you can turn under the seam allowances on the curved edge of each B piece and appliqué Bs in place instead. Press seam allowances toward Bs.

3. Position 2 F leaves on each C triangle and appliqué. Place and appliqué D circles as shown; then add E circles. Press.

4. Sew appliquéd C triangles onto sides of A/B unit as shown. Press seam allowances toward Cs.

5. Make 22 flower blocks.

6. Lay out blocks, X setting squares, Y side triangles, and Z corner triangles in diagonal rows (**Setting Diagram**). Move blocks around to achieve a nice balance of color. When satisfied with block placement, join units in each row. Press seam allowances toward setting squares (or triangles) whenever possible.

7. Lay out rows to verify correct placement of units; then join rows.

8. For top border, join 14 Gs and 13 Hs in a horizontal row as shown (**Setting Diagram**). Refer to photos and diagram for color placement. Assemble bottom border in same manner.

Setting Diagram

9. For each side border, join 17 Gs and 16 Hs as shown.

10. Join each border to quilt, easing to fit as necessary.

11. Join 3 I pieces for each corner unit, referring to photos and diagram for color placement. Make 4 corner units.

12. Sew corner units in place with a set-in seam. (See page 10 for tips on sewing a set-in seam.) It may be necessary to tack middle I piece at corner.

Quilting and Finishing

1. Make stencils of Tea Leaf Quilting Pattern (inside Pattern A) and Feather Wreath Quilting Pattern on page 122; mark quilt top. Quilt tea leaf in center of each A piece. Quilt wreath in each setting square. Quilt shown also has outline quilting at seam lines, with echo quilting moving out from seams at 1" intervals.

2. See page 17 for instructions on making bias binding. Make 8⅞ yards of binding from reserved white fabric. Apply binding to quilt edges.

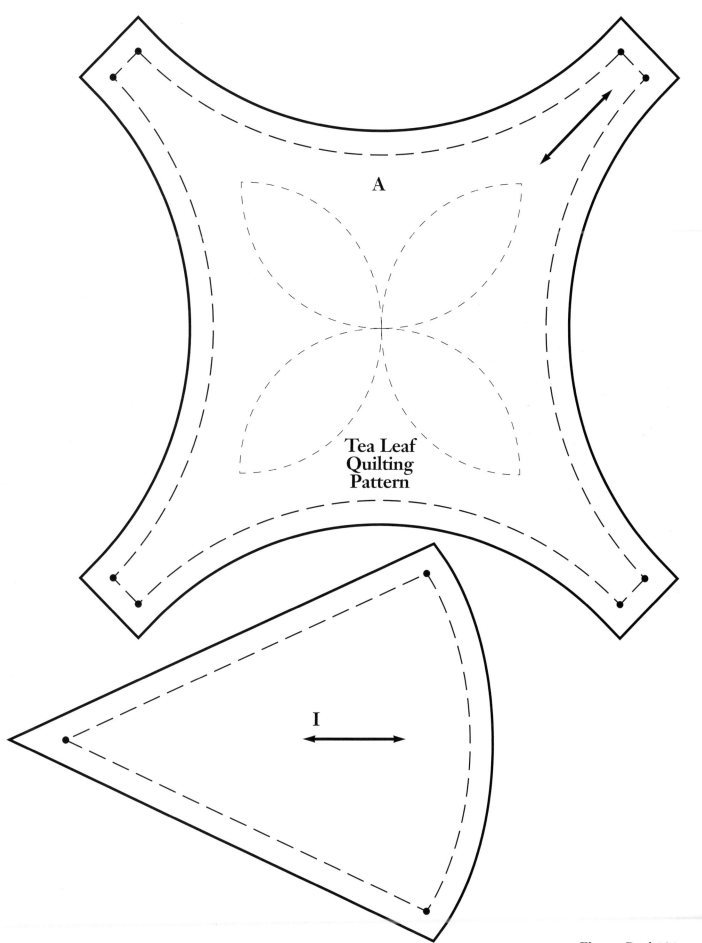

A

Tea Leaf
Quilting
Pattern

I

Flower Reel 121

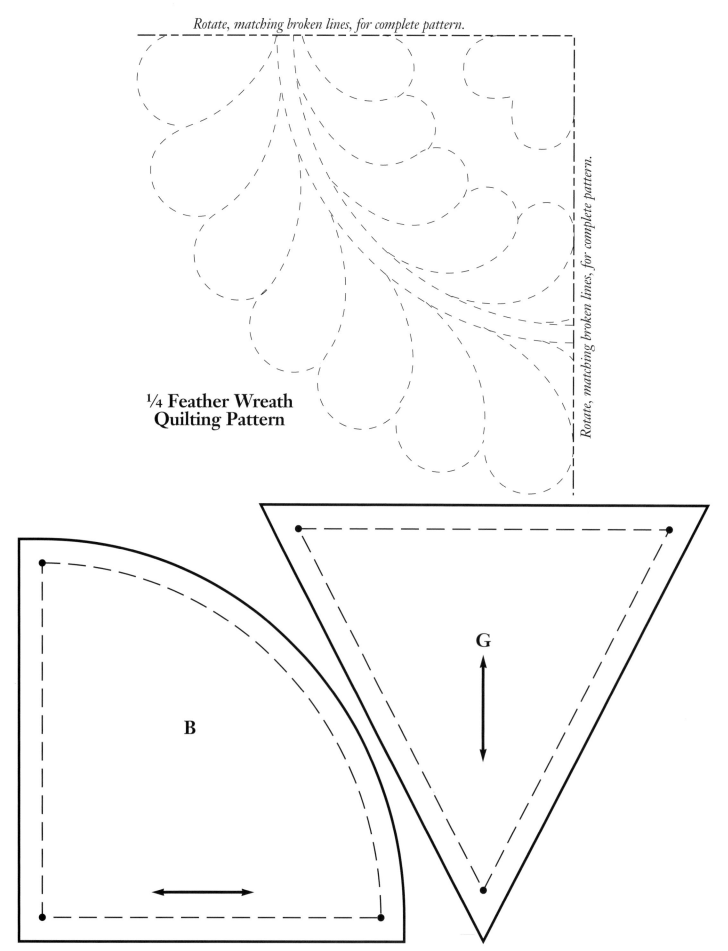

Rotate, matching broken lines, for complete pattern.

Rotate, matching broken lines, for complete pattern.

**¼ Feather Wreath
Quilting Pattern**

B

G

122 Flower Reel

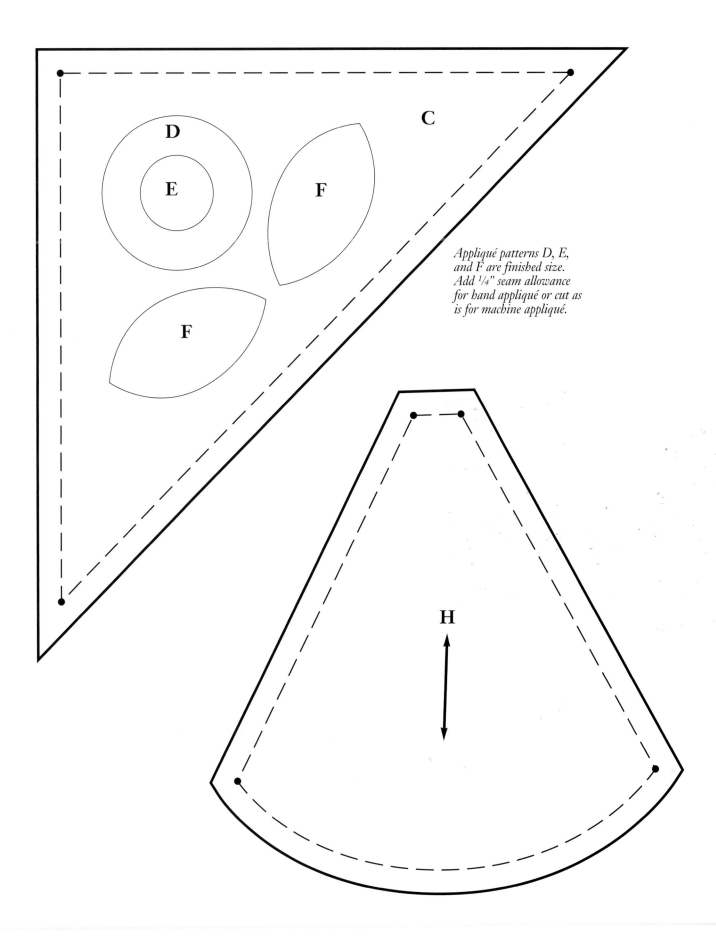

C

D

E

F

F

Appliqué patterns D, E, and F are finished size. Add ¼" seam allowance for hand appliqué or cut as is for machine appliqué.

H

Flying Geese

Do you have lots of scraps looking for a place to live? If so, this is the quilt for you. There are more than 400 triangles in various shades of red in this quilt. Make a flock in your favorite hue or use scraps of many colors, letting the border fabric determine the predominant color.

Quilt by Lara Kline
Springfield, Massachusetts

Finished Quilt Size

76" x 76"

Fabric Requirements

Cranberry prints   9 fat quarters*
Multi-striped print   3¼ yards**
Beige print   4½ yards
Binding fabric   ¾ yard
Backing   4⅝ yards

*Fat quarter = 18" x 22".
**Required *finished* widths of 2 stripes are
 2" and 3⅜", respectively. Fabric between
 stripes is not used.

Cutting

Instructions are for rotary cutting.
For traditional cutting, make templates of patterns A–F on page 126.

From cranberry prints
• 30 (3½" x 22") strips. From these,
  cut 328 (2" x 3½") A pieces.
• 15 (2⅞" x 22") strips. From
  these, cut 80 (2⅞") squares. Cut
  each square in half diagonally to
  get 160 C triangles.

From multi-striped print
• 4 (3⅞" x 63") border strips, centering 3⅜"-wide stripe.
• 4 (2½" x 63") border strips, centering 2" stripe.
• 7 (2½" x 40") sashing strips, centering 2" stripe.
• 62 (2") squares (center any stripe
  or combination of stripes in each
  square). Cut each square in half
  diagonally to get 124 C triangles.
• 8 (2" x 3½") A pieces.

From beige print
• 2 (2" x 56") and 6 (1½" x 56")
  lengthwise border strips.
• 20 (6⅞") squares. Cut each
  square in half diagonally to get
  40 E triangles.
• 5 (9¼") squares. Cut each square
  in quarters diagonally to get 20 F
  triangles.
• 32 (2"-wide) strips. From these,
  cut 672 (2") B squares.
• 9 (2¼"-wide) strips. From these,
  cut 160 (2¼") squares. Cut each
  square in half diagonally to get
  320 D triangles.
• 4 (8½") G squares.

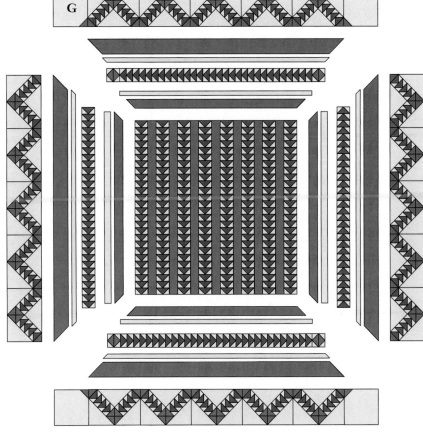

Setting Diagram

Quilt Top Assembly

1. See page 12 for instructions
on Diagonal-Corners Method for
Flying Geese units. Use cranberry
A pieces and beige B squares to
make 208 Flying Geese units. For
traditional piecing, sew beige Bs to
sides of each A to get 208 units.

2. Join 26 A/B units in a vertical
row to make a Flying Geese column. Make 8 columns.

3. Join columns, alternating with
2½" x 40" sashing strips **(Setting
Diagram)**. Sew 2½"-wide striped
borders to quilt, mitering corners.

4. Sew 2"-wide beige border
strips to quilt sides. Sew 2 (1½"-
wide) beige strips to top and bottom edges of quilt.

5. Make 4 Flying Geese rows,
with 30 A/B units in each row. Join
1 row to each side of quilt.

6. Sew beige Bs to each striped A.
Join 2 A/B units to make a pieced
square. Make 4 pieced squares. Join
squares to ends of remaining
Flying Geese rows. Join rows to
top and bottom edges of quilt.

7. Sew 1½"-wide beige border
strips to quilt, mitering corners.
Add 3⅞"-wide striped borders to
quilt, mitering corners.

8. Join beige Ds to sides of each
cranberry C to make 160 Flying
Geese units. (These are not suit-
able for diagonal-corner technique
because of odd size.) Join 8 C/D
units with striped Cs, Es, and Fs to
make each border block **(Border
Block Piecing Diagram)**. Make
20 border blocks.   *continued*

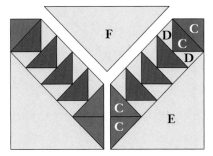

Border Block Piecing Diagram

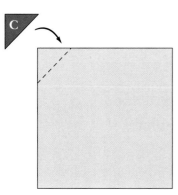

Corner Piecing Diagram

9. Make 4 border rows, with 5 border blocks in each row. Sew 2 rows to quilt sides with E triangles on outside edge of quilt **(Setting Diagram)**.

10. Sew 1 striped C to 1 corner of each 8½" beige print square **(Corner Piecing Diagram).** Trim excess fabric of square under triangle, leaving ¼" seam allowance.

11. Sew corner blocks to opposite ends of remaining borders, noting position of C. Join borders to top and bottom edges of quilt.

Quilting and Finishing

1. Outline-quilt ¼" inside and outside seam lines of all cranberry As and Cs. Outline-quilt ½" inside seam lines of Es and Fs; then add echo quilting ½" from previous line of quilting. Quilt along designs on striped borders as desired.

2. See pages 16 amd 17 for instructions on making binding. Make 8¾ yards of 2½"-wide bias or straight-grain binding from reserved fabric. Apply binding to quilt edges.

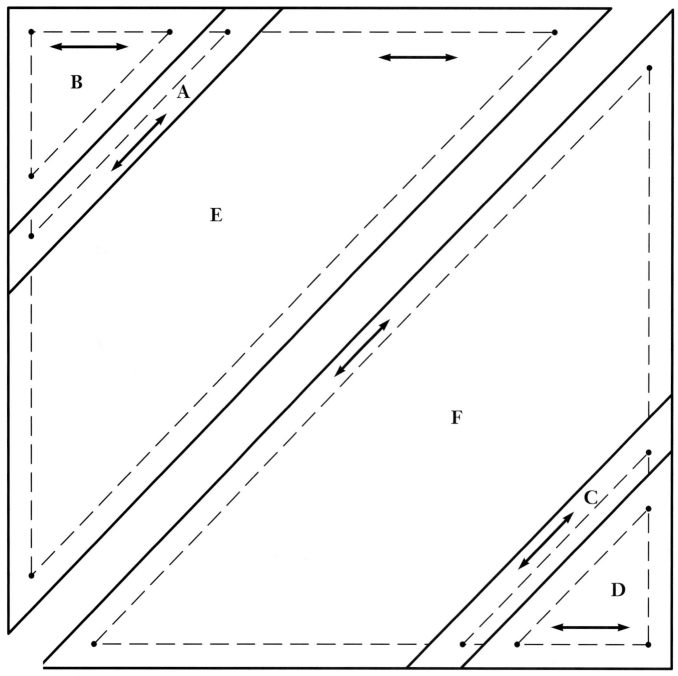

Fruit Basket

Pieced in the rich colors of an autumn harvest, this quilt top dates from the 1930s. To enhance your baskets with the theme of nature's bounty, add quilting designs of fruits and grains.

Antique quilt, maker unknown

Finished Quilt Size
81" x 109"

Number of Blocks and Finished Size
35 blocks   10" x 10"

Fabric Requirements
Red print   4¾ yards*
White print   3⅛ yards
Tan print   2¾ yards
Backing   6¾ yards
*Includes fabric for binding.

Cutting
From red print fabric
- 2 (4" x 86") and 2 (4" x 114") lengthwise strips for border.
- 4 (2½" x 114") lengthwise strips for straight-grain binding.
- 3 (12" x 43") crossgrain strips. From these, cut 16 (7" x 12") rectangles for quick-pieced A triangles.
- 18 (6⅞") squares. Cut each square in half diagonally to get 35 B triangles (and 1 extra).
- 35 (2⅞") squares. Cut each square in half diagonally to get 70 A triangles.

From white print fabric
- 2 (2¼" x 79") and 2 (2¼" x 108") lengthwise strips for border.
- 4 (12" x 34") strips. From these, cut 16 (7" x 12") rectangles for quick-pieced A triangles.
- 3 (4⅞" x 34") strips. From these, cut 18 (4⅞") squares. Cut each square in half diagonally to get 35 D triangles (and 1 extra).
- 14 (2½" x 34") strips. From these, cut 70 (2½" x 6½") C pieces.
- 18 (6⅞") squares. Cut each square in half diagonally to get 35 B triangles (and 1 extra).

From tan print fabric
- 5 (15½") squares. Cut each square in quarters diagonally to get 20 F side setting triangles.
- 24 (10½") E squares.
- 2 (8") squares. Cut each square in half diagonally to get 4 G corner triangles.

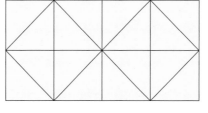

Diagram 1

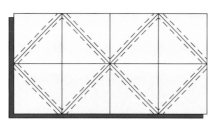

Diagram 2

Quick Piecing
1. On wrong side of a 7" x 12" white piece, mark a 2- x 4-square grid of 2⅞" squares **(Diagram 1)**. Draw diagonal lines through squares as shown.

2. With right sides facing, pin white piece to a red print piece. Machine-stitch ¼" from each side of all *diagonal* lines **(Diagram 2)**. Cut on *all* grid lines to separate 16 A triangle-squares. Press seam allowances toward red print.

3. Repeat with remaining 7" x 12" pieces to get a total of 245 triangle-squares (and 11 extra).

Color Variations
This classic basket block is appealing in many color combinations. Here are some other color schemes to inspire you.

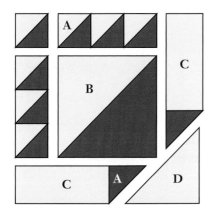

Block Assembly Diagram

Quilt Top Assembly

1. Join red print and white print B triangles as shown **(Block Assembly Diagram).** Press seam allowances toward red.

2. Join 3 A triangle-squares in a horizontal row as shown. Sew row to top of white print B triangle.

3. Join 4 A triangle-squares in a vertical row as shown. Sew row to left side of white print B triangle.

4. Select 2 C pieces for each block. Sew a red print A triangle to 1 end of each C, positioning triangles as shown. Press seam allowances toward red. Sew A/C pieces to red sides of B triangle-square.

5. Add D triangle to complete block, making sure to center D.

6. Make a total of 35 blocks.

7. Arrange blocks and E squares in diagonal rows, turning blocks on point as shown **(Setting Diagram).** Add G and G triangles to row ends as shown. Join units in each diagonal row; then join rows.

8. Matching centers, join white print and red print border strips in pairs to make a 2-strip border for each quilt edge. Sew longer strips to quilt sides; then sew shorter strips to top and bottom edges. Miter border corners.

Quilting and Finishing

1. Outline-quilt basket blocks. Add other quilting as desired.

2. Join red print strips end-to-end to make 11 yards of continuous straight-grain binding. See page 17 for instructions on applying binding.

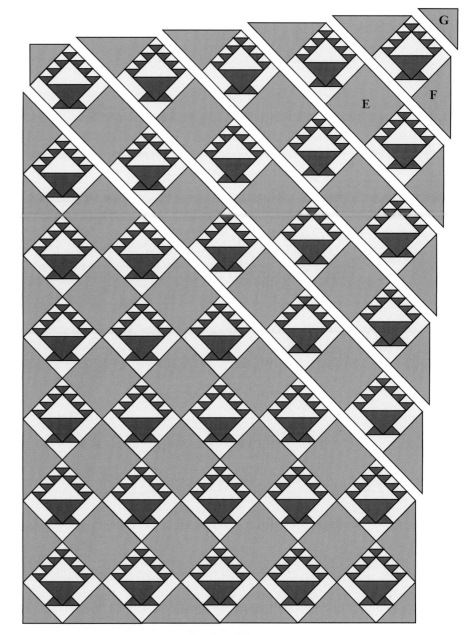

Setting Diagram

Make Your Own Quilt Label
See page 366 for instructions.

Garden of Friendship

Cheery scrap fabrics combine with salmon pink and green solid fabrics for a quilt with a distinctive 1930s look. Check fabric stores and quilt shops for reproduction '30s prints.

Quilt by Henrietta Kroening and Mattie Borntreger
Owned by Karen G. Veldboom
Waukesha, Wisconsin

Finished Quilt Size
77" x 100"

Number of Blocks and Finished Size
59 full blocks   8" x 8"

Fabric Requirements
Salmon pink   7⅝ yards
Green   3 yards
11 assorted prints   ⅜ yard each
7 blue prints   ⅛ yard each
Backing   6 yards

Cutting
Make templates of patterns A–H on pages 132 and 133. Cut all strips cross-grain except as indicated.

From salmon pink fabric
- 2 (4" x 72") and 2 (4" x 95") lengthwise strips for border. Use 27" x 95" remainder for next 2 cuts.
- 70 *each* of Template G and Template G reversed.
- 77 of Template D.
- 21 (6"-wide) strips. From these, cut 70 of Template E, 70 of Template E reversed, 75 of Template H, and 75 of Template H reversed.
- 9 (4½"-wide) strips. From these, cut 77 of Template B.
- 4 (7½") squares for inner border.

From green fabric
- 2 (7½" x 83") and 2 (7½" x 58") lengthwise strips for border.
- 75 *each* of Template F and Template F reversed.
- 4 (4") border squares.

From each assorted print fabric
- 7 of Template A.
- 12 (5") squares for prairie points.

From each blue print fabric
- 11 of Template C.

Quilt Top Assembly
1. For each block, select 1 each of A, B, C, D, E, E reversed, F, F rev., G, G rev., H, and H rev.

2. See page 11 for tips on stitching curved seams. Join A and B **(Block Assembly Diagram).**

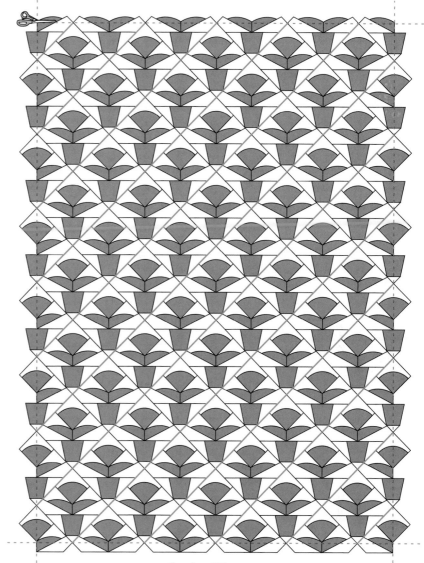

Setting Diagram

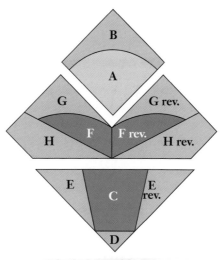

Block Assembly Diagram

3. Sew E and E reversed to sides of C flowerpot piece; add D triangle at bottom of unit.

4. Join F and G; then join F reversed to G reversed in same manner. Add H and H reversed to bottom of each unit. Sew center seam to join both units.

5. Sew flowerpot unit to bottom of flower/leaf section. Set A/B flower unit into opening at top to complete block. (See page 10 for tips on sewing a set-in seam.)

6. Make 59 blocks.

7. Make 6 blocks without F/G/H reversed pieces for right side of quilt **(Setting Diagram)**. Make 6 more blocks for left side of quilt, omitting F/G/H unit. Leave edges of these blocks uneven until after quilt is assembled.

continued

Garden of Friendship   131

8. Make 6 partial blocks without A, B, G, and G reversed for top edge **(Setting Diagram)**. Eliminate 1 side of leaf section on 2 blocks for corners.

9. For bottom edge, make 6 partial blocks without C/D/E flowerpot units. Eliminate half of leaf section for 2 corner blocks.

10. Join blocks in diagonal rows **(Setting Diagram)**. Be sure to note type of partial block needed at end of row. Join rows.

11. Measure width of quilt. Trim 58"-long green strips to match width. Sew pink squares to ends of each strip. Press seam allowances toward borders. Set aside.

12. Sew 83"-long green border strips to quilt sides, stitching over partial blocks. Trim border ends as needed; then trim partial blocks even with seam allowance. Press seam allowances toward borders.

13. Sew reserved borders to top and bottom edges of quilt. Trim excess fabric of partial blocks from seam allowances.

14. Join long pink borders to sides of quilt. Trim ends as needed. Add top and bottom borders with green corner squares in same manner as for inner border.

Quilting and Finishing

1. Outline-quilt blocks. Quilt borders as desired. Trim batting and backing even with quilt top.

2. Fold each 5" square in half twice to make a small triangle **(Figure 1)**. Press.

3. Starting at corner and aligning raw edges, pin 27 points each across top and bottom edges. Space them evenly and overlap adjacent points. Pin 38 points on each side.

4. Stitch points in place with a ½" seam **(Figure 2)**. Press points to right side of quilt. Fold under ½" hem on backing to cover raw edges of points **(Figure 3)**. Blind-stitch in place.

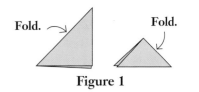

Fold. Fold.

Figure 1

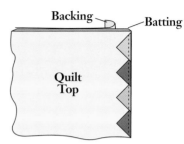

Backing — Batting

Quilt Top

Figure 2

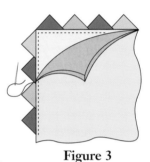

Figure 3

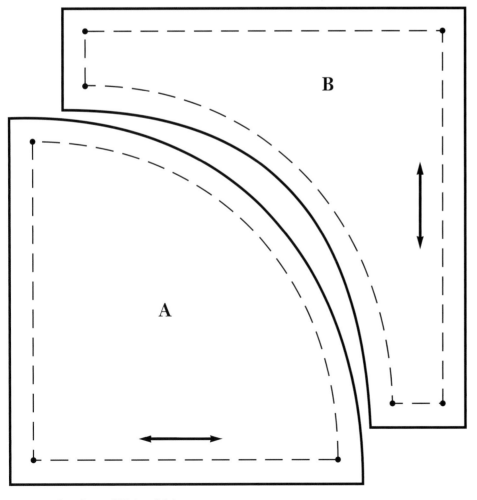

B

A

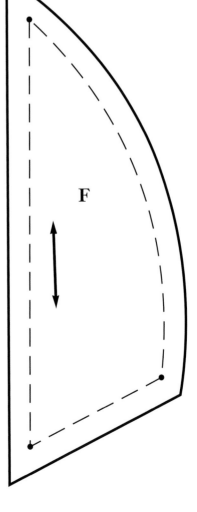

F

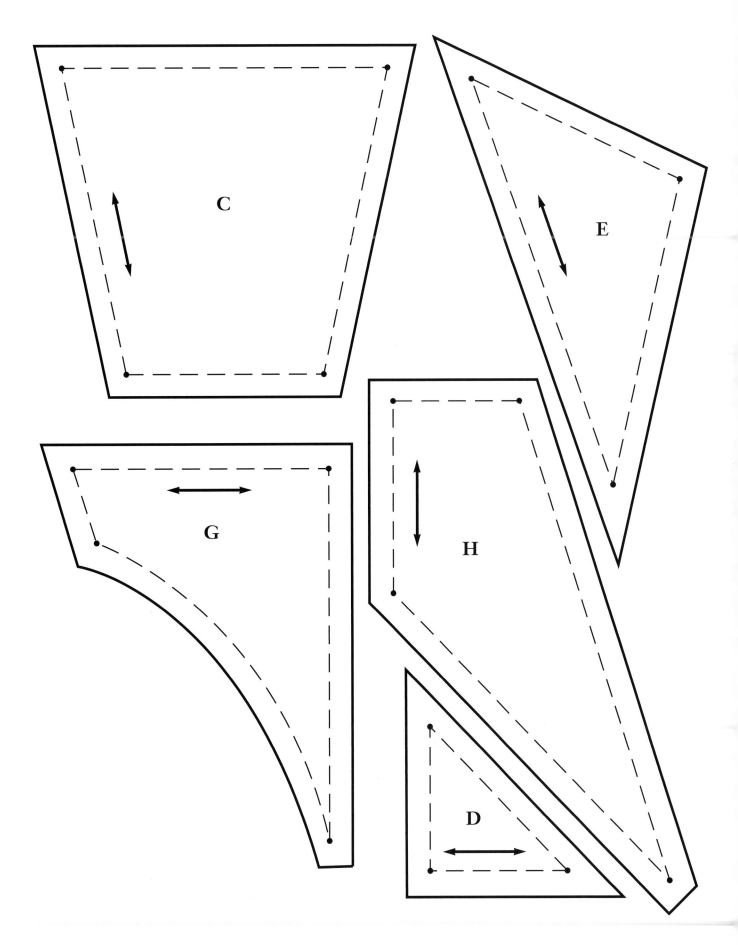

Gingham Dog & Calico Cat

This nursery quilt, which features three-dimensional ears and bows, is inspired by the opening lines of Eugene Field's poem, "The Duel":

The Gingham Dog and the Calico Cat
Side by side on the table sat;
'Twas half past 12, and (what do you think!)
Nor one nor t'other had slept a wink!
The old Dutch clock and the Chinese plate
Appeared to know as sure as fate
There was going to be a terrible spat.

Quilt by Gussie A. Moore
Mt. Olive, Alabama

Finished Quilt Size
45" x 58"

Number of Blocks and Finished Size
12 blocks   10½" x 10½"

Fabric Requirements
Blue   2 yards*
White   1½ yards
6 assorted ginghams   ¼ yard each
6 assorted prints   ¼ yard each
12 coordinating solids   scraps
Red   scraps
Backing   3½ yards
*Includes fabric for binding.

Other Materials
Black embroidery floss

Cutting
Make templates of patterns A–L on pages 136 and 137.
From blue fabric
- 2 (3" x 63") and 2 (3" x 50") lengthwise strips for straight-grain binding.
- 12 (11") squares.

From white fabric
- 4 (5" x 50") and 3 (2¾" x 37") lengthwise strips for sashing.
- 8 (2¾" x 11") strips for sashing.

From each gingham fabric
- 1 of Template A.
- 1 of Template B and 1 of Template B reversed.
- 1 of Template C.
- 1 of Template D.

From each print fabric
- 1 of Template H.
- 1 of Template I.
- 1 of Template J.

From each of 6 solid fabrics
- 1 of Template F.
- 1 of Template G and 1 of Template G reversed.

From each remaining 6 solid fabrics
- 3 of Template L and 3 of Template L reversed.
- 1 of Template K.

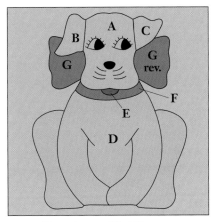

Dog Assembly Diagram

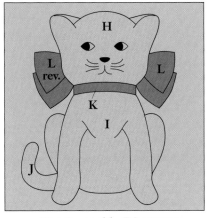

Cat Assembly Diagram

From red fabric
- 12 of Template E.

Quilt Top Assembly
1. For 1 dog, select a matching set of pieces A, B, B rev., C, and D. Select a coordinating set of 1 F, 1 G and 1 G rev. Lightly trace embroidery lines on A and D.

2. With right sides facing, seam B and B reversed, leaving opening as indicated on pattern. Trim seam allowance, clip curves, and turn right side out through opening.

3. Join 2 Es in same manner, leaving straight edges open for turning. Trim and clip seam allowance; then turn through opening.

4. Position dog pieces on 1 blue background square **(Dog Assembly Diagram)**. Tack raw edge of E in place, leaving finished edge of tongue loose. Appliqué D (body), and then F (collar).

5. Appliqué 1 G and 1 G rev. (bow) on each side of head (A). Stitch C (ear) in place. Sew B (ear) in place at raw edge only, leaving finished edge loose. Appliqué A in place, covering edges of B, C, E, F, and Gs.

6. Make a total of 6 dog blocks.

7. For 1 cat, select a matching set of 1 each of pieces H, I, and J. Select a coordinating set of 1 K, 3 L and 3 L reversed. Lightly trace embroidery details onto H and I.

8. With right sides facing, seam 1 L and 1 L reversed, leaving opening for turning. Trim seam

allowance and turn right side out. Make second bow unit in same manner.

9. Position cat pieces on 1 background square **(Cat Assembly Diagram)**. Use faced Ls for top bow loops. When satisfied with placement, appliqué J (tail) and then I (body). Appliqué bottom bow loops in place; then tack raw edge of top bows in place, leaving bow loops to flop. Appliqué H (head), covering edges of all bow loops. Appliqué K (collar) in place to cover edges of head and body.

10. Make a total of 6 cat blocks.

11. Referring to stitch diagrams on page 137, use 2 strands of floss to embroider details as shown.

12. Referring to photograph, lay out blocks in 4 horizontal rows of 3 blocks each. Join blocks in each row, sewing 1 (11") sashing strip between each pair. Then join rows, sewing a 37"-long sashing strip between rows, easing to fit as needed.

13. Referring to instructions for straight borders on page 14, sew white borders to quilt. Press seam allowances toward borders.

Quilting and Finishing
1. Outline-quilt cats and dogs. Add additional quilting in sashing as desired. Select a cable design to quilt in white borders.

2. See page 16 for instructions on making binding. Make straight-grain binding from reserved blue strips. Apply binding to quilt edges.

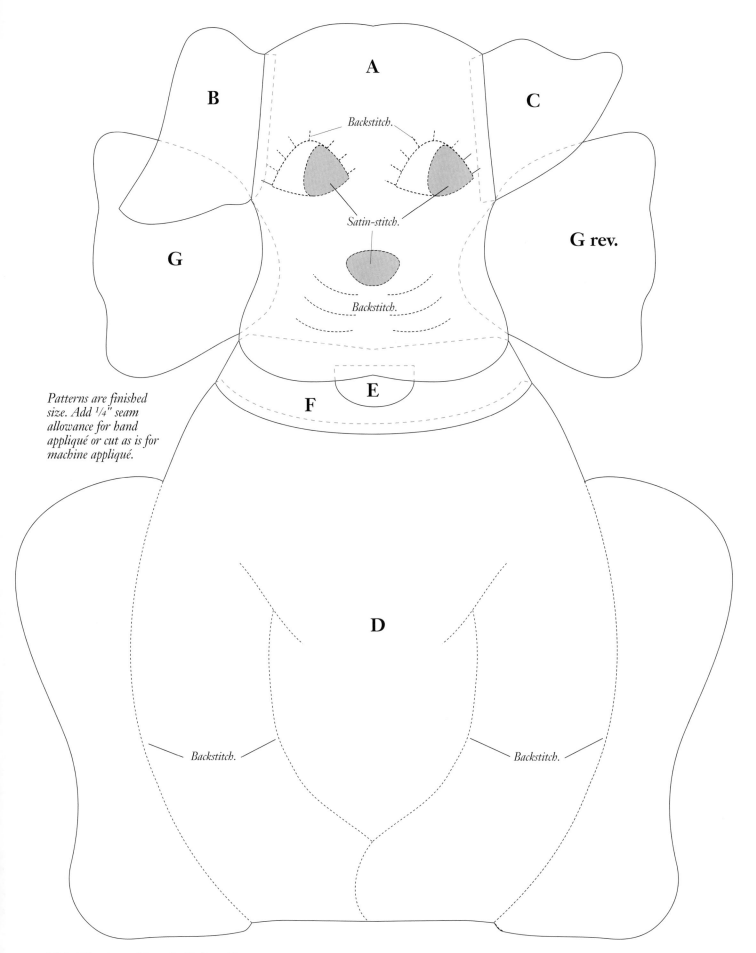

Backstitch.

B

A

C

G

Satin-stitch.

G rev.

Backstitch.

F

E

Patterns are finished
size. Add ¼" seam
allowance for hand
appliqué or cut as is for
machine appliqué.

D

Backstitch.

Backstitch.

136 Gingham Dog & Calico Cat

Backstitch

Satin Stitch

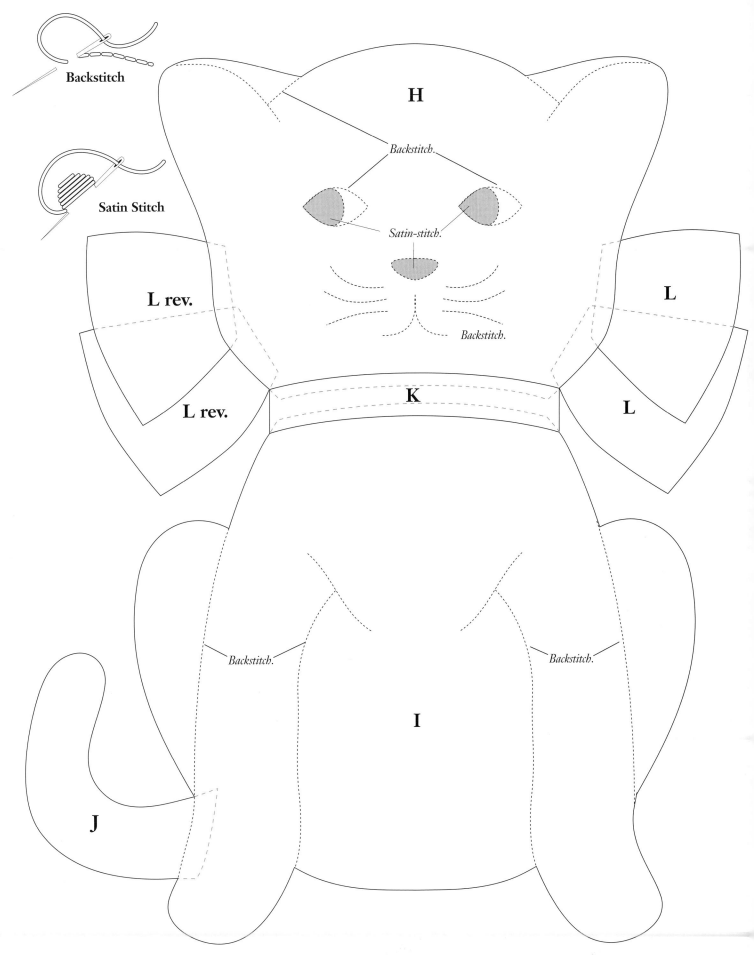

H

Backstitch.

Satin-stitch.

Backstitch.

L rev.

L rev.

L

L

K

Backstitch.

Backstitch.

I

J

Glorified Nine-Patch

Friendship quilts were popular during the 1930s.
This one might have been made by church
women to welcome a new pastor to their pulpit.

Vintage quilt owned by Susan Ramey Cleveland
Leeds, Alabama

Finished Quilt Size
71" x 81"

Number of Blocks
56 nine-patch units

Fabric Requirements
White or muslin	1⅜ yards
28 assorted prints	12" x 14" each
Yellow	5 yards*
Backing	5 yards

*Includes fabric for binding.

Cutting
Make templates of patterns A–D on pages 140 and 141. Cut all strips cross-grain.

From white fabric
- 12 (2½"-wide) strips. From these, cut 56 of Template A and 112 of Template B.

From each print fabric
- 8 of Template C (makes 2 blocks).

From yellow fabric
- 127 of Template D.

Quilt Top Assembly
1. Referring to Figures 1–6, make 56 nine-patch units as shown. (If this is a friendship quilt, you may prefer to have each piecer construct a Center Block as shown in Figure 2, with D pieces to be added when blocks are joined. Each piecer should embroider or sign her name with an indelible pen on piece A of her block as shown in photograph.)
2. Referring to **Setting Diagram** on page 140, join units.

Quilting and Finishing
1. Quilt as desired.
2. See page 17 for instructions on making bias binding. Make 10 yards of 2½"-wide (or narrower) bias binding from remaining yellow fabric. Apply binding to quilt's scalloped edges, pivoting carefully at each inside corner.

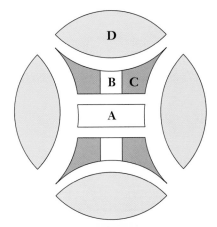

Figure 1—Whole Block
Make 28.

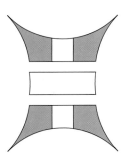

Figure 2—Center Block
Make 15.

Figure 3—Top and Bottom Unit
Make 5.

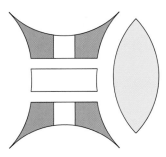

Figure 4—Side Unit
Make 6.

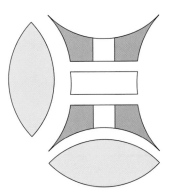

Figure 5—Bottom Left Corner Unit
Make 1.

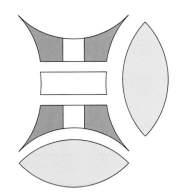

Figure 6—Bottom Right Corner Unit
Make 1.

Block Assembly Diagrams

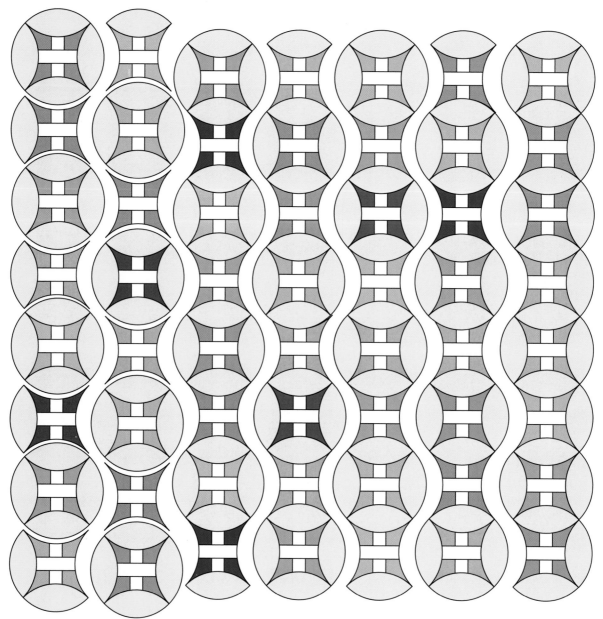

Setting Diagram

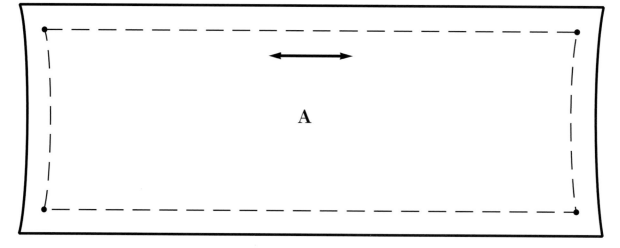

A

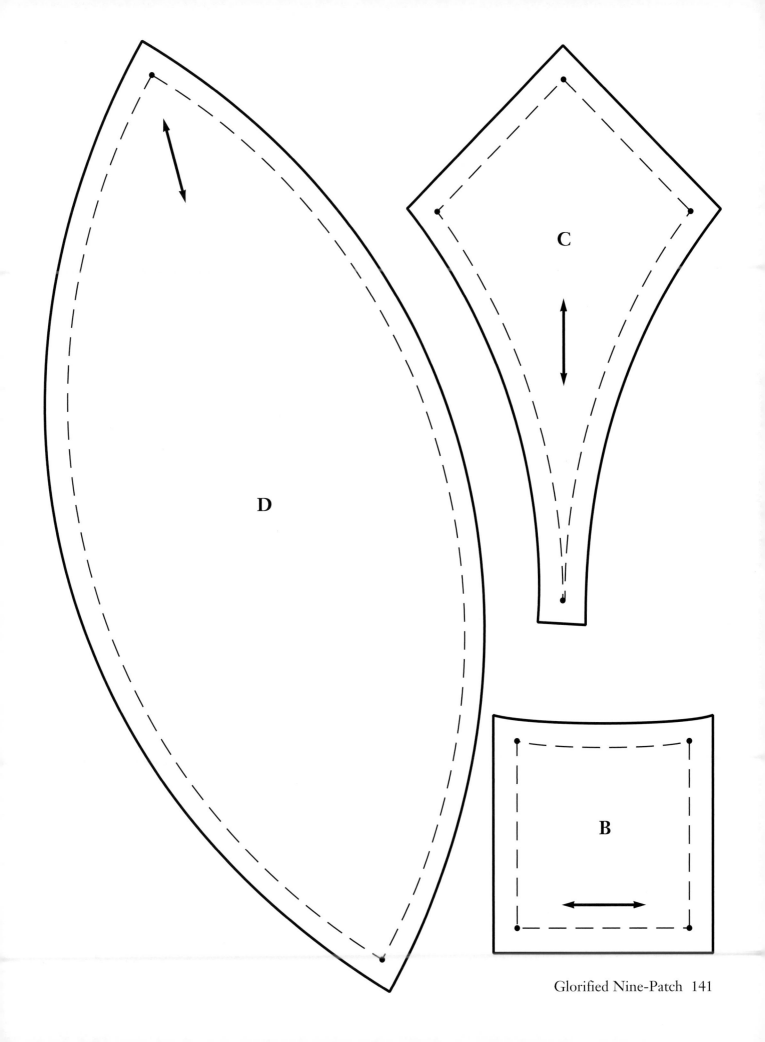

C

D

B

Golden Double Wedding Ring

An avid quiltmaker who learned the craft at her grandmother's knee, Linda Houghton devotes two to four hours a day to her quilting. She stitched this quilt by hand, carrying the pieces around in a shoebox so that she could seize every opportunity to piece. She suggests that Golden Double Wedding Ring is a good quilt on which to practice piecing challenging curves and precise points, but she doesn't recommend that it be your first quilt. The set-in pieces and scalloped edges also require considerable expertise.

Quilt by Linda Houghton
Rocky Hill, New Jersey

Finished Quilt Size
84" x 96½"

Fabric Requirements
Muslin	7 yards
Pink	2¼ yards
Pink print	1¾ yards
Blue print	3⅜ yards
Blue	1⅜ yards
Binding fabric	1 yard
Backing	8¼ yards

Cutting
Make templates of patterns A–P on pages 145 and 146. Cut all strips cross-grain.

From muslin
- 36 (3¼"-wide) strips. From these, cut 288 of Template C.
- 33 (2¾"-wide) strips. From these, cut 165 of Template D.
- 6 each of templates K and K rev.
- 30 of Template P.

From pink
- 30 (2¼"-wide) strips. From these, cut 300 of Template A, 360 of Template E, 6 of Template I, and 6 of Template I rev.

From pink print
- 30 (1¾"-wide) strips. From these, cut 330 each of templates F and F rev., and 6 each of templates L, L rev., O, and O rev.

From blue print
- 21 (3¼"-wide) strips. From these, cut 294 of Template B.
- 27 (1⅝"-wide) strips. From these, cut 330 each of templates G and H, and 12 each of templates M and M rev.
- 6 each of templates J and J rev.

From blue
- 27 (1⅝"-wide) strips. From these, cut 330 each of templates G rev. and H rev., and 6 each of templates M, M rev., N and N rev.

Quilt Top Assembly
1. Join 6 As to form a star (**Diagram 1**). Sew Bs and Cs to star (**Diagram 2**). Make 46 star units.
2. Join 1 each of E, F, G, H, H rev., G rev., and F rev. to make a pieced arc (**Diagram 3**). Make 330 arcs with E at 1 end only as shown. Join arcs to Ds as shown to make ring segments.
3. Sew ring segments to stars, adding Es at ends as necessary to fit rings together (**Diagram 4**).
4. Make 6 half-stars (**Diagram 5**). Using L, Ms, N, and O, make arcs for each half-star. Join arcs to half-stars.
5. Starting from 1 side, join 4 vertical rows of stars; then join rows with remaining stars and half-stars (**Diagram 6**). Use Ps to join ring segments on outside edges.

Quilting and Finishing
1. Outline-quilt patchwork or quilt as desired.
2. Referring to instructions on page 17, make 12 yards of 2"-wide continuous bias binding. Apply binding to quilt edges, easing bias along curves and pivoting at corners along scalloped edge. Miter or tuck these corners. Fold binding to back and blindstitch in place.

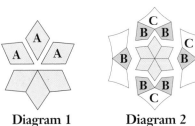

Diagram 1

Diagram 2

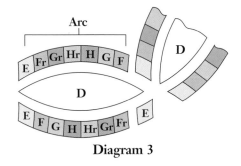

Diagram 3

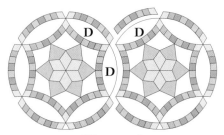

Diagram 4

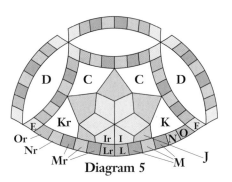

Diagram 5

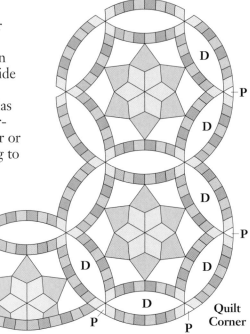

Diagram 6

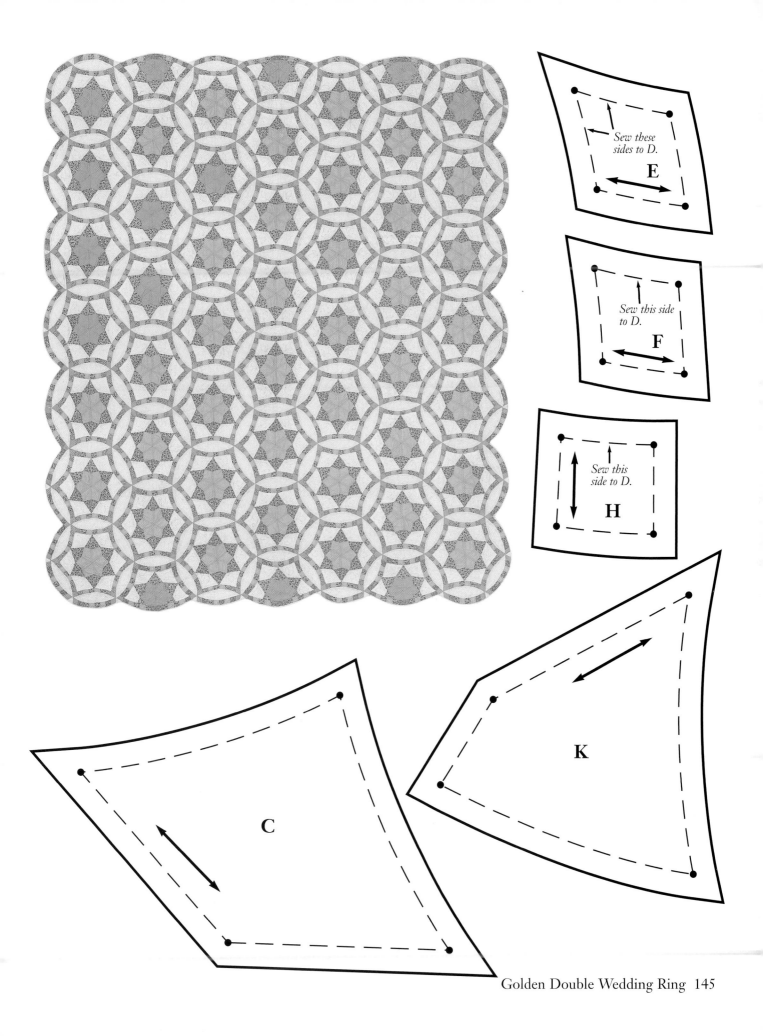

Sew these sides to D.

E

Sew this side to D.

F

Sew this side to D.

H

K

C

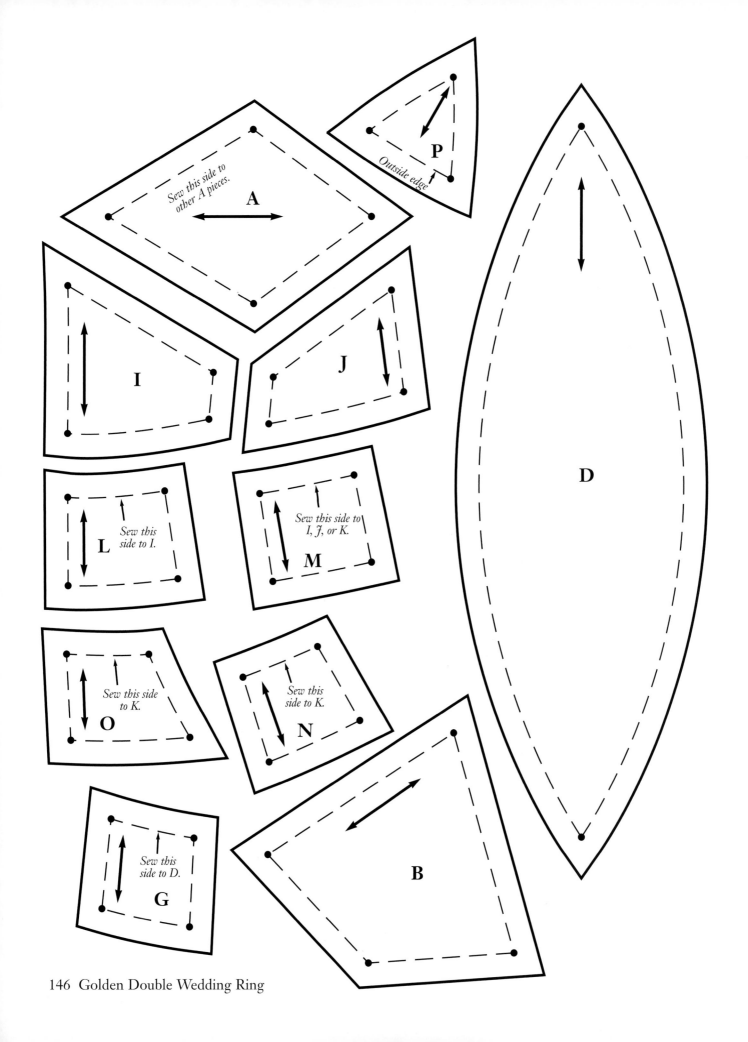

Sew this side to other A pieces.

A

Outside edge

P

I

J

D

Sew this side to I.

L

Sew this side to I, J, or K.

M

Sew this side to K.

O

Sew this side to K.

N

Sew this side to D.

G

B

Gone Fishin'

Use your brightest fabrics to make an ocean of tropical fish. These blocks blend hot prints with cool white to keep summer's colors vivid long after vacation is over.

Quilt designed by Susan Ramey Cleveland, Leeds, Alabama
Made by Radine Robinson, Decatur, Georgia

Finished Quilt Size
65" x 81"

Number of Blocks and Finished Size
12 blocks   16½" x 16½"

Fabric Requirements
White   3½ yards
Turquoise   1⅜ yards
Tropical print   1⅜ yards
Rainbow stripe   2 yards*
Backing   5 yards
*Includes fabric for bias binding.

Cutting
Make templates of patterns A–H on pages 149 and 150. Cut all strips cross-grain except as indicated.
From white
- 8 (2⅛"-wide) strips. From these, cut 96 of Template D.
- 7 (5¾"-wide) strips. From these, cut 24 (5¾") squares. Cut each square in half diagonally to get 48 E triangles.
- 3 (5"-wide) strips. From these, cut 32 each of templates F, G, and G reversed.
- 17 (2¾"-wide) strips. From these and scraps, cut 96 of Template C and 32 each of templates H and H reversed.

From turquoise
- 8 (3¼"-wide) strips. From these, cut 64 of Template A.
- 5 (3⅛"-wide) strips. From these, cut 64 (3⅛") squares. Cut each square in half diagonally to get 128 B triangles.

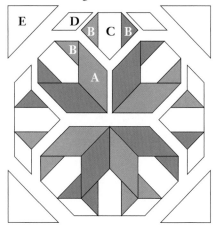

Block Assembly Diagram

From tropical print
- 8 (3¼"-wide) strips. From these, cut 64 of Template A.
- 5 (3⅛"-wide) strips. From these, cut 64 (3⅛") squares. Cut each square in half diagonally to get 128 B triangles.

From rainbow stripe
- 2 (4" x 67") and 2 (3¾" x 58") lengthwise border strips.
- 1 (28") square for bias binding.
- 4 (4¾") squares for border corners.

Quilt Top Assembly
See page 10 for tips on sewing a set-in seam.

1. Join 1 turquoise A and 1 tropical print A to form fish pair **(Block Assembly Diagram)**. Make 4 pairs for each block. Set aside 16 As and 32 Bs of each color for fish border.

2. Join 1 B to opposite sides of each C—make 4 of these units with tropical print Bs on the right and turquoise Bs on the left; reverse placement for remaining 4 units.

3. Set 1 B/C/B unit into opening of each fish pair, matching colors of As and Bs **(Block Assembly Diagram)**.

4. Join fish pairs.

5. Sew 1 D to sides of each remaining B/C/B unit. Set unit

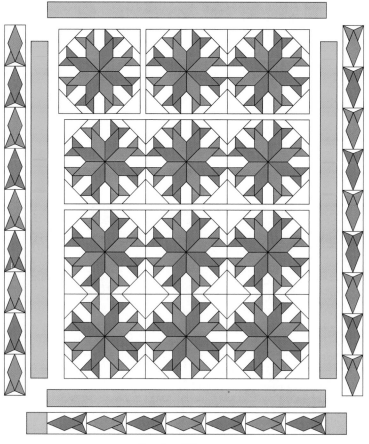

Setting Diagram

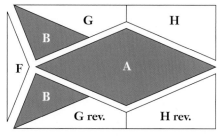

Border Block Assembly Diagram

into each new opening as shown.

6. Join 1 E at corners to complete block. Make 12 blocks.

7. Join blocks in 4 horizontal rows with 3 blocks in each row **(Setting Diagram)**. Join rows.

8. Join 4" x 67" borders to side edges of quilt. Join 3¾" x 58" borders to top and bottom edges. Press seam allowances toward borders.

9. Use remaining As and Bs to make 16 tropical print border blocks and 16 turquoise border blocks **(Border Block Assembly Diagram)**.

10. Join 9 border blocks, alternating colors, for each side border **(Setting Diagram)**. Join side borders to quilt top, easing to fit as necessary.

11. Join 7 border blocks as shown for top border, joining 1 rainbow stripe square to each end. Join border to top edge of quilt. Repeat for bottom border.

Quilting and Finishing

1. Outline-quilt patchwork.

2. See page 17 for instructions on making continuous bias binding. Make 8⅜ yards of 2½"-wide binding. Apply binding to quilt edges.

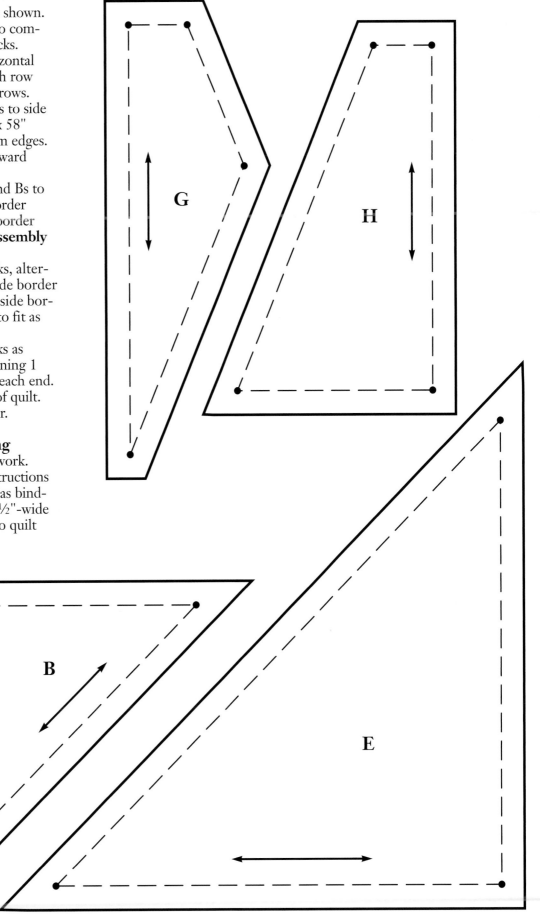

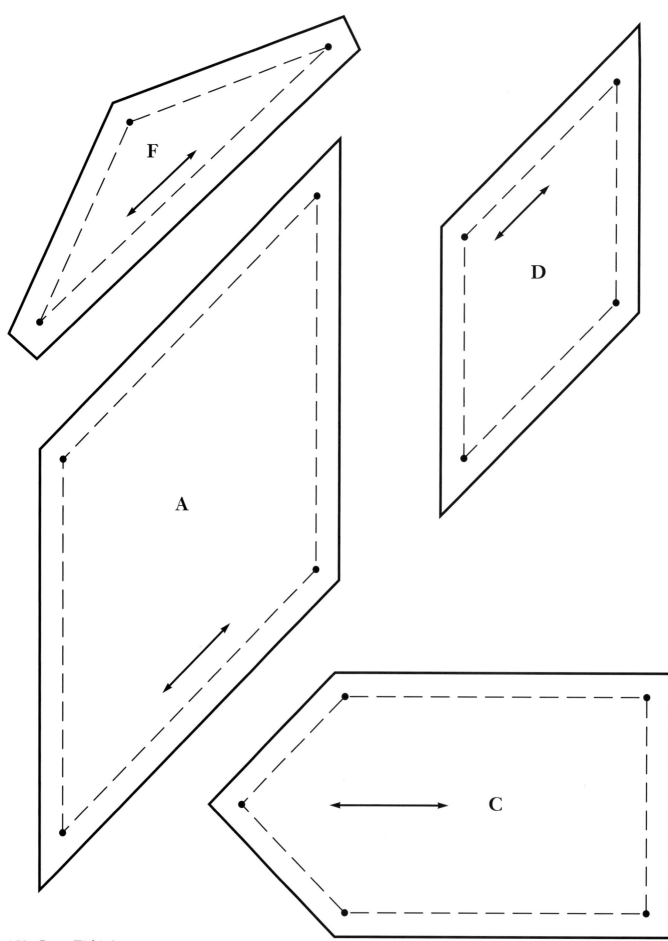

Grandmother's Fan

In Victorian times, ladies pieced this pattern from lavish silks, satins, and velvets, and embellished it with embroidery, lace, ribbons, and beading. During the lean Depression years, quilters dug into their scrap bags to make this favorite design. Mable Webb used beautiful contemporary florals, combined with muslin, to make this quilt for her granddaughter.

Quilt by Mable Azbill Webb
Jackson, Tennessee

Finished Quilt Size
82" x 100"

Number of Blocks and Finished Size
40 blocks   9" x 9"

Fabric Requirements
Rose   3 yards
Assorted florals   14 fat quarters*
Muslin   5½ yards
Binding fabric   1 yard
Backing   6 yards
* Fat Quarter = 18" x 22".

Cutting
Make templates of patterns A, B, and C. Cut all strips cross-grain except as noted.
From rose
- 2 (5½" x 84") and 2 (5½" x 102") lengthwise border strips.
- 40 of Template A.

From florals
- 120 (2" x 22") strips. From these, cut 360 of Template B.

From muslin
- 20 (9½"-wide) strips. From these, cut 40 (9½") setting squares and 40 of Template C.

Quilt Top Assembly
1. Join 9 Bs in a fan **(Block Assembly Diagram).** Sew 1 A and 1 C to curved edges to complete block Make 40 blocks.

2. Referring to photo at right for placement, join blocks and setting squares in 10 horizontal rows, with 4 blocks and 4 setting squares in each row. Press seam allowances toward setting squares. Join rows.

3. Sew borders to quilt edges and miter corners.

Quilting and Finishing
1. Make a stencil of Fan Quilting Pattern and mark each setting square; quilt. Quilt border with desired pattern.

2. See pages 16 and 17 for instructions on making binding. Make 10½ yards of 2½"-wide bias or straight-grain binding. Apply binding to quilt edges.

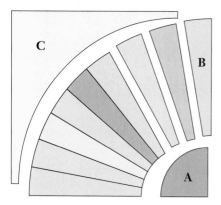

Block Assembly Diagram

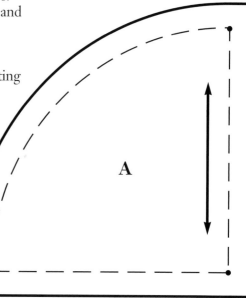

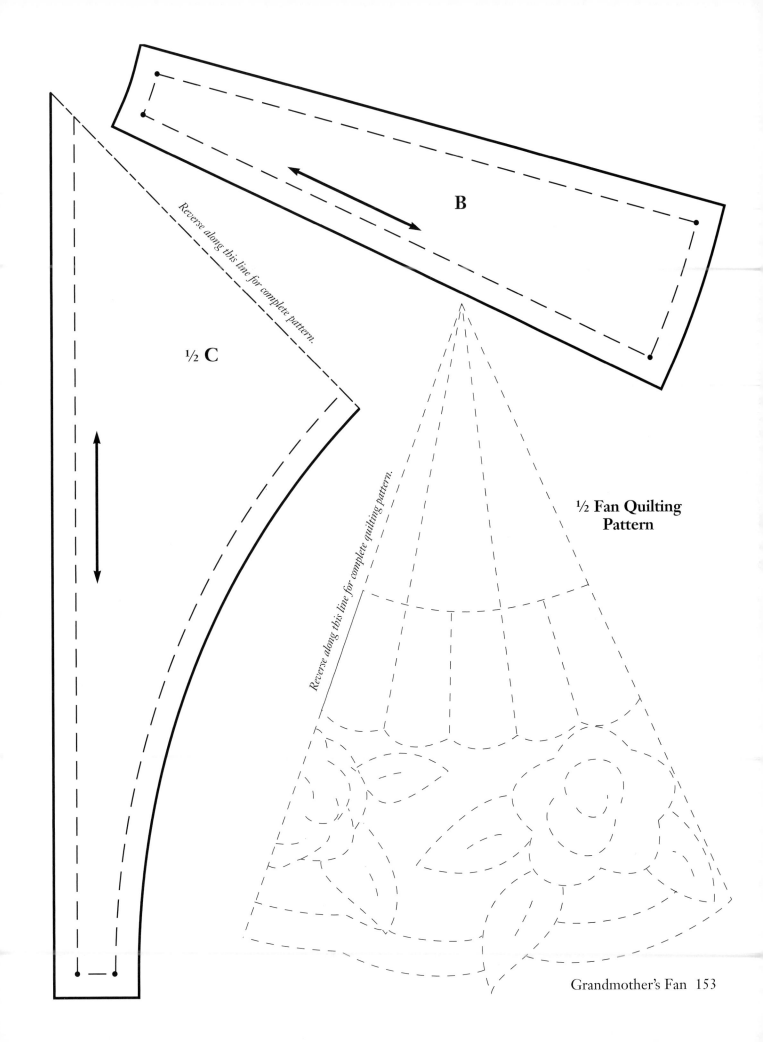

B

½ **C**

Reverse along this line for complete pattern.

Reverse along this line for complete quilting pattern.

½ **Fan Quilting Pattern**

Grandmother's Fan 153

Grandmother's Flower Garden

Quilts made from hexagons are characteristic of English patchwork brought to America by early settlers. English quilters call hexagon designs "honeycomb quilts," and the hexagons themselves are known as "sixes." Grandmother's Flower Garden is the hexagon pattern most familiar to Americans.

Quilt by Mary E. Ramey
Leeds, Alabama

Finished Quilt Size

Full-size   71" x 89¼"
King-size   104" x 106¾"

Fabric Requirements

Full-size
  Assorted prints   11 fat quarters*
  Yellow   3¼ yards
  Green   4 yards**
  Pink   ½ yard
  Backing   5½ yards
King-size
  Assorted prints   21 fat quarters*
  Yellow   5¾ yards
  Green   5¾ yards**
  Backing   3⅛ yards, 120" wide
*Fat quarter = 18" x 22".
**Includes 1 yard for bias binding.

Cutting

Make template of hexagon pattern selected from page 156.

From assorted prints
• 680 for full-size; 1,273 for king.

From yellow
• 808 for full-size; 1,460 for king.

From green
• 623 for full-size; 1,122 for king.

Quilt Top Assembly

See page 10 for tips on sewing a set-in seam.

1. For each flower, select 19 print hexagons and 18 yellow. For each half flower (full-size quilt only), choose 12 print hexagons and 10 yellow. Make needed number of flowers and half flowers (**Flower Assembly Diagram** and **Half-Flower Assembly Diagram**).

2. Set flowers and half flowers together with green hexagons (**Setting Diagram** for desired quilt; see page 156 for king-size diagram).

3. For full-size quilt, cut 166 pink hexagons; join to quilt for first border (**Setting Diagram**).

4. Add 172 yellow hexagons for full-size quilt's second border, or 254 for king-size quilt's first border.

5. Add 178 green hexagons for full-size quilt's outer border, or 260 for king-size quilt's outer border.

Setting Diagram (for Full-Size)

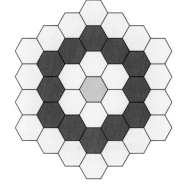

Flower Assembly Diagram
Full-size: Make 32.   King-size: Make 67.

Half-Flower Assembly Diagram
Full-size: Make 6.

Quilting and Finishing

1. Quilt in-the-ditch around each hexagon, or quilt as desired.

2. See page 17 for instructions on making bias binding. Make 13 yards of 2"-wide binding for full-size, or 18 yards for king-size. Trim uneven edges of hexagons so you can sew binding in a straight seam. Apply binding to quilt edges, mitering each corner.

Grandmother's Flower Garden 155

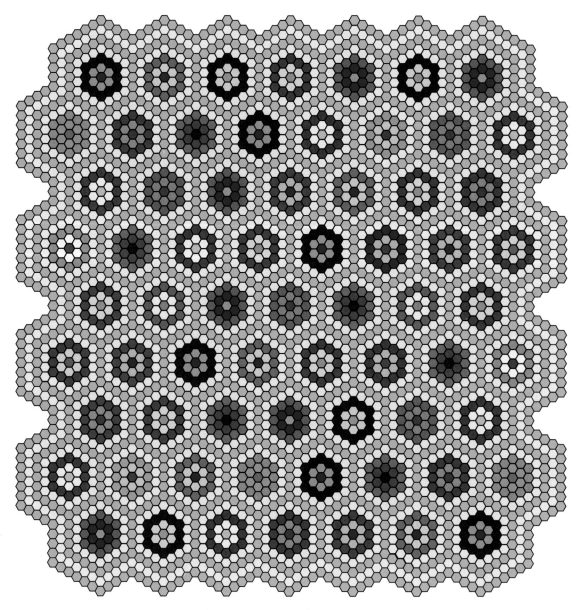

Setting Diagram (for King-size)

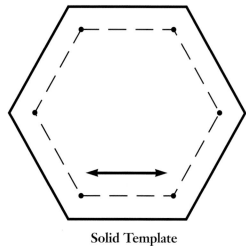

Solid Template

Cut on solid line.

For this design, you have a choice of two templates. The window template is recommended for hand piecing. Cut out the window template on the outside line. Then cut out the middle of the template on the inside line. Lay the template on your fabric and trace both outside and inside edges. On the fabric, the outside line is your cutting line; the inside line is the stitching line.

Use the solid template if you plan to piece by machine. It is not necessary to mark the stitching line when machine piecing, since your seam allowance should be marked on your presser foot or throat plate.

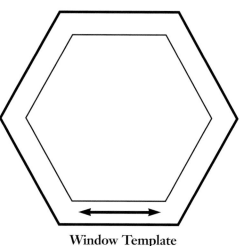

Window Template

Cut on both solid lines and remove center.

Hanover Tulip

This quilt was made for the Richmond Quilting Guild's quilt exhibit. Beverley Cosby was asked to design a quilt to be completed by the Piecemakers and raffled to raise funds for the exhibit. "I began with the simple heart shape," says Beverley. "When I added the bud at the top and a stem and leaves, it became a tulip."

Quilt by Piecemakers
Mechanicsville, West Virginia

Finished Quilt Size
82¼" x 97¾"

Number of Blocks and Finished Size
20 blocks   11" x 11"

Fabric Requirements
Muslin	5⅝ yards
Green	3⅛ yards
Maroon	3 yards
Pink	1⅝ yards
Binding fabric	⅞ yard
Backing	6 yards

Cutting
Make templates of appliqué patterns A, B, C, and D. Cut all strips cross-grain except as noted.

From muslin
- 4 (8¼" x 100") lengthwise border strips.
- 32 (11½") squares.

From green
- 9 (1"-wide) strips. From these, cut 62 (1" x 6") A stem pieces.
- 124 of Template B.

From maroon
- 2 (1½" x 100"), 4 (1½"x 86"), and 2 (1½" x 70") lengthwise border strips.
- 102 of Template D.

From pink
- 8 (2¼"-wide) strips. From these, cut 102 of Template C.
- 4 (16¾") squares. Cut each square in quarters diagonally to get 14 side triangles (and 2 extra).
- 2 (8⅝") squares. Cut each square in half diagonally to get 4 corner triangles.

Quilt Top Assembly
1. Fold 1 muslin square in quarters vertically, horizontally, and diagonally; finger-press creases for placement guides.
2. Position 4 A stems, 4 B leaves, 4 C buds, and 4 D flowers on square **(Placement Diagram)**. Appliqué pieces in place in alphabetical order.

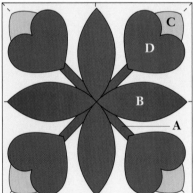

Placement Diagram

3. Make 20 blocks.
4. Lay out blocks, setting squares, side triangles, and corner triangles in diagonal rows **(Setting Diagram)**. Join units in each row; then join rows.

Setting Diagram

5. Sew 70"-long maroon borders to top and bottom edges of quilt and 86"-long borders to quilt sides; miter border corners. Press seam allowances toward maroon.

6. Join muslin borders to quilt edges and miter corners. Press seam allowances toward maroon.

7. Referring to photograph at left, lay out single tulips on borders. Align border tulips with tulips in blocks as shown. Trim remaining A stems as indicated on pattern. Appliqué tulips, stems, and leaves in alphabetical order.

8. Stitch 100"-long maroon borders to quilt sides and 86"-long borders to top and bottom edges; miter border corners. Press seam allowances toward borders.

Quilting and Finishing

1. Outline-quilt appliqué pieces and seam lines of appliquéd blocks. Quilt shown also has a feather motifs quilted in each setting square and side triangle.

2. See pages 16 and 17 for instructions on making binding. Make 10¼ yards of 2½"-wide bias or straight-grain binding. Apply binding to quilt edges.

Appliqué patterns are finished size. Add ¼" seam allowance for hand appliqué or cut as is for machine appliqué.

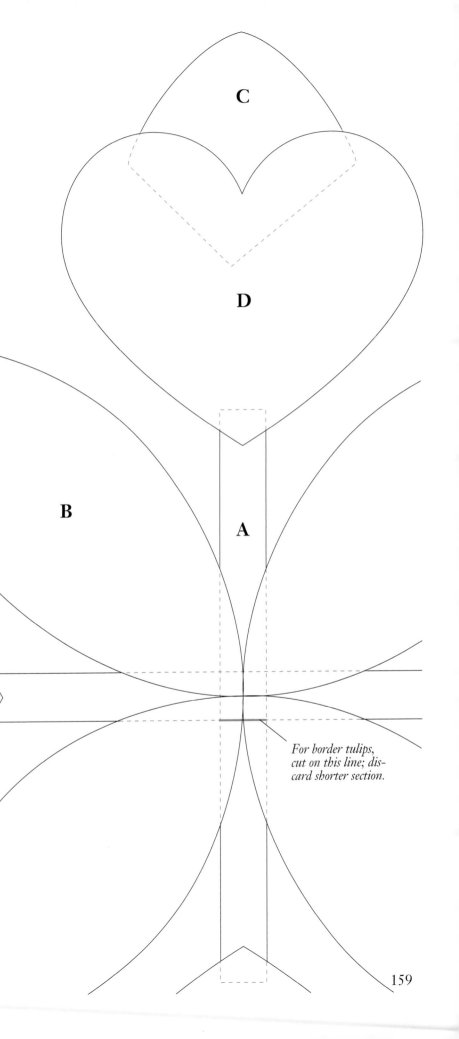

For border tulips, cut on this line; discard shorter section.

159

Hens A-Peckin'

Anyone who has fed chickens or gathered eggs can relate to Jane Eakin's cheerful quilt. She strip-pieced the checkerboard sashing for a country look reminiscent of old feed sacks. With the help of three friends, Jane's wall hanging was as easy to make as scrambled eggs!

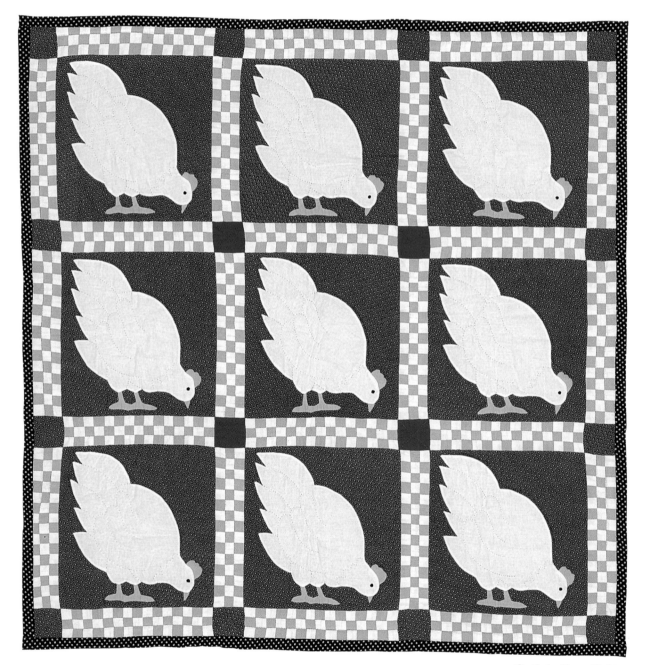

Quilt by Jane Eakin
Wilmette, Illinois

Finished Quilt Size
44" x 44"

Number of Blocks and Finished Size
9 chicken blocks   11¼" x 11¼"

Fabric Requirements
Red/black print   1⅛ yards
White   1½ yards
Gold   ⅛ yard
Tan   ¾ yard
Blue   4 (2¾") squares
Navy binding fabric   ¾ yard
Backing   2¾ yards

Other Materials
Red quilting thread
Black embroidery floss

Cutting
Make templates of appliqué patterns A, B, C, and D on page 162. Cut all strips cross-grain except as noted.

From red print
- 9 (11¾") squares for blocks.
- 12 (2¾") sashing squares.

From white
- 2 (13½"-wide) strips. From these, cut 9 of Template A.
- 17 (1¼"-wide) strips for checkerboard sashing.

Appliqué Placement Diagram

From gold
- 2 (2"-wide) strips. From these, cut 9 each of templates B, C, and D.

From tan
- 16 (1¼"-wide) strips for checkerboard sashing.

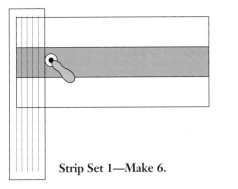

Strip Set 1—Make 6.

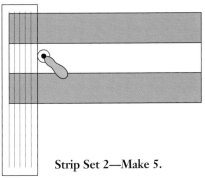

Strip Set 2—Make 5.

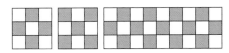

Sashing Diagram

Quilt Top Assembly
1. Using 3 strands of floss, satin-stitch 1 eye on each A piece. (See page 137 for stitch diagram.)

2. Center and pin 1 A on each red square (**Appliqué Placement Diagram**). Position beak (B), comb (C), and feet (D) as shown. Appliqué B, C, and D; then stitch A in place. Appliqué 9 blocks.

3. For Strip Set 1, sew a tan strip between 2 white strips as shown (**Strip Set 1 Diagram**). Make 6 of Strip Set 1. For Strip Set 2, sew a white strip between 2 tan strips as shown (**Strip Set 2 Diagram**). Make 5 of Strip Set 2. Press all seam allowances toward tan.

4. Cut 1¼"-wide units across strip sets. Cut 192 units from Strip Set 1 and 168 units from Strip Set 2.

5. For each sashing unit, select 8 Strip Set 1 segments and 7 Strip Set 2 segments. Join 15 units in a row, alternating colors as shown (**Sashing Diagram**). Make 24 checkerboard sashing strips.

continued

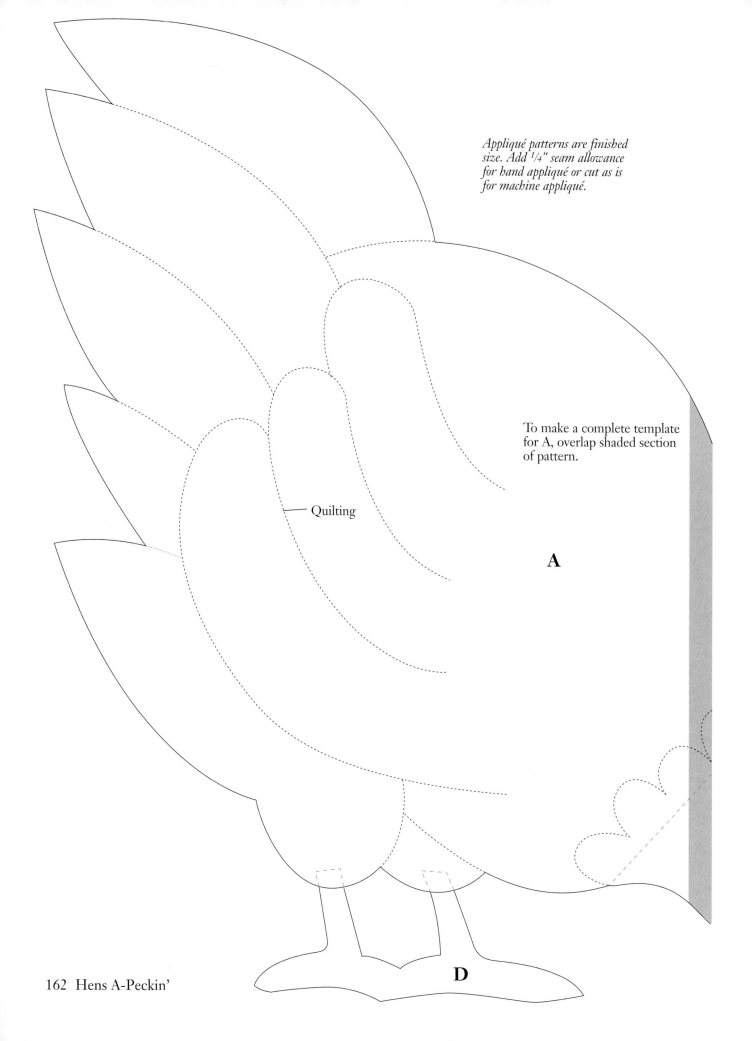

Appliqué patterns are finished size. Add ¼" seam allowance for hand appliqué or cut as is for machine appliqué.

To make a complete template for A, overlap shaded section of pattern.

Quilting

A

D

Setting Diagram

6. Lay out blocks in 3 rows, with 3 blocks in each row **(Setting Diagram).** Place checkerboard sashing strips between blocks and at row ends. Join blocks and sashing strips in each row. Press seam allowances toward blocks.

7. For sashing rows, lay out 3 sashing strips in a horizontal row, placing sashing squares between sashing strips and at row ends. Use red sashing squares in first and fourth sashing rows. In second and third sashing rows, place 2 blue squares in center of row and red squares at row ends as shown **(Setting Diagram).** Press seam allowances toward sashing squares.

8. Join rows as shown to assemble quilt top.

Quilting and Finishing

1. Quilt shown has feathers quilted on each chicken as shown on pattern. Outline-quilt chickens and seams of blocks. Quilt Xs in sashing squares.

2. See pages 16 and 17 for instructions on making binding. Make 5⅛ yards of 2½"-wide bias or straight-grain binding. Apply binding to quilt edges.

Satin-stitch.

C

B

Hidden Circles

When someone spends much time and talent to achieve a goal, the satisfaction upon completion is that much greater. That is probably why Mary Ann Keathley calls this her favorite of the many quilts she has made. In 1990, *Hidden Circles* won blue ribbons at the Silver Dollar City Quilt Show in Missouri and at the Arkansas Quilter's Guild Show.

Quilt by Mary Ann Keathley
Jacksonville, Arkansas

Finished Quilt Size
84" x 101"

Number of Blocks and Finished Size
32 blocks   12" x 12"

Fabric Requirements
Muslin	8¼ yards
Scraps	20 (¼- yard) pieces
Floral print*	2 yards
Green	1¼ yards
Rust	7" x 10" scrap
Light rust	5" x 7" scrap
Backing	6 yards

*Includes yardage for border flowers, appliquéd border strip, and bias binding.

Cutting
Make templates of patterns A–P on pages 168 and 169. Cut strips cross-grain except as noted.

From muslin
- 2 (9" x 106") and 2 (9" x 90") lengthwise strips for border. Use remainder for Ds.
- 8 (2¾"-wide) strips. From these and remainder from borders, cut 426 of Template D.
- 46 (3"-wide) strips. From these, cut 132 of Template G, 14 of Template H and 14 of Template H reversed.
- 14 (6⅞") squares. Cut each square in half diagonally to get 28 I triangles.

From scraps
- 142 each of templates A, B, B reversed, E, and F.
- 284 of Template C.

From floral print
- 1 (23") square for bias border.
- 1 (32") square for bias binding.
- 24 of Template J.
- 32 of Template P.

From green
- 1 (22"-wide) strip for bias vines.
- 4 (2"-wide) strips. From these, cut 10 of Template M, 10 of Template M reversed, 8 of Template N, 8 of Template N reversed, and 16 of Template O.

From rust
- 6 of Template K.

From light rust
- 6 of Template L.

Other Materials
¼"- and ½"-wide bias bars

Quilt Top Assembly
1. Join pieces A through F to form a unit **(Diagram 1)**. Make 4 units for each block.

2. Join 2 units at sides of As to form a section, as shown. Make 2 sections; then join sections.

continued

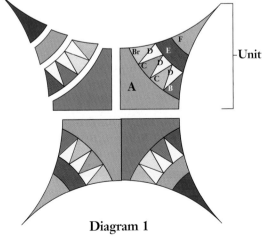

Diagram 1

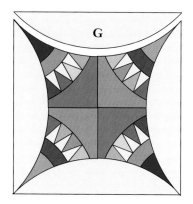

Diagram 2

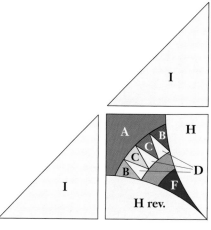

Setting Triangle Diagram

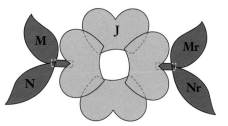

Border Flower Piecing Diagram

3. Join G pieces to sides of units to complete block **(Diagram 2)**.

4. Make 32 blocks.

5. For each side triangle, join A–F, H, and H reversed to make a pieced square **(Setting Triangle Diagram)**. Add 2 I triangles to sides of square to make a triangle as shown. Piece 14 setting triangles.

6. Lay out blocks in 8 diagonal rows **(Setting Diagram 1)**. Join blocks in each row. Add G pieces at corners as shown.

Border Assembly

1. Measure quilt length through middle of pieced section. Find center of each 106"-long border; measuring out in both directions from center point, measure length

on border strip and mark.

2. Measure quilt width through middle of pieced section. Mark this measurement on 90"-long muslin border strips in same manner as for longer strips.

3. Sew muslin border strips to each other, not to pieced section, mitering corners. (See page 14 for instructions on sewing a mitered seam.)

4. Center pieced section of quilt on top of border frame. Baste quilt in place **(Setting Diagram 2)**. Leave border corners square until quilting is complete.

5. See page 17 for directions on making continuous bias. Use 23" square of floral print to make 9 yards of 1¼"-wide continuous bias.

Fold strip in half lengthwise with *wrong* sides facing; stitch raw edges together with a ¼"-wide seam. Center tube on ½"-wide bias bar and press seam allowances open, centering seam on flat surface of bar. Center bias strip over basted edge of pieced quilt with seam allowance face down; appliqué strip to quilt and border. Where ends meet, turn second end under and overlap first end slightly.

6. Measure 22" from 1 corner of 22"-wide green strip and mark. Trim a triangle from corner to mark **(Diagram 3)**. Measuring from cut edge, cut 8 (1" x 30") bias strips for vines. Fold strip in half lengthwise with *wrong* sides facing and stitch edges together. Press

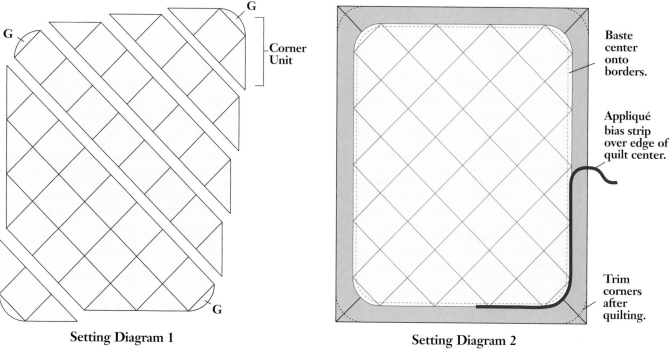

Setting Diagram 1

Setting Diagram 2

Baste center onto borders.

Appliqué bias strip over edge of quilt center.

Trim corners after quilting.

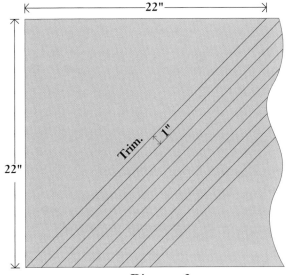

Diagram 3

each strip on ¼"-wide bias bar, centering seam on 1 side.

7. From green scraps, cut 4 (1" x 2") strips for side flower stems. Pin stems, M and N leaves, and J petals at center of each side border **(Border Flower Piecing Diagram).** Appliqué pieces in place on border. Appliqué flower centers (K and L) at center of each flower.

8. Position J flower petals at border corners. Referring to quilt photograph on page 165, pin vines on border as shown. From green scraps, cut 8 short 1"-wide bias strips. Pin these stems in place on vines for flower buds. Pin remaining leaves in place as desired. Appliqué vines and leaves in place; then appliqué J flower petals. Stitch flower centers (K and L) in place at center of each flower.

9. Pin O pieces in place at ends of each bud stem.

10. Join 2 P pieces, right sides facing, leaving 1 long edge unsewn. Turn right side out. Run a basting

thread through both layers at open edge and gather. Slip gathered edge under an O **(Bud Piecing Diagram).** Appliqué O pieces in place, leaving buds loose.

Quilting and Finishing

1. Quilt in-the-ditch of seam lines of each unit. Outline-quilt ¼" inside seam lines of A pieces. Make a stencil of feather pattern below and quilt design in muslin G pieces. Outline-quilt around appliqué pieces and print border strip. Quilt shown diagonal lines, 1⅜" apart, quilted in borders.

2. Use Template G to mark round corners on borders.

3. Make 10⅝ yards of 2½"-wide continuous bias binding from 32" square of floral print. Stitch binding to quilt, stitching on marked line for round corners. Trim excess fabric from corners, leaving ¼" seam allowance. Turn binding to back of quilt and blindstitch binding on backing.

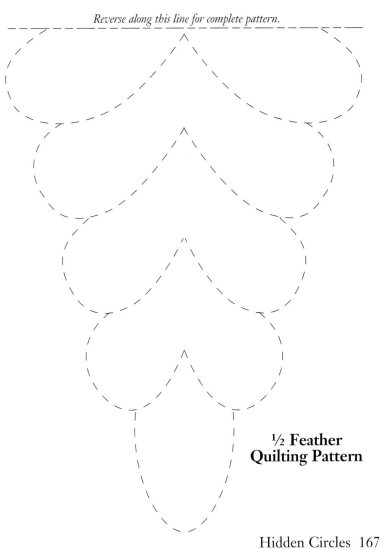

Reverse along this line for complete pattern.

½ Feather Quilting Pattern

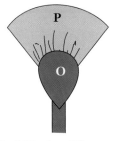

Bud Piecing Diagram

Hidden Circles 167

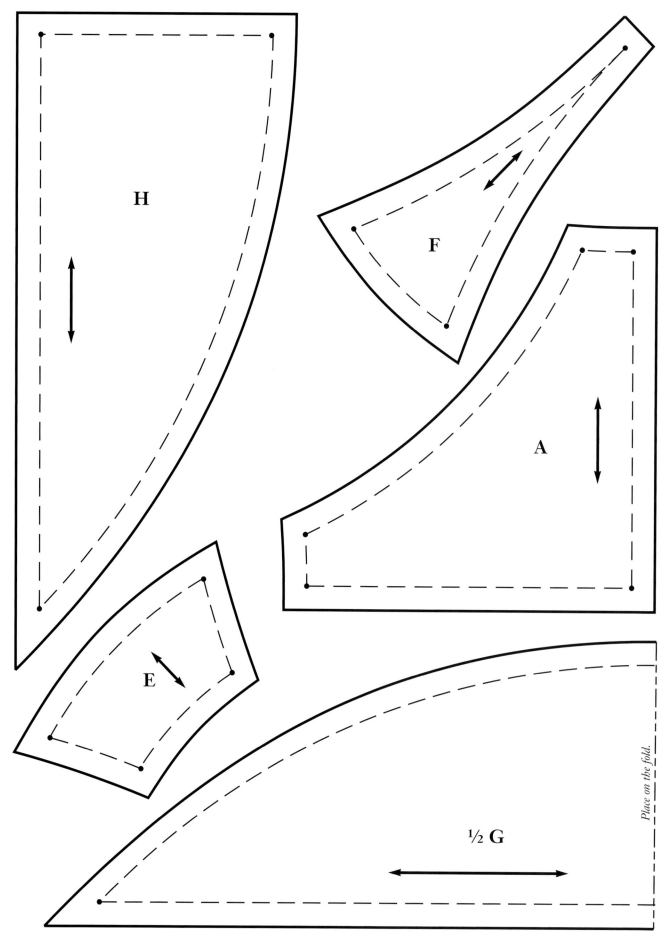

H

F

A

E

½ G

Place on the fold.

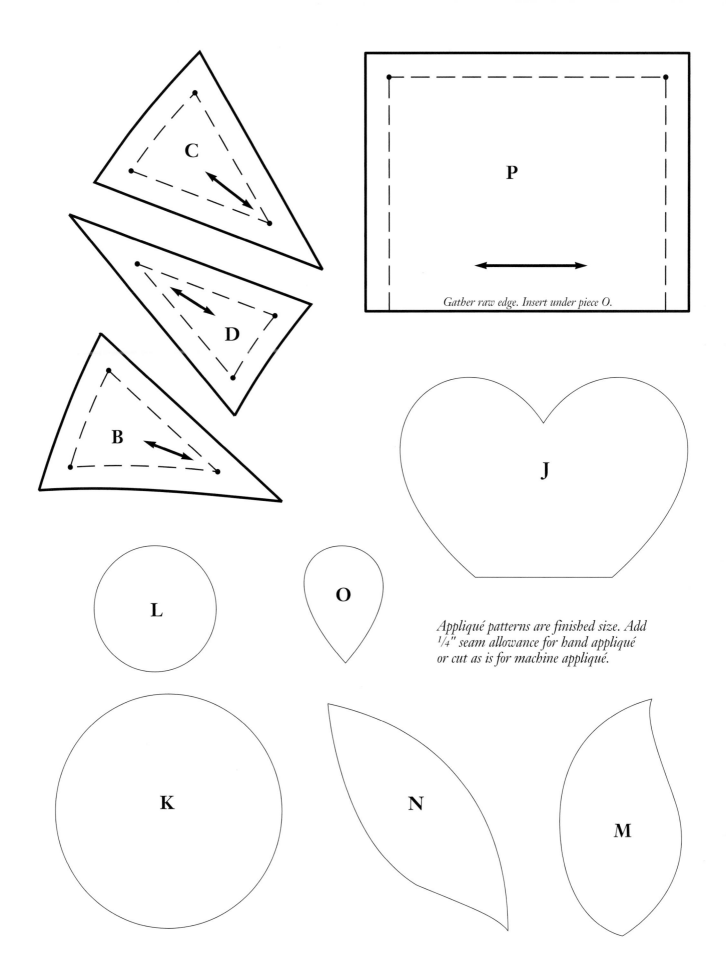

C

D

B

P

Gather raw edge. Insert under piece O.

J

L

O

*Appliqué patterns are finished size. Add
1/4" seam allowance for hand appliqué
or cut as is for machine appliqué.*

K

N

M

Hollyhock

Floral wreaths have been popular with American quilters since the 19th century. Mary Conover's variation of the traditional Hollyhock Wreath adds four buds to the ring. "I've always admired red and green quilts," says Mary, "and since my daughter loves hollyhocks, this was the perfect design to make for her."

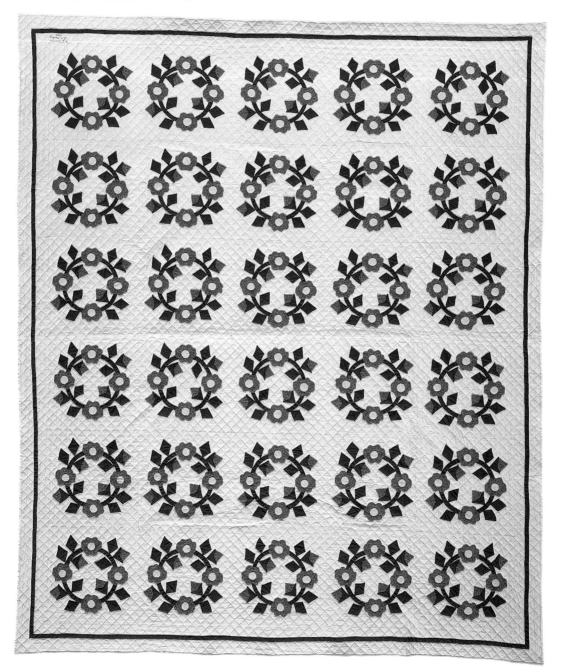

Quilt by Mary Jurgensen Conover
West Simsbury, Connecticut

Finished Quilt Size
75½" x 89"

Number of Blocks and Finished Size
30 blocks   13½" x 13½"

Fabric Requirements
Muslin	5¼ yards*
Green	3¾ yards
Red print	1¾ yards
Yellow	¼ yard
Binding fabric	1 yard
Backing	5¼ yards

* Prewashed muslin must be 44" wide.

Other Materials
¼"-wide bias pressing bar

Cutting
Make templates of appliqué patterns A, B, C, D, and E. Cut all strips cross-grain except as noted.

From muslin
• 4 (2" x 94") and 4 (2" x 80") lengthwise strips for borders.
• 30 (14") squares.

From green
• 2 (1½" x 94") and 2 (1½" x 80") lengthwise strips for borders.
• 2 (20"-wide) strips for bias vines.
• 33 (2½" x 37") strips. From these, cut 240 of Template C and 120 of Template E.

From red print
• 19 (3"-wide) strips. From these, cut 120 *each* of templates A and D.

From yellow
• 120 of Template B.

Placement Diagram

Appliqué patterns are finished size. Add ¼" seam allowance for hand appliqué or cut as is for machine appliqué.

Quilt Top Assembly
1. Measure 20" from 1 corner of 20"-wide green strip and mark. Trim triangle from corner to mark **(Bias Vines Diagram).** Measuring from cut edge, cut 30 (1⅛" x 27") bias strips for wreaths. Fold strip in half lengthwise with *wrong* sides facing; stitch edges together. Press each strip on pressing bar, centering seam on 1 side of bar.

2. Fold a muslin square in quarters; finger-press creases to mark guidelines. Lightly mark 8½"-diameter circle on square. Appliqué bias strip on marked circle, butting raw ends at top or bottom of circle.

3. Appliqué 4 As, 4 Bs, 8 Cs, 4 Ds, and 4 Es around wreath in alphabetical order **(Placement Diagram).** One A should cover raw ends of bias strip

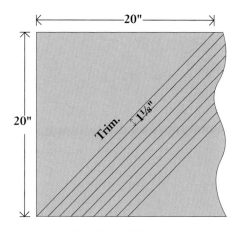

Bias Vines Diagram

---

4. Make 30 blocks.

5. Join blocks in 6 rows, with 5 blocks in each row. Join rows.

6. Join 2 (94"-long) muslin borders and 1 green border for each side of quilt. Join 80"-long borders for top and bottom edges in same manner. Sew borders to quilt and miter corners.

Quilting and Finishing
1. Outline-quilt appliqué pieces and green borders. Quilt background with 1" cross-hatch grid.

2. See pages 16 and 17 for instructions on making binding. Make 9½ yards of 2½"-wide bias or straight-grain binding. Apply binding to quilt edges.

In the Bleak Midwinter

As a haunting melody transforms Christina Rossetti's poem of winter chill into a favorite hymn, so can seemingly stark fabrics mix to prove that easy piecing can have dramatic results. Judy Cantwell collected black prints for years with the idea of making this quilt someday.

Quilt by Judy Cantwell
Cahaba Heights, Alabama

Finished Quilt Size
76½" x 88"

Number of Blocks and Finished Size
30 blocks   11½" x 11½"

Fabric Requirements
Light gray   4 yards
Black print for border   2¼ yards
Assorted black
  prints and solids   11 fat quarters*
Binding fabric   1 yard
Backing   5¼ yards
*Fat quarter = 18" x 22".

Cutting
See Alternate Quick Piecing instructions before cutting.
From light gray fabric
• 4 (3½" x 72") lengthwise strips for inner borders.
• 480 of Template A *or* 24 (9" x 21") pieces for quick-piecing.

From black border fabric
• 4 (7" x 81") lengthwise strips for outer borders. Add remaining fabric to black scraps for blocks.

From black print fabrics
• 480 of Template A *or* 24 (9" x 21") pieces for quick-piecing.

Quilt Top Assembly
1. Join 1 black triangle and 1 gray triangle to make a triangle-square **(Piecing Diagram)**. Make 480 triangle-squares.

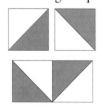

Piecing Diagram

2. Join triangle-squares in pairs; then combine pairs to make a 4-square unit as shown.

3. Join 4 pieced units to make each block **(Block Assembly Diagram)**. Make 30 blocks.

4. Referring to photograph, lay out blocks in 6 horizontal rows of 5 blocks each. Join blocks in rows. Join rows to assemble quilt top.

Alternate Quick Piecing
Quick piecing eliminates the labor of making a template, tracing it repeatedly on fabric, cutting out each piece, and joining one pair at a time. This technique involves marking a grid on the wrong side of one fabric piece and stitching diagonal lines through the grid.

1. Instead of using Template A, cut 24 (9" x 21") pieces from gray fabric. Cut 24 matching pieces from assorted black prints.

2. On wrong side of each gray piece, mark a 2- x 5-square grid of 3¾" squares **(Diagram 1)**. Draw diagonal lines through squares as shown.

3. Pin a gray rectangle to each black piece, right sides facing.

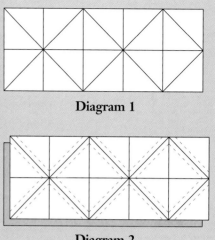

Diagram 1

Diagram 2

Machine-stitch ¼" from each side of all *diagonal* lines **(Diagram 2)**.

4. Cut on *all* grid lines to separate 20 triangle-squares.

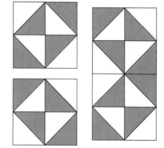

Block Assembly Diagram

5. Mark centers of each gray border strip and each black border strip. Join gray and black borders. Matching centers of borders and quilt, join border strips to all edges. See page 14 for instructions on mitering corners.

Quilting and Finishing
1. Quilt each block as shown in **Quilting Diagram**. Extend lines of quilting from blocks into borders.

2. See pages 16 and 17 for instructions on making binding. Make 9¼ yards of 2½"-wide bias or straight-grain binding. Apply binding to quilt edges.

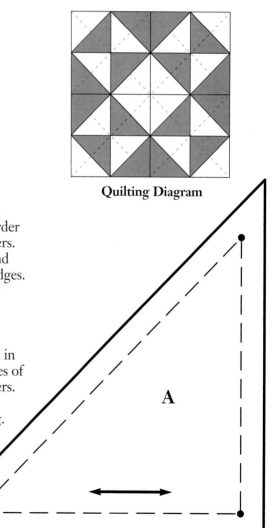

Quilting Diagram

A

Indian Summer

Susan Cleveland reached deep into her scrap bag for the prints she used in this quilted interpretation of a shower of autumn leaves. Susan began this quilt in 1980. Over the years, she brought out the autumn leaf project occasionally, but put it away as other quilt ideas were born.

"Each year, sometime in late summer, I'd get nostalgic for October and stitch a few more autumn leaf blocks," says Susan. "But as Christmas got closer, I'd long to make something red and green, and I'd put the leaf quilt away again."

When Susan stitched the last of these blocks, she added plaid sashing and finished the project by echo-quilting around each leaf. Now, when muggy August afternoons make her pine for October evenings, this quilt reminds her that Indian Summer is just a couple of full moons away.

Finished Quilt Size
77½" x 87"

Number of Blocks and Finished Size
72 blocks   8" x 8"

Fabric Requirements
Scraps or 12 assorted prints   ¼ yard each
Muslin   4½ yards*
Brown plaid   2 yards
Brown solid   ⅜ yard
12 assorted prints   ¼ yard each
Backing   5¼ yards
*Includes fabric for binding.

Other Materials
Black embroidery floss

Quilt by Susan Ramey Cleveland
Leeds, Alabama

Appliqué pattern is finished size. Add ¼" seam allowance for hand appliqué or cut as is for machine appliqué.

Outline Stitch

Center

Leaf Pattern

Cutting

Make template of Leaf Pattern.

From assorted print fabrics
• 72 of Leaf Pattern.

From muslin
• 72 (8½") squares.

From brown plaid
• 8 (8½" x 42") strips. From these, cut 161 (2" x 8½") sashing strips.

From brown solid fabric
• 90 (2") sashing squares.

Quilt Top Assembly

1. Fold each muslin square in half vertically, horizontally, and diagonally, creasing folds to make appliqué placement guidelines.

2. Place a square over leaf pattern, matching center of fabric with marked center on pattern. Lightly trace leaf and stem outlines on muslin. Pin leaf in place on muslin, aligning turned edges with traced outlines. Appliqué leaves to make 72 blocks.

3. Use 2 strands of embroidery floss to outline-stitch leaf veins and stems. (See page 182 for outline-stitch diagram.)

4. Join 8 blocks and 9 sashing strips to make each block row **(Row Assembly Diagram)**. Make 9 block rows.

5. Join 8 sashing strips and 9 sashing squares to make 1 sashing row. Make 10 sashing rows.

6. Join rows, alternating sashing rows and block rows.

Quilting and Finishing

1. Outline-quilt leaves and sashing squares.

2. See page 17 for instructions on making bias binding. Make 9½ yards of 2½"-wide continuous bias binding from remaining muslin. Apply binding to quilt edges.

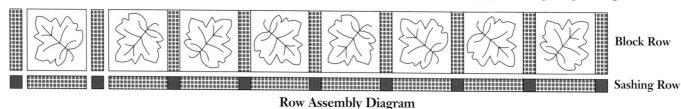

Block Row

Sashing Row

Row Assembly Diagram

Indiana Rose

The lovely appliquéd blocks of Debra Wagner's *Indiana Rose* are surrounded by the lush roses of a preprinted stripe fabric. Look for fabrics with wide printed stripes to make an elegant border for your own quilt.

Quilt by Debra Wagner
Hutchinson, Minnesota

Finished Quilt Size
42" x 42"

Number of Blocks and Finished Size
9 blocks   9" x 9"

Fabric Requirements
Ecru tone-on-tone print	¾ yard
Pink print	¼ yard
Blue print	¼ yard
Navy print	¼ yard
Green print	⅝ yard
Border stripe*	1 yard**
Backing	1⅜ yards

* Choose a fabric with a 7½"-wide stripe or use any other print fabric.

**Use narrow stripe from border fabric for straight-grain binding. Depending on stripe design, additional yardage may be necessary. Or purchase ⅜ yard of another fabric for straight-grain binding.

Cutting
Make templates of appliqué patterns A, B, C, and D. Cut all strips cross-grain except as noted.

From ecru print
- 9 (9½") squares.

From pink print
- 12 of Template A.
- 3 of Template C.

From blue print
- 12 of Template A.
- 3 of Template C.

From navy print
- 12 of Template A.
- 3 of Template C.

From green print
- 5 (3¾"-wide) strips. From these, cut 36 of Template B and 9 of Template D.

From border stripe
- 4 (8" x 45") lengthwise strips.

Appliqué Placement Diagram

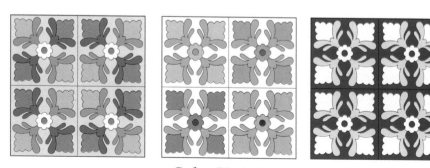

Color Variations
These are some suggestions for other color schemes.

Quilt Assembly

1. Fold each ecru square in half diagonally in both directions and finger-press to make creases for placement guides.

2. On 1 ecru square, position C flower in center; then position A and B pieces on diagonal placement guides as shown (**Appliqué Placement Diagram**). When satisfied with placement of pieces, appliqué A, B, and C pieces in alphabetical order. Stitch D in place last.

3. Appliqué 9 blocks.

4. Referring to photo, lay out blocks in 3 rows, with 3 blocks in each row. Join blocks in each row; then join rows.

5. Sew borders to quilt edges and miter corners. (See page 14 for tips on sewing mitered corners.)

Quilting and Finishing

1. Outline-quilt appliqué. Add additional quilting as desired.

2. See pages 16 and 17 for instructions on making binding. Make 5 yards of 2½"-wide bias or straight-grain binding. Apply binding to quilt edges.

Appliqué patterns are finished size. Add ¼" seam allowance for hand appliqué or cut as is for machine appliqué.

Make Your Own Quilt Label

See page 366 for instructions.

Iris in My Garden

Zelda Fasciano used a traditional Iris pattern to create her quilt. She appliquéd and embroidered each flower in a combination of bright springtime colors, repeating the iris as a quilting design in the muslin setting squares.

Quilt by Zelda Wheeler Fasciano
Greenville, North Carolina

Finished Quilt Size
71¾" x 85"

Number of Blocks and Finished Size
20 blocks   9½" x 9½"

Fabric Requirements
Muslin   5¼ yards
Green   4 yards*
Pastel solids   38 (4" x 7") scraps
                    38 (4"-square) scraps
Backing   5¼ yards
*Includes fabric for binding

Other Materials
Embroidery floss to match pastel
    fabrics
Gold or yellow embroidery floss
Tracing paper
⅜"-wide bias pressing bar

Cutting
Make templates of appliqué patterns
A–H on pages 182 and 183. Cut
strips cross-grain except as noted.
From muslin
• 4 (9½" x 90") lengthwise border
  strips.
• 32 (10") squares.
• 4 (14⅝") squares. Cut each
  square in quarters diagonally to
  get 14 side triangles (and 2 extra).
• 2 (7⅝") squares. Cut each square
  in half diagonally to get 4 corner
  triangles.

From green
• 2 (4"-wide) strips for bias stems.
• 20 *each* of templates A, B, and C.
• 4 *each* of Template F.
• 18 *each* of templates G and H.

From pastel solids
• 1 *each* of Template D and Template D reversed from each
  4" x 7" scrap.
• 1 of Template E from each
  4" scrap.

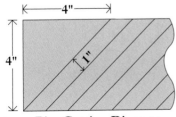

Bias Cutting Diagram

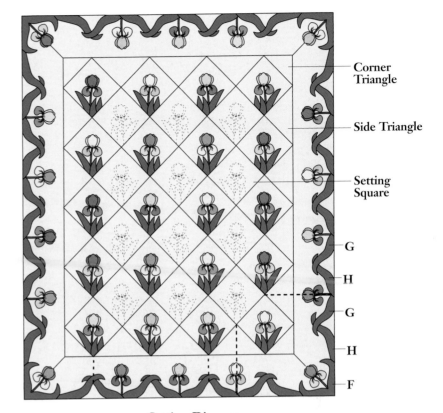

Setting Diagram

Corner Triangle

Side Triangle

Setting Square

G

H

G

H

F

Quilt Assembly
1. Trace **Placement Diagram**
on page 182 onto tracing paper.
Lightly trace pattern on 16 muslin
squares; turn pattern over and trace
reversed placement pattern on 16
squares (darken lines if necessary to
see them through fabric). Set aside
6 squares from each tracing for setting squares.

2. Lightly trace embroidery
details on D and E pieces.

3. Measure 4" from corner of 1
green strip and trim triangle (**Bias
Cutting Diagram**). Measuring
from cut edge, cut 20 (1"-wide)
bias stem pieces for iris blocks.
Each stem should be about 5" long.
From second green strip, cut 18
(1" x 4¼") stems for border irises.

4. Center pressing bar on top of
each bias strip. Press edges of strip
over bar, overlapping raw edges.

5. Aligning pieces with traced
outline, appliqué stem and 1 each
of A, B, C, D, D rev., and E to
muslin square in alphabetical order.

6. Appliqué 20 squares.

7. Use 2 strands of gold floss to
outline-stitch "beards" on D petals.
With same or coordinating color of
floss, work running stitches on
each side of outline-stitched details.

Use 2 strands of floss matched to
color of petal to outline-stitch
around each E petal; work running-
stitch detail at bottom of petal.

8. Lay out appliquéd blocks, setting squares, side triangles, and
corner triangles in diagonal rows
(**Setting Diagram**). (Note that all
reversed blocks are placed on right
side of quilt.) Join units in each
row. Press seam allowances toward
setting squares. Then join rows.

9. Sew borders to each quilt side
and miter corners. (See page 14 for
tips on sewing mitered corners.)

10. Pin F leaves at border corners as shown. Lay out remaining
leaves, stems, and irises. (Each stem
should be in line with tip of setting
triangle directly above it and leaves
cross at a point in line with tip of
appliquéd block.)

continued

11. Appliqué stems and border pieces in place in alphabetical order. Embroider petals.

Quilting and Finishing

1. Outline-quilt all appliquéd pieces. Quilt iris design traced in setting squares. In quilt shown, remainder of background is quilted with a 7/8" cross-hatch grid.

2. See pages 16 and 17 for instructions on making binding. Make 9 yards of 2½"-wide bias or straight-grain binding. Apply binding to quilt edges.

Appliqué patterns are finished size. Add ¼" seam allowance for hand appliqué or cut as is for machine appliqué.

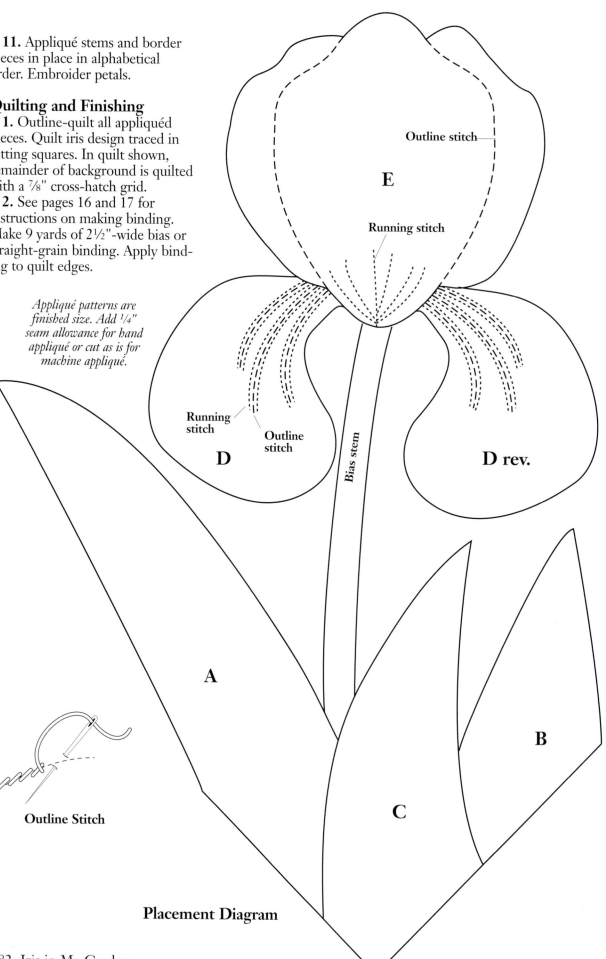

Outline stitch

E

Running stitch

Running stitch

Outline stitch

D

Bias stem

D rev.

A

B

C

Outline Stitch

Placement Diagram

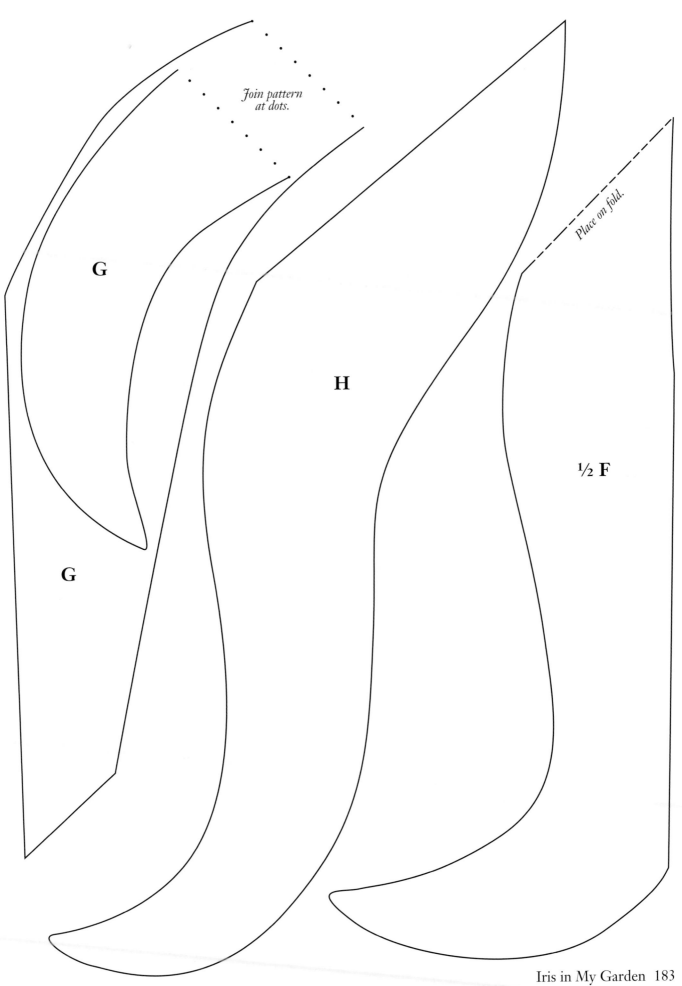

Join pattern
at dots.

G

G

H

½ F

Place on fold.

Irish Crosses

Salute St. Patrick's Day and the new spring with a fabulous scrap quilt. You can celebrate the wearing o' the green or choose another cheerful color scheme from your scrap bag.

Quilt designed by Susan Ramey Cleveland, Leeds, Alabama
Made by Annie Phillips, Hayden, Alabama

Finished Quilt Size
96" x 96"

Number of Blocks and Finished Size
64 blocks   12" x 12"

Fabric Requirements
10 light green prints   ½ yard each
10 dark green prints   ½ yard each
White shamrock print   2¼ yards
Binding fabric   ⅞ yard
Backing   2⅞ yards 104" wide

Cutting
Cut all strips cross-grain except as noted.

From each light green print
- 4 (4¼"-wide) strips. Cut 10 (4¼") squares from each strip. Cut each square in quarters diagonally to get 160 A triangles from each fabric. (You need a total of 1,536 triangles; fabric allows for plenty of extras.)

From each dark green print
- 4 (4¼"-wide) strips. Cut 10 (4¼") squares from each strip. Cut each square in quarters diagonally to get 160 A triangles from each fabric. (You need a total of 1,536 triangles; fabric allows for plenty of extras.)

From shamrock print
- 11 (6½"-wide) strips. From these, cut 64 (6½") B squares.

Setting Diagram

Quilt Top Assembly
1. Select 12 light green A triangles. Join triangles side-by-side in rows of 5 and 7 as shown **(Block Assembly Diagram)**. Join rows to form 1 light triangle segment . Make 128 light triangle segments. Repeat procedure with dark A triangles to make 128 dark triangle segments.

2. Arrange 2 light segments and 2 dark segments around 1 print B square. Sew each segment to square, leaving ¼" seam allowance unsewn at both ends of each seam. Then stitch diagonal corner seams to join segments and complete block.

3. Make 64 blocks.

4. Join blocks in 8 horizontal rows of 8 blocks each, turning blocks as shown to make dark and light crosses **(Setting Diagram)**. Join rows to complete quilt top assembly.

Quilting and Finishing
1. Outline-quilt patchwork as shown **(Block Quilting Diagram)**.

2. See pages 16 and 17 for instructions on making binding. Make 11 yards of 2½"-wide bias or straight-grain binding from reserved fabric. Apply binding to quilt edges.

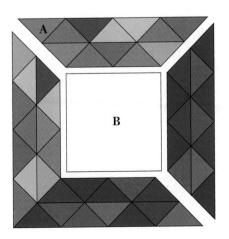

Block Assembly Diagram

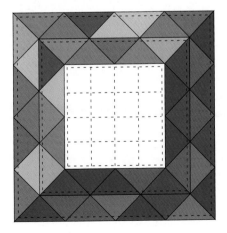

Block Quilting Diagram

Jewels in My Flower Garden

After taking a class on the Jewel Box pattern, Jean Sumner began to play with the possibilities of the design. "Each year, the Museum of the American Quilter's Society holds a contest on new interpretations of traditional patterns," Jean says. "Jewel Box wasn't on their list, but the contest gave me the idea to do my own version of this pattern."

Quilt by Elgenia B. Sumner
Birmingham, Alabama

Finished Quilt Size
81½" x 93½"

Number of Blocks and Finished Size
30 blocks   12" x 12"

Fabric Requirements
White   2¾ yards
Assorted prints   12 fat quarters*
Floral stripe for inner
    and outer borders   2¾ yards
Floral print for border   2¾ yards
Binding fabric   1 yard
Backing   5¾ yards
*Fat quarter = 18" x 22".

Cutting
Cut all strips cross-grain.
From white
- 23 (2"-wide) strips. From these, cut 480 (2") A squares.
- 11 (3⅞"-wide) strips. From these, 120 (3⅞") squares. Cut each square in half diagonally to get 240 B triangles.

From each fat quarter
- 4 (2" x 22") strips. From total of these (48 strips), cut 480 (2") A squares.
- 2 (3⅞" x 22") strips. From total of these (24 strips), cut 120 (3⅞") squares. Cut each square in half diagonally to get 240 B triangles.

Setting Diagram

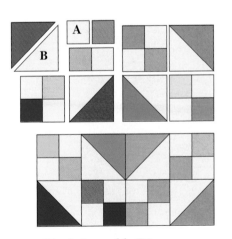

Block Assembly Diagram

Quilt Top Assembly
1. Sew a print A square to each white A. Sew a print B triangle to each print B. Press all seam allowances toward print fabrics.

2. For each block, select 16 A units and 8 B units. Join A units in pairs (**Block Assembly Diagram**). Join 2 A four-patches and 2 B units in each quadrant as shown. Join quadrants in pairs to make a half-block; then join halves to complete block. Make 30 blocks.

3. Lay out blocks in 6 horizontal rows with 5 blocks in each row (**Setting Diagram**). Join blocks in each row; then join rows.

4. From floral stripe, cut 4 (1¾" x 97") strips and 4 (1¾" x 85") strips. From floral, cut 2 (8¾" x 97") strips and 2 (8¾" x 85") strips.

5. Sew stripe strips to each long edge of floral border strip, matching lengths. Mark centers on edges of each border strip and on edges of quilt. Matching centers of borders and quilt edges, sew 1 border strip to each edge. Miter border corners. (See page 14 for tips on sewing a mitered corner.)

Quilting and Finishing
1. Quilt all pieces in-the-ditch. Echo-quilt white As and Bs at ¼"-intervals. Quilt around flower motifs in floral border print.

2. See pages 16 and 17 for instructions on making binding. Make 10 yards of 2½"-wide bias or straight-grain binding from reserved fabric. Apply binding to quilt edges.

Joseph's Coat

"Now Israel loved Joseph more than all his children, because he was the son of his old age; and he made him a coat of many colours."   Genesis 37:3

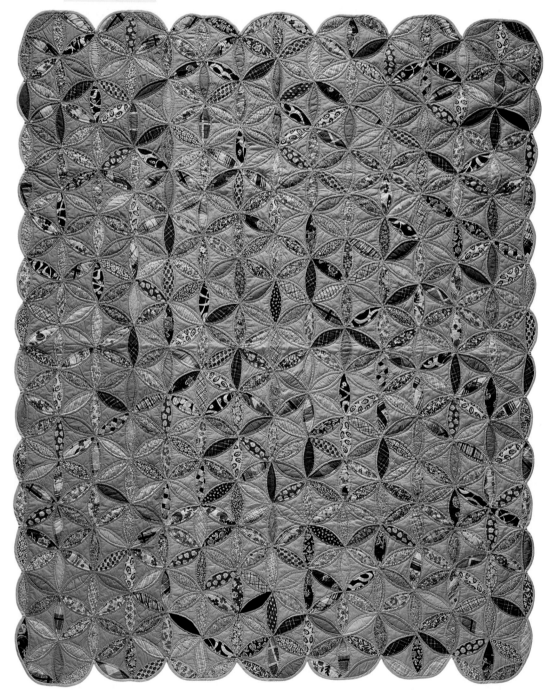

Quilt by Lorene Payne
Austin, Arkansas

Finished Quilt Size
68¾" x 82½"

Number of Blocks and Finished Size
49 blocks   11" diameter

Fabric Requirements
Pink solid	9⅝ yards*
Scraps	27 fat quarters**
Backing	4¼ yards

*Includes 1 yard for binding.
**Fat quarter = 18" x 22".

Cutting
Make templates of patterns A and B on page 190. Cut all strips cross-grain. Cut pieces in order listed to get best use of yardage.
From pink solid
• 30" square for bias binding.
• 50 (6¼"-wide) strips. From these, and scrap from binding square, cut 406 of Template B.

From fat quarters
• 80 (6½" x 18") strips. From these, cut 637 of Template A.

Quilt Top Assembly
1. For each block, select 12 As and 6 Bs. Join As and Bs in a circle (**Block Diagram**). Then join As around outside edge to complete block. Make 49 blocks.

2. For End Unit, select 5As and 4 Bs. Join As and Bs in a row as shown; then join 2 remaining Bs at top edge (**End Unit Diagram**). Make 5 end units.

3. For each side unit, join 1 A and 1 B as shown (**Side Unit Diagram**). Make 12 side units.

4. For each corner unit, select 6 As and 4 Bs. Join 3 As and 3 Bs in a row as shown; then add 3 As to outside edge (**Corner Units Diagram**). For bottom left corner unit, add remaining B to right side. For bottom right corner unit, add remaining B to left side as shown.

5. Join blocks, end units, side units, corner units, and remaining Bs in vertical rows (**Setting Diagram**). Join rows.

continued

Setting Diagram

Joseph's Coat is not recommended for the beginning quilter, as the piecing requires practiced skill with curved seams. However, if you have pieced a top or two and are comfortable with curved seams, don't shy away from this one. Curved seams can be fun; and the sense of accomplishment you'll get upon seeing the finished quilt will be worth the effort. For control and accuracy, we suggest hand piecing this quilt.

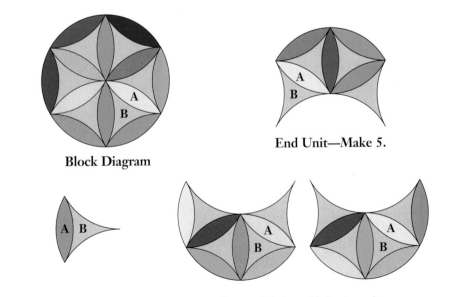

Block Diagram

End Unit—Make 5.

Side Unit—Make 12.

Corner Units—Make 1 each.

Quilting and Finishing

1. Outline-quilt all pieces.

2. See page 17 for instructions on making continuous bias binding. Make 10 yards of 2"-wide bias binding. Apply binding to quilt edges, mitering corners of binding around each A piece.

A

B

Kaleidoscope

Careful placement of light and dark fabrics gives this quilt its complex sense of movement and creates the illusion of circles in the patchwork. All the seams are straight in this easy-to-sew design.

Quilt by Gaynelle Hardy
Norcross, Georgia

Finished Quilt Size
88" x 99"

Number of Blocks and Finished Size
168 blocks   5½" x 5½"

Fabric Requirements
Dark fabrics   11 fat quarters*
Light fabrics   17 fat quarters*
Black   ½ yard
Brown print for border   2½ yards
Binding fabric   1 yard
Backing   9 yards
*Fat quarter = 18" x 22".

Cutting
Make a template of Pattern X. A template for Pattern Y is optional, since it can be rotary cut. Cut all strips cross-grain except as noted.

From dark fat quarters
• 62 (3⅝" x 18") strips. From these, cut 672 of Template X **(Triangle Cutting Diagram).** To be sure you don't cut your template, place acrylic ruler on top of template, matching edges, and use ruler as a cutting edge.

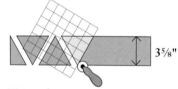

3⅝"

Triangle Cutting Diagram

From light prints
• 62 (3⅝" x 18") strips. From these, cut 672 of Template X in same manner as for dark fabrics.
• 48 (2½" x 18") strips. From these, cut 336 (2½") squares. Cut each square in half diagonally to get 672 Y triangles.

From black
• 8 (1½"-wide) strips for inner border.

From brown print
• 4 (10½" x 90") lengthwise strips for outer borders.

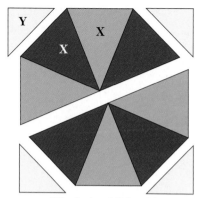

Block A—Make 84.

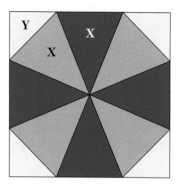

Block B—Make 84.

Quilt Top Assembly
1. For each block, select 4 light Xs and 4 dark Xs.

2. For Block A, join X triangles as shown **(Block A Diagram)**. Join Y triangles to edges of each dark X. Press seam allowances toward Ys. Make 84 of Block A.

3. For Block B, join X triangles as shown **(Block B Diagram)**. Then join Y triangles to edges of each light X. Make 84 of Block B.

4. Lay out blocks in 14 horizontal rows, with 12 blocks in each row, alternating A blocks and B blocks **(Setting Diagram)**. Join blocks in each row; then join rows.

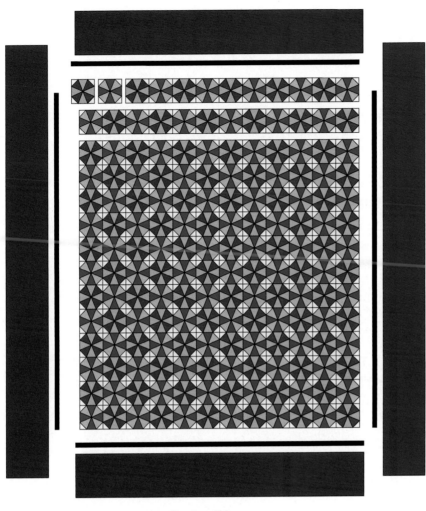

Setting Diagram

5. Join 2 black strips end-to-end to make a border for each quilt edge. Trim 2 borders to match quilt length and stitch these to side edges. Press seam allowances toward borders. Trim 2 remaining borders to match quilt width, including side borders, and stitch these to top and bottom edges.

6. Sew 2 brown border strips to side edges of quilt. Press seam allowances toward borders. Sew remaining borders to top and bottom edges of quilt.

Quilting and Finishing

1. Outline-quilt blocks. Quilt a 1" diagonal cross-hatch pattern in borders, or quilt as desired.

2. See pages 16 and 17 for instructions on making binding. Make 10½ yards of 2½"-wide bias or straight-grain binding. Apply binding to quilt edges.

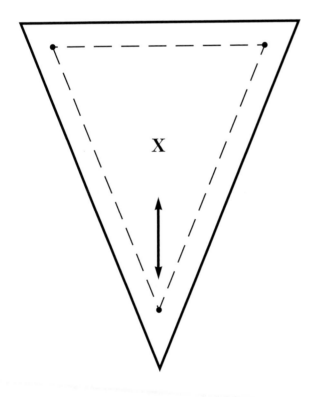

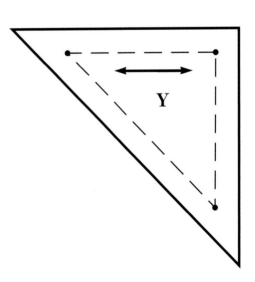

Kansas Sunflower

Mary Alice Russell pieced the blocks in this quilt during the Depression. In 1984, her granddaughter, Evelyn Russell, hand-quilted the top. And in 1991, Evelyn displayed the quilt at the Russell family reunion.

Quilt pieced by Mary Alice Russell
Quilted by Evelyn Russell
Electric City, Washington

Finished Quilt Size
74" x 91"

Number of Blocks and Finished Size
20 blocks   12" x 12"

Fabric Requirements
Yellow   ¼ yard
Assorted prints   20 fat quarters*
Assorted solids   20 fat eighths*
White   1⅝ yards
Pink   4 yards
Backing   5½ yards
Binding fabric   1 yard
*Fat quarter = 18" x 22" and
 fat eighth = 9" x 22".

Cutting
Make templates of patterns A, B, and C on page 197. Templates for patterns D and E are optional, as these pieces can be rotary cut. Cut strips cross-grain except as noted.
From yellow
• 20 of Template A.

From each print fat quarter
• 8 of Template B.

From each solid fat eighth
• 8 of Template C.

From white
• 8 (4"-wide) strips. From these, cut 80 (4") E squares.
• 3 (6¼"-wide) strips. From these, cut 20 (6¼") squares. Cut each square in quarters diagonally to get 80 D triangles.

From pink
• 2 (3½" x 80") and 2 (3½" x 90") lengthwise strips for borders.
• 12 (12½") setting squares.
• 4 (18¼") squares. Cut each square in quarters diagonally to get 14 side triangles (and 2 extra).
• 2 (9⅜") squares. Cut each square in half diagonally to get 4 corner triangles.

Quilt Top Assembly
1. For each block, select 1 set of B pieces and 1 coordinating set of C pieces, as well as 4 D triangles and 4 E squares.

2. Sew 2 Cs to sides of 1 B. Make 4 B/C petals **(Block Assembly Diagram)**. Join B/C petals with remaining Bs to form flower. Leave center open. Set in D triangles and E squares. (See page 10 for tips on sewing a set-in seam.)

3. Run a gathering thread across bottom of each C piece. Gather Cs until open center of flower is slightly smaller than A template. Appliqué yellow A over open center of flower to complete block.

4. Make 20 flower blocks.

5. Lay out blocks, setting squares, side triangles, and corner triangles in diagonal rows **(Setting Diagram)**. When satisfied with placement, join units in each row. Press seam allowances toward setting squares and side triangles. Then join rows.   *continued*

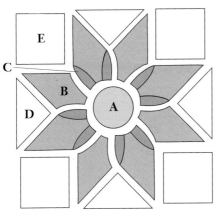

Block Assembly Diagram

Setting Diagram

Reverse along broken line for complete quilting pattern.

**½ Sunflower
Quilting Pattern**

6. Sew 90"-long borders to sides of quilt. Press seam allowances toward borders. Join 80"-long borders to top and bottom of quilt and press.

Quilting and Finishing

1. Transfer Sunflower Quilting Pattern to setting squares, corner triangles, and side triangles as shown **(Setting Diagram).**

2. Outline-quilt block pieces. Quilt flower pattern in setting pieces. Quilt borders as desired.

3. See pages 16 and 17 for instructions on making binding. Make 9½ yards of 2½"-wide bias or straight-grain binding. Apply binding to quilt edges.

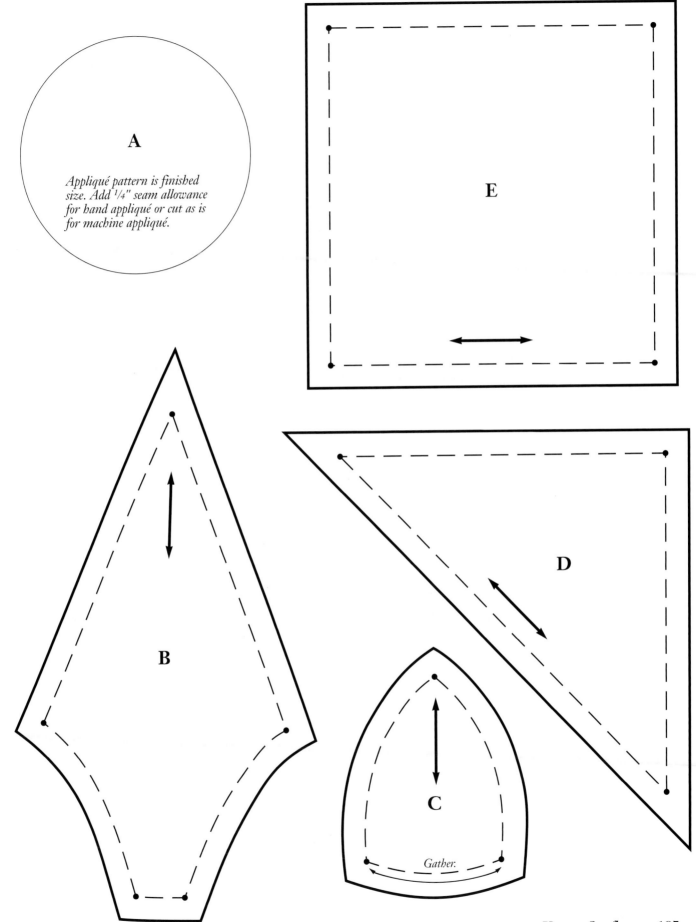

A

Appliqué pattern is finished size. Add ¼" seam allowance for hand appliqué or cut as is for machine appliqué.

E

B

D

C

Gather.

Kit Carson

Kit Carson's mother, Rebecca Robinson Carson, made the antique quilt that inspired this one. Laverne Mathews created her own version after seeing the heirloom at the Kit Carson Museum in Taos, New Mexico. Patterns for Laverne's lovely quilting designs are on pages 201 and 202.

Quilt by Laverne Noble Mathews
Orange, Texas

Finished Quilt Size
67" x 81¼"

Number of Blocks
36 feathered triangles
8 feathered half-triangles

Fabric Requirements
Muslin   4½ yards
Red   3½ yards*
Red print   ⅞ yard
Backing   5 yards
*Includes fabric for binding.

Cutting
Cut all strips cross-grain except as noted. Rotary-cut pieces in order listed to get best use of yardage.

From muslin
- 4 (5½" x 78") lengthwise strips for borders.
- 2 (15½"-wide) strips. From these and scrap from borders, cut 9 (15½") squares. Cut each square in quarters diagonally to get 36 C setting triangles.
- 6 (8"-wide) strips. From 1 strip, cut 4 (8") squares. Cut each square in half diagonally to get 8 B triangles. From remaining strips, cut 15 (8" x 14") pieces for quick-pieced D triangles.
- 4 (2⅞") squares. Cut each square in half diagonally to get 8 D triangles.
- 36 (2½") A squares.

From red
- 4 (2¾" x 82") lengthwise strips for sawtooth border. Use lengthwise scrap for next 2 cuts.
- 8 (2⅞" x 31") strips. From these, cut 40 (2⅞") squares. Cut each square in half diagonally to get 80 D triangles.
- 5 (8"-wide) strips. From these, cut 15 (8" x 14") pieces for quick-pieced D triangles.

From red print
- 3 (9¾"-wide) strips. From these, cut 9 (9¾") squares. Cut each square in quarters diagonally to get 36 E triangles. From remainder, cut 4 (5⅛") squares. Cut each square in half diagonally to get 8 F triangles.

Quick Piecing
See page 11 for tips on sewing quick-pieced triangle-squares.

1. On wrong side of each 8" x 14" muslin piece, mark a 2- x 4-square grid of 2⅞" squares (**Diagram 1**). Draw diagonal lines through squares as shown.

2. Match 1 muslin piece to a red piece, right sides facing. Machine-stitch ¼" from each side of all *diagonal* lines (**Diagram 2**). Cut on *all* grid lines to get 16 D triangle-squares. Press seam allowances toward red.

3. Repeat procedure with remaining 8" x 14" pieces to get a total of 240 red/muslin D triangle-squares.

Note: If you prefer traditional piecing, use 8" x 14" pieces of red and muslin to cut 120 (2⅞") squares of each color; cut each square in half diagonally to get 240 D triangles. Join pairs of triangles to make 240 triangle-squares.

Quilt Top Assembly
1. Join 3 triangle-squares in a row (**Feathered Triangle Assembly Diagram**). Make 2 rows. Join 1 row to side of E triangle as shown. Press seam allowances toward E.

2. Join an A square to end of remaining row and join to adjacent side of E triangle.

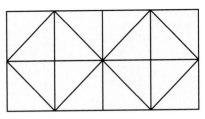

Diagram 1

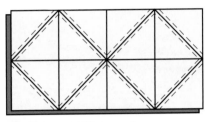

Diagram 2

3. Sew a red D triangle to end of each triangle-square row as shown to complete feathered triangle block.

4. Make 36 feathered triangle blocks.

5. For half-triangle block, join 3 triangle-squares in a row (**Feathered Half-Triangle Assembly Diagram**). Join row to diagonal edge of red print F triangle. Press seam allowances toward F.

6. Sew 1 muslin D triangle and 1 red D triangle to ends of triangle-square row as shown to complete half-triangle block.

7. Make 8 half-triangle blocks.
continued

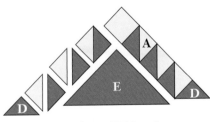

**Feathered Triangle
Assembly Diagram**

**Feathered Half-Triangle
Assembly Diagram**

Setting Diagram

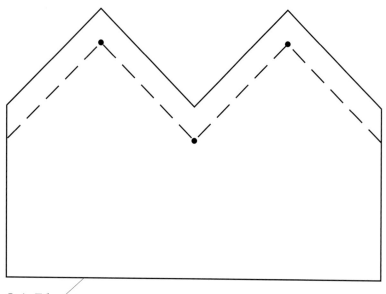

Strip Edge

Sawtooth Border Guide

8. Lay out triangle blocks and half-triangle blocks with B and C setting triangles (**Setting Diagram**). When satisfied with layout, join units in 8 vertical rows as shown. Join rows.

9. See page 14 for tips on measuring and sewing border strips. Measure and trim 2 border strips to match quilt length; sew these to quilt sides. Repeat to join remaining border strips to top and bottom edges of quilt. Press seam allowances toward borders.

10. Make a window template of sawtooth border guide at left. (See page 8 for tips on making a window template.)

11. Trim red border strips to match length and width of quilt. Starting at center of each border strips, match straight edge of template with edge of strip and mark sawtooth pattern along length of strip. Mark cutting edge as well as sewing line. Cut out sawtooth edge of each strip.

12. Lay sawtooth border strips on each quilt side, aligning straight edges. Appliqué triangle points to muslin border and miter corners.

Quilting and Finishing

1. Make stencils of quilting patterns on pages 201 and 202. Mark feather on C triangles of outside rows. Mark vertical areas of muslin (Cs and Bs) with flowered vine. Mark pineapple on B corner triangles and rope pattern in borders.

2. Outline-quilt ⅛" inside seams of all D triangles and A squares, but only on sides adjacent to red triangles. Quilt vertical parallel lines, 1" apart, in E and F triangles.

3. Quilt all marked designs.

4. Quilt area around vines with diagonal lines, ⅜" apart. Quilt area around feathers with vertical lines, ½" apart.

5. Outline-quilt ⅛" outside sawtooth seam line.

6. See pages 16 and 17 for instructions on making binding. Make 8½ yards of 2½"-wide bias or straight-grain binding. Apply binding to quilt edges.

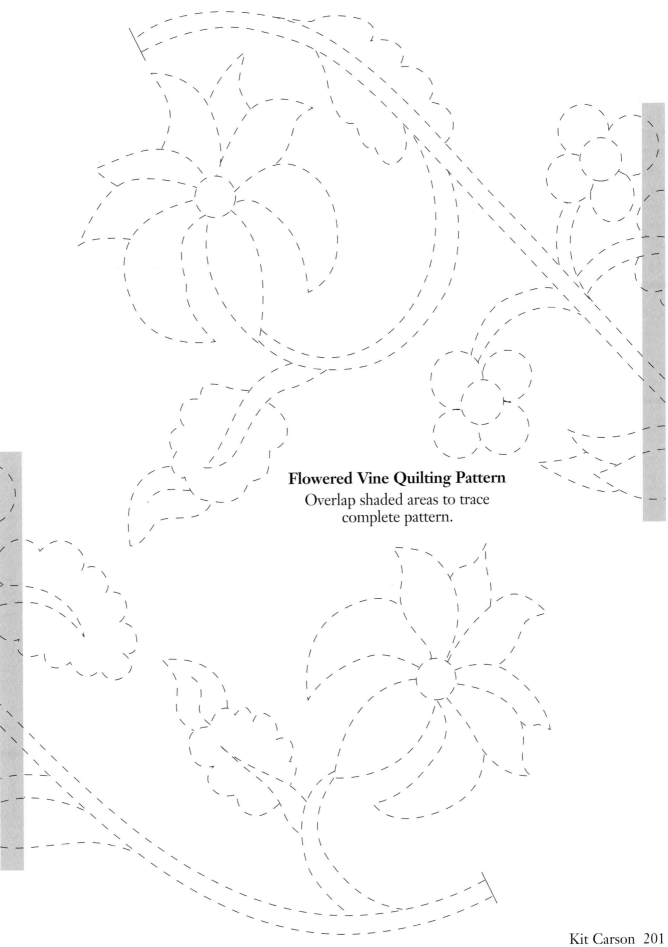

Flowered Vine Quilting Pattern
Overlap shaded areas to trace
complete pattern.

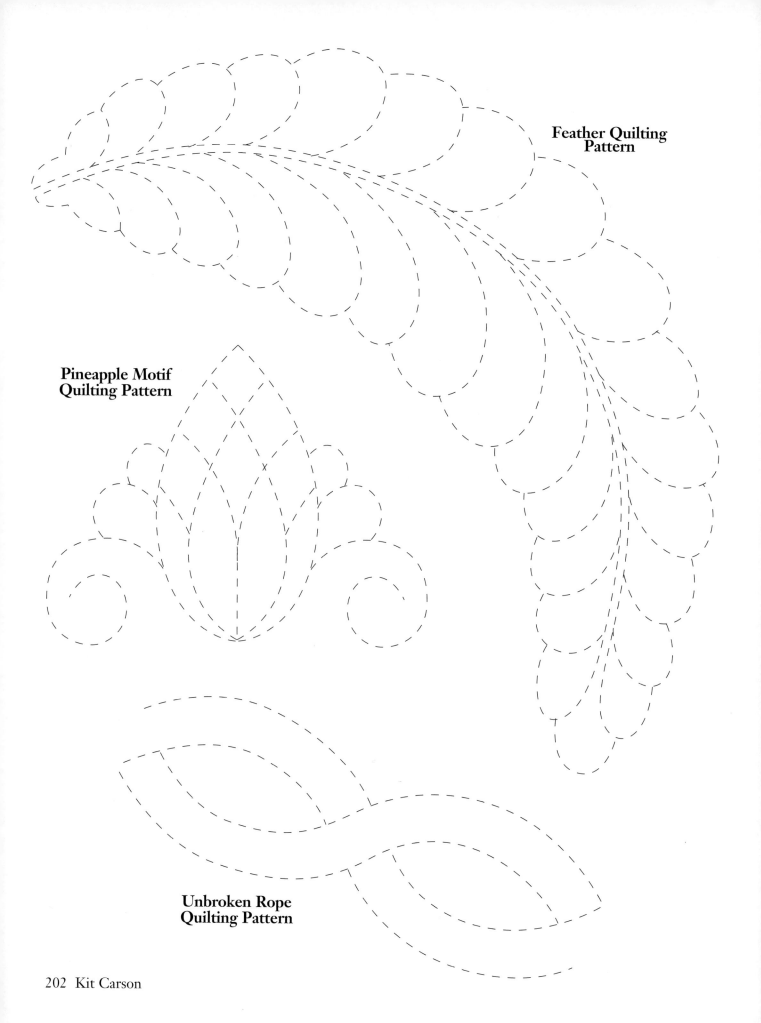

Feather Quilting Pattern

Pineapple Motif Quilting Pattern

Unbroken Rope Quilting Pattern

202 Kit Carson

Lilies of the Field

"Consider the lilies of the field, how they grow; they toil not, neither do they spin: and yet I say unto you, that even Solomon in all his glory was not arrayed like one of these."   Matthew 6:28

Quilt from The Fosters
Pittsfield, Illinois

Finished Quilt Size
75" x 75"

Number of Blocks and Finished Size
36 blocks   8" x 8"

Fabric Requirements
White or muslin	5¾ yards
Navy	5 yards
Binding fabric	1 yard
Backing	4½ yards

Cutting
Make a template of Pattern F. Cut all strips cross-grain. Cut pieces in order listed to get best use of yardage. When possible, pieces are listed in order needed, so you don't have to cut everything all at once.

Before cutting, decide if you prefer traditional or quick-piecing methods for patchwork. See pages 11 and 12 for tips on quick-piecing techniques for triangle-squares and flying geese. Instructions are for quick-piecing techniques.

From white
- 4 (4½"-wide) strips. From these, cut 36 (4½") A squares.
- 3 (3⅛"-wide) strips. From this, cut 36 (3⅛") squares. Cut each square in half diagonally to get 72 C triangles.
- 5 (6"-wide) strips. From these, cut 20 (6" x 10") pieces for quick-pieced C triangle-squares. For traditional piecing, cut 162 (2⅛") squares; cut each square in half diagonally to get 324 C triangles.
- 3 (7"-wide) strips. From these, cut 18 (7") squares. Cut each square in quarters diagonally to get 72 D triangles.
- 2 (12⅝"-wide) strips. From these, cut 5 (12⅝") squares and 2 (6½") squares. Cut each larger square in quarters diagonally to get 20 setting triangles; cut smaller squares in half diagonally to get 4 corner triangles.
- 5 (8½"-wide) strips. From these, cut 25 setting squares.

- 15 (2⅜"-wide) strips. From these and scraps, cut 152 (2⅜" x 4¼") H rectangles for flying geese border units.

From navy
- 6 (¾"-wide) strips. From these, cut 36 (¾" x 5¾") strips for stems.
- 6 (1¾"-wide) strips. From this, cut 36 of Template F and 36 of Template F reversed.
- 4 (3⅝"-wide) strips. From these, cut 36 (3⅝") squares. Cut each square in half diagonally to get 72 B triangles.
- 3 (3⅛"-wide) strips. From these, cut 36 (3⅛") E squares.
- 5 (6"-wide) strips. From these, cut 20 (6" x 10") pieces for quick-pieced C triangle-squares. For traditional piecing, cut 162 (2⅛") squares; cut each square in half diagonally to get 324 C triangles.
- 24 (3¼"-wide) strips. From these, cut 304 (3¼") G squares.

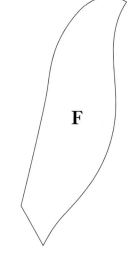

F

Appliqué pattern is finished size. Add ¼" seam allowance for hand appliqué or cut as is for machine appliqué.

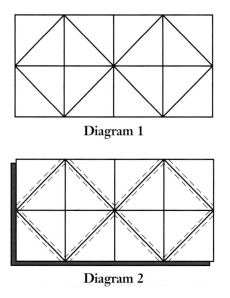

Diagram 1

Diagram 2

Corner triangle   Side triangle

Setting square

Seting Diagram.

Quilt Top Assembly

1. On wrong side of each 6" x 10" white piece, mark a 2- x 4-square grid of 2⅛" squares (**Diagram 1**). Draw diagonal lines through squares as shown.

2. Match 1 white piece to a navy piece, right sides facing. Machine-stitch ¼" from each side of all *diagonal* lines (**Diagram 2**). Cut on *all* grid lines to get 16 C triangle-squares. Stitch 20 grids to get a total of 320 triangle-squares. Press seam allowances toward navy.

3. From scraps, cut 2 (2⅛") squares each of white and navy; cut each square in half to get 4 triangles of each color. Piece 4 more triangle-squares traditionally to get a total of 324, 9 for each block.

4. Press under ¼" on long edges of each stem strip. Appliqué 1 F, 1 F reversed and 1 stem strip to each A square.

5. Join 2 C triangle-squares; then sew a white C triangle to end of row as shown (**Block Assembly Diagram**). Sew this row to B triangle. Make 2 B/C units; then join D triangles as shown.

6. Join 2 C triangle-squares; then join this pair to 1 E square. Join 3 more triangle-squares and join row to adjacent side of E.

7. Join assembled units in pairs; then join pairs to complete 1 block. Make 36 blocks.

8. Join blocks, setting squares, side triangles, and corner triangles in diagonal rows (**Setting Diagram**). Join rows.

9. Following directions on page 12 for Diagonal-Corners quick-piecing method, sew G squares to H rectangles. Make 152 flying geese units for border.

10. For each side border, join 36 geese units in a row (**Setting Diagram**). Join borders to sides of quilt as shown, easing to fit as needed.

11. For top and bottom borders, join 36 geese units in a row. For each border corner, join 2 geese units with Hs together to make a square as shown; make 4 border corners. Sew corners to ends of border strips; then stitch pieced borders to top and bottom edges of quilt, easing to fit as needed.

Quilting and Finishing

1. Outline-quilt all patchwork. Quilt a cross-hatch pattern in setting squares, setting triangles, and corner triangles; or quilt as desired.

2. See pages 16 and 17 for instructions on making binding. Make 11½ yards of 2½"-wide bias or straight-grain binding. Apply binding to quilt edges.

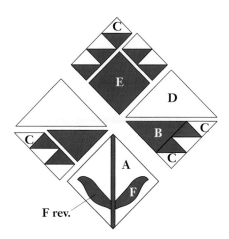

Block Assembly Diagram

Lilies of the Field 205

Log Cabin

In England, all the variations of this string-pieced pattern are known simply as Log Cabin. But in America, variations in the arrangement of light and dark fabrics have names such as Barn Raising, Straight Furrows, Open Windows, and Courthouse Steps. On the following pages you'll find instructions for making these four variations.

Quilt by Beryl G. Moran
Manchester, Missouri

Log Cabin Basics

Log Cabin blocks can be assembled with or without templates. These instructions are for machine piecing Log Cabin blocks without templates. Instructions for quilts in this book give measurements for cutting the Log Cabin square and strips.

Log Cabin Block Assembly

The size of the center square and log strips will vary with the type of Log Cabin block you are making, and should be specified in the instructions. All pieces are joined with ¼" seam allowance.

1. Cut a square (A) for the center. With right sides facing, match any light strip (B) to 1 side of square and stitch **(Diagram 1)**. Trim B even with A **(Diagram 2)**. Press seam allowance toward B.

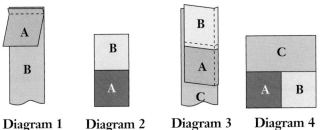

Diagram 1   **Diagram 2**   **Diagram 3**   **Diagram 4**

2. Turn unit so Log B is at top. Match another light strip (C) to next edge and stitch **(Diagram 3)**. Trim C even with A/B **(Diagram 4)**. Press seam allowance toward Log C.

3. Turn unit so Log C is at top. Match a dark strip (D) to next edge of square and stitch **(Diagram 5)**. Trim log even with bottom of unit and press seam allowance toward Log D **(Diagram 6)**.

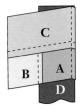

Diagram 5

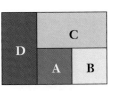

Diagram 6

4. Continue adding strips in this fashion until desired block size is reached **(Diagram 7)**. Always press seam allowances toward newest log; then rotate unit to put it at top edge to add next log.

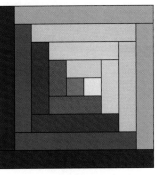

Diagram 7

Types of Log Cabin Blocks

Alternation of color tones changes the character of the traditional spiraling Log Cabin block **(Diagram 8)**.

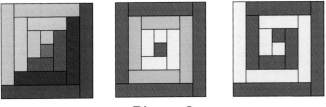

Diagram 8

Chimney and Cornerstone blocks repeat the center square throughout the block, often seen as a large X across the block **(Diagram 9)**.

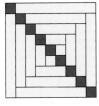

Diagram 9

Use log strips of 2 different widths to shift the center square off-center. An Off-Center block is assembled in the same way as the traditional spiraling block **(Diagram 10)**.

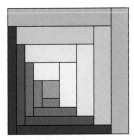

Diagram 10

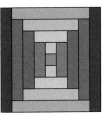

Diagram 11

The Courthouse Steps block is assembled by joining log strips of equal width to each side of the center square **(Diagram 11)**. Varied square and strip dimensions as well as color placement alter the block's appearance.

Finished Quilt Sizes

Barn Raising	96" x 96"
Straight Furrows	96" x 96"
Open Windows	96" x 96"
Courthouse Steps	96" x 96"

Number of Blocks and Finished Size

Block	12" x 12"
Barn Raising	64 blocks
Straight Furrows	64 blocks
Open Windows	64 blocks
Courthouse Steps	64 blocks

Fabric Requirements

Barn Raising, Straight Furrows, Open Windows

Dark fabrics	20 fat quarters*
Light fabrics	20 fat quarters*
Center square fabric	⅜ yard
Binding fabric	1 yard
Backing fabric	5¾ yards

Courthouse Steps

Dark fabrics	22 fat quarters*
Light fabrics	19 fat quarters*
Center square fabric	⅜ yard
Binding fabric	1 yard
Backing	5¾ yards

*Fat quarter = 19" x 22".

Cutting

It is not necessary to make templates for this block, as all pieces are easily rotary cut.

Barn Raising, Straight Furrows, Open Windows

From dark fabrics
• 240 (1½" x 22") strips.

From light fabrics
• 224 (1½" x 22") strips.

From center square fabric
• 64 (2½") squares.

Courthouse Steps

From dark fabrics
• 256 (1½" x 22") strips.

From light fabrics
• 208 (1½" x 22") strips.

From center square fabric
• 64 (2½") squares.

Quilt Top Assembly

Barn Raising, Straight Furrows, Open Windows

1. For each Basic Log Cabin block, select 1 center square, 5 light fabric strips, and 5 dark fabric strips.

2. Referring to Log Cabin basics on page 207 and diagram below, sew strips around center square until block is complete.

3. Make 64 Log Cabin blocks.

4. Select desired arrangement of blocks from **Setting Diagrams** opposite. Lay out blocks in 8 horizontal rows, with 8 blocks in each row. Join blocks in each row; then join rows.

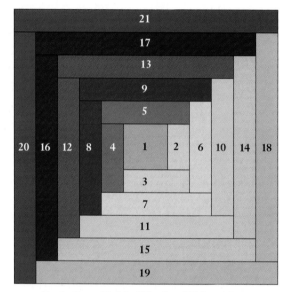

Basic Log Cabin Block—Make 64.

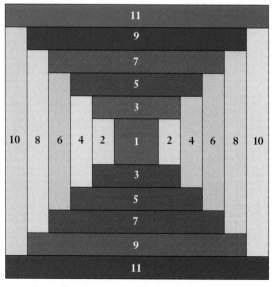

Courthouse Steps Block—Make 64.

Courthouse Steps

1. For each Courthouse Steps block, select 1 center square, 5 light fabric strips, and 5 dark fabric strips.

2. Sew light strips (#2) to opposite sides of center square **(Courthouse Steps Block Diagram).** Press seam allowances toward strips and trim ends of strip even with square.

3. Sew dark strips (#3) to opposite sides of center unit. Press seam allowances toward dark strips and trim ends of strip even with center unit.

4. Continue adding logs in this manner, always pressing seam allowances toward newest log.

5. Make 64 Courthouse Steps blocks.

6. Lay out blocks in 8 horizontal rows, with 8 blocks in each row as shown. Join blocks in each row; then join rows.

Quilting and Finishing

1. Quilt as desired.

2. See pages 16 and 17 for instructions on making binding. Make 11 yards of 2½"-wide bias or straight-grain binding. Apply binding to quilt edges.

Barn Raising

Straight Furrows

Open Windows

Courthouse Steps

Mary's Fan

Mary Ann Keathley has a lifelong affinity for all kinds of needlework. "I am happiest when I have a needle in my hand," says Mary. "Quilting has been a salvation, especially since my retirement." Inspired by an antique quilt of Grandmother's Fans set in this arrangement, Mary was delighted to find a quilt design in which she could use so many fabric scraps.

Quilt by Mary Ann Keathley
Jacksonville, Arkansas

Finished Quilt Size

92" x 92"

Number of Blocks and Finished Size

64 blocks   11½" x 11½"

Fabric Requirements

Dark green print	2¼ yards
Scrap fabrics	22 (¼-yard) pieces
Muslin	7½ yards
Binding fabric	1 yard
Backing	2⅞ yards 104" wide

Cutting

Make a templates of patterns A, B, and C on pages 211 and 212.

From dark green print
• 64 of Template A.

From scrap fabrics
• 64 (2¾" x 44") strips. From these, cut 448 of Template B.

From muslin
• 64 of Template C.

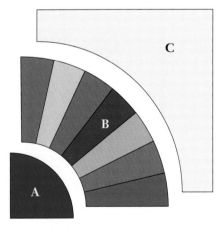

Block Assembly Diagram

Quilt Top Assembly

1. Join 7 B fan blades along long edges **(Block Assembly Diagram).** Sew A and C pieces to fan edges as shown. Make 64 blocks.

2. Lay out blocks in 8 horizontal rows, with 8 blocks in each row **(Setting Diagram).** Be sure blocks are positioned correctly. (Note that top half of quilt is a mirror image of bottom half.) Join blocks in each row; then lay out rows to verify correct position of blocks. When satisfied with placement, join rows.

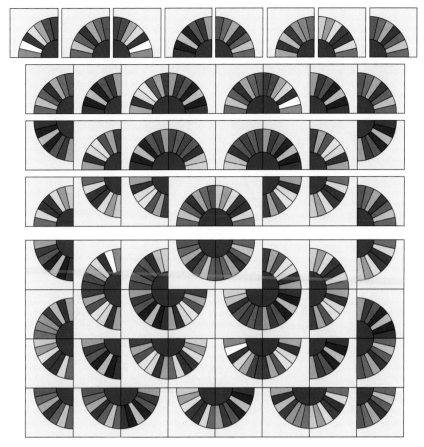

Setting Diagram

Quilting and Finishing

1. Quilt in-the-ditch or outline-quilt seam lines.

2. See pages 16 and 17 for instructions on making binding. Make 10¼ yards of 2½"-wide bias or straight-grain binding. Apply binding to quilt edges.

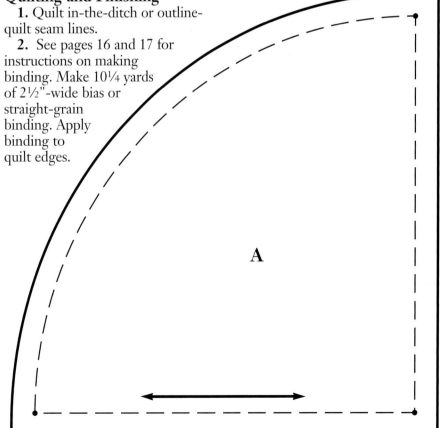

A

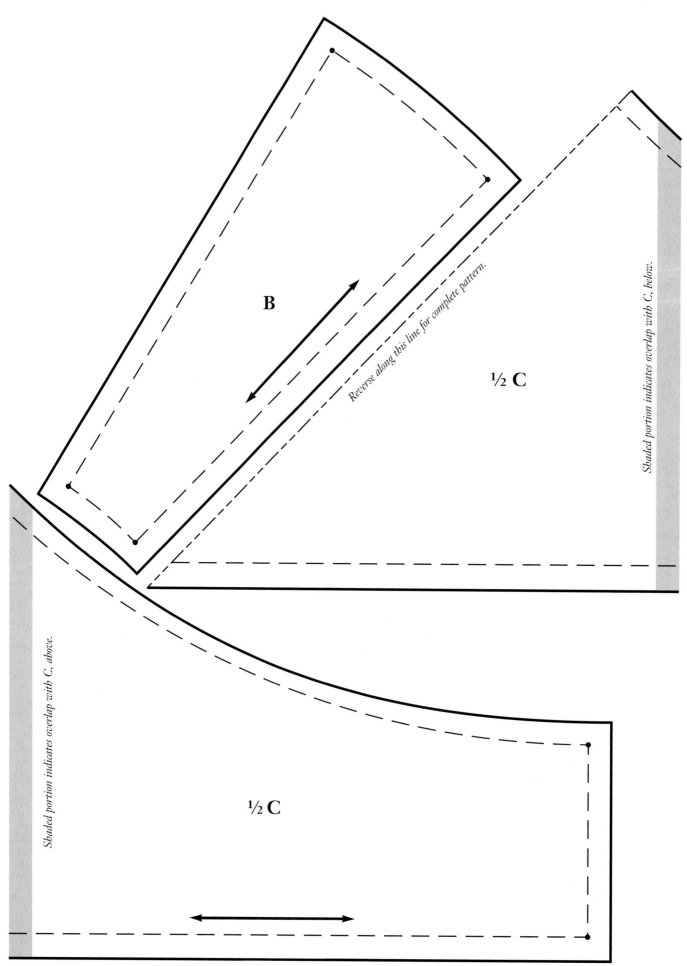

B

½ C

Reverse along this line for complete pattern.

Shaded portion indicates overlap with C, below.

Shaded portion indicates overlap with C, above.

½ C

Memory Chain

This is Marianna Frost's adaptation of a traditional pattern she has had since the 1960s. To unify the scraps, Marianna chose a novelty print of teddy bears on a green background for the repeating squares on point. "The colors are not placed randomly," she says. "I try to place each fabric next to a piece with a similar or complementary color. Then I always use a lot of red for drama!"

Quilt by Marianna Frost
Calvert, Texas

Finished Quilt Size
73½" x 88½"

Number of Blocks and Finished Size
90 blocks   7½" x 7½"

Fabric Requirements
Muslin	3½ yards
Scrap fabrics	14 fat quarters*
Dark print	½ yard**
Border/binding fabric	2¾ yards
Backing	5½ yards

* Fat quarter = 18" x 22".

** You can eliminate this yardage if you cut A squares from border/binding fabric.

Cutting
Make templates of patterns D and E. Templates for A, B, and C are not necessary, since they can be rotary cut. Cut all strips cross-grain except as noted.

From muslin
- 99 (2¾") squares. Cut each square in half diagonally to get 198 B triangles.
- 32 (2⅜"-wide) strips. From these, cut 180 of Template D, 18 of Template E, and 18 of Template E reversed.

From scrap fabrics
- 66 (2⅜" x 22") strips. From these, cut 594 (2⅜") C squares.
- 26 (2¾" x 22") strips. From these, cut 207 (2¾") squares. Cut each square in half diagonally to get 414 B triangles.

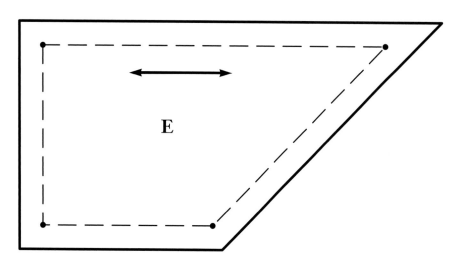

From dark print fabric
- 45 (3⅛") A squares.

From border/binding fabric
- 2 (3½" x 95") and 2 (3½" x 80") lengthwise strips for borders.
- 1 (30") square for binding.

Quilt Top Assembly
1. For Block 1, select 1 A, 2 Ds, and 4 each of muslin Bs, scrap Bs, and C squares.

2. Sew muslin Bs to sides of A square (**Block 1 Assembly Diagram**). Press seam allowances toward Bs.

3. Join Cs in pairs. Sew these to top and bottom of A/B unit.

4. Sew scrap Bs to Ds as shown. Join B/D units to sides of center unit as shown to complete block.

5. Make 45 of Block 1.

6. For each Half-Block 1, select 1 each of E and E reversed, 2 muslin Bs, 4 scrap Bs, and 2 scrap Cs. Sew scrap Bs to Es and muslin Bs as shown (**Half-Block 1 Assembly Diagram**). Press seam allowances toward scrap Bs. Join B triangle-squares to a scrap C square; press seam allowances toward C. Join units in rows to complete Half-Block 1. Make 9 of Half-Block 1.

7. For each Block 2, select 2 Ds, 4 scrap Bs, and 8 scrap C squares. Sew Bs to ends of D as shown (**Block 2 Assembly Diagram**); press seam allowances toward Bs. Join Cs in 2 rows as shown. Join

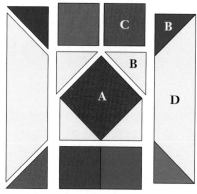

Block 1 Assembly Diagram
Make 45.

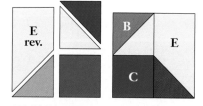

Half-Block 1 Assembly Diagram
Make 9.

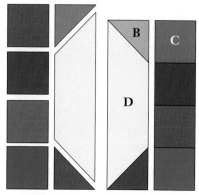

Block 2 Assembly Diagram
Make 45.

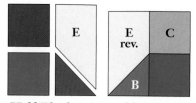

Half-Block 2 Assembly Diagram
Make 9.

rows to complete Block 2 as shown. Make 45 of Block 2.

8. For each Half-Block 2, select 1 each of E and E reversed, 2 scrap Bs, and 4 C squares. Sew Bs to Es (**Half-Block 2 Assembly Diagram**). Join Cs in pairs as shown. Join rows to complete Half-Block 2. Make 9 of Half-Block 2.

Setting Diagram

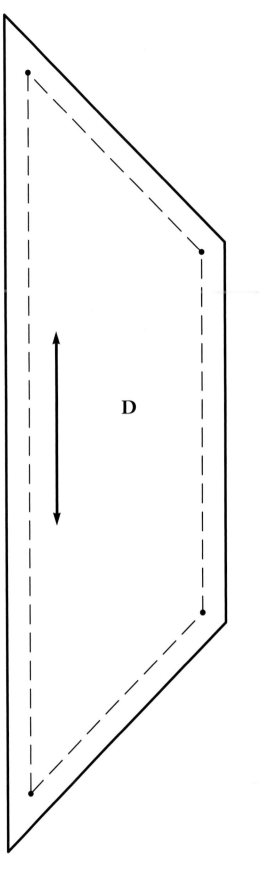

D

9. Lay out blocks and half blocks in 12 horizontal rows as shown **(Setting Diagram).** For Row 1, lay out 4 of Half-Block 1 and 5 of Half-Block 2, beginning with Half-Block 2 and alternating half-blocks. In same manner, lay out 5 of Half-Block 1 and 4 of Half-Block 2 for Row 12, beginning with Half-Block 1 and alternating half-blocks.

For rows 2, 4, 6, 8, and 10, lay out 5 of Block 1 and 4 of Block 2, beginning with Block 1 and alternating blocks. For rows 3, 5, 7, 9, and 11, lay out 4 of Block 1 and 5 of Block 2, beginning with Block 2 and alternating blocks.

10. When satisfied with layout of blocks, join units in each row. Return rows to layout to verify correct placement; then join rows.

11. Sew borders to quilt edges and miter border corners.

Quilting and Finishing

1. Quilt in-the-ditch or as desired.

2. See pages 16 and 17 for instructions on making binding. Make 9¼ yards of 2½"-wide bias or straight-grain binding. Apply binding to quilt edges.

Mexican Star

This lovely quilt was pieced and quilted entirely by machine. With your rotary-cutting tools and the instructions that follow, you can make your own version—without templates!

Quilt by Norma J. Snyder
Montpelier, Ohio

Finished Quilt Size
83" x 98"

Number of Blocks and Finished Size
20 blocks   11¾" x 11¾"

Fabric Requirements
Navy print   5¼ yards*
White print   3¼ yards
Blue pindot   ½ yard
Navy pindot   1 yard
Backing   6 yards
*Includes fabric for binding.

Strip Set 1—Make 2.

Strip Set 2—Make 1.

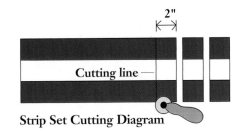

Strip Set Cutting Diagram

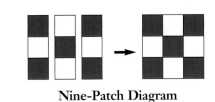

Nine-Patch Diagram

Cutting
Cut all strips cross-grain except as noted. Pieces are listed in order needed, so it's not necessary to cut everything all at once.

From navy print
- 18 (2"-wide) strips. Set aside 5 strips for strip sets. From remaining strips, cut 80 (2" x 6⅝") B rectangles.
- 6 (3½"-wide) strips. From these, cut 18 (3½" x 12½") strips and 4 (3½") squares for sashing.
- 1 (4¼") strip. From this, cut 7 (4¼") squares. Cut each square in quarters diagonally to get 28 E triangles for pieced sashing squares.
- 4 (11" x 85") lengthwise strips for borders.
- 1 (32") square for binding.

From white print
- 4 (2"-wide) strips for strip sets.
- 8 (3"-wide) strips. From these, cut 80 (3") squares. Cut each square in half diagonally to get 160 C triangles.
- 4 (6½"-wide) strips. From these, cut 20 (6½") squares. Cut each square in quarters diagonally to get 80 D triangles.
- 1 (4¼") strip. From this, cut 7 (4¼") squares. Cut each square in quarters diagonally to get 28 E triangles for pieced sashing squares.
- 11 (3½"-wide) strips. From these, cut 31 (3½" x 12¼") strips and 12 (3½") squares for sashing.

From navy pindot
- 18 (2"-wide) strips for A pieces.

From blue pindot
- 8 (2"-wide) strips for A pieces.

Quilt Top Assembly
1. For Strip Set 1, join 2 navy print strips and 1 white print strip as shown **(Strip Set 1 Diagram)**. For Strip Set 2, join 2 white print strips and 1 navy print strip as shown **(Strip Set 2 Diagram)**. Make 2 of Strip Set 1 and 1 of Strip Set 2. Press seam allowances toward navy print.

2. Cut 2"-wide segments from each strip set **(Strip Set Cutting Diagram)**. Cut 40 segments of Strip Set 1 and 20 segments of Strip Set 2.

3. Join 2 Strip Set 1 segments and 1 Strip Set 2 segment to make a nine-patch **(Nine-Patch Diagram)**. Make 20 nine-patch units.

4. With right sides facing and raw edges aligned, lay 1 blue pindot strip on top of another. Measure 4⅝" from 1 end on bottom of strip and mark **(Trapezoid A Cutting Diagram, Figure 1)**. Place top of quilter's ruler at mark and 45° angle line of ruler along bottom edge of strip **(Figure 2)**. Cut angle through both layers of fabric to get a mirror-image set of A trapezoids **(Figure 3)**. Measure 4⅝" from end on top of remaining strip and repeat steps to cut next set of A pieces **(Figure 4)**. Cut 24 mirror-image sets of trapezoids from blue pindot and 56 sets from navy pindot strips. *continued*

Trapezoid A Cutting Diagram

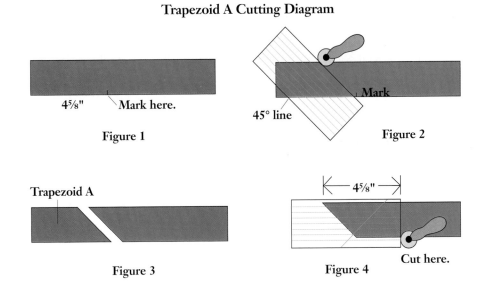

4⅝"   Mark here.

Figure 1

Mark

45° line

Figure 2

Trapezoid A

Figure 3

4⅝"

Cut here.

Figure 4

Block Assembly Diagram

Finished Block

Setting Diagram

5. For 1 block, select 1 nine-patch, 4 sets of navy or blue A pieces, 4 Bs, 8 C triangles, and 4 D triangles. Sew Cs to ends of each A piece **(Block Assembly Diagram).** Sew A/C units to both sides of each B, matching square ends of As with 1 end of B. Press seam allowances toward Bs. Trim corners of B pieces in line with C triangles.

6. Join 2 A/B/C units to opposite sides of nine-patch.

7. Sew D triangles to both sides of 2 remaining A/B/C units. Join these to center unit to complete block.

8. Make 6 Mexican Star blocks with blue pindot A pieces and 14 blocks with navy pindot A pieces.

9. For pieced sashing squares, join navy print E triangles and white print E triangles in pairs to make a larger triangle. Join 2 pairs to make a pieced square. (See pieced sashing squares in **Setting Diagram**). Make 14 navy/white pieced sashing squares.

10. Lay out blocks in 5 horizontal rows, with 4 blocks in each row as shown. (Note that blue pindot blocks are at center in rows 2, 3, and 4.) Place navy sashing strips at ends of each row and white sashing strips between blocks. Join blocks and sashing in each row. Press seam allowances toward sashing.

11. Lay out remaining sashing strips and sashing squares in 6 horizontal rows as shown. Join units in each row. Press seam allowances toward sashing strips.

12. Join rows.

13. Sew 2 border strips to quilt sides. Press seam allowances toward borders. Join remaining border strips to top and bottom edges of quilt.

Quilting and Finishing

1. Outline-quilt or quilt as desired.

2. See pages 16 and 17 for instructions on making binding. Make 10⅜ yards of 2½"-wide bias or straight-grain binding. Apply binding to quilt edges.

Mountain Rose

Few sights are as lovely as wild mountain roses covering a hillside. This delightful vision might have inspired a pioneer quilter to design this lovely appliqué pattern.

*Quilt from The Antique Quilt Source
Carlisle, Pennsylvania*

Finished Quilt Size
74½" x 74½"

Number of Blocks and Finished Size
25 blocks   9" x 9"

Fabric Requirements
Muslin   5 yards
Light pink   1 yard
Dark pink   ¾ yard
Green   1 yard
Binding fabric   ⅞ yard
Backing   4⅜ yards

Cutting
Make templates of appliqué patterns A, B, C, and D. Cut all strips cross-grain except as noted.
From muslin
- 4 (6" x 80") strips for borders.
- 49 (9½") squares.

From light pink
- 5 (7"-wide) strips. From these, cut 25 of Template B.

From dark pink
- 7 (3¼"-wide) strips. From these, cut 25 of Template A and 100 of Template D.

From green
- 16 (2"-wide) strips. From these, cut 100 of Template C and 100 of Template C reversed.

Quilt Top Assembly
1. Fold 1 muslin square in quarters horizontally, vertically, and diagonally, finger-pressing creases to make placement guidelines.

2. For each block, select 4 each of C, C reversed, and D, and 1 each of A and B. Center B on muslin square; then position other pieces as shown (**Appliqué Placement Diagram**). Be sure D pieces are aligned with diagonal placement guidelines.

3. Appliqué Ds and Cs in place; then stitch B and A.

4. Appliqué 25 blocks.

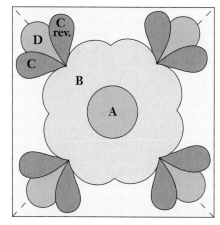

Appliqué Placement Diagram

5. Lay out blocks and setting squares in 7 horizontal rows, with 7 blocks and squares in each row (**Setting Diagram**). Alternate Mountain Rose blocks with setting squares as shown.

6. When satisfied with layout, join blocks and setting squares in each row. Press seam allowances toward setting squares. Join rows.

7. See page 14 for instructions on stitching mitered border corners. Mark centers on edges of each border strip and on each edge of quilt. Matching centers of borders and quilt top, sew 1 border strip to each edge. Miter border corners.

Quilting and Finishing
1. Quilt as desired. On quilt shown, appliqué pieces are outline-quilted, and concentric circles are quilted in B pieced about 1" apart. Appliqué design is repeated in quilting in setting squares.

2. See pages 16 and 17 for instructions on making binding. Make 8½ yards of 2½"-wide bias or straight-grain binding. Apply binding to quilt edges.

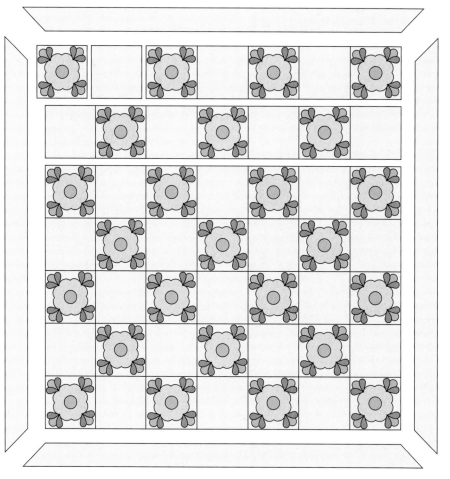

Setting Diagram

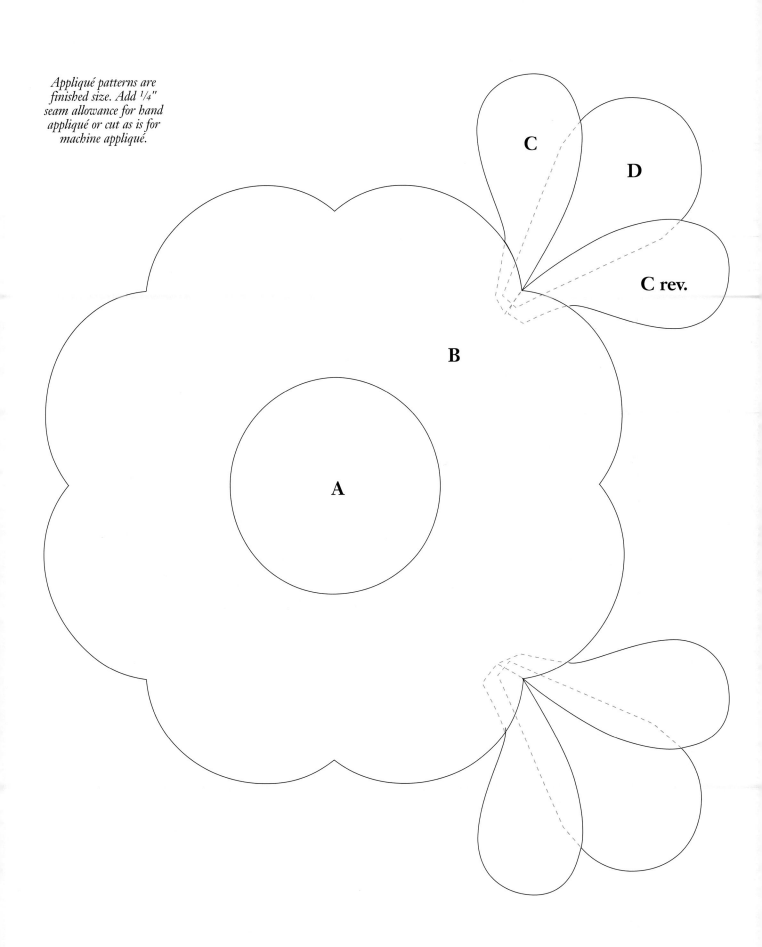

Appliqué patterns are finished size. Add ¼" seam allowance for hand appliqué or cut as is for machine appliqué.

C

D

C rev.

B

A

Oak Leaf

After a lifetime of sewing, Ethel Hickman became passionate about quiltmaking, especially handwork like appliqué and hand quilting. Her exceptional quilts have won numerous awards, and one is in the permanent collection of the American Quilter's Society Museum in Paducah, Kentucky. *Oak Leaf* is one of Ethel's favorite blue-ribbon winners. The classic blocks are framed by an inner border of sawtooth triangles and an outer border elegantly appliquéd in a swag-and-tassel design.

Quilt by Ethel Hickman
Camden, Arkansas

Finished Quilt Size
85" x 103"

Number of Blocks and Finished Size
12 blocks   18" x 18"

Fabric Requirements
Muslin	8½ yards
Green	2½ yards
Red	2¼ yards
Binding fabric	1 yard
Backing	2⅝ yards 120" wide

Cutting
Make templates of patterns A–E on pages 225 and 226. Cut pieces in order listed to get best use of yardage. Cut all strips cross-grain except as noted.

From muslin
- 2 (112") lengths. From 1 length, cut 1 (14" x 110") and 2 (14" x 93") lengthwise border strips. From second length, cut 1 (14" x 110") lengthwise border strip and 6 (18½") squares for blocks. Use remaining strip for next cut.
- 3 (18½"-wide) strips. From these, cut 6 (18½") squares.
- 8 (8" x 14") pieces for border quick-pieced triangle-squares.

From green
- 4 (10½"-wide) strips. From these, cut 28 of Template E.
- 8 (5"-wide) strips. From these, cut 48 of Template C.

From red
- 2 (5½"-wide) strips. From these, cut 12 of Template A.
- 6 (3"-wide) strips. From these, cut 48 of Template B.
- 5 (3½"-wide) strips. From these, cut 28 of Template D.
- 3 (8"-wide) strips. From these, cut 8 (8" x 14") pieces for quick-pieced triangle-squares.

Quilt Top Assembly
1. Fold 1 muslin square in half diagonally and crease folds to make placement guidelines.
2. Center an A piece on square, aligning arms of A with guidelines

Oak Leaf Block Diagram

(Oak Leaf Block Diagram). Position 4 B pieces around A. Finally, place 4 C pieces, aligned with placement lines. Appliqué A and Cs; then stitch Bs last.

3. Appliqué 12 Oak Leaf blocks.
4. Lay out blocks in 4 horizontal rows, with 3 blocks in each row **(Setting Diagram).** Join blocks in each row; then join rows.
5. See page 11 for tips on sewing quick-pieced triangle-squares. On wrong side of each 8" x 14" muslin piece, mark a 2- x 4-square grid of 2⅞" squares **(Diagram 1).** Draw diagonal lines through squares as shown.
6. Match 1 muslin piece to a red piece, right sides facing. Machine-stitch ¼" from each side of all *diagonal* lines **(Diagram 2).** Cut on *all* grid lines to get 16 triangle-squares. Repeat with remaining 8" x 14" pieces to get a total of 128 (2½") red/muslin triangle-squares. Press seam allowances toward red.

Setting Diagram

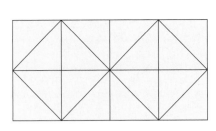

Diagram 1

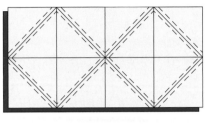

Diagram 2

7. From scrap, cut 1 (2⅞") each from red and muslin. Cut each square in half diagonally to get 2 triangles of each color. Join red and muslin triangles in pairs to get 2 more red/muslin triangle-squares, for a total of 130.

8. Join 36 triangle-squares in a vertical row for each side border. Join borders to quilt sides, easing to fit as needed.

9. Join 29 triangle-squares in a horizontal row, turning units at row ends as shown **(Setting Diagram).** Sew borders to top and bottom edges of quilt.

10. Sew muslin borders to quilt edges, mitering corners.

11. Place 1 D tassel on each mitered seam. Space 7 Ds and 8 Es on each side border and 5 Ds and 6 Es along top and bottom borders, with bottom of Ds about 5½" from raw edge of border (see photo on page 222). When satisfied with placement, appliqué pieces in place, stitching Ds over ends of Es where they meet.

Quilting and Finishing

1. Outline-quilt appliqué pieces and sawtooth triangles or quilt as desired.

2. See pages 16 and 17 for instructions on making binding. Make 8½ yards of 2½"-wide bias or straight-grain binding. Apply binding to quilt edges.

Appliqué patterns are finished size. Add ¼" seam allowance for hand appliqué or cut as is for machine appliqué.

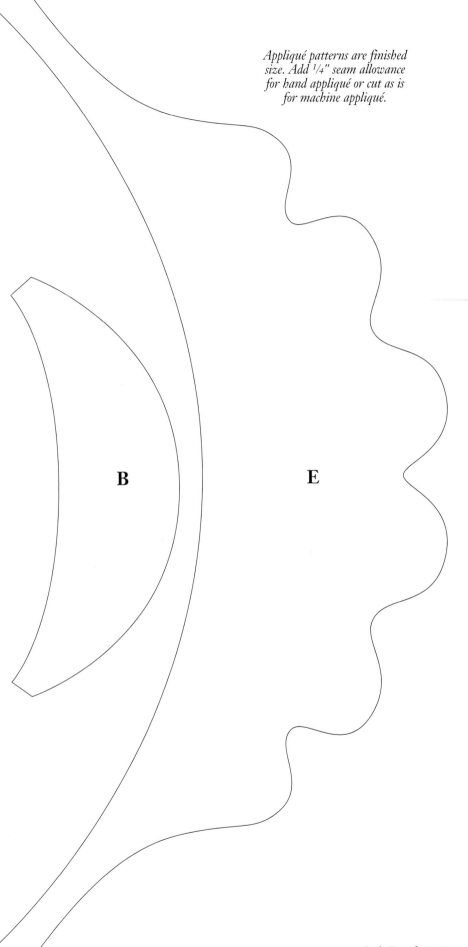

B

E

Oak Leaf 225

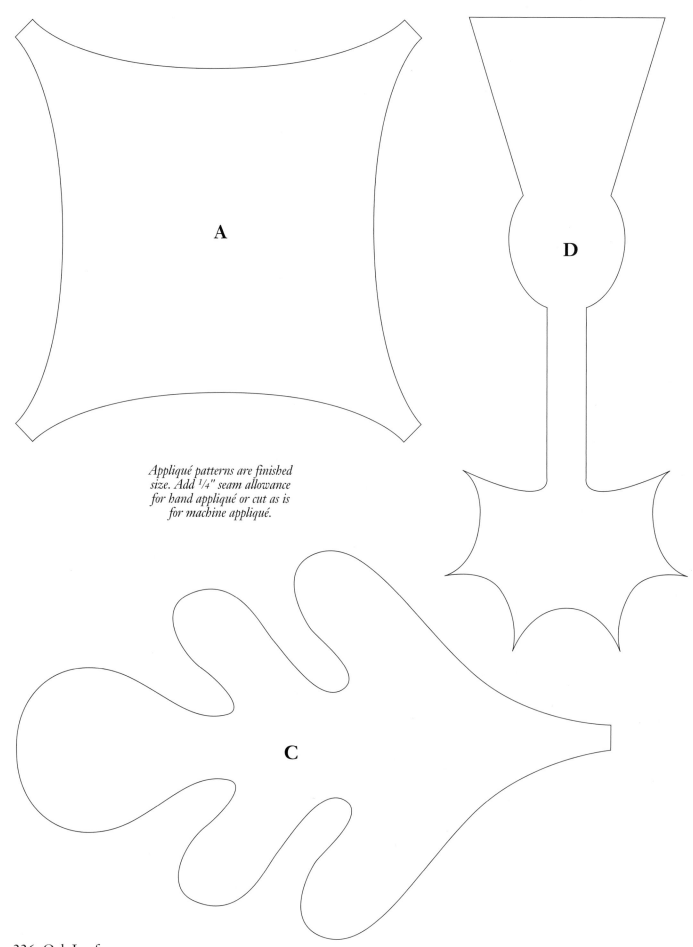

A

D

Appliqué patterns are finished size. Add ¼" seam allowance for hand appliqué or cut as is for machine appliqué.

C

Ocean Waves

This scrappy design is a favorite of traditional Amish quilters, who are famous for their use of bold solid colors, often set against black. Today's quick-piecing techniques make this a fast and fun project to make.

Quilt by the Narrows Connection Quiltmakers
Gig Harbor and Tacoma, Washington

Finished Quilt Size
75½" x 95½"

Number of Blocks and Finished Size
18 blocks   14" x 14"

Fabric Requirements
Assorted solids   15 fat quarters*
Black   2¾ yards
Blue   ⅝ yard**
Binding fabric   1 yard
Backing   5¾ yards

*Fat quarter = 18" x 22". Include a few polished cottons for a little sparkle.
**Yardage is for borders cut cross-grain and pieced. If you prefer to cut inner borders lengthwise, you will need 2½ yards.

Cutting
Cut all strips cross-grain except as noted. All pieces can be rotary cut, so templates are not needed. Pieces are listed in order needed, so it's not necessary to cut everything all at once.

From fat quarters
- 58 (4¼" x 22") strips. From these, cut 288 (4¼") squares. Cut each square in quarters diagonally to get 1,152 A triangles.

From black
- 2 (6½" x 82") and 2 (6½" x 102") lengthwise border strips.
- 2 (7½" x 16") strips. From these, cut 18 (7½") B squares.
- 3 (11⅛") squares. Cut each square in quarters diagonally to get 10 C triangles (and 2 extra).
- 2 (5⅞") squares. Cut each square in half diagonally to get 4 D triangles.

From blue
- 8 (2½"-wide) strips for inner border.

Quilt Top Assembly
1. Join 2 A triangles of different colors to make a triangle-square. Make 288 triangle-squares.

Setting Diagram

2. Sew 2 A triangles to adjacent sides of each triangle-square to make 288 larger triangle units **(Block Assembly Diagram)**.

3. Select 12 units for each block. Sew 1 unit to each side of B square. Press seam allowances toward B.

4. Join remaining triangle units in pairs to get 4 larger triangles. Join large triangles to center unit as shown to complete block. Make 18 blocks.

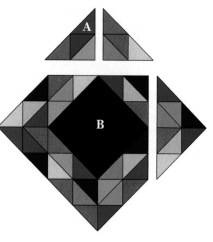

Block Assembly Diagram

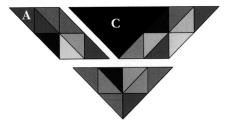

Half-Block Assembly Diagram

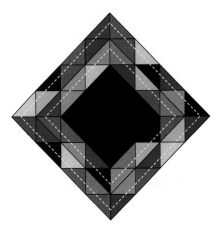

Corner Block Assembly Diagram

5. For each half-block, select 6 triangle units and 1 C triangle. Join triangle units in pairs **(Half-Block Assembly Diagram).** Sew 1 pair to each leg of C triangle. Press seam allowances toward C. Then join remaining triangle unit as shown to complete half-block. Make 10 half-blocks.

6. For each corner block, select 3 triangle units and 1 D triangle. Join triangle units in a row as shown **(Corner Block Assembly Diagram).** Sew D triangle to center unit in row to make 1 corner block. Make 4 corner blocks.

7. Lay out blocks in 6 diagonal rows as shown **(Setting Diagram).** Add half-blocks and corner blocks to ends of each row as shown. Join units in each row; then join rows. Add remaining corner blocks to complete piecing.

8. Trim 4 blue border strips to 36" long. Join trimmed strips in pairs to get 2 (71"-long) borders. Join remaining pairs and 7"-long trimmed pieces to get 2 (92"-long) borders.

9. Mark centers on edges of each blue and black border strip. Matching centers, join 92"-long blue borders to 102"-long black border strips. Join remaining border strips in same manner, matching centers.

10. See page 14 for instructions on mitering border corners. Mark

centers on each edge of quilt. Matching centers of borders and quilt top, sew shorter borders to top and bottom edges and longer borders to quilt sides. See page 14 for instructions on mitering border corners.

Quilting and Finishing

1. Quilt block centers as desired. Quilt triangles as shown **(Block Quilting Diagram).** Quilt block centers and borders as desired.

2. See pages 16 and 17 for instructions on making binding. Make 10 yards of 2½"-wide bias or straight-grain binding. Apply binding to quilt edges.

Block Quilting Diagram

Ohio Rose

The design of this lovely quilt is a variation of a pattern that was printed on the packaging of Mountain Mist batting purchased by Ruth Ann Hatfield's mother, Beatrice Pelter Dean, in 1939. Beatrice never completed the project, however. Ruth Ann took a quilting class in 1989 so she could finish the quilt her mother had started 50 years earlier.

Quilt by Ruth Ann Dean Hatfield
South Charleston, West Virginia

Finished Quilt Size
64" x 81"

Number of Blocks and Finished Size
12 blocks   17" x 17"

Fabric Requirements
Muslin   3½ yards
Rose   2¼ yards
Pink   ¾ yard
Green   3⅜ yards*
Backing   4 yards
*Includes fabric for binding.

Cutting
Make templates of appliqué patterns A–E on page 232. Cut all strips cross-grain except as noted.

From muslin
- 4 (1¼" x 78") lengthwise strips for middle border.
- 12 (17½") squares.

From rose
- 2 (3½" x 72") and 2 (3½" x 60") lengthwise strips for inner border.
- 48 of Template D.
- 48 of Template A.

From pink
- 7 (3½"-wide) strips. From these, cut 48 of Template C and 12 of Template E.

From green
- 2 (3" x 80") and 2 (3" x 68") lengthwise strips for outer border.
- 1 (31") square for bias binding.
- 48 of Template B.

Quilt Top Assembly
1. Fold 1 muslin square in half diagonally, finger-pressing creases to make placement guidelines.
2. For each block, select 1 E and 4 each of A, B, C, and D. Center E on muslin square; then pin other pieces in place as shown (**Placement Diagram**). Be sure As, Bs, Cs, and Ds are aligned with diagonal placement lines.
3. Appliqué pieces to square in alphabetical order.
4. Appliqué 12 blocks.

5. Lay out blocks in 4 horizontal rows, with 3 blocks in each row. Join blocks in rows; then join rows.
6. Join longer rose borders to quilt sides, easing to fit as needed.

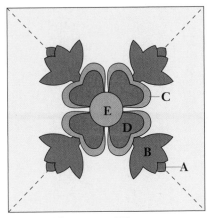

Placement Diagram

Join remaining rose borders to top and bottom edges of quilt. Press seam allowances toward borders.
7. Join muslin and green borders to quilt in same manner, adding borders to sides first and then to top and bottom edges.

Quilting and Finishing
1. Outline-quilt appliqué and muslin border. Quilt Rose Leaf quilting pattern (page 232) in rose and green borders. Quilt remainder of quilt with a 1" diagonal cross-hatch grid.
2. See pages 16 and 17 for instructions on making binding. Make 8⅜ yards of 2½"-wide bias or straight-grain binding. Apply binding to quilt edges.

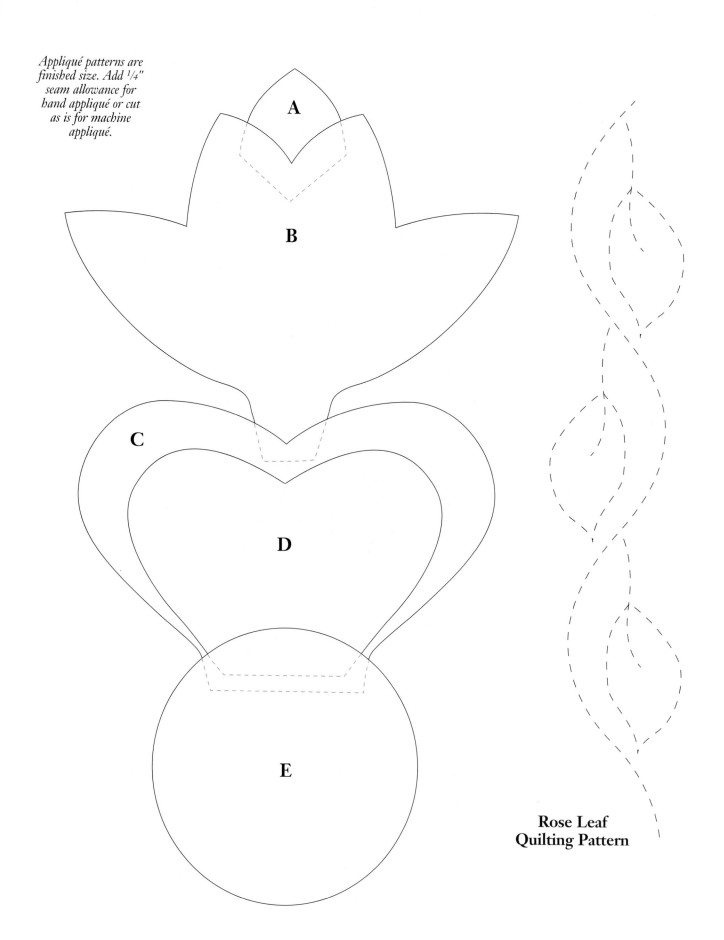

Appliqué patterns are finished size. Add ¼" seam allowance for hand appliqué or cut as is for machine appliqué.

A

B

C

D

E

**Rose Leaf
Quilting Pattern**

Oklahoma Dogwood

Pauline Bryant enjoyed the challenge of hand-piecing the tiny pieces in each of these blocks. Pauline's brother insisted that she enter the quilt in the 1992 Oklahoma State Fair. Even though he was ill at the time, he drove 140 miles to Oklahoma City to see his sister's quilt win the blue ribbon for Best of Show.

Quilt by Pauline Bryant
McAlester, Oklahoma

Finished Quilt Size
85" x 95"

Number of Blocks and Finished Size
4 Block As   14" x 14"
11 Block Bs   7½" x 7½"

Fabric Requirements
Pink   5¾ yards
Mauve   2½ yards
Burgundy   3½ yards*
Backing   2⅝ yards 104" wide
*Includes fabric for binding.

Cutting
Make a templates of patterns B–G on page 236 (pieces A and H are rotary cut without templates). Cut all strips cross-grain except as noted. Cut pieces in order listed to get best use of yardage.

From pink
- 1 (95") length. From this, cut 2 (3¼" x 95") and 2 (3¼" x 85") lengthwise border strips. Use remainder for next 3 cuts.
- 6 (8" x 30") strips. From these, cut 12 (8" x 14½") sashing strips.
- 5 (4" x 30") strips. From these, cut 32 of Template F.
- 5 (3⅜" x 30") strips. From these, cut 44 of Template G.
- 2 (31¼") squares. Cut each square in half diagonally to get 4 corner triangles. From scrap, cut 1 (11⅞") square. Cut this square in quarters diagonally to get 2 side triangles (and 2 extra).
- 9 (3⅜"-wide) strips. From these and remaining scraps, cut 136 (3⅜") squares. Cut each square in half diagonally to get 272 H triangles.

From mauve
- 2 (2¾" x 78") and 2 (2¾" x 88") lengthwise border strips.
- 28 (2¼" x 33") strips. From these, cut 304 (2¼") squares. Set aside 244 squares for A. From remainder, cut 60 of Template B.
- 160 of Template D.

From burgundy
- 2 (2½" x 72") and 2 (2¾" x 83") lengthwise border strips.
- 28 (2¼" x 33") strips. From these, cut 304 (2¼") squares. Set aside 244 squares for A. From remainder, cut 60 of Template B.

- 10 (1¼" x 33") strips. From these, cut 128 of Template E.
- 5 (1" x 33") strips. From these, cut 32 of Template C and 32 of Template C reversed.
- 1 (32") square for binding.

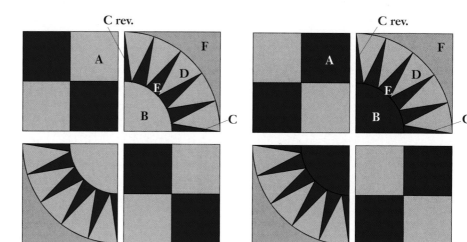

Unit 1—Make 8.   Unit 2—Make 8.

Unit Assembly Diagrams

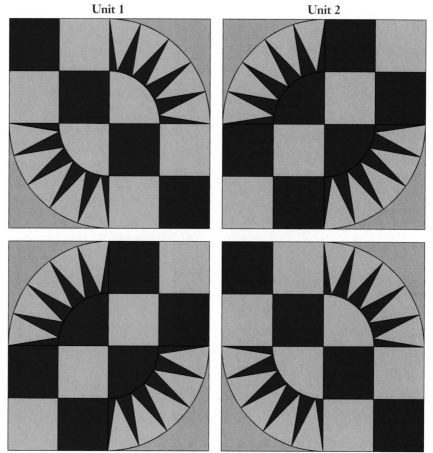

Block A Assembly Diagram

234   Oklahoma Dogwood

Quilt Top Assembly

1. Join mauve and burgundy A squares in 222 pairs. (Save remaining 44 A squares for B blocks.) Press all seam allowances toward burgundy. Then join 2 segments to make each of 111 four-patch units. Set aside 68 units for border, 32 for Block A and 11 for Block B.

2. For Unit 1, select 2 mauve Bs, 2 Cs, 2 Cs rev., 10 Ds, 8 Es, and 2 Fs. For each quarter-block section, join C, 4 Es, 5 Ds, and C rev. in a row **(Unit Assembly Diagrams, Unit 1).** Press seam allowances toward Ds. Sew B and F to opposite sides of each arc. Join a four-patch unit to 1 side of each arc unit as shown; then join rows to complete Unit 1. Make 8 of Unit 1.

3. Make Unit 2 in same manner, this time using burgundy Bs **(Unit Assembly Diagram, Unit 2).** Make 8 of Unit 2.

4. For Block A, join 2 of Unit 1 and 2 of Unit 2 as shown **(Block Assembly Diagram).** Make 4 of Block A. *continued*

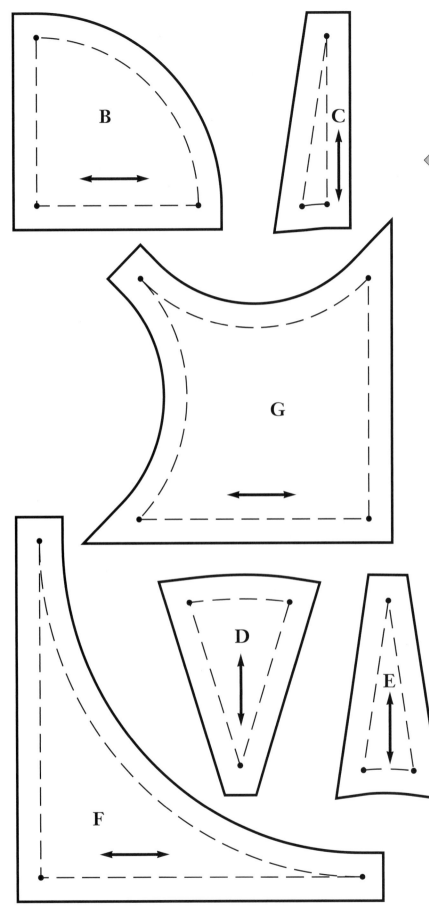

Block B Assembly Diagram

5. For each Block B, select 1 four-patch unit, 2 mauve A squares, 2 burgundy A squares, 4 mauve Bs, 4 burgundy Bs, and 4 Gs. Sew a B of each color to each G (**Block B Assembly Diagram).** Join 2 of these units to opposite sides of four-patch. Sew A squares to ends of remaining G units and add these to remaining sides of four-patch to complete block. Unstitched edges of corner A squares will be appliquéd onto quilt top later. Make 11 of Block B.

6. Lay out 4 of Block A in 2 rows, with sashing strips between blocks and at row ends (**Setting Diagram).** Be sure blocks are positioned as shown. Join blocks and sashing in each row. Press seam allowances toward sashing.

7. Join 7 of Block B, remaining sashing, and side triangles in sashing rows as shown. Pin loose corners of Block B away from seams. Join block rows and sashing rows to complete center medallion.

8. Sew corner triangles to center medallion. Appliqué loose corners of B blocks onto sashing and corner triangles.

9. Position remaining B blocks on corner triangles at edge of quilt top, aligning A squares with those in center medallion. Appliqué B blocks in place on corner triangles.

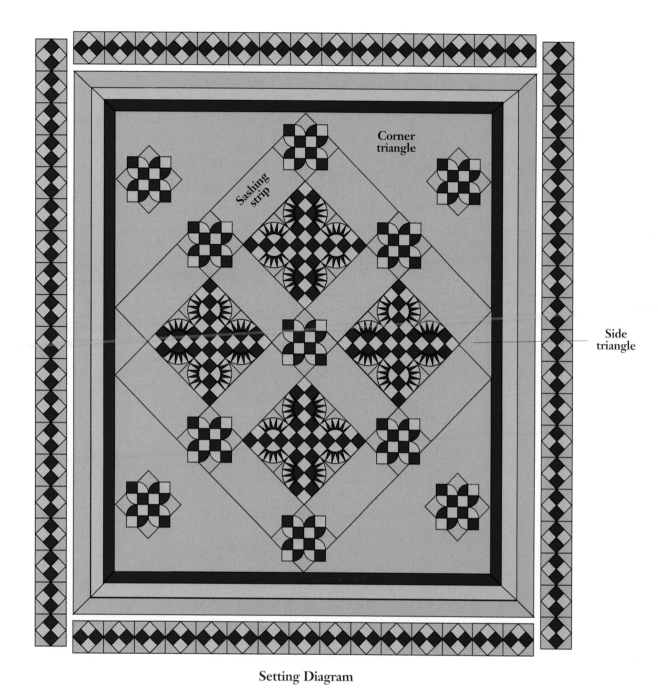

Setting Diagram

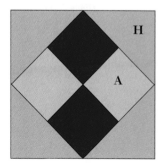

Border Block Assembly Diagram

10. Mark centers on each border strip. Matching centers, join 3 long border strips (1 of each color) to make a single border unit for each quilt side. Matching centers of borders and quilt edges, join border units to quilt sides. Repeat for top and bottom borders. See page 14 for tips on mitering border corners.

11. Sew H triangles to sides of 68 remaining four-patches **(Border Block Assembly Diagram)**.

12. Join 15 border blocks in each horizontal row for top and bottom border. Be sure to position blocks as shown **(Setting Diagram)**. Sew borders to quilt edges, easing to fit as needed. Join 19 blocks in each vertical row for side borders. Join pieced borders to quilt sides.

Quilting and Finishing

1. Outline-quilt pieces in blocks and border blocks. Quilt 1" cross-hatch pattern in corner triangles. Quilt borders and sashing strips as desired.

2. See pages 16 and 17 for instructions on making binding. Make 10¼ yards of 2½"-wide bias or straight-grain binding. Apply binding to quilt edges.

Oklahoma Dogwood 237

Overall Sam

Overall Sam, Sue's shy friend, is also known as Overall Andy and Suspender Sam. Like his pal Fisherman Fred on page 109, Overall Sam is often used for little boys' quilts.

Quilt by Ginger Kean Berk
Ambler, Pennsylvania

Finished Quilt Size
55" x 76"

Number of Blocks and Finished Size
12 blocks   10" x 12"

Fabric Requirements
Solid-colored scraps	12 (6" x 11")
Ginghams	6 (¼-yard) pieces
White	1¼ yards
Blue	2¼ yards
Backing	3½ yards

Other Materials
Scraps of yarn for tying (optional)
Black embroidery floss (optional)

Cutting
Make templates of patterns A, B, C and D on page 240. Cut all strips cross-grain except as noted.

From each *scrap*
- 1 of Template B (overall/hat).

From each *gingham*
- 2 (3½"-wide) strips. From these, cut 15 (2½" x 3½") pieces for pieced binding (a total of 90) and 13 (1½" x 3½") strips for pieced border (a total of 72 and 6 extra).
- 2 of Template A (shirt).
- 2 of Template C (pocket).
- 2 of Template D (hatband).

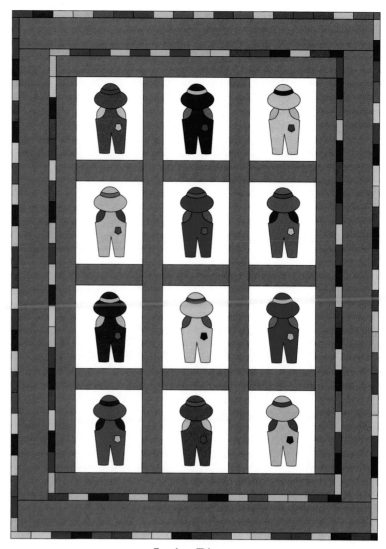

Setting Diagram

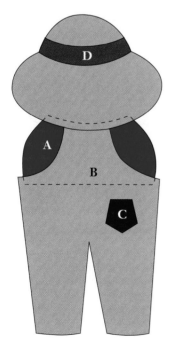

Appliqué Placement Diagram

From white
- 12 (10½" x 12½") rectangles.

From blue
- 2 (5¾" x 68") and 2 (5¾" x 58") lengthwise border strips.
- 4 (3½" x 60") lengthwise sashing strips.
- 2 (3½" x 53") lengthwise strips. From these, cut 9 (3½" x 10½") sashing strips.
- 2 (3½"-wide) strips for cross-wise sashing.

Quilt Top Assembly
1. Fold a white rectangle in half vertically and horizontally, finger-pressing creases to make appliqué placement guidelines.

2. For each block, select 1 B piece and 1 coordinating set of A, C, and D. Center B piece on block; then pin remaining pieces in place, slipping A piece under B as shown **(Appliqué Placement Diagram).** When satisfied with placement, appliqué pieces in place in alphabetical order. Appliqué 12 blocks.

3. Quilt shown is machine appliquéd, so hat detail is accomplished by machine satin stitch. If your blocks are appliquéd traditionally, use black embroidery floss to work a line between hat and overalls in satin stitch or backstitch. (See page 136 for stitch diagrams.)

4. Lay out blocks in 3 vertical rows with 4 blocks in each row and 10½"-long sashing strips between blocks **(Setting Diagram).** Join blocks and strips in each row. Press seam allowances toward sashing.

continued

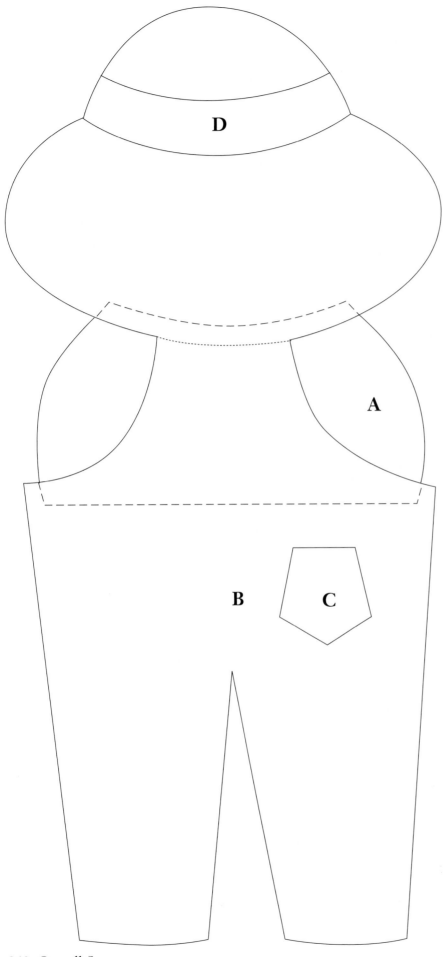

5. Lay out rows with 60"-long sashing strips between rows and at outside edges. Join sashing strips and rows. Trim excess length from sashing strips as needed. Sew 44"-long strips to top and bottom edges of quilt. Press seam allowances toward sashing.

6. To make each pieced side border, join 21 (1½" x 3½") gingham strips end-to-end. Join pieced strips to sides of quilt, easing to fit as needed. Press seam allowances toward blue borders. In same manner, join 15 gingham strips each for top and bottom borders. Join borders to top and bottom edges of quilt, easing to fit.

7. Sew 68"-long blue borders to quilt sides. Press seam allowances toward blue borders. Join 58" blue borders to top and bottom edges of quilt and press.

Quilting and Finishing

1. Outline-quilt appliqué pieces, blocks, and borders, or quilt as desired. Quilt shown has yarn bows tied at intersections of sashing strips. Tie bows if desired.

2. See pages 16 and 17 for instructions on making binding. Join 2½" x 3½" gingham strips end-to-end to make 7½ yards of straight-grain binding. Apply binding to quilt edges.

Appliqué patterns are finished size. Add ¼" seam allowance for hand appliqué or cut as is for machine appliqué.

Pennsylvania Tulip

Pretty pink tulips rise gracefully from pieced baskets in this beautiful quilt, which was pieced in 1932. Lovingly tucked away for many years, the top was quilted 47 years later, making it a classic example of the timeless appeal of patchwork baskets.

Quilt by Jessie M. Krueger
Owned by her daughter, Chrystal Sinn
Minier, Illinois

Finished Quilt Size
74" x 89½"

Number of Blocks and Finished Size
20 blocks   11" x 11"

Fabric Requirements
Muslin   6⅜ yards*
Green   1¼ yards
Pink   ¾ yard
Rose   ¾ yard
Backing   5½ yards
*Includes fabric for binding.

Cutting
Make templates of patterns A–H on page 244. (Templates are recommended for odd-sized squares and triangles.) Cut all strips cross-grain except as noted. Cut pieces in order listed for best use of yardage.

From muslin
- 2 (6½" x 78") and 2 (6½" x 94") lengthwise strips for border. (Use leftover strip for next 3 cuts.)
- 4 (16¾") squares. Cut each square in quarters diagonally to get 14 Y triangles (and 2 extra).
- 80 of Template B.
- 20 (1⅞") N squares.
- 3 (4⅝"-wide) strips. From these, cut 20 (4⅝") squares. Cut each square in half diagonally to get 40 L triangles.
- 3 (2½"-wide) strips. From these, cut 40 of Template C.
- 1 (2¼"-wide) strip. From this, cut 20 (2¼") squares. Cut each square in half diagonally to get 40 D triangles.
- 2 (4¼"-wide) strips. From these, cut 20 of Template E.
- 1 (8"-wide) strip. From this and scrap from previous cuts, cut 40 (2¼" x 8") K pieces.
- 10 (4⅜") squares. Cut each square in half diagonally to get 20 F triangles.
- 1 (30") square for binding. Use leftover strip to cut 2 (8⅝") squares; cut each square in half diagonally to get 4 Z triangles.
- 4 (11½"-wide) strips. From these, cut 12 (11½") X squares.

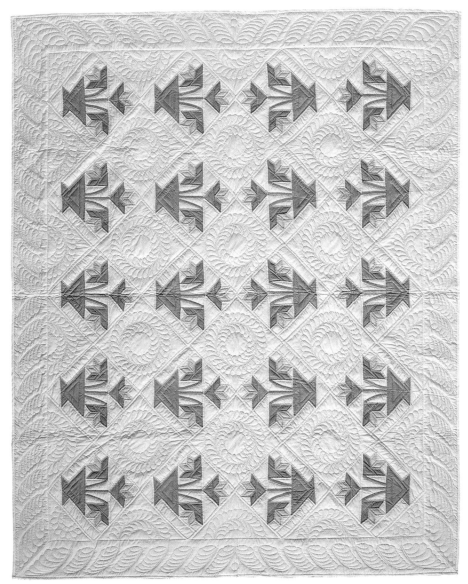

From green
- 2 (6½"-wide) strips. From these, cut 20 of Template G.
- 5 (1½"-wide) strips. From these, cut 20 of Template H and 20 of Template H reversed.
- 1 (4¼"-wide) strip. From this, cut 20 (⅞" x 4¼") J strips.
- 3 (4¼"-wide) strips. From these, cut 30 (4¼") squares. Cut each square in half diagonally to get 60 M triangles.
- 2 (2⅝"-wide) strips. From these, cut 20 (2⅝") squares. Cut each square in half diagonally to get 40 O triangles.

From pink
- 4 (2½"-wide) strips. From these, cut 60 of Template A.
- 4 (2½"-wide) strips. From these, cut 60 of Template A reversed.

From rose
- 4 (2½"-wide) strips. From these, cut 60 of Template A.
- 4 (2½"-wide) strips. From these, cut 60 of Template A reversed.

Quilt Top Assembly

1. For each tulip, select 2 pink As, 2 rose As, and 1 green M.

2. Join pink and rose As **(Block Assembly Diagram 1).** Sew M triangle to base of A tulip. Make 60 tulips, 3 for each block.

3. Select 1 tulip for Unit 1. Set in 2 B triangles and 1 N square **(Block Assembly Diagram 1).** (See page 10 for tips on sewing a set-in seam.) Add L triangles to sides to complete unit.

4. Select 2 tulips for Unit 2. Set in B and D triangles as shown; then add 1 C square.

Turn under seam allowances on side edges of J, H, and H reversed to get 3 stems approximately 5/16" wide. Appliqué stems to 1 E rectangle. Sew tulips to sides of E to complete Unit 2.

5. Join units 1 and 2. Add G triangle to bottom as shown.

6. Join 1 O triangle to each of 2 K rectangles **(Block Assembly Diagram 2).** Join these to block sides as shown. Add 1 F triangle to bottom to complete block.

7. Make 20 blocks.

8. Lay out basket blocks and X squares in diagonal rows, turning blocks as shown **(Setting Diagram).** Add Y and Z triangles to row ends as shown.

9. Join pieces in each row. Press seam allowances toward setting squares and triangles. Join rows.

10. Sew border strips to all quilt sides. Miter corners.

Quilting and Finishing

1. Quilt shown has feathered wreaths quilted in setting squares and triangles—use an 8" or 9"-diameter wreath stencil to mark quilting design. Mark border quilting designs as desired. Outline-quilt basket blocks; then quilt marked designs.

2. See pages 16 and 17 for instructions on making binding. Make 9¼ yards of 2½"-wide bias or straight-grain binding from reserved muslin. Apply binding to quilt edges.

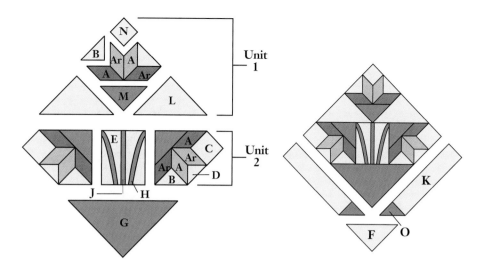

Block Assembly Diagram 1   **Block Assembly Diagram 2**

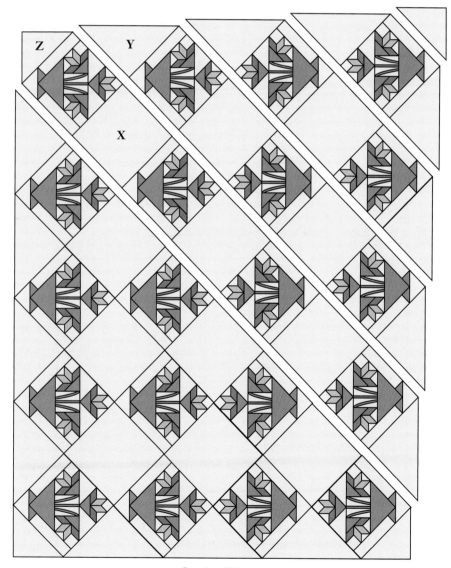

Setting Diagram

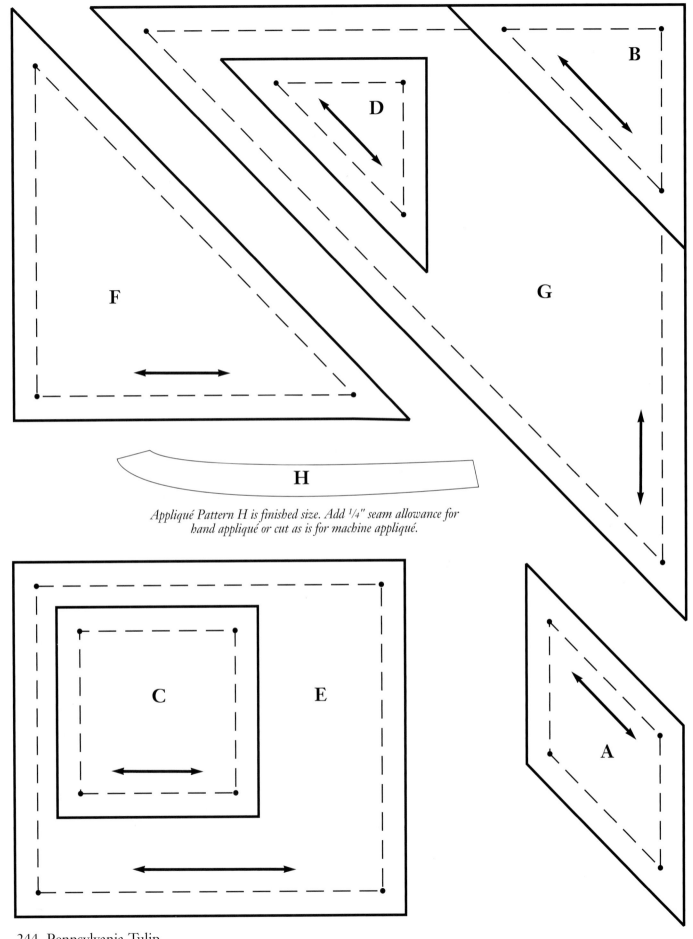

B

D

F

G

Appliqué Pattern H is finished size. Add ¹/₄" seam allowance for
hand appliqué or cut as is for machine appliqué.

H

C

E

A

Peony

Whether you call them peonies, starflowers, lilies, or poinsettias, the pieced flowers in this quilt block continue to charm quilters. Through the years, the stems and leaves have been twisted and turned, straightened, and pruned to create a multitude of variations. Yet, with each twist and turn, the flowers maintain their radiant appeal.

Quilt by Susan Craig Campbell
Flint, Texas

Finished Quilt Size
85" x 102"

Number of Blocks and Finished Size
20 blocks   12" x 12"

Fabric Requirements
Green	1½ yards*
Red print	2¼ yards*
Muslin or white	5¾ yards
Red	3 yards
Backing	2⅝ yards 120" wide

* Includes fabric for bias binding.

Other Materials
½"-wide bias pressing bar

Cutting
Make templates of patterns A and F. (Remaining pieces can be rotary cut.) Cut strips cross-grain except as noted. Cut pieces in order listed for best use of yardage.

From green
- 3 (7¾"-wide) strips for bias vines.
- 8 (1¾"-wide) strips. From these, cut 120 of Template A.
- 20 (2½") E squares.
- 20 *each* of Template F and Template F reversed.

From red print
- 23 (1¾"-wide) strips. From these, cut 360 of Template A.

From muslin
- 1 (2¾-yard) length. From this, cut 4 (3"x 99") lengthwise strips for middle border. Use remainder for next 3 cuts.
- 4 (18¼") squares. Cut each square in quarters diagonally to get 14 side triangles (and 2 extra).

Flower Piecing Diagram

246 Peony

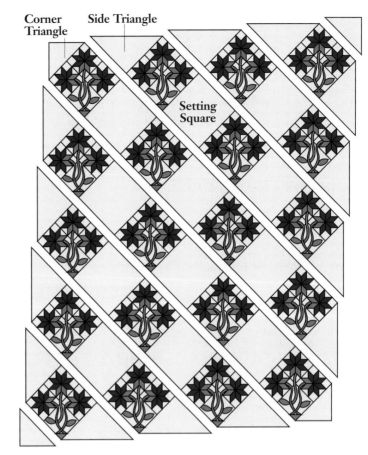

Quilt Top Assembly Diagram

- 20 (6½") D squares.
- 2 (9½") squares. Cut each square in half diagonally to get 4 corner triangles.
- 4 (12"-wide) strips. From these, cut 12 (12") setting squares.
- 13 (2¼"-wide) strips. From these, cut 240 (2¼") B squares.
- 120 (2⅝") squares. Cut each square in half diagonally to get 240 C triangles.

From red
- 4 (2½" x 95") lengthwise strips for inner border.
- 4 (4¼" x 108") lengthwise strips for outer border.

Quilt Top Assembly
1. See page 10 for tips on sewing set-in seams. For 1 flower, join 6 red print As and 2 green As **(Flower Piecing Diagram)**. Be careful not to stitch into seam allowances. Press seam allowances open.

2. Set Bs and Cs between diamonds, leaving a part of 1 seam

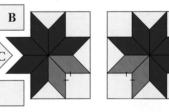

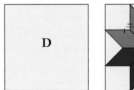

Leave seams open for stem.

Block Piecing Diagram

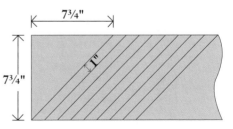

Bias Cutting Diagram

Appliqué Placement Diagram

Quilting and Finishing

1. Outline-quilt petals, stems, and leaves. Quilt setting squares, triangles, and borders as desired.

2. See pages 16 and 17 for instructions on making binding. Make 10⅝ yards of 2½"-wide bias or straight-grain binding from remaining red print. Apply binding to quilt edges.

unstitched for insertion of stem **(Block Piecing Diagram).** Make 3 flower squares.

3. Join 3 flower squares and 1 D as shown. (E will be added later.)

4. On 1 corner of each 7¾"-wide green strip, measure and cut a 7¾" triangle **(Bias Cutting Diagram).** Measuring from cut edge, cut 1"-wide bias strips. Cut 40 (10"-long) and 20 (8"-long) bias stems. Press edges of bias strips over pressing bar.

5. Lightly trace Stem Guide on each block, flipping guide to trace third stem **(Appliqué Placement Diagram).** Appliqué 2 leaves (1 F and 1 F reversed). Align stem pieces with traced outlines and appliqué, inserting ends through unstitched openings in seam lines. Stitch seams closed, catching stems.

6. See page 12 for instructions on diagonal-corner quick-piecing technique. Following those instructions, sew E square to corner of D, catching ends of stems in seam.

7. Make 20 blocks.

8. Lay out blocks, side triangles, setting squares, and corner triangles in diagonal rows as shown **(Quilt Top Assembly Diagram).** When satisfied with layout, join units in each row. Press seam allowances toward setting pieces. Join rows.

9. Mark center of each border strip. Matching centers, join 1 of each border to make a 3-strip border unit. Sew borders to edges of quilt and miter corners.

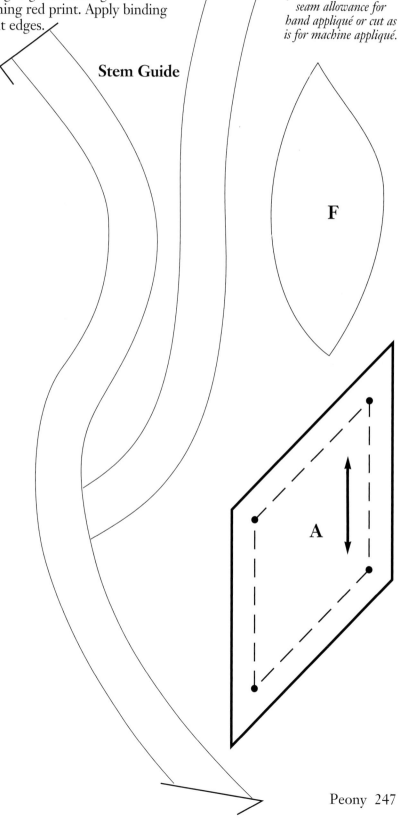

Appliqué Pattern F is finished size. Add ¼" seam allowance for hand appliqué or cut as is for machine appliqué.

Stem Guide

F

A

Peony 247

Pinwheel Star

Charm quilts, in which no two pieces are cut from the same fabric, are a fabric lover's delight. Lorraine Vignoli advertised in a quilt magazine inviting readers to participate with her in a fabric swap. The fabrics in this quilt are the results of these exchanges. Lorraine collected fabrics from charm traders in the U.S., England, and Australia.

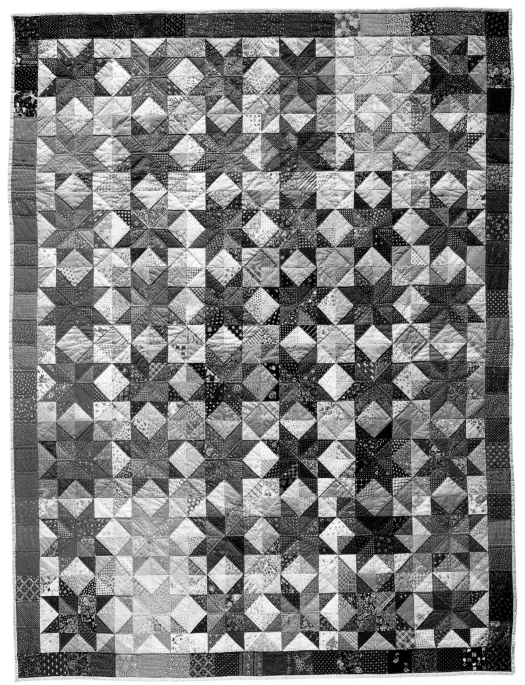

Quilt by Lorraine Vignoli
Commack, New York

Finished Quilt Size
80" x 104"

Number of Blocks and Finished Size
48 blocks   12" x 12"

Fabric Requirements
This is a great quilt to make with friends so you can share fabrics.

Scraps   1,536 (3⅞") A squares*
                88 (3½") B squares
Binding fabric   1 yard
Backing   6 yards

*For good visual results, select approximately 768 dark fabrics and 768 light/medium fabrics.

Cutting
From A squares
- Cut each 3⅞" square in half diagonally to get 2 sets of 1,536 A triangles. Keep 1 set for your quilt and share the other set with a friend.

Quilt Top Assembly
1. For each block, select 8 dark triangles for star points, 4 dark and 4 medium triangles for center pinwheel, and 16 light triangles for outer edges of block.

2. Join dark and medium triangles in pairs for pinwheel **(Block Assembly Diagram)**. Join dark triangles for star points to light triangles in pairs. Then join remaining light triangles in pairs for block corners. Press all seam allowances toward darker fabric in each pair. Join triangle-square units in rows as shown; join rows to complete block.

3. Make 48 blocks.

4. Lay out blocks in 8 horizontal rows, with 6 blocks in each row **(Setting Diagram)**. Join blocks in each row; then join rows.

5. Join 24 (3½") B squares for each side border. Sew borders to quilt sides, easing to fit as needed. Join 20 Bs each for top and bottom borders. Join borders to top and bottom edges of quilt.

Quilting and Finishing
1. Outline-quilt pieces or quilt as desired.

2. See pages 16 and 17 for instructions on making binding. Make 10½ yards of 2½"-wide bias or straight-grain binding. Apply binding to quilt edges.

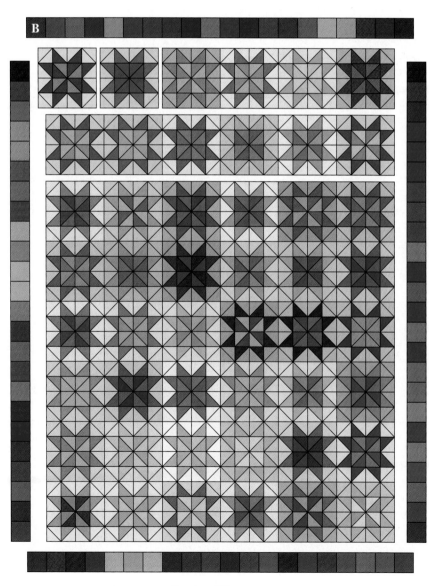

Setting Diagram

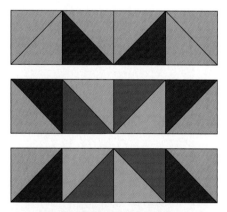

Block Assembly Diagram

Repeating Crosses

Rotary cutting and easy strip piecing make fast work of the triangle units that form this interesting design.

Quilt by Helen Whitson Rose, Nauvoo, Alabama
Quilted by Millie Atkins

Finished Quilt Size
85" x 97"

Number of Blocks and Finished Size
42 blocks   12" x 12"

Materials
Cream print   4 yards
Brown print   4 yards
Brown solid   2¾ yards*
Brown floral print   2½ yards
Backing   2⅝ yards, 104" wide
*Includes fabric for straight-grain binding.

Cutting
Cut all strips cross-grain except as noted. All pieces can be rotary cut, so templates are not needed.
From cream print
• 68 (2"-wide) strips.

From brown print
• 68 (2"-wide) strips.

From brown solid
• 8 (2" x 98") lengthwise strips for inner and outer borders.
• 4 (2½" x 98") lengthwise strips for straight-grain binding.

From brown floral
• 4 (6" x 90") lengthwise strips for middle border.

Quilt Top Assembly
1. Join cream print strips and brown print strips in pairs to make 68 strip sets 3½" wide. Press seam allowances toward brown in 34 sets and toward cream in remaining 34 sets.

2. Measure 3½" from top left corner of strip set as shown (**Cutting Diagram**). Mark this point; then mark off every 7¼" along top edge of strip. Mark 7¼" segments along bottom edge of strip.

3. Measuring from bottom left corner to first mark, rotary-cut end triangle and discard. Then cut from mark to mark as shown to cut 10 triangles from strip set—5 triangles with cream points and 5 with brown print points.

4. Repeat steps 2 and 3 with strip set to get 672 triangles. Make separate stacks of cream-tipped triangles and brown-tipped triangles.

5. For each quarter-block, select 2 brown-tipped triangles with seam allowances pressed in opposite directions, and 2 cream-tipped triangles with opposite pressings. Matching short sides, join brown-tipped triangles to make a larger triangle unit (**Block Assembly Diagram**). Repeat with cream-tipped triangles. Join these units to make a quarter-block section.

6. Make 4 quarter-block sections. Join quarter-block sections as shown to complete block. Make 42 blocks.

7. Lay out blocks in 7 horizontal rows, with 6 blocks in each row. Join blocks in rows; then join rows.

8. Sew 2"-wide brown solid border strips to quilt sides. Press seam allowances toward border and trim borders even with quilt edges. Add border strips to top and bottom edges.

9. Add middle and outer borders in same manner, joining border strips to sides first and then joining remaining border strips to top and bottom edges.

Quilting and Finishing
1. Outline-quilt patchwork and borders or quilt as desired.

2. See pages 16 and 17 for instructions on making binding. Make 10⅜ yards of 2½"-wide straight-grain binding from brown strips. Apply binding to quilt edges.

Block Assembly Diagram

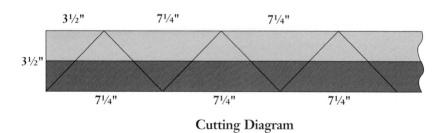

Cutting Diagram

Road to Jericho

This challenging design is known by several names, including Baby Bunting and Mohawk Trail. As *Road to Jericho*, it reminds us of the biblical tale of the Israelites who wandered in the desert for 40 years until they reached the Promised Land. "And the Lord said unto Joshua, 'See, I have given into thine hand Jericho, and the king thereof, and the mighty men of valour.' " *Joshua 6:2*

Quilt from The Patchwork Palace
Franklin, Tennessee

Finished Quilt Size
72" x 94½"

Number of Blocks and Finished Size
12 blocks   18" x 18"

Fabric Requirements
Pink   7 yards*
White   6½ yards
Backing   5⅝ yards
*Includes fabric for binding.

Cutting
Make templates of patterns A–E on page 254. Cut all strips cross-grain.
From pink
- 4 (18½"-wide) strips. From these, cut 31 (5" x 18½") sashing strips.
- 1 (30") square for binding.
- 58 (2½"-wide) strips. From these and scraps from previous steps, cut 192 of Template A, 768 of Template B, 192 of Template D, and 192 of Template D reversed.

From white
- 27 (5"-wide) strips. From these, cut 20 (5") sashing squares and 192 of Template E.
- 59 (1½"-wide) strips. From these and scraps from previous step, cut 960 of Template C.

Quilt Top Assembly
1. For each fan section, select 4 Bs, 5 Cs, and 1 each of A, D, D reversed, and E.
2. Join Bs and Cs in an arc **(Fan**

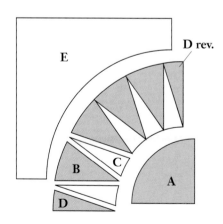

Fan Unit Assembly Diagram

Setting Diagram

Unit Assembly Diagram). Add D and D reversed at row ends as shown. Press seam allowances toward Bs. Sew A and E pieces to edges of arc. Make 192 fan units.

3. Lay out 16 units for each block, rotating units as shown **(Block Assembly Diagram).** Join units in rows; then join rows to complete 1 block. Make 12 blocks.

4. Lay out blocks in 4 horizontal rows, with 3 blocks in each row **(Setting Diagram).** Place sashing strips between blocks and at row ends. Join blocks and sashing strips in each row. Press seam allowances toward sashing strips.   *continued*

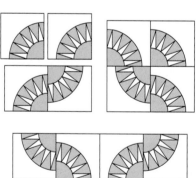

Block Assembly Diagram

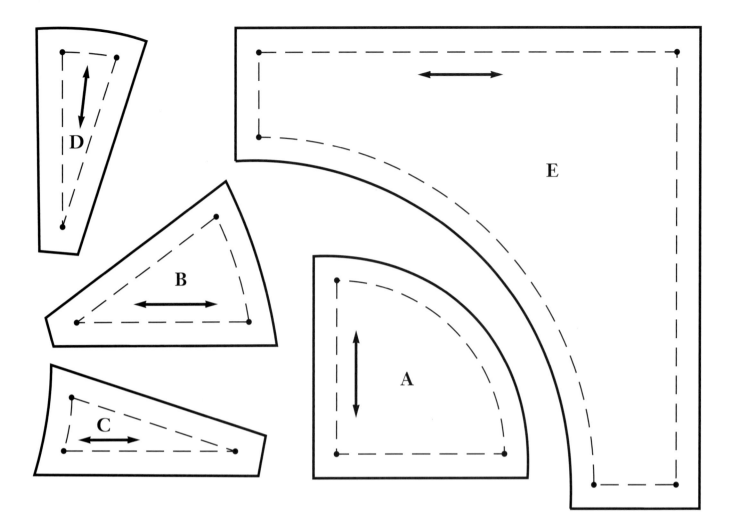

Color Variations

This challenging patchwork is appealing in any color scheme. Here are some other ideas to inspire you.

5. Join 3 sashing strips and 4 sashing squares in a row as shown. Make 5 sashing rows.

6. Join block rows and sashing rows to complete quilt top.

Quilting and Finishing

1. Outline-quilt patchwork. Quilt sashing and sashing squares as desired.

2. See pages 16 and 17 for instructions on making binding. Make 9½ yards of 2½"-wide bias or straight-grain binding from reserved pink fabric. Apply binding to quilt edges.

Roads

Becky Johnson made *Roads* as a gift for her nephew, Matthew. "It seemed appropriate for him," Becky says, "because he loves to play with toy cars, and the blue arcs make perfect roads for his vehicles." This pattern is also known as Drunkard's Trail, Snake Trail, and the Rainbow Quilt.

Quilt by Becky Olson Johnson
Badger, Minnesota

Finished Quilt Size
63½" x 95½"

Number of Blocks and Finished Size
60 blocks   8" x 8"

Fabric Requirements
Light prints   18 fat quarters*
Dark prints   18 fat quarters*
Blue   4 yards**
Backing   5¾ yards
*Fat quarter = 18" x 22".
**Includes fabric for binding.

Cuting
Make templates of patterns A, B, and C. Cut pieces in order listed to get best use of yardage. Cut all strips cross-grain.
From light prints
- 18 (3" x 22") strips and 1 (6½" x 22") strip. From these, cut 54 (3" x 6½") and 4 (3½" x 6½") pieces for border.
- 60 each of templates A and B.

From dark prints
- 18 (3" x 22") strips and 1 (6½" x 22") strip. From these, cut 54 (3" x 6½") and 4 (3½" x 6½") pieces for border.
- 60 each of templates A and B.

From blue
- 8 (2¼"-wide) strips for borders.
- 120 of Template C.

Setting Diagram

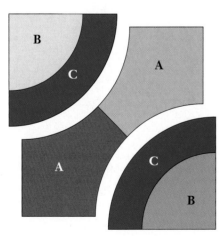

Block Assembly Diagram

Quilt Top Assembly
1. Sew a C to each B. (See page 11 for tips on sewing curved seams.)
2. Join any 2 A pieces **(Block Assembly Diagram)**. Join 2 B/C units to As. Make 60 blocks.
3. Lay out blocks in 10 horizontal rows, with 6 blocks in each row **(Setting Diagram)**. Be careful to orient each block as shown to create the "road" pattern. Join blocks in each row; then join rows.
4. Join pairs of blue border strips end-to-end. Sew borders to quilt sides; trim borders even with quilt edges and press seam allowances toward borders. Add borders to top and bottom edges in same manner.
5. For each pieced side border, join 31 (3" x 6½") strips, alternating dark and light prints. Add a 3½" x 6½" strip to ends of both borders. Join borders to quilt sides, easing to fit as needed.
6. For each top and bottom border, join 23 (3" x 6½") strips, alternating dark and light prints. Add a 3½" x 6½" strip to ends of both borders. Sew pieced borders to top and bottom edges of quilt.

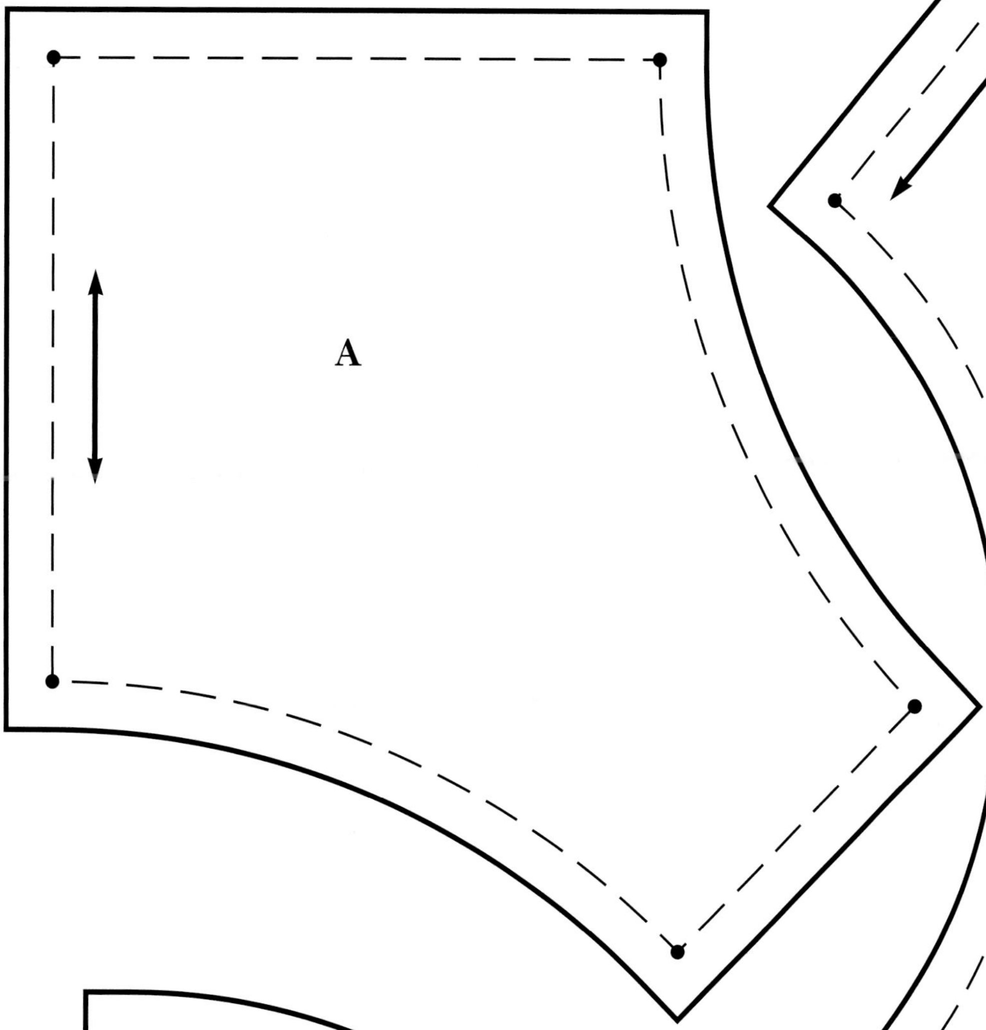

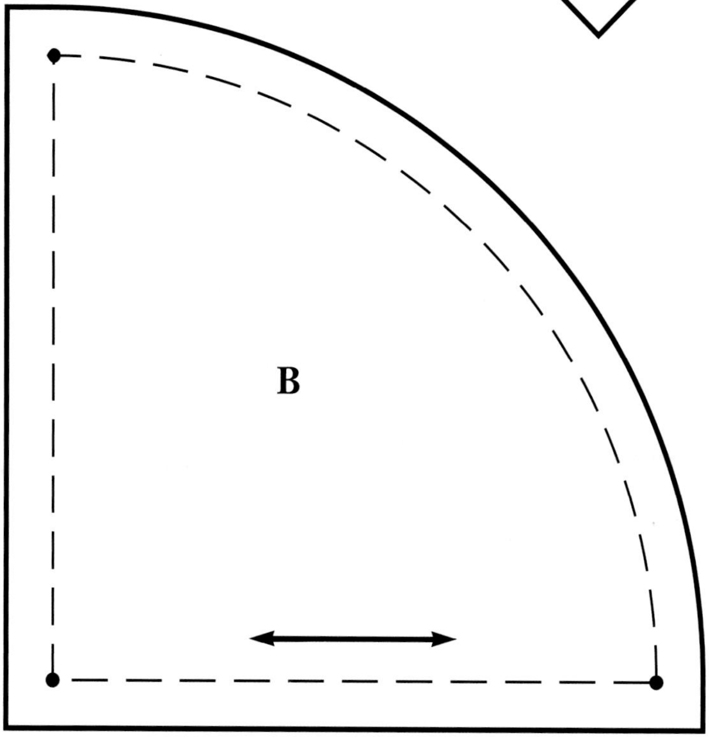

A

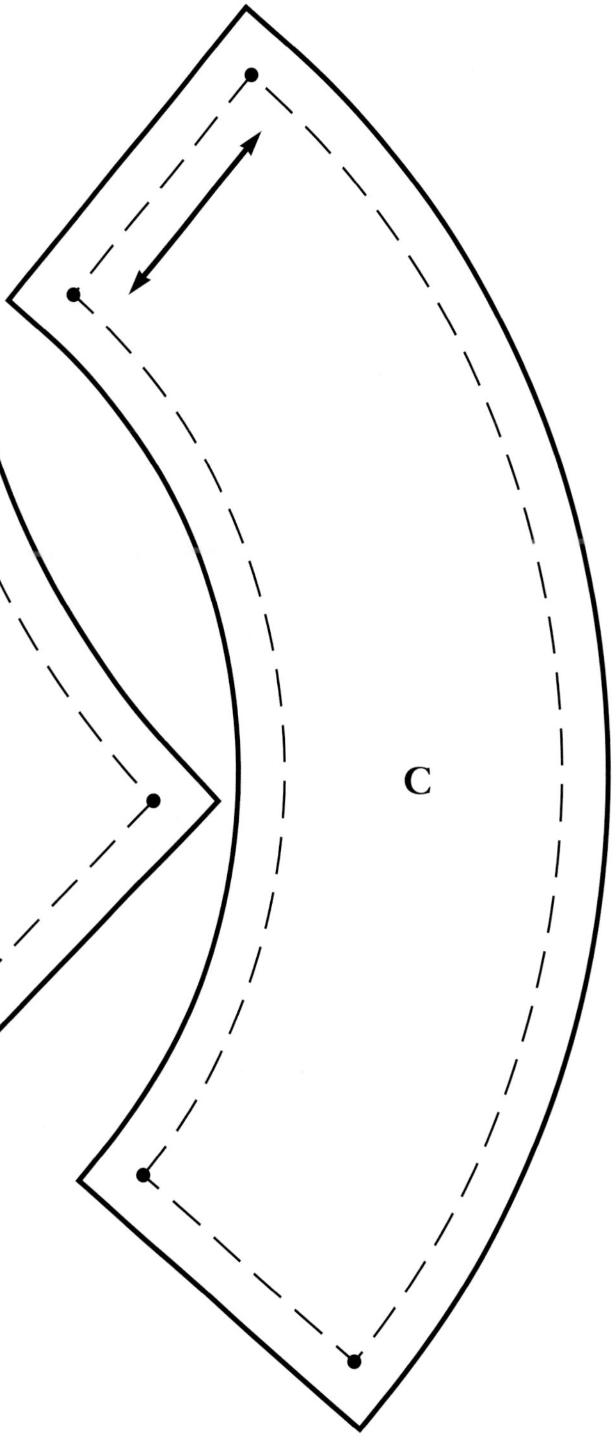

B

C

Quilting and Finishing
   1. Quilt each seam in-the-ditch, or quilt as desired.
   2. See pages 16 and 17 for instructions on making binding. Make $9\frac{1}{8}$ yards of $2\frac{1}{2}$"-wide bias or straight-grain binding from reserved blue fabric. Apply binding to quilt edges.

Rock Star

Bright colors against a dark background give this quilt's design a sense of movement as patterns merge and change. The star points are cut from strip-pieced bands. Leftover bands are cut and pieced into multi-colored binding for a stellar finishing touch. This block is also known as World Without End or Rocky Road to Kansas.

Quilt by Charlotte Hagood
Birmingham, Alabama

Finished Quilt Size
72" x 92"

Number of Blocks and Finished Size
12 blocks   20" x 20"

Fabric Requirements
Navy   4 yards
12 solid fabrics for
  block centers   8¾" square each
13 assorted bright
  solid fabrics for
  strip piecing   ¼ yard each*
Backing   5½ yards
*Includes fabric for binding.

Cutting
Make templates for patterns A and B on pages 260 and 261. (Trace both parts of pattern to make a complete template.) Cut all strips cross-grain except as noted. Cut

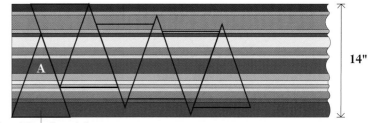

Place Template A here.

Cutting Diagram

pieces in order listed to get best use of yardage.

From navy
- 2 (6½" x 84") and 2 (6½" x 64") lengthwise border strips.
- 8 (5⅜"-wide) strips. From these and scrap from previous step, cut 48 of Template B and 48 of Template B reversed.

From each solid square
- Cut square in quarters diagonally to get 4 C triangles.

From assorted bright fabrics
- Cut each fabric into cross-wise strips in widths ranging from ¾" to 2".

Quilt Top Assembly
1. Join a variety of bright strips along long edges to make a 14"-wide strip set. Make 7 strip sets. Press all seam allowances in 1 direction.

2. Use Template A to cut 7 strip-pieced A triangles from each strip set, staggering triangles across width of band for variety (**Cutting Diagram**). You should have 48 A triangles plus 1 extra. Set aside remainder of strip sets for binding.

3. Sew 1 B and 1 B rev. to sides of each A triangle as shown (**Block Assembly Diagram**). Press seam allowances toward Bs.

4. Select 4 A/B units for each block. Then choose 4 C triangles, 2 each of 2 colors. Sew C triangles to bottom of A triangles as shown. Press seam allowances toward Cs.

5. Join units in pairs; then join pairs to complete block. Make 12 blocks.   *continued*

Setting Diagram

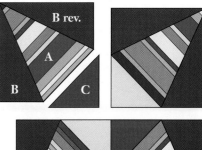
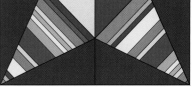

Block Assembly Diagram

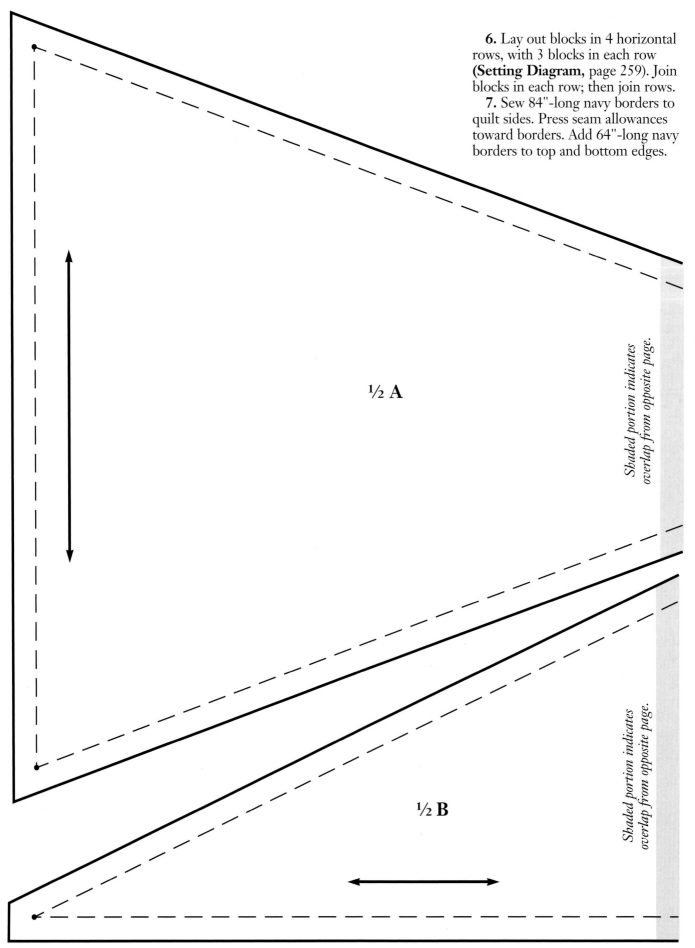

½ A

½ B

Shaded portion indicates overlap from opposite page.

Shaded portion indicates overlap from opposite page.

6. Lay out blocks in 4 horizontal rows, with 3 blocks in each row **(Setting Diagram,** page 259). Join blocks in each row; then join rows.

7. Sew 84"-long navy borders to quilt sides. Press seam allowances toward borders. Add 64"-long navy borders to top and bottom edges.

Quilting and Finishing

1. Outline-quilt C triangles. Quilt remaining areas as desired.

2. From remainder of pieced strip sets, cut 25 or 26 (2½" x 14") strips. Join these end-to-end to make a continuous strip approximately 9⅜ yards long for binding. See page 17 for instructions on applying binding to quilt edges.

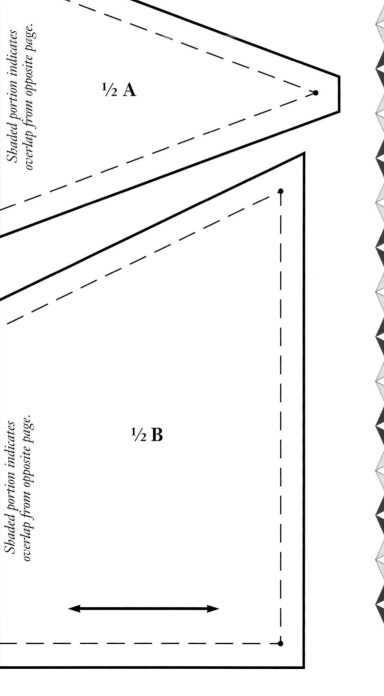

Shaded portion indicates overlap from opposite page.

½ **A**

½ **B**

Shaded portion indicates overlap from opposite page.

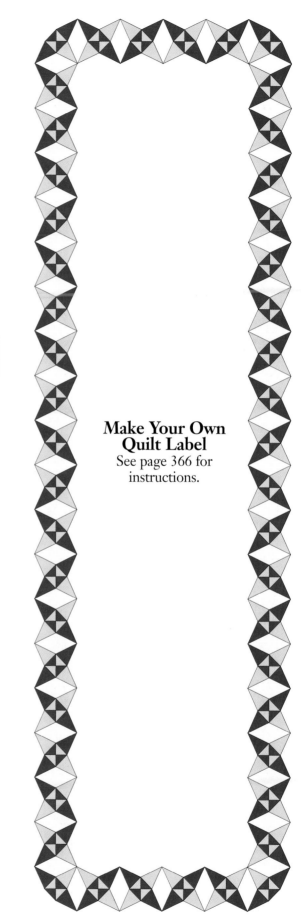

Make Your Own Quilt Label
See page 366 for instructions.

Rose & Tulip

Ami Simms drafted this block design from a picture of a 19th-century variation of a Whig Rose pattern. She complemented the block with a graceful vine-and-flower border and lovely feather quilting. Even though this quilt seems to use yards of bias strips, Ami recommends cutting stems and vines using the templates provided.

Quilt by Ami Simms
Flint, Michigan

Finished Quilt Size
79" x 79"

Number of Blocks and Finished Size
9 blocks   17" x 17"

Fabric Requirements
White or muslin   6 yards
Red print   ¾ yard
Red   ⅝ yard
Navy print   ⅞ yard
Navy   scrap or ⅛ yard
Green   3¾ yards
Binding fabric   1 yard
Backing   4¾ yards

Cutting
Make templates of appliqué patterns A–N on pages 264–267. (Make 4 templates of Pattern L; see Step 7 on cutting vine.) Cut all strips cross-grain except as noted.

From white
- 4 (14½" x 88") lengthwise strips for borders.
- 9 (17½") squares.

From red print
- 28 of Template A.

From red
- 68 of Template C.
- 52 of Template E.

From navy print
- 68 of Template B.

From navy
- 13 of Template F.

From green
- 1 (6¾"-wide) strip. From this, cut 20 (⅞" x 6¾") G stems.
- 2 (4"-wide) strips. From these, cut 20 of Template H.
- 2 (2½"-wide) strips. From these, cut 20 of Template I, 4 of Template N, and 4 of Template N reversed.
- 16 (3"-wide) strips. From these and scraps from previous steps, cut 12 of Template J, 12 of Template J reversed, and 292 of Template D.
- 8 (7"-wide) strips for border vines.

Block 1 Placement Diagram

Block 2 Placement Diagram

Quilt Top Assembly
1. Fold each white square in quarters diagonally and finger-press creases to make placement guidelines for appliqué.

2. For Block 1, center F piece on square; then pin A flowers and G stems on diagonal placement lines **(Block 1 Placement Diagram)**. Pin E flowers, H and I stems, B/C flowers, and D leaves in place as shown. When satisfied with placement of pieces, appliqué stems; then appliqué flowers and leaves. Make 5 of Block 1.

3. For Block 2, center F piece on square; then pin E flowers in place **(Block 2 Placement Diagram)**. Pin a B/C flower and 2 D leaves in each corner. Appliqué pieces in place. Make 4 of Block 2.

4. Before joining blocks, lightly mark Feathered Wreath quilting design on each Block 2. (See pattern on page 267.)

5. Lay out blocks in 3 vertical rows, with 3 blocks in each row, alternating blocks 1 and 2 as shown. Join blocks in each row; then join rows.

6. Sew border strips to center section and miter corners. (See page 14 for tips on sewing mitered border corners.)

7. Match ends of templates K, L, and M as shown **(Template Placement Diagram,** page 266). Lay combined template on each 7"-wide green strip; cut 8 border vine units.

8. Pin vines, stems, and leaves in place on border strips **(Border Placement Diagram)**. Pin flowers in place as shown. (Left half of border is shown; right half is mirror image.) When satisfied with placement of all pieces, appliqué vine, stems, and leaves; then appliqué flowers. Appliqué F piece to corner flowers on mitered seam.

continued

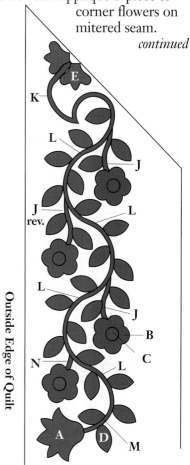

Border Placement Diagram

Quilting and Finishing

1. For border, make stencil of Feathered Wave pattern on this page. Starting at center of each side, lightly mark design on each border (see photograph, page 262).

2. Outline-quilt all appliqué. Quilt Feathered Wreath in center of each Block 2. Also in Block 2, add an arched line of quilting from D leaf to D leaf as shown in photograph. Quilt Feathered Wave motifs on each border strip.

3. See pages 16 and 17 for instructions on making binding. Make 9 yards of 2½"-wide bias or straight-grain binding. Apply binding to quilt edges.

Corner Section

Feathered Wave Quilting Pattern

Repeat this section for feathered waves quilting.

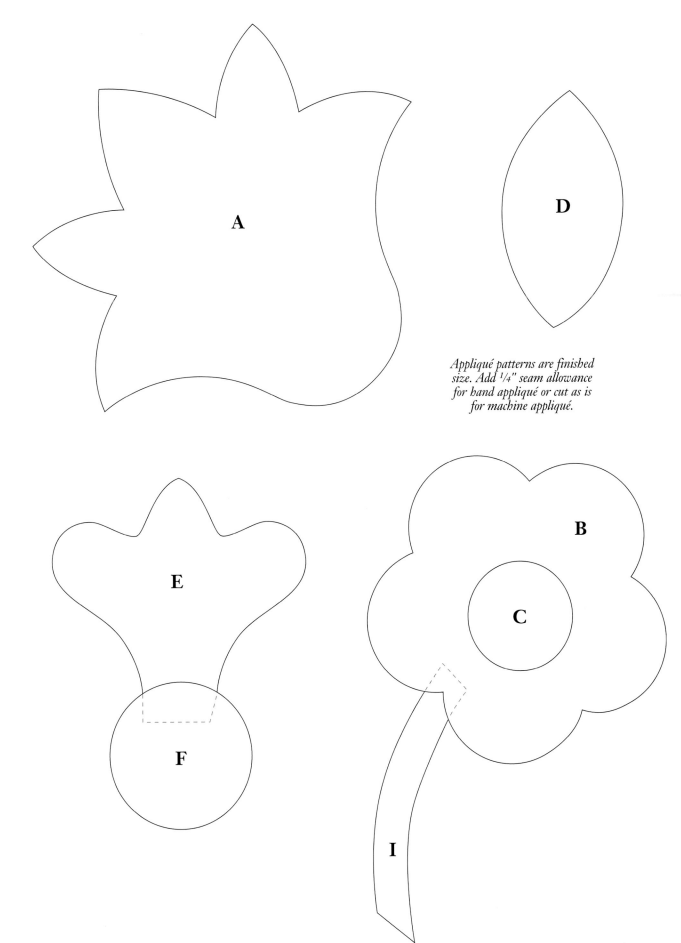

A

D

Appliqué patterns are finished size. Add ¼" seam allowance for hand appliqué or cut as is for machine appliqué.

E

B

C

F

I

Rose & Tulip 265

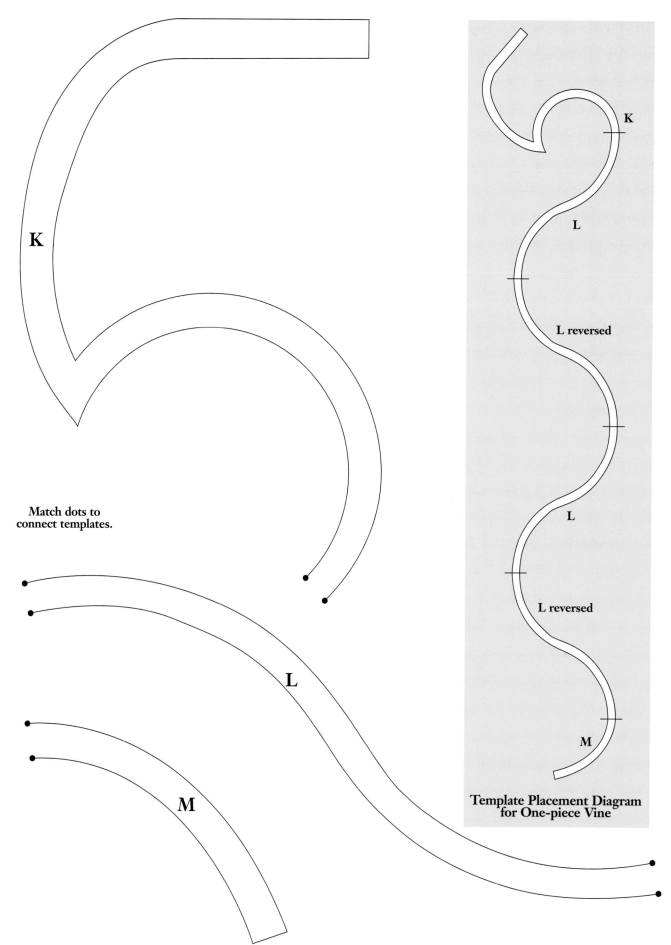

K

Match dots to connect templates.

L

M

K

L

L reversed

L

L reversed

M

Template Placement Diagram for One-piece Vine

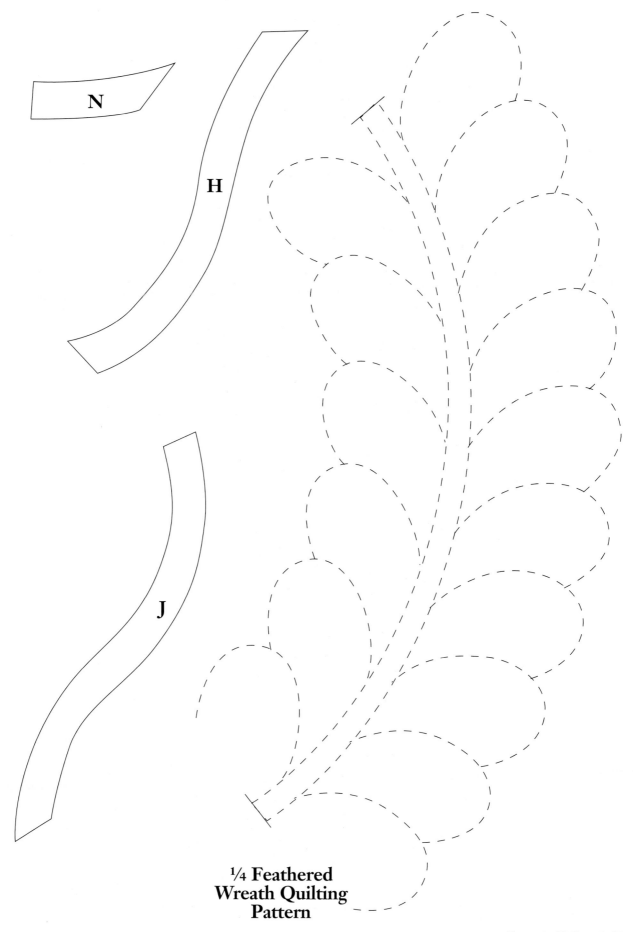

**¼ Feathered
Wreath Quilting
Pattern**

Rose of Sharon

The Quilt 'n' Patch Quilters, a 10-woman quilting bee, makes fund-raising quilts for the Sunshine Children's Home, a service for children with severe medical needs. This quilt, made for the 1996 auction, is an adaptation of an antique quilt. It upholds the tradition of heirloom quilts with meticulous appliqué and fine hand quilting.

Quilt by Quilt 'n' Patch Quilters, Toledo, Ohio
Owned by Katherine Frey, Archbold, Ohio

Finished Quilt Size
90" x 110"

Number of Blocks and Finished Size
12 blocks   20" x 20"

Fabric Requirements
White or muslin   6½ yards
Green   5½ yards*
Dark red   1½ yards
Dark pink print   ⅞ yard
Medium pink print   ¾ yard
Backing   3¼ yards 104" wide
*Includes fabric for binding.

Other Materials
¼"-wide bias pressing bar

Cutting
Make templates for appliqué patterns A–E on page 271. Cut all strips cross-grain except as noted. Cut pieces in order listed to get best use of yardage.

From white
- 2 (8½" x 100") and 2 (8½" x 80") lengthwise border strips.
- 12 (20½") squares.

From green
- 2 (6½" x 116") and 2 (6½" x 96") lengthwise border strips. Use leftover strip for next step.
- 30 (3" x 17") strips. From these, cut 240 of Template D.
- 2 (4"-wide) strips. From these and remaining scraps, cut 48 of Template A.
- 4 (6¼"-wide) strips for bias stems.
- 1 (35"-wide) strip. From this, cut 1 (35") square for bias binding and 6 (1" x 35") strips for second border (sides).
- 4 (1"-wide) strips for second border (top and bottom).

From dark red
- 2 (6¼"-wide) strips. From these, cut 12 of Template B.
- 6 (3½"-wide) strips. From these, cut 64 of Template E.
- 10 (1"-wide) strips for third border.

From dark pink
- 2 (5"-wide) strips. From these, cut 12 of Template C.
- 5 (3½"-wide) strips. From these and scrap from previous step, cut 68 of Template E.

From medium pink
- 6 (3½"-wide) strips. From these, cut 68 of Template E.

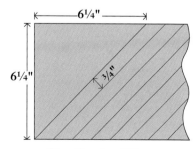

Bias Cutting Diagram

Preparing Bias Stems
1. Measure 6¼" from 1 corner of each 6¼"-wide green strip and mark. Trim triangles from corner to mark (**Bias Cutting Diagram**).
2. Measuring from cut edges, cut ¾"-wide bias strips for stems. Cut at least 30 stems from each strip.
3. With right side of fabric face-up, fold each stem over pressing bar and press, centering raw edges on 1 side of bar.

continued

Appliqué Placement Diagram

Quilt Top Assembly

1. Fold a white square in half horizontally, vertically, and diagonally; finger-press creases to mark guidelines. Center 1 B on block and pin (**Appliqué Placement Diagram**). Pin C on top of B so B fabric shows through center circle of C. Pin 4 A leaves on diagonal placement guides.

2. Select 8 bias stems. Pin 4 stems at center of each side of B, tucking ends under B. Trim 1" from remaining 4 stems; place these branching off first stems as shown. Position 20 D leaves as shown. Select 8 E flowers (4 dark pink and 4 medium pink) and pin Es at ends of each stem, centering flowers on opposite sides of diagonal placement lines.

3. When satisfied with placement of all pieces, appliqué stems. Appliqué remaining pieces in alphabetical order.

4. Make 12 blocks. Save remaining E flowers for appliqué after quilt is assembled.

5. Lay out blocks in 4 horizontal rows, with 3 blocks in each row (**Setting Diagram**). Join blocks in each row; then join rows.

6. Sew white borders to quilt and miter corners. Press seam allowances toward borders.

7. Pin dark red E flowers in place on block seam lines to complete flower circles. Pin remaining E flowers in place on borders to complete flower circles at outside edges (see photograph on page 269). Appliqué flowers in place.

8. Join 2 (1" x 44") green strips end-to-end for each top and bottom border and 3 (1" x 35") strips for each side border. Join red strips for third border in same manner. Join green and red borders of same length to make a 2-strip border unit for each side of quilt.

9. Sew a 6½"-wide green border to red strip of each 2-border unit. Sew combined border units to quilt and miter corners.

Quilting and Finishing

1. Mark Wreath Quilting Pattern (page 272) in center of each wreath circle.

2. Outline-quilt appliqué pieces and borders. Quilt wreath design in each circle. Add other quilting as desired. Quilt shown has cross-hatching quilted in background areas, large feather motifs in quilt corners, and a feathered swag quilted in green borders.

3. See pages 16 and 17 for instructions on making binding. Make 11⅜ yards of 2½"-wide bias or straight-grain binding. Apply binding to quilt edges.

Setting Diagram

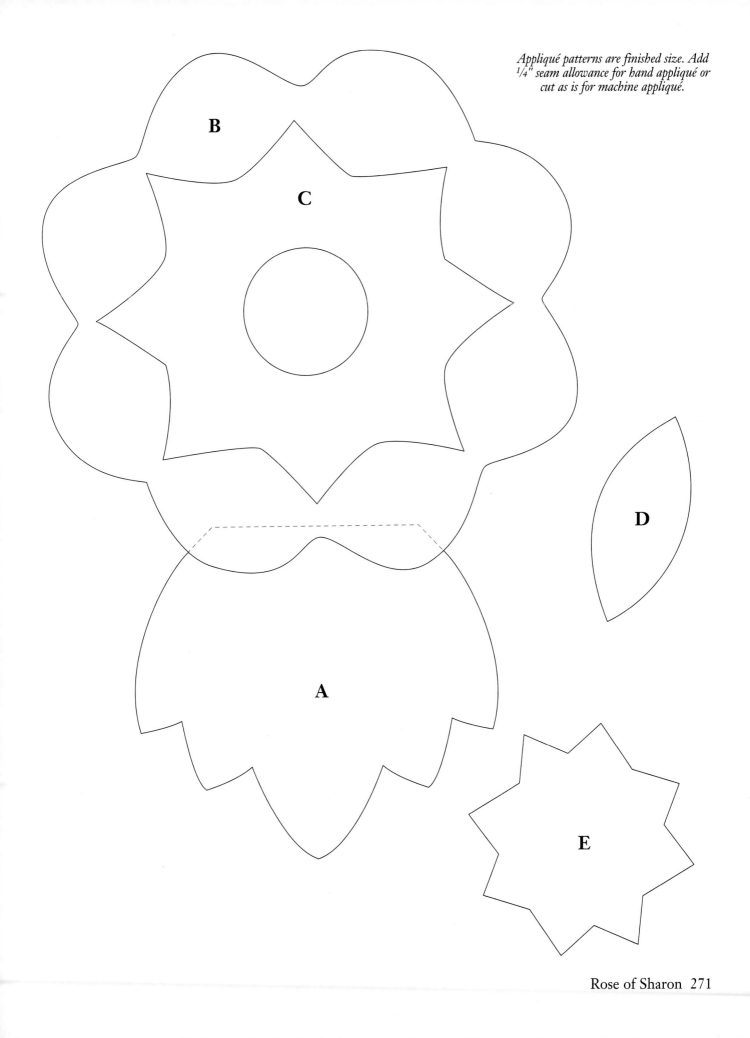

Appliqué patterns are finished size. Add ¼" seam allowance for hand appliqué or cut as is for machine appliqué.

B

C

D

A

E

Rose of Sharon 271

Wreath Quilting Pattern

Color Variations
These are some suggestions for other color schemes.

Row Houses

The smell of fresh paint was still in the air when Flavin Glover designed these houses. She and her husband had just completed a new house; and after spending hours with the color chips in every paint store in town, the design for *Row Houses* came naturally to mind. Color chips play a role in the design; they circle the houses like a rainbow, echoing the colors of the houses.

Quilt by Flavin Glover
Auburn, Alabama

Finished Quilt Size
83" x 107"

Number of Blocks and Finished Size
192 Log Cabin blocks   4½" x 4½"

Fabric Requirements
16 brights (houses
   and chips)   1 fat quarter* each
4 blues (sky)   1 fat quarter* each
4 earth tones
   (roofs)   1 fat quarter* each
Gray (border, windows)   1 yard
Peach (border, windows)   ¾ yard
Black   3⅛ yards
Black pinstripe   3⅛ yards**
Backing   6⅛ yards
*Fat quarter = 18" x 22".
**Includes fabric for straight-grain binding.

Cutting
Templates are not needed, as all pieces can be rotary cut. Cut all strips cross-grain except as noted.
From each *bright fat quarter*
- 1 (2½" x 22") strip for chips.
- 15 (1" x 22") strips for houses.

From each *blue and* each *earth tone fat quarter*
- 18 (1" x 22") strips.

From black
- 52 (1"-wide) strips and 1 (2"-wide) strip for roofs, windows, doors, etc. Set aside 17 (1"-wide) strips for chip borders.
- 20 (2"-wide) strips and 18 (1"-wide) strips for borders.

From gray
- 10 (2"-wide) strips for borders. Use remainder for roofs, chip borders, windows, etc. as desired.

From peach
- 8 (2"-wide) strips for borders. Use remainder for roofs, chips, or windows as desired.

From black pinstripe
- 2 (3" x 112") and 2 (3" x 86") lengthwise strips for outer border.
- 2 (2½" x 86") and 2 (2½" x 56") lengthwise strips for sashing.

Row House Assembly
Before you begin, see Log Cabin Basics on page 207.

1. There are 8 styles of "downstairs" blocks. (See diagrams on opposite page; blocks differ slightly in size and shape of windows and doors.) For first house, choose a downstairs block style and cut 2 block centers as indicated under diagram (includes seam allowance), using peach, gray, black, or other fabric as desired.

2. Select 1 strip of house fabric. Following Log Cabin Basics instructions, add logs around center piece as shown in diagram for downstairs block. (Choice of block style determines if 3 or 4 rows of logs are needed.) Make second block a mirror image of first downstairs block. Join blocks as shown.

3. For each upstairs block, cut a 1½" x 2" window for center. Using same house fabric, add logs to complete block **(Row House Assembly Diagram)**. Make a mirror-image second block. Join blocks.

4. For each roof block, cut a 1" center square from selected roof fabric. Add logs to complete block, referring to diagram for placement of roof and house strips. Make a mirror-image second block. Join blocks as shown.

5. For each roof/sky block, cut a 1" center square of blue fabric. Add logs to complete block, referring to diagram for placement of sky and roof strips. Make a mirror-image second block. Join blocks.

6. Join rows as shown to complete 1 house.

7. Make a total of 22 pairs of downstairs blocks. For half-houses, make 2 right downstairs blocks and 2 left downstairs blocks. Blocks can be all same style or mixed styles.

Quilt Top Assembly

1. Lay out houses in 4 rows, with 5 houses and 2 half-houses in rows 1 and 3 and 6 houses in remaining rows. Join blocks in each row.

2. Join rows, with 56"-long sashing between house rows. Press seam allowances toward sashing.

continued

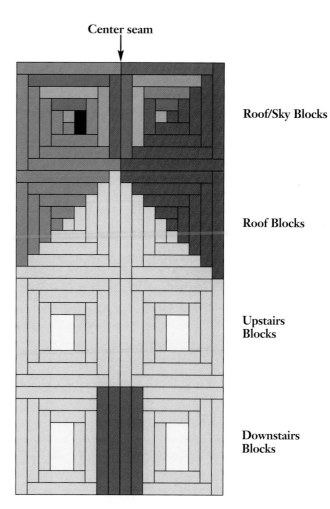

Row House Assembly Diagram

Center seam

Roof/Sky Blocks

Roof Blocks

Upstairs Blocks

Downstairs Blocks

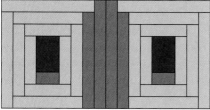

Block Center = 1½" x 2"

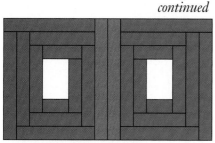

Block Center = 1½" x 2"

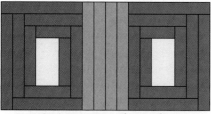

Block Center = 1½" x 2½"

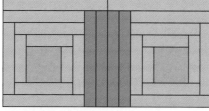

Block Center = 2" square

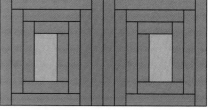

Block Center = 1½" x 2½"

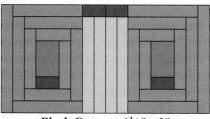

Block Center = 1½" x 2"

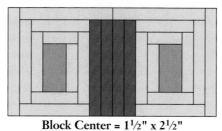

Block Center = 1½" x 2½"

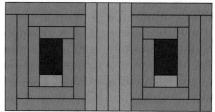

Block Center = 1½" x 2"

Downstairs Blocks

3. Sew 86"-long sashing strips to sides of quilt and press.

4. Piece 1"-wide black strips end-to-end to make 4 (66"-long) borders and 4 (90"-long) borders. Piece 2 peach border strips of each length. Sew black border strips to both sides of peach strip of matching length. Join borders to quilt and miter corners.

5. From reserved fabric strips, cut 104 (2½") squares for color chips. From reserved black strips, cut 120 (1" x 2½") pieces and 120 (1" x 3½") pieces. Sew shorter black pieces to opposite sides of 60 squares; then sew longer black pieces to remaining sides. Cut border strips for remaining 40 squares from peach, gray, and remaining scraps; join these to squares in same manner. Press seam allowances toward border strips.

6. Join 29 squares end-to-end for each side border. Sew borders to quilt sides, easing to fit as needed. Press seam allowances toward previous black border.

7. Join 23 squares end-to-end for each top and bottom border. Sew borders to top and bottom edges of quilt, easing to fit as needed.

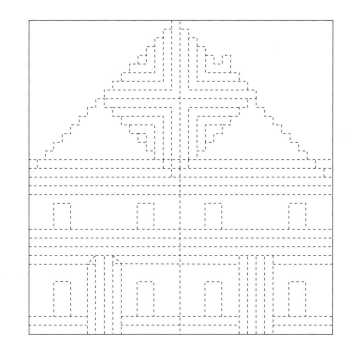

Quilting Diagram

8. Piece 2"-wide black strips end-to-end to make 4 (86"-long) borders and 4 (112"-long) borders. Piece 2 gray border strips of each length. Sew black border strips to both sides of each gray strip of matching length. Add pinstripe borders to 1 edge of each set to make a 4-strip border for each side of quilt. Join borders to quilt and miter corners. Press seam allowances toward black.

Quilting and Finishing

1. Outline-quilt roof edges, between houses, along door strips, and inside windows. See Quilting Diagram for suggestion for additional quilting.

2. See pages 16 and 17 for instructions on making binding. Make 10⅞ yards of 2½"-wide straight-grain binding from remaining black and/or pinstripe. Apply binding to quilt edges.

Make Your Own Quilt Label
See page 366 for instructions.

Sadie's Choice

Through the centuries, quilters have invented many variations of appliquéd rose and tulip designs. Perennial favorites include Rose of Sharon (page 268) and Whig Rose (page 362). This block was an obvious choice for the Krazy Quilters, who made the quilt to honor their founder, Sadie Bell.

Quilt by The Krazy Quilters Club
Temple Terrace, Florida

Finished Quilt Size
96" x 120"

Number of Blocks and Finished Size
12 blocks   17" x 17"

Fabric Requirements
Pink   9 yards
Teal   1¾ yards
Black floral   1¾ yard
Dark pink   1½ yards
Gold   ¼ yard
White floral   1 yard
Binding fabric   1 yard
Backing   4½ yards

Other Materials
⅜"-wide bias pressing bar

Cutting
Make templates of patterns A–K on pages 279–281 (patterns C and D are for piecing, others are for appliqué). Cut all strips cross-grain. Cut pieces in order listed to get best use of yardage.

From pink
- 3 (25¼") squares. Cut each square in quarters diagonally to get 11 side triangles (and 1 extra).
- 28 (17½") squares.
- 2 (9"-wide) strips for corners.

From teal
- 8 (4¾"-wide) strips. From these, cut 48 of Template G.
- 5 (3½"-wide) strips. From these, cut 116 of Template I.
- 12 of Template J.

From black floral
- 1 (24") square for bias vines.
- 12 of Template B.
- 48 of Template E.

From dark pink
- 15 (2¾"-wide) strips. From these, cut 188 of Template D.
- 2 (4½"-wide) strips. From these and scrap from previous step, cut 48 of Template F.
- 48 of Template H.

From gold
- 40 of Template A.

From white floral
- 8 (3"-wide) strips. From these, cut 144 of Template C and 12 of Template K.

Quilt Top Assembly
1. Piece 12 C pieces and 12 D pieces in a ring **(Block Assembly Diagram)**. Press seam allowances toward Ds. Turn under outside edge for appliqué.

2. Fold a pink square in half vertically, horizontally, and diagonally; finger-press creases to make placement guidelines for appliqué.

3. Center pieced C/D ring on pink square; pin or baste in place.

4. Position 4 E/F flowers and 4 G/H flowers as shown, tucking E and G ends under Ds. Appliqué Fs and Hs; then appliqué Es and Gs.

5. Appliqué outer edge of C/D

ring in place. Center B on top of ring and appliqué; then stitch A on top of B to complete block.

6. Make 12 blocks.

7. See page 17 for instructions on making continuous bias. Make

Block Assembly Diagram

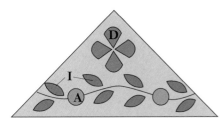

Side Triangle Placement Diagram

450" of 1"-wide continuous bias from 24" square of black floral.

8. Cut bias into 12 (30"-long) lengths and 2 (45"-long) lengths. Center bias bar on wrong side of each strip and press edges over bar.

9. On 1 side triangle, pin 4 Ds, 1 (30"-long) bias strip, 2 As, and 8 I pieces **(Side Triangle Placement Diagram)**. When satisfied with placement, appliqué pieces in place. Appliqué 11 side triangles.

10. Lay out appliquéd blocks, setting squares, and side triangles in diagonal rows **(Setting Diagram)**. Join units in each row; press seam allowances toward setting squares. Join rows.

11. Fold each 9"-wide pink strip in half; mark center. From center, measure along edges as shown and mark **(Corner Cutting Diagram)**. Draw lines to connect marked points; cut corner units on lines.

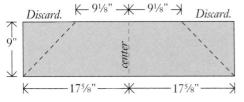

Corner Cutting Diagram

12. Pin a 45"-long bias strip, 3 As and 14 Is on each corner unit **(Corner Placement Diagram)**. Appliqué pieces in place. Sew corner units to corners at top of quilt.

Corner Placement Diagram

13. Pin a K flower at corner of each outer setting square **(Setting Diagram)** and appliqué. Appliqué a J piece at base of each K.

continued

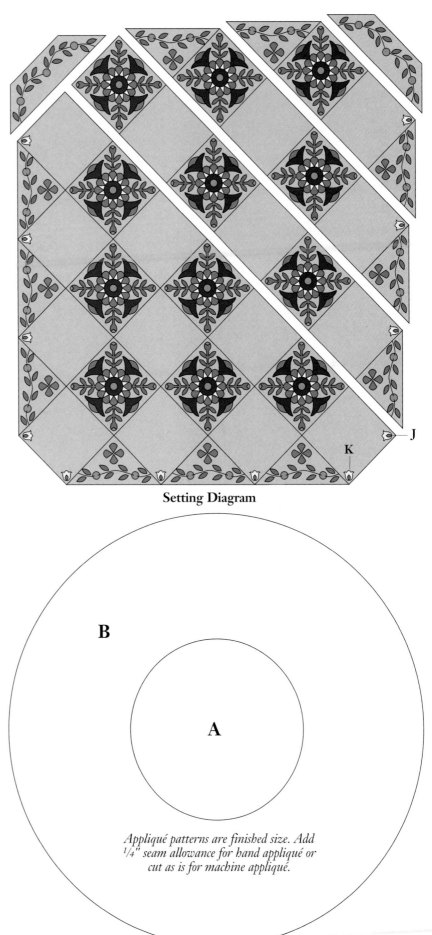

Setting Diagram

Appliqué patterns are finished size. Add ¹⁄₄" seam allowance for hand appliqué or cut as is for machine appliqué.

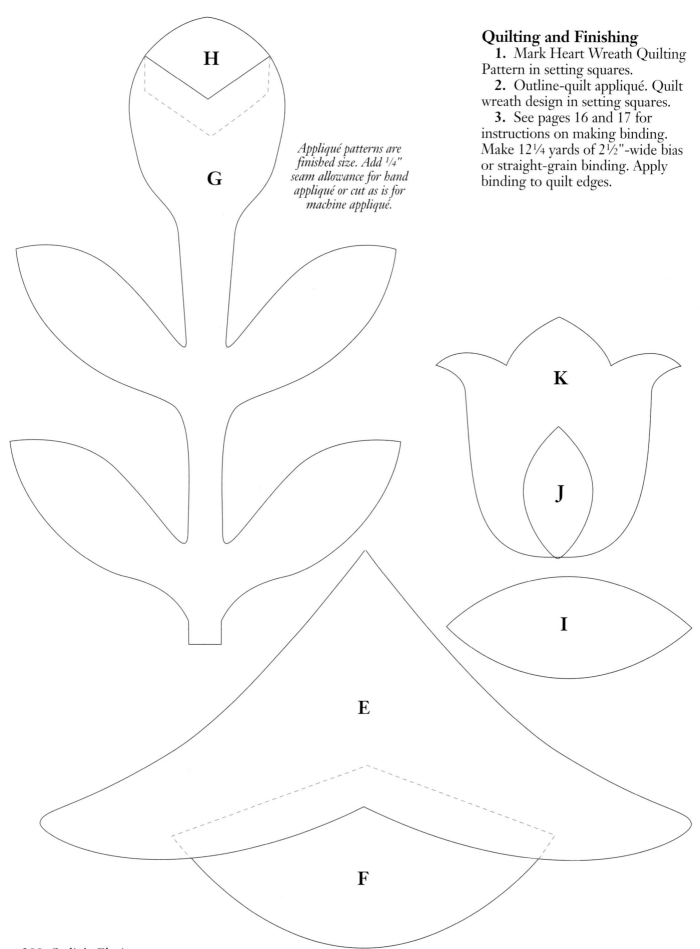

Appliqué patterns are finished size. Add 1/4" seam allowance for hand appliqué or cut as is for machine appliqué.

Quilting and Finishing

1. Mark Heart Wreath Quilting Pattern in setting squares.

2. Outline-quilt appliqué. Quilt wreath design in setting squares.

3. See pages 16 and 17 for instructions on making binding. Make 12¼ yards of 2½"-wide bias or straight-grain binding. Apply binding to quilt edges.

H

G

K

J

I

E

F

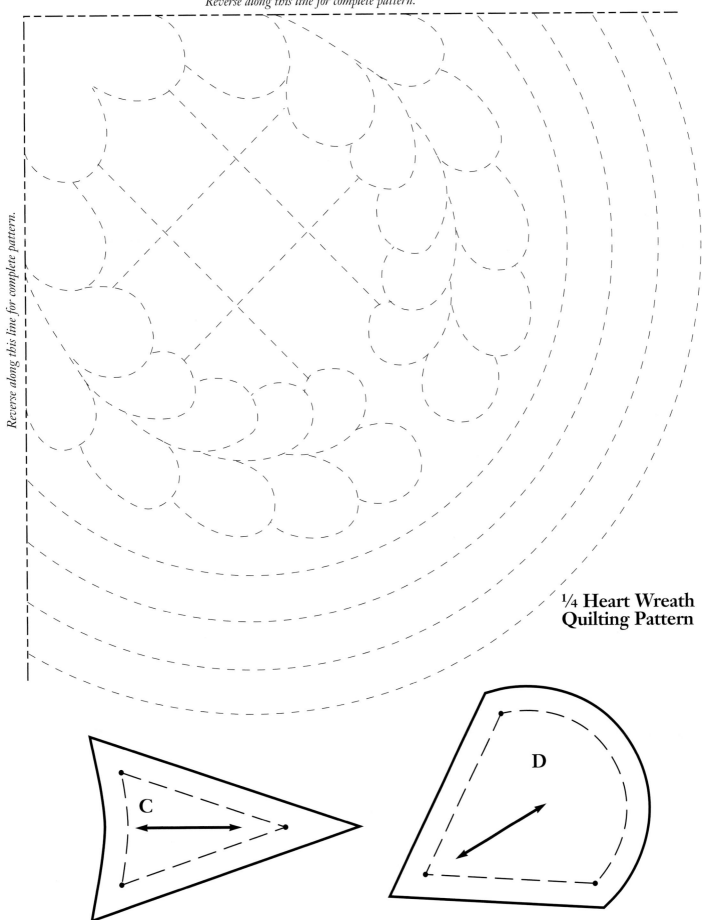

Reverse along this line for complete pattern.

Reverse along this line for complete pattern.

¼ Heart Wreath Quilting Pattern

C

D

Sailboats

Summer's warmth brings to mind breezy days spent on the water. This endearing little quilt is perfect for a child or as a wall hanging. Quick-piecing techniques make navigating fabric waters a breeze.

Quilt by Joanne R. Cage
Birmingham, Alabama

Finished Quilt Size
40" x 52½"

Number of Blocks and Finished Size
12 blocks   10" x 10"

Fabric Requirements
White   2½ yards
6 blue prints   1 fat eighth each*
Binding fabric   ⅜ yard
Backing   1⅝ yards
*Fat eighth = 9" x 22".

Cutting
See alternate instructions for quick-pieced triangle-squares on page 11 before cutting. Cut all strips cross-grain except as noted.
From white fabric
• 2 (3" x 54") lengthwise strips for side borders.
• 5 (3" x 37") strips for top and bottom borders and sashing.
• 6 (3" x 37") strips. From these, cut 72 (3") A squares.
• 8 (3" x 11") strips for sashing.
• 48 (3⅜") squares for traditional piecing; cut each square in half diagonally to get 96 B triangles. For quick piecing, cut 6 (9" x 16") pieces.

From each blue print
• 8 (3⅜") squares for traditional piecing; cut each square in half diagonally to get 16 B triangles. For quick piecing, cut 1 (9" x 16") piece.
• 4 (3") A squares.

Quilt Top Assembly
1. For traditional piecing, sew 1 blue B to 1 white B to make 1 B/B square. For quick piecing, follow instructions and diagram on page 11, drawing a 2-square by 4-square grid of 3⅜" squares. Make a total of 96 B/B triangle-squares.

2. Join 2 B/B squares and 2 white As for each sail row **(Block Assembly Diagram)**. Make 3 sail rows. For boat row, join 2 blue As and 2 B/B squares as shown. Join rows to complete block.

3. Make 6 blocks. Make 6 more blocks in same manner, turning

B/B squares to reverse direction of sails **(Setting Diagram)**.

4. Lay out blocks in 4 rows of 3 blocks each, with sashing strips between blocks as shown. Alternate direction of sails in each row. Join blocks and sashing in each row.

5. Sew a 3" x 37" sashing strip to top edge of each row. Join rows. Sew remaining sashing strip to bottom row. Join remaining borders to sides of quilt.

Quilting and Finishing
1. Outline-quilt patchwork. Quilt an X in each white A. If desired, quilt water lines at bottom of each boat. Quilt sashing and borders as desired.

2. See pages 16 and 17 for

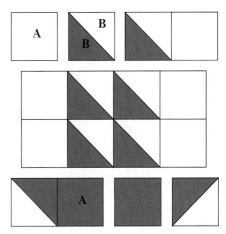

Block Assembly Diagram

instructions on making binding. Make 5½ yards of 2½"-wide bias or straight-grain binding. Apply binding to quilt edges.

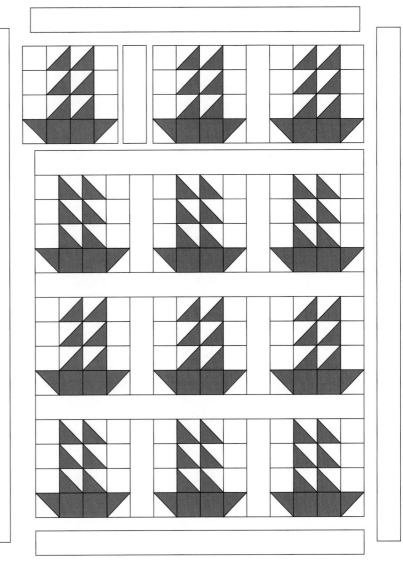

Setting Diagram

Schoolhouse

Brown County State Park, located east of Bloomington, Indiana, is famous for its log cabin tours. Linda Sage honors the beauty and heritage of these historic buildings with this quilt, which she calls *Brown County Log Cabins*. Using the traditional Schoolhouse block, sometimes known as Log Cabin, Linda selected fabrics to mimic the rustic texture of log cabins in the piney woods.

Quilt by Linda Karel Sage
Morgantown, Indiana

Finished Quilt Size
73½" x 96"

Number of Blocks and Finished Size
20 cabin blocks   12" x 12"

Fabric Requirements
Scraps of solids, dots,
 and stripes   30 (6" x 22") strips*
Yellow   9" square
Black   3¼ yards
Sashing fabric   2⅜ yards
Green   1 yard
Dark green   2¼ yards
Stripe border fabric   ¾ yard
Backing   2¼ yards 104" wide
*Equivalent to 10 fat quarters.
 Fat quarter = 18" x 22".

Cutting
Make templates of patterns A, D, E, F, G, N, and O on pages 287 and 288 (other pieces can be rotary cut). Cut all strips cross-grain except as noted.

Note: Yardage assumes 5 houses have yellow windows and doors for a "lights on" look, 5 houses have black windows and doors ("lights out"), and remaining houses have black windows and colored doors.

From each of 10 scrap strips
• 2 of Template E.
• 4 (2") B squares.
• 1 (1½" x 3") L piece.

From each of 20 scrap strips
• 1 of Template G.
• 1 (3½" x 4") I piece.
• 2 (2" x 7½") H pieces.
• 3 (2" x 3") J pieces.
• 2 (1¾" x 3") K pieces.

From yellow
• 3 (3" x 9") strips. From these, cut 10 (1¾" x 3") K pieces and 5 (1½" x 3") L pieces.

From black
• 2 (3½"-wide) strips. From these, cut 10 (3½" x 8") pieces. Cut 2 of Template A from each piece.
• 2 (7" x 76") and 2 (7" x 100") lengthwise strips for outer border.
• 3 (6" x 15") strips. From these, cut 20 (2" x 6") C pieces.

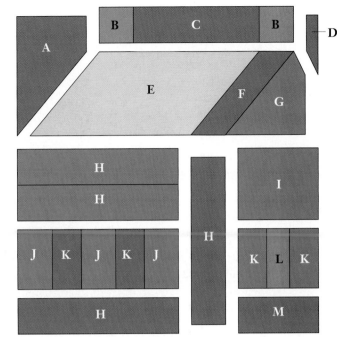

Block Assembly Diagram

• 4 (1" x 15") strips. From these, cut 20 of Template D.
• 10 (1⅝" x 15") strips. From these, cut 20 of Template F.
• 20 (2" x 15") strips. From these, cut 40 (2" x 7½") H pieces.
• 6 (1¾" x 15") strips. From these, cut 30 (1¾" x 3") K pieces.
• 5 (1½" x 3") L pieces.
• 20 (2" x 4") M pieces.

From sashing fabric
• 2 (4" x 60") and 2 (4" x 84") lengthwise strips for inner border.
• 3 (4" x 76") lengthwise strips and 16 (4" x 12½") sashing strips.

From green
• 180 of Template N.

From dark green
• 180 of Template O.

Quilt Top Assembly
1. For each block, select 2 black Hs, 2 matching Bs, and 1 each of A, C, D, E, F, and M. Select 1 set of house pieces (1 G, 2 H, 1 I, 3 J, and 2K). Also select 1 set of window/door pieces (2 K and 1 L), choosing all yellow, all black, or black windows (K) and a colored door (L).

2. Join pieces in rows as shown **(Block Assembly Diagram)**. Join

units in window section and door section; then join both sections to center black H. Sew B/C chimney row to top of E/F roof row; then set in pieces A and D (see page 10 for tips on sewing a set-in seam). Join top and bottom sections to complete block.

3. Make 20 cabin blocks.

4. Lay out blocks in 4 vertical rows, with 5 blocks in each row and 4 sashing strips between blocks. Intermingle cabins with "lights on" among those with "lights out." Join units in each row.

5. Join rows with 3 (76"-long) sashing strips, alternating block rows and sashing as shown.

6. Join 60"-long border strips to top and bottom edges of quilt. Join 84"-long strips to quilt sides.

7. Sew 100"-long black strips to quilt sides. Sew remaining black strips to top and bottom edges.

8. Referring to instructions on page 17, make 10 yards of 1¼"-wide bias from stripe border fabric. Cut 2 (100") lengths; stitch these to quilt sides, handling them carefully to avoid stretching bias edges. Cut remaining bias in half; stitch strips to top and bottom edges.

continued

Quilting and Finishing

1. Quilting is varied in each block. Some blocks are quilted with diagonal parallel lines, 1½" apart, while others have horizontal or cross-hatched quilting lines across the cabin. Quilt blocks as desired.

2. Outline-quilt sashing seam lines. Quilt parallel wavy lines, 1¼" apart, along sashing strips. Quilt shown also has mountain and sunrise pattern quilted in black borders, placed so that suns meet at corners to form a half circle **(Quilting Diagram)**.

3. Fold each green and dark green pine tree point (N and O) as shown **(Folding Diagram)**; press. To keep points from unfolding, stack and weight them until you are ready to use them.

4. Center each small point (N) on a large point (O) and pin.

5. With right sides facing and raw edges aligned, pin 49 pine tree points, side by side, to each quilt side **(Pine Tree Points Diagram, Figure 1)**. Pin 41 points to top and bottom edges. Space points evenly along each edge. When satisfied with placement, stitch points in place ¼" from raw edges, being careful to keep backing fabric away from stitching.

6. Turn edges of backing under and blindstitch in place to cover raw edges of pine tree points .

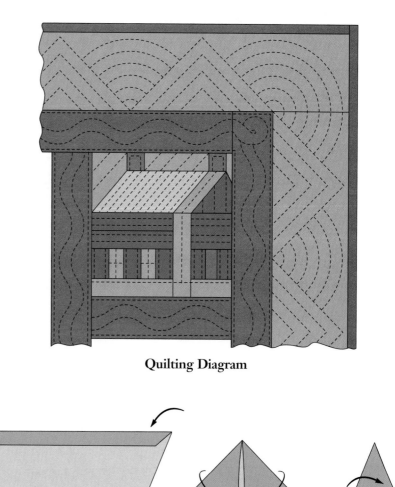

Quilting Diagram

Figure 1   **Figure 2**   **Figure 3**

Folding Diagram

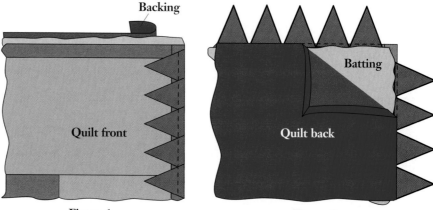

Figure 1   **Figure 2**

Pine Tree Points Diagram

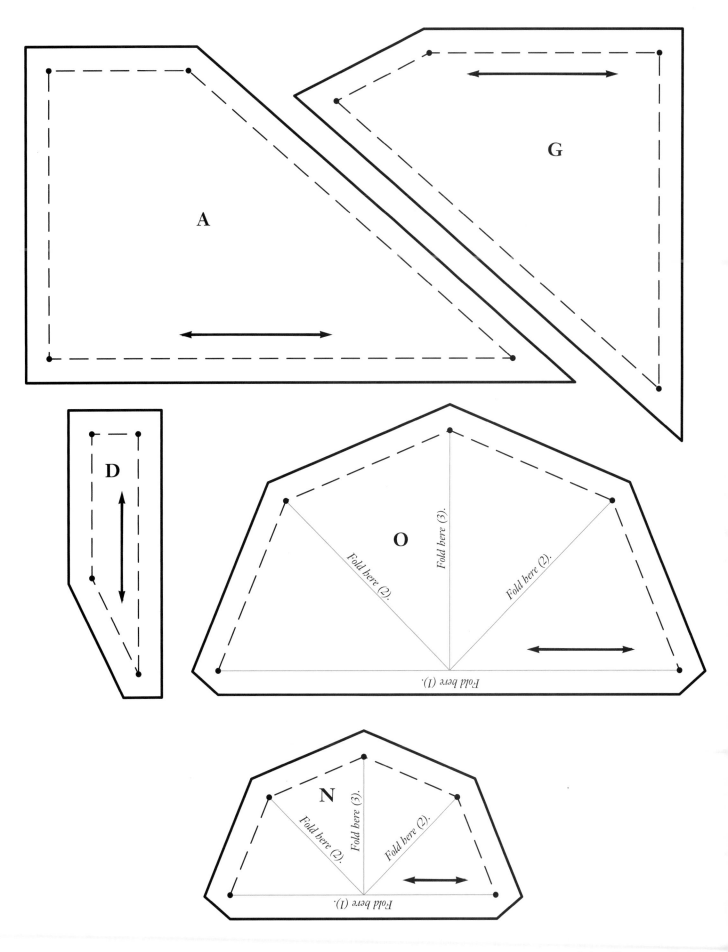

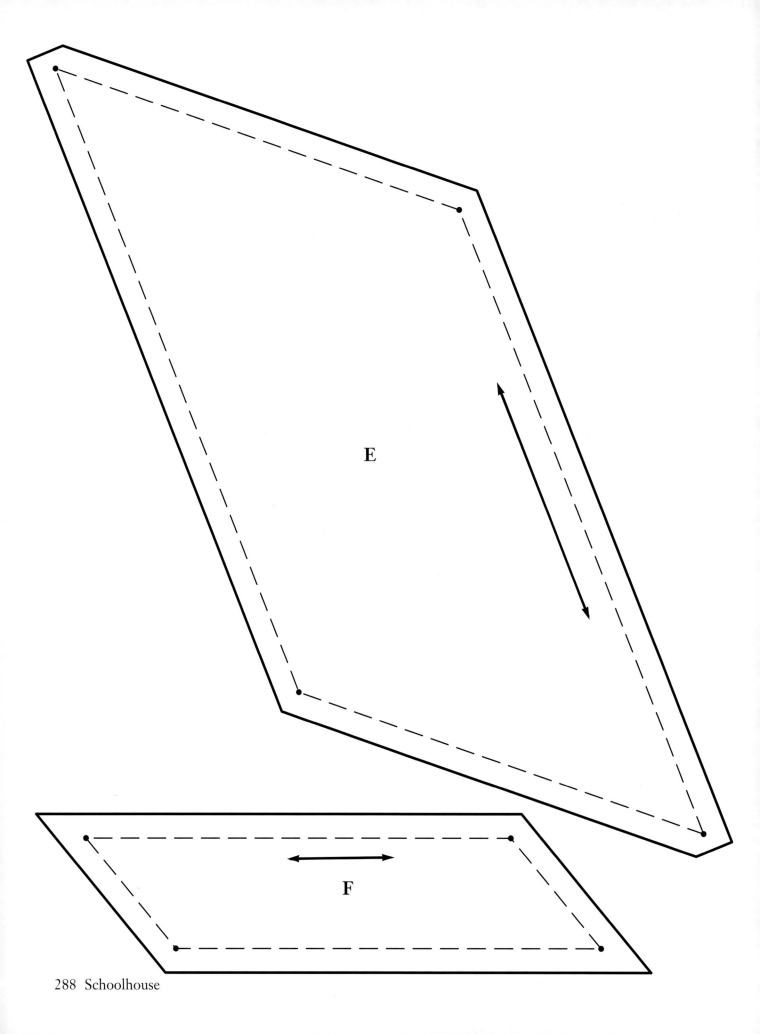

E

F

Seven Sisters

This traditional pieced block is inspired by seven sisters of Greek myth who were turned into stars by the gods. The block is a hexagon instead of the usual square.

Quilt by Judy Cantwell
Cahaba Heights, Alabama

Finished Quilt Size
70" x 87⅝"

Number of Blocks and Finished Size
20 blocks   13⅛" x 15"

Fabric Requirements
Muslin   3¼ yards
Blue print   2¾ yards
Red print   3 yards*
Backing   2⅛ yards 104" wide
*Includes fabric for straight-grain binding.

Cutting
Make templates of patterns A–D on page 291. Cut all strips cross-grain except as noted. Cut pieces in order listed to get best use of yardage.

From muslin
- 4 (7¼"-wide) strips. From these, cut 30 of Template C.
- 34 (1⅞"-wide) strips. From these, cut 360 of Template A and 120 of Template B.
- 2 (4½"-wide) strips. From these, cut 10 of Template D and 10 of Template D reversed.

From blue print
- 47 (1⅞"-wide) strips. From these, cut 840 of Template A.

Star Diagram

From red print
- 4 (5½" x 92") lengthwise strips for borders.
- 4 (3½" x 62") lengthwise strips for sashing.

Quilt Top Assembly
1. Join 6 blue As to make a star **(Star Diagram)**. Make 140 stars.
2. Join 7 stars with 18 muslin As and 6 Bs **(Block Assembly Diagram)**. (See page 10 for tips on sewing set-in seams.) Make 20 blocks.
3. Lay out blocks in 5 horizontal rows of 4 blocks each **(Row Assembly Diagram)**. Join blocks in each row with Cs as shown, ending each row with D and D reversed pieces. Press seam allowances toward Cs and Ds.
4. Join rows, alternating block rows and sashing strips.
5. Add borders, mitering corners.

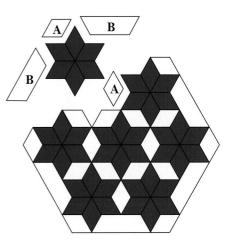

Block Assembly Diagram

Quilting and Finishing
1. Make stencils for flag and cable quilting designs. (See page 15 for tips on making stencils.) Mark flags in muslin triangles, positioning flags as shown on Pattern C. Mark cables in sashing strips.
2. Outline-quilt patchwork. Quilt flags and cables as marked and borders as desired.
3. See page 16 for instructions on making binding. Make 9 yards of 2½"-wide straight-grain binding from remaining red print fabric. Apply binding to quilt edges.

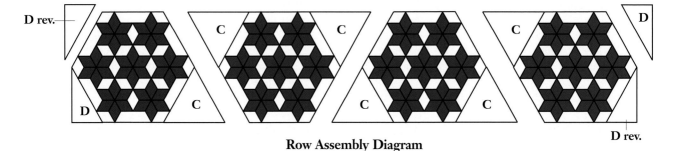

Row Assembly Diagram

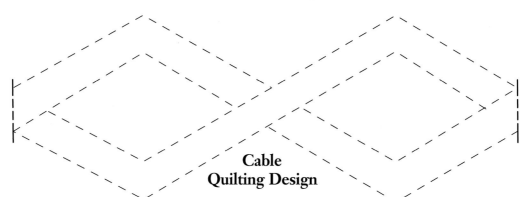

Cable Quilting Design

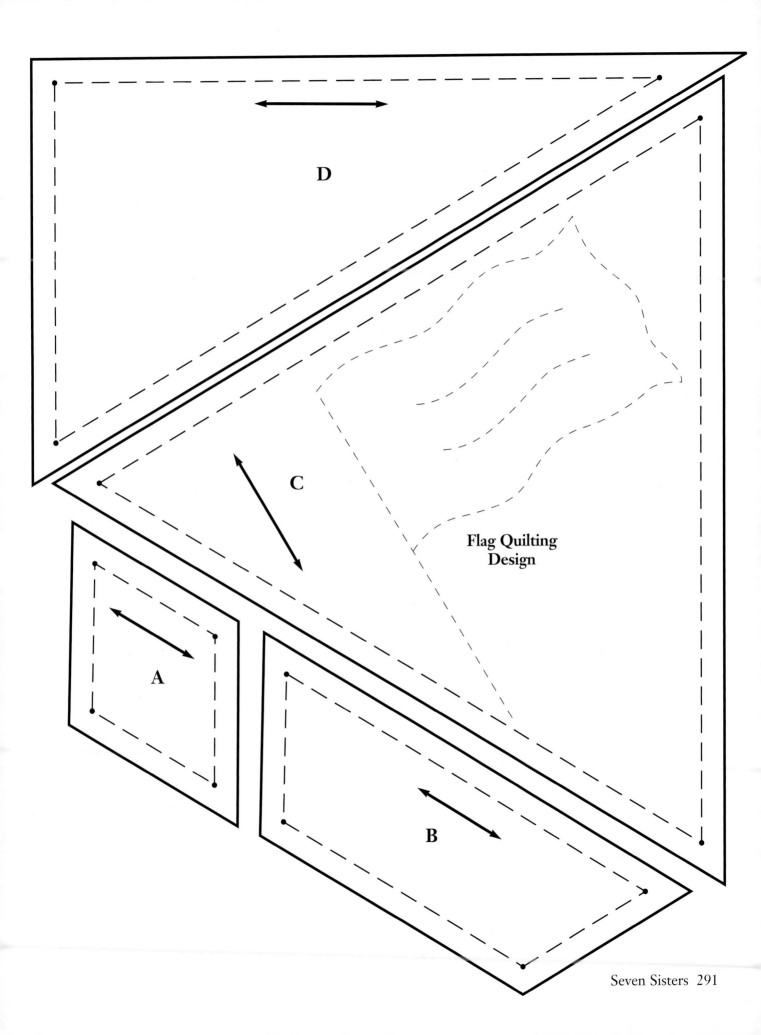

D

C

Flag Quilting
Design

A

B

Spider Web

Brew up a great Halloween combination with the traditional Spider Web design and a fun novelty print. Quilt bats in the borders for an extra touch of boo!

Quilt by Susan Ramey Cleveland
Leeds, Alabama

Finished Quilt Size
63" x 67¼"

Number of Blocks and Finished Size
18 blocks   11¼" x 13"
4 half blocks

Fabric Requirements
Black solid   5½ yards*
Black print   1 yard
Orange   1¾ yards
Binding   ¾ yard
*Includes backing fabric.

Cutting
Make templates of patterns A, B, and C on page 295. Mark seam placement lines on Templates A and C. Cut all strips cross-grain except as noted.

From black
• 2 (72" x 33") pieces for backing.
• 4 (4½" x 72") lengthwise strips for outer borders.
• 24 (2"-wide) strips.

From black print
• 4 (6⅜"-wide) strips. From each of 3 strips, cut 1 of Template C, 1 of Template C reversed, and 9 of Template A as shown **(Cutting Diagram 1)**. From fourth strip, cut 3 of Template C, 3 of Template C reversed and 7 of Template A to get a total of 34 A triangles, 6 C triangles, and 6 C reversed.
• 22 of Template B.

From orange
• 30 (2"-wide") strips. Set aside 6 strips for inner borders.

Quilt Top Assembly
1. Join 1 orange strip and 2 black strips to make Strip Set 1 as shown **(Cutting Diagram 2)**. Make 8 of Strip Set 1. Press seam allowances toward black.

2. Aligning seam placement lines on templates with strip-set seam lines, cut 1 C, 1 C reversed, and 7 A triangles from each of 2 strip sets **(Cutting Diagram 2)**. Note that points of templates will extend past strip unit.

3. Cut 8 As from each remaining Strip Set 1 **(Cutting Diagram 3)**.

4. In same manner, join 2 orange strips and 1 black strip to make Strip Set 2. Make 8 of Strip Set 2. Press seam allowances toward black. Cut 62 A triangles, 2 Cs, and 2 C reversed from Strip Set 2.

5. For each block, select 3 A triangles from each strip set and 1 B. Join short top edge of 1 A to 1 side of B, being careful not to stitch into seam allowance at ends of seam **(Block Assembly Diagram)**. Join a contrasting A triangle to adjacent edge of B in same manner; then join adjacent As. Continue to alternate As around B to complete block. Make 18 blocks.

6. Use remaining As, Cs, and Cs reversed to make 2 of each half-block shown **(Half-Block Assembly Diagram)**. Trim Bs to align with raw edges of Cs and Cs reversed.

continued

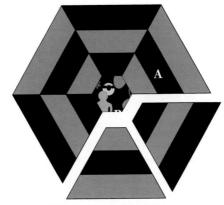
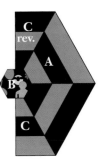

Block Assembly Diagram   **Half-Block Assembly Diagram**

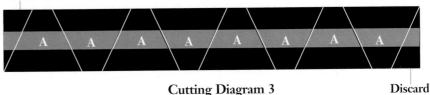

Cutting Diagram 1

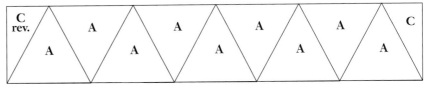

Cutting Diagram 2

Discard

Cutting Diagram 3   Discard

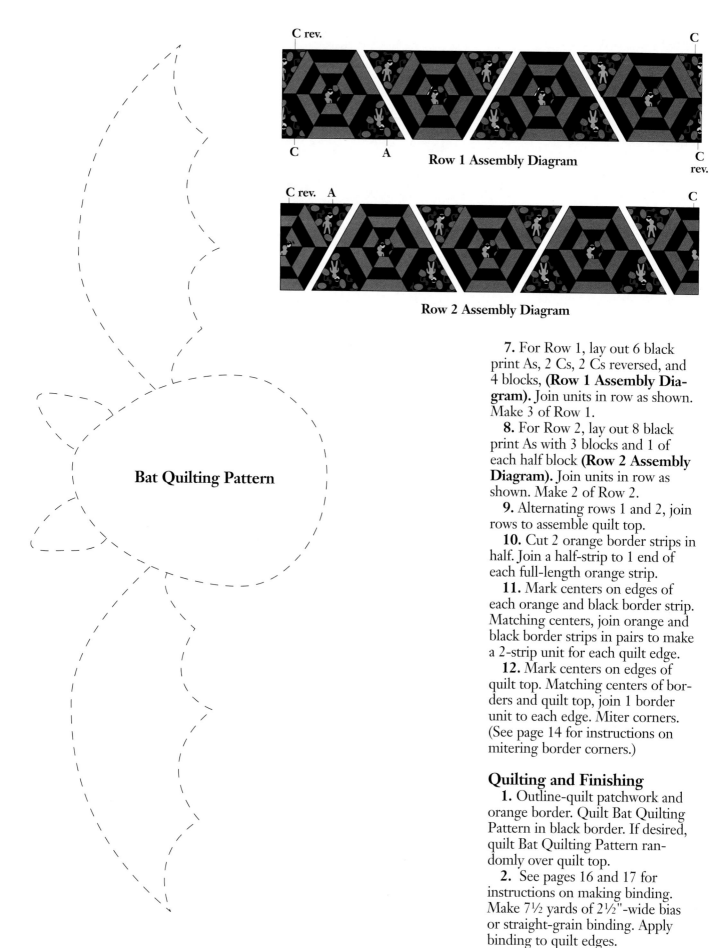

Row 1 Assembly Diagram

Row 2 Assembly Diagram

Bat Quilting Pattern

7. For Row 1, lay out 6 black print As, 2 Cs, 2 Cs reversed, and 4 blocks, **(Row 1 Assembly Diagram).** Join units in row as shown. Make 3 of Row 1.

8. For Row 2, lay out 8 black print As with 3 blocks and 1 of each half block **(Row 2 Assembly Diagram).** Join units in row as shown. Make 2 of Row 2.

9. Alternating rows 1 and 2, join rows to assemble quilt top.

10. Cut 2 orange border strips in half. Join a half-strip to 1 end of each full-length orange strip.

11. Mark centers on edges of each orange and black border strip. Matching centers, join orange and black border strips in pairs to make a 2-strip unit for each quilt edge.

12. Mark centers on edges of quilt top. Matching centers of borders and quilt top, join 1 border unit to each edge. Miter corners. (See page 14 for instructions on mitering border corners.)

Quilting and Finishing
1. Outline-quilt patchwork and orange border. Quilt Bat Quilting Pattern in black border. If desired, quilt Bat Quilting Pattern randomly over quilt top.

2. See pages 16 and 17 for instructions on making binding. Make 7½ yards of 2½"-wide bias or straight-grain binding. Apply binding to quilt edges.

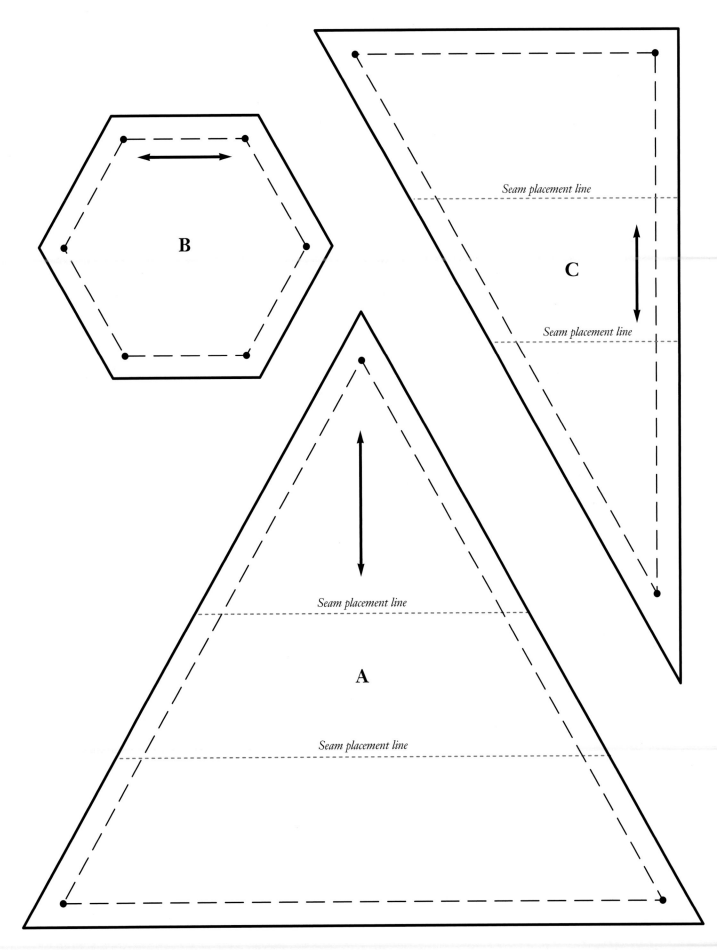

B

Seam placement line

C

Seam placement line

Seam placement line

A

Seam placement line

Spring Beauties

Rosie Grinstead's *Spring Beauties* captures the brilliance and freshness of spring. Rosie used as many different prints as she could to make her 144 buttercups, but you don't have to have 144 different fabrics. One pastel print, one beige print, and one green print make each buttercup, but you can use the same prints again in other buttercups.

Spring Beauties won Best Scrap Quilt and Color Award, National Quilting Association Show, 1989; First Place and Judge's Choice ribbons, Silver Dollar City Show, 1989; and Third Place in the 1991 Mid-Atlantic Quilt Festival at Williamsburg, Virginia.

Quilt by Rosie Grinstead
Mission Hills, Kansas

Finished Quilt Size
88" x 88"

Number of Blocks and Finished Size
36 blocks   12" x 12"

Fabric Requirements
3 beige prints   2 yards each
10 green prints   1 fat eighth each*
7 peach prints   1 fat eighth each*
7 yellow prints   1 fat eighth each*
7 blue prints   1 fat eighth each*
7 pink prints   1 fat eighth each*
8 lavender prints   1 fat eighth each*
Peach solid   1 fat eighth each*
Yellow solid   1 fat eighth each*
Blue solid   1 fat eighth each*
Pink solid   1 fat eighth each*
Lavender solid   1 fat eighth each*
Binding fabric   ⅞ yard
Backing   2¾ yards 104" wide
*Fat eighth = 9" x 22".

Cutting
Make a template of Pattern A. All remaining pieces are rotary cut. Cut all strips cross-grain.

From each beige print
- 14 (2⅞"-wide) strips. From these, cut 48 of Template A, 48 of Template A reversed, and 96 (2⅞") squares. Cut each square in half diagonally to get 192 D triangles.
- 10 (2½"-wide) strips. From these, cut 144 (2½") C squares for blocks and 17 (2½") C squares for border units. Cut 1 more C square for border from any scrap.

From green prints
- 28 (2⅞" x 22") strips total. From these, cut 196 (2⅞") squares. Cut each square in half diagonally to get 392 D triangles, 288 for blocks and 104 for border units.

From each print fat eighth
- 1 (2⅞" x 22") strip. From each strip, cut 4 (2⅞") squares; cut each square in half diagonally to get 8 D triangles. From remainder of each strip, cut 4 (2½") C squares.

From remaining print fabrics
- 8 (2⅞" x 22") strips. From these, cut 52 (2⅞") squares. Cut each square in half diagonally to get 104 D triangles for border units.
- 61 (2½" x 22") strips. From these, cut 484 (2½") C squares for border units.

From each solid fabric
- 28 (1½") B squares. Cut 4 additional squares of lavender solid for a total of 32 lavender.

Quilt Top Assembly
1. For each flower unit, select 1 C square and 2 D triangles of same print fabric, 1 coordinating B, 2 Ds of same green fabric, and a set of beige background pieces—1 A, 1 A reversed, 3 C squares, and 4 Ds. Join pieces in 3 horizontal rows **(Flower Unit Piecing Diagram)**. Join rows to complete unit.

2. Make 28 flower units each with peach, yellow, blue, and pink print flowers. Make 32 lavender units, for a total of 144 units.

3. For each block, join 4 units with same color flowers **(Block Piecing Diagram)**. Make 36 blocks—7 each of peach, yellow, blue, and pink and 8 lavender.

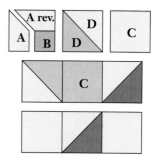

Flower Unit Piecing Diagram

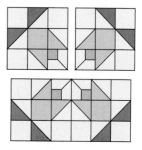

Block Piecing Diagram

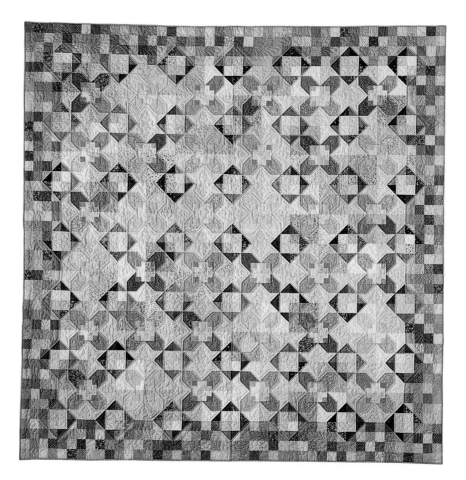

298 Spring Beauties

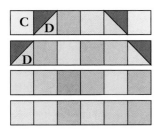

Border Unit—Make 24.

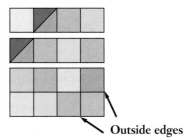

Corner Unit—Make 4.

Outside edges

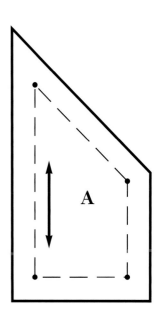

A

4. Lay out blocks in 6 horizontal rows, with 6 blocks in each row. Arrange blocks to get a pleasing balance of color. When satisfied with placement, join blocks in each row; then join rows.

5. For each border unit, select 2 beige C squares, 18 print Cs, 4 print D triangles, and 4 green Ds. (Use same green fabric for both triangles in each corner.) Join squares and triangles in rows as shown; then join rows to complete unit **(Border Unit Diagram)**. Make 24 border units.

6. For each corner unit, select 1 beige C square, 13 print Cs, 2 print D triangles and 2 matching green Ds. Join squares and triangles in rows as shown; then join rows to complete unit **(Corner Unit Diagram)**. Make 4 corner units.

7. Join 6 border units in a row to make a border. Make 4 borders. Sew borders to top and bottom edges of quilt, easing to fit as necessary **(Setting Diagram)**. Add corner units to ends of each remaining row and sew borders to quilt sides, easing to fit as needed.

Quilting and Finishing

1. Outline-quilt seam lines. Quilt shown also has a heart quilted in each flower C square and a continuous feather design quilted in borders **(Quilting Diagram)**. Purchase similar designs or draft your own.

2. See pages 16 and 17 for instructions on making binding. Make 10 yards of 2½"-wide bias or straight-grain binding. Apply binding to quilt edges.

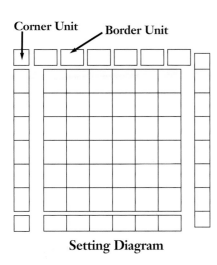

Corner Unit   Border Unit

Setting Diagram

Quilting Diagram

Star & Crescent

An appliquéd border frames these Star & Crescent blocks,
a design also known as Four Winds and Alaska Chinook.
The block piecing is challenging, so precision is the key to
success. Refer to the Workshop (page 8) for tips on careful
cutting, piecing curved seams, and pressing seam allowances.

Quilt by Pauline F. Spieks
Stone Mountain, Georgia

Finished Quilt Size
102" x 117"

Number of Blocks and Finished Size
42 blocks   15" x 15"

Fabric Requirements
Muslin   12 yards
Red print   5¾ yards*
Backing   3½ yards 120" wide
*Includes 1 yard for binding.

Cutting
Make templates of patterns A–G on pages 302 and 303. Cut all strips cross-grain except as noted.

From muslin
- 4 (6½" x 121") lengthwise strips for borders.
- 6 (3¾"-wide) strips. From these and scrap from borders, cut 168 of Template B.
- 34 (8¼"-wide) strips. From these, cut 168 of Template D.

From red print
- 21 (3⅜"-wide) strips. From these, cut 168 of Template A.
- 12 (3¾"-wide) strips. From these, cut 168 of Template C.
- 1 (36") square for binding.
- 11 (4"-wide) strips. From these and scrap from binding, cut 78 of Template E and 4 of Template F.
- 3 (1½"-wide) strips. From these, cut 82 of Template G.

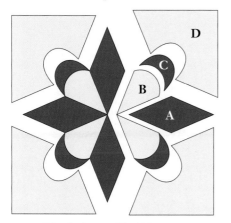

Block Assembly Diagram

Quilt Top Assembly
1. Join 1 B to C to make a pieced cone unit **(Block Assembly Diagram).** Make 168 cones. Press seam allowances toward Bs.

2. For each block, join 4 cones and 4 A diamonds to make a star. Add D corner pieces to complete block as shown. Make 42 blocks.

3. Lay out blocks in 7 horizontal rows, with 6 blocks in each row. Join blocks in rows; then join rows.

4. Mark centers of each border strip and each quilt edge. Matching centers, sew border strips to all edges. See page 14 for instructions on mitering border corners.

5. Center 1 F over each mitered seam and pin. Pin 18 Es on top and bottom borders and 21 Es on each side border as shown. Pin Gs over ends where scallops meet. Appliqué all pieces.

Quilting and Finishing
1. Outline-quilt patchwork and appliqué. Add other quilting as desired.

2. See pages 16 and 17 for instructions on making binding. Make 12⅜ yards of 2½"-wide bias or straight-grain binding. Apply binding to quilt edges.

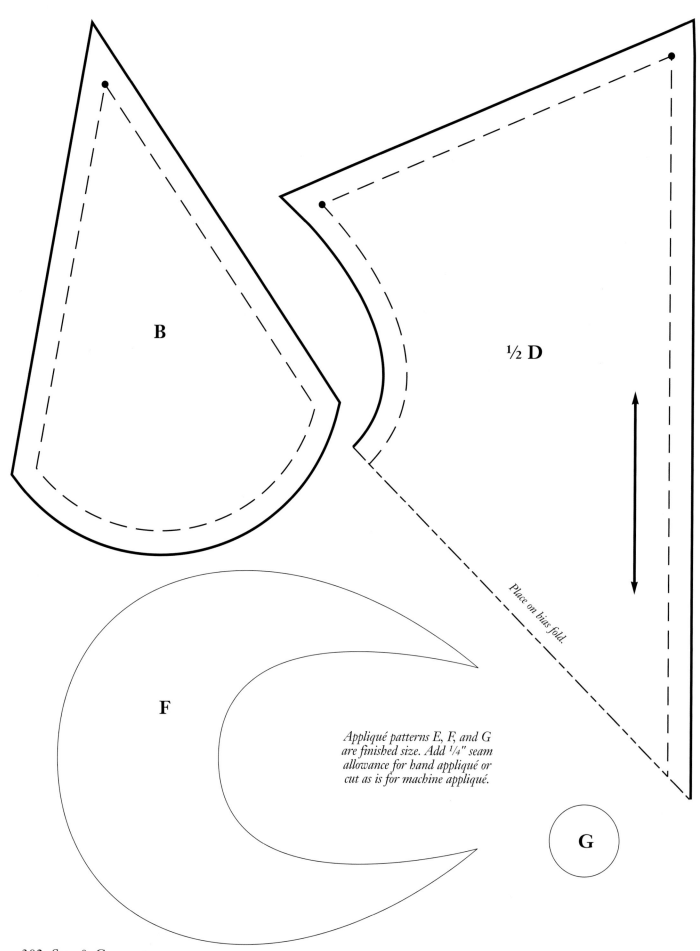

B

½ D

Place on bias fold.

F

Appliqué patterns E, F, and G are finished size. Add ¼" seam allowance for hand appliqué or cut as is for machine appliqué.

G

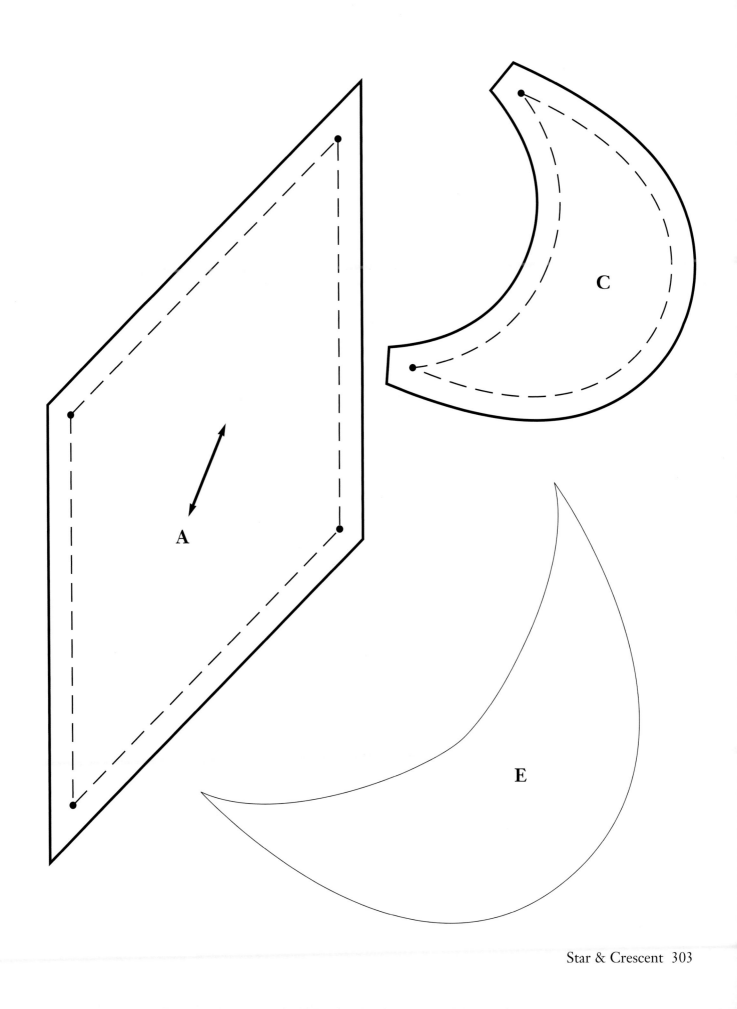

A

C

E

Starlight Nights

A special fabric sparked the idea for this quilt. "I love cats," Judith Hindall says, "and I enjoy using cat fabric when I can find it." This block showcases cat faces Judy found hiding among the flowers in a print fabric. Our instructions for this block suggest a partial-seam technique to eliminate the need for set-in seams.

Quilt by Judith Hindall
Stow, Ohio

Finished Quilt Size
84" x 84"

Number of Blocks and Finished Size
25 blocks   10" x 10"

Fabric Requirements
Blue   5¼ yards
Navy   1½ yards
Floral print   1½ yards*
Green   ¼ yard
White   ¼ yard
Binding fabric   1 yard
Backing   7½ yards

*More fabric may be necessary, depending upon repeat of desired motif in print. The floral cat fabric used in *Starlight Nights* is a discontinued Springs Industries print designed by Marti Michell. Look for a similar fabric with floral or other motifs to use in your quilt.

Cutting
Make a template of Pattern A on page 307. If you want to frame a special motif in the piece, make a window template (see page 8 for notes on window templates). Cut strips lengthwise except as noted.
From blue
- 4 (3" x 86") lengthwise strips for outer border. Use 32" x 86" strip remaining for next cut.
- 24 (10½") setting squares.
- 25 (3⅞"-wide) strips. From these, cut 150 (3⅞") squares. Cut each square in half diagonally to get 300 B triangles.
- 3 (3½"-wide) strips. From these, cut 30 (1½" x 3½") E pieces, 20 (2" x 3½") F pieces, and 7 (2½" x 3½") G pieces.

From navy
- 12 (2⅜"-wide) strips. From these, cut 200 (2⅜") squares. Cut each square in half diagonally to get 400 D triangles.
- 2 (3½"-wide) strips. From these and remainder from previous step, cut 29 (1½" x 3½") E pieces, 19 (2" x 3½") F pieces, and 5 (2½" x 3½") G pieces.
- 8 (2"-wide) strips for inner border.

From floral print
- 4 (4⅝"-wide) strips. From these, cut 25 of Template A.
- 10 (2"-wide) strips. From these, cut 200 C squares.
- 3 (3½"-wide) strips. From these, cut 16 (1½" x 3½") E pieces, 10 (2" x 3½") F pieces, 6 (2½" x 3½") G pieces, 12 (3" x 3½") H pieces, and 4 (3½") squares for border corners.

From green
- 2 (3½"-wide) strips. From these, cut 27 (1½" x 3½") E pieces and 9 (2" x 3½") F pieces.

From white
- 2 (3½"-wide) strips. From these, cut 37 (1½" x 3½") E pieces.

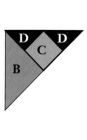
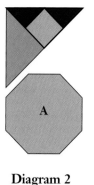
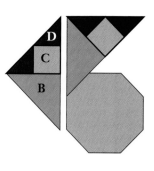

Diagram 1   **Diagram 2**   **Diagram 3**

Quilt Top Assembly
1. Sew 2 D triangles to adjacent sides of 1 C square. Press seam allowances toward Ds **(Diagram 1)**. Add a B triangle to 1 side as shown. Make 8 B/C/D units.

2. Join 1 unit to A, stitching about half the seam **(Diagram 2)**. Leave remainder of seam open for now. Working in a counterclockwise direction, join a second unit to A **(Diagram 3)**. Continue in this manner to join all 8 units **(Diagram 4)**. When last unit is in place, align first unit with edge and complete partially sewn seam.

3. Add 1 B to each corner to complete block **(Diagram 5)**. Press seam allowances toward Bs.

4. Make 25 blocks.

continued

Diagram 4

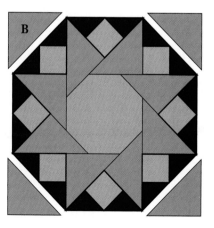

Diagram 5

5. For Row 1, join 4 blocks and 3 setting squares in a horizontal row as shown **(Setting Diagram).** Make 4 of Row 1. Make 3 of Row 2 in same manner, joining 3 blocks and 4 setting squares as shown. Press seam allowances toward setting squares.

6. Join rows, alternating rows 1 and 2 as shown.

7. Sew 2 navy border strips end-to-end to make a border for each quilt side. Stitch borders to quilt sides; then join borders to top and bottom edges of quilt. Press seam allowances toward borders.

8. Measure quilt sides. Join Es, Fs, Gs, and Hs in random order to make 2 pieced borders to match length (about 74½"). Begin and end each border strip with a navy F. Join borders to quilt sides.

9. Make top and bottom pieced borders in same manner. Join 1 (3½") floral print square to ends of each border. Join borders to top and bottom edges of quilt.

10. Join blue border strips to quilt sides; then sew remaining borders to top and bottom edges. Press seam allowances toward blue borders.

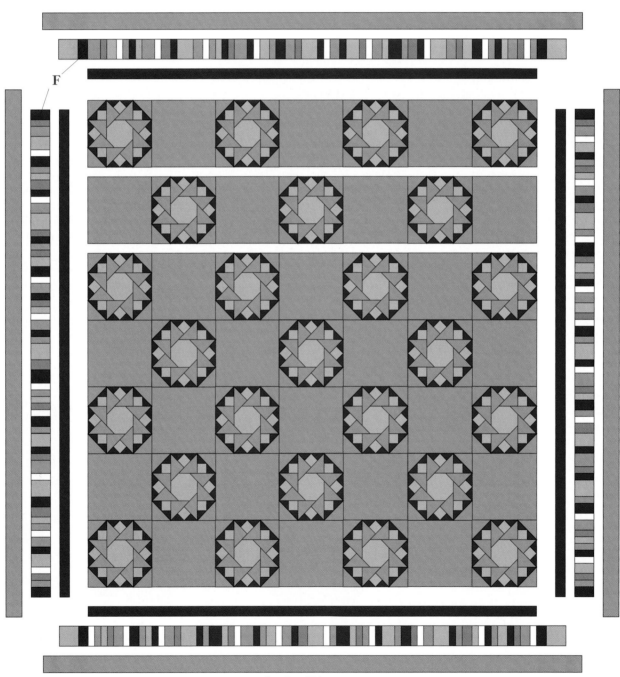

Setting Diagram

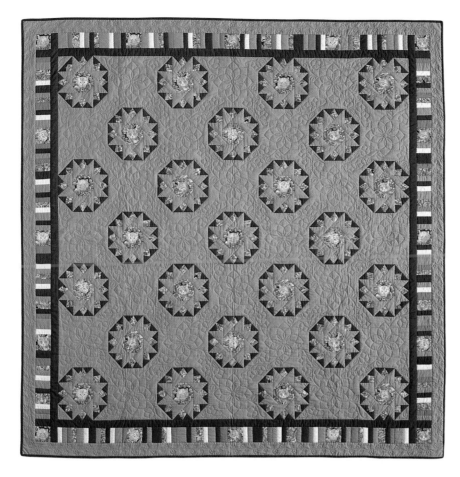

Quilting and Finishing

1. Make stencils of rose and rosebud quilting patterns on page 308. Mark rose design in setting squares. Mark rosebud vine design diagonally between blocks and on outer border as shown.

2. Outline-quilt stars. Quilt rose and rosebud designs. Quilt navy border in-the-ditch.

3. See pages 16 and 17 for instructions on making binding. Make 9½ yards of 2½"-wide bias or straight-grain binding. Apply binding to quilt edges.

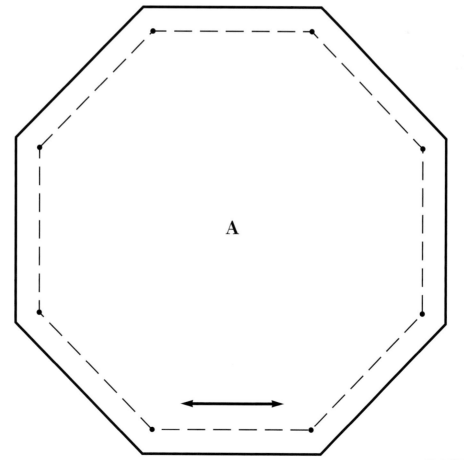

A

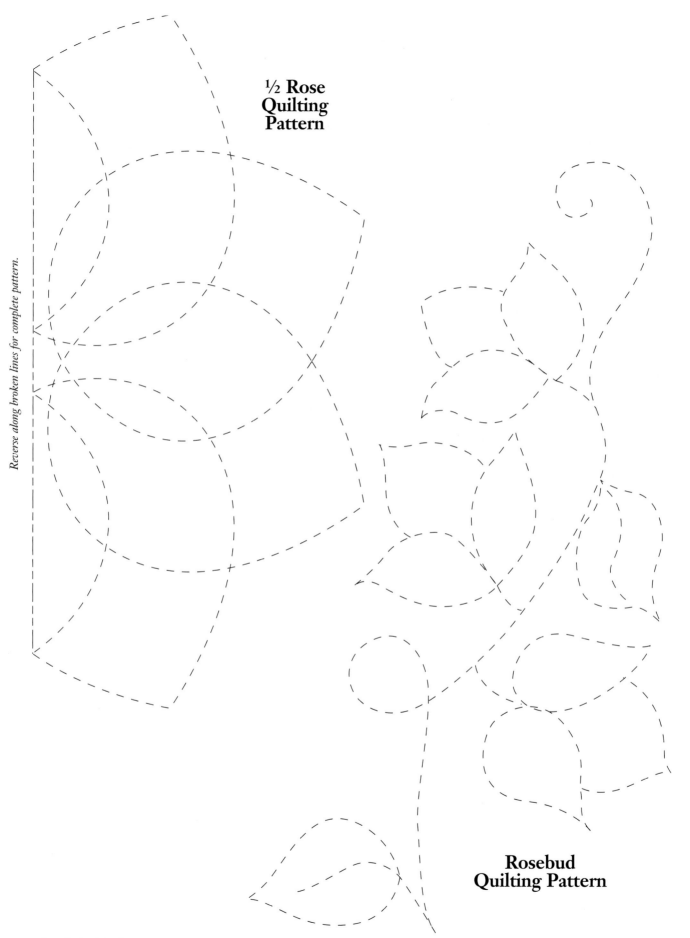

½ **Rose
Quilting
Pattern**

Reverse along broken lines for complete pattern.

**Rosebud
Quilting Pattern**

Stepping Stones

This quilt is an elegant pairing of red and white, but you can be more daring with the fabrics—use a mix of red scraps instead of one print, or reverse the placement of dark and light for a dramatic look. With timesaving techniques and rotary cutting, you can get the piecing done between Christmas and New Year's Eve.

Quilt by Annie C. Phillips
Hayden, Alabama

Finished Quilt Size
82" x 100"

Number of Blocks and Finished Size
12 blocks   16" x 16"

Fabric Requirements
Red   3¾ yards
Muslin   7¼ yards*
Backing   6 yards

*Includes fabric for binding.

Cutting
Make a template of Pattern D on page 311. All other pieces are rotary cut. Cut all strips cross-grain except as noted.

From red
- 2 (2½" x 99") and 2 (2½" x 84") lengthwise strips for outer border. Use 32"-wide strip leftover for next 3 cuts.
- 2 (4½" x 32") strips. From these, cut 12 (4½") E squares.
- 16 (2½" x 32") strips. From these, cut 48 of Template D and 48 of Template D reversed.
- 11 (2½" x 32") strips. From these, cut 124 (2½") A squares for sashing and border.
- 9 (2½"-wide) strips for quick piecing.

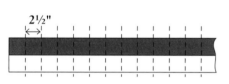

Strip Set 1—Make 6.

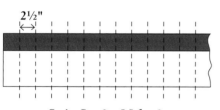

Strip Set 2—Make 3.

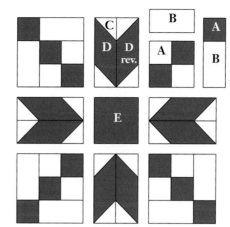

Block Assembly Diagram

From muslin
- 1 (2¾-yard) length. From this, cut 2 (4½" x 99"), 2 (4½" x 85"), 2 (4½" x 72"), and 2 (4½" x 58") lengthwise strips for borders. Use scraps for next cut.
- 96 (2⅞") squares. Cut each square in half diagonally to get 192 C triangles.
- 3 (4½"-wide) strips and 6 (2½"-wide) strips for quick piecing.
- 3 (4½"-wide) strips. From these, cut 48 (2½" x 4½") B pieces.
- 5 (4"-wide) strips. From these, cut 50 (4") squares. Cut each square in quarters diagonally to get 200 F triangles.
- 16 (2½"-wide) strips. From these, cut 31 (2½" x 16½") sashing strips.
- 8 (2¼") squares. Cut each square in half diagonally to get 16 G triangles.

Quick Piecing
1. Join pairs of red and muslin 2½"-wide strips as shown to make Strip Set 1 (**Strip Set 1 Diagram**). Make 6 strip sets. Press seam allowances toward red.

2. Cut 16 (2½"-wide) segments from each strip set to get 96 A units. Join 2 units to make a four-patch (**Block Assembly Diagram**). Make 48 four-patch units.

3. Join each remaining 2½"-wide red strip to a 4½"-wide muslin strip to make Strip Set 2 (**Strip Set 2 Diagram**). Make 3 strip sets. Press seam allowances toward red.

4. Cut 2½"-wide segments from these strip sets to get 48 A/B units (**Block Assembly Diagram**).

Quilt Top Assembly
1. For each block, select 4 four-patch units, 4 A/B units, and 4 B pieces. Sew B to 1 edge of each four-patch as shown (**Block Assembly Diagram**). Press seam allowances toward Bs.

2. Sew A/B unit to adjacent side of four-patch.

3. Select 16 C triangles and 4 each of D and D reversed. Sew Cs to each D piece as shown. Join D and D reversed units to get 4 diamond units.

4. Lay out assembled block units in rows as shown, adding E square in center row (**Block Assembly Diagram**). Join units in rows; then join rows to complete block.

5. Make 12 blocks.

6. Referring to Setting Diagram, Lay out blocks in 4 horizontal rows, with 3 blocks in each row. Place sashing strips between blocks and at row ends. Join blocks and sashing in each row. Press seam allowances toward sashing.

7. For each sashing row, join 4 red A squares and 3 sashing strips as shown. Make 5 rows. Press seam allowances toward sashing.

8. Join block rows and sashing rows as shown.

9. Join 58" muslin borders to top and bottom edges of quilt. Trim borders even with quilt sides; press seam allowances toward borders.

10. Measure length of quilt through middle of quilt top. Trim 85" muslin borders to this length, but do not join yet.

11. Join red As to Fs and Gs to make units for middle borders (**Border Piecing Diagram**). Using a scant ¼" seam, make 28 G/A/F units for each side border. Join units to make border strip. Compare

Strip Set 1—Make 6.

Setting Diagram

length of pieced borders with trimmed muslin borders; then adjust piecing as necessary to make borders match. Join pieced borders to muslin borders as shown; then join border unit to quilt sides.

12. Join 24 G/A/F units each for top and bottom border in same manner as for side borders. Adjust seams as necessary to fit borders to width of quilt. Join pieced borders to top and bottom edges of quilt.

13. Join 72" border strip to top and bottom edges.

14. Matching long edges, join 99"-long red and muslin borders. Add these units to quilt sides as shown. Join remaining red borders to top and bottom edges.

Quilting and Finishing
1. Use a purchased stencil to mark a 3"-wide cable design in muslin borders.

2. Outline-quilt patchwork and sashing; then quilt marked borders.

3. See pages 16 and 17 for instructions on making binding. Make 10⅜ yards of 2½"-wide bias or straight-grain binding from remaining muslin. Apply binding to quilt edges.

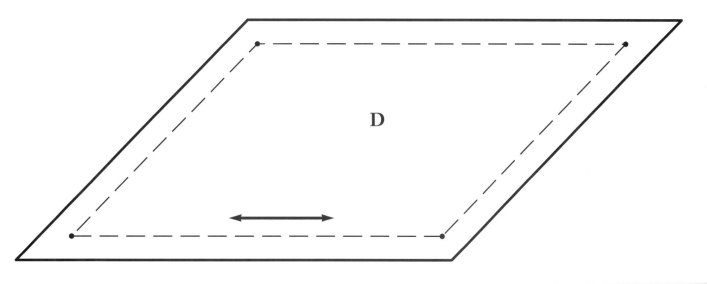

D

Stepping Stones 311

Storm at Sea

The pieced sashing in this dramatic quilt creates an illusion of stars on a storm-tossed sea. An all-time favorite, this block is often interpreted in nautical blue and white fabrics. Different color schemes, even a scrap-bag approach, are guaranteed to please.

Quilt by Arthur A. Bluj
Winston-Salem, North Carolina

Finished Quilt Size
76" x 88"

Number of Blocks and Finished Size
42 large blocks   8" x 8"
56 small blocks   4" x 4"
97 sashing blocks   4" x 8"

Fabric Requirements
White   3½ yards
Blue   3 yards
Navy   3 yards
Binding fabric   1 yard
Backing   5¼ yards

Cutting
Make templates of patterns D and E on page 314. Other pieces are rotary cut. Cut all strips cross-grain.

From white
- 8 (3¾"-wide) strips. From these, cut 84 (3¾") squares. Cut each square in half diagonally to get 168 B triangles.
- 15 (4½"-wide) strips. From these, cut 194 of Template E and 194 of Template E reversed.
- 7 (2⅜"-wide) strips. From these, cut 112 (2⅜") squares. Cut each square in half diagonally to get 224 G triangles.

From blue
- 5 (4½"-wide) strips. From these, cut 42 (4½") A squares.
- 11 (4⅞"-wide) strips. From these, cut 84 (4⅞") squares. Cut each square in half diagonally to get 168 C triangles.
- 4 (2½"-wide) strips. From these, cut 56 (2½") F squares.

From navy
- 14 (4⅜"-wide) strips. From these, cut 97 of Template D.
- 8 (2⅞"-wide) strips. From these, cut 112 (2⅞") squares. Cut each square in half diagonally to get 224 H triangles.

Quilt Top Assembly
1. Sew 4 B triangles to sides of each A square **(Block Assembly Diagram)**. Press seam allowances toward Bs. Join 4 Cs as shown to corner to complete block. Press seam allowances toward Cs. Make 42 large blocks.

2. Join Fs, Gs, and Hs in same manner to make 56 small blocks.

3. Sew 4 Es to each D **(Sashing Block Assembly Diagram)**. Press seam allowances toward Ds. Make 97 sashing blocks.

4. Lay out 7 small blocks in a row, alternating with 6 sashing blocks. Join blocks to make 1 sashing row. Make 8 sashing rows.

5. Lay out 6 large blocks in a row, alternating with 7 sashing blocks. Join blocks to make 1 block row. Make 7 block rows.

6. Beginning with a sashing row, lay out rows, alternating sashing rows and block rows as shown. Join rows to complete quilt top.

continued

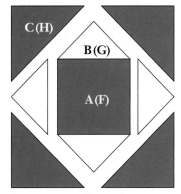

(Letters in parentheses indicate pieces for small blocks.)

Block Assembly Diagram

Sashing Block Assembly Diagram

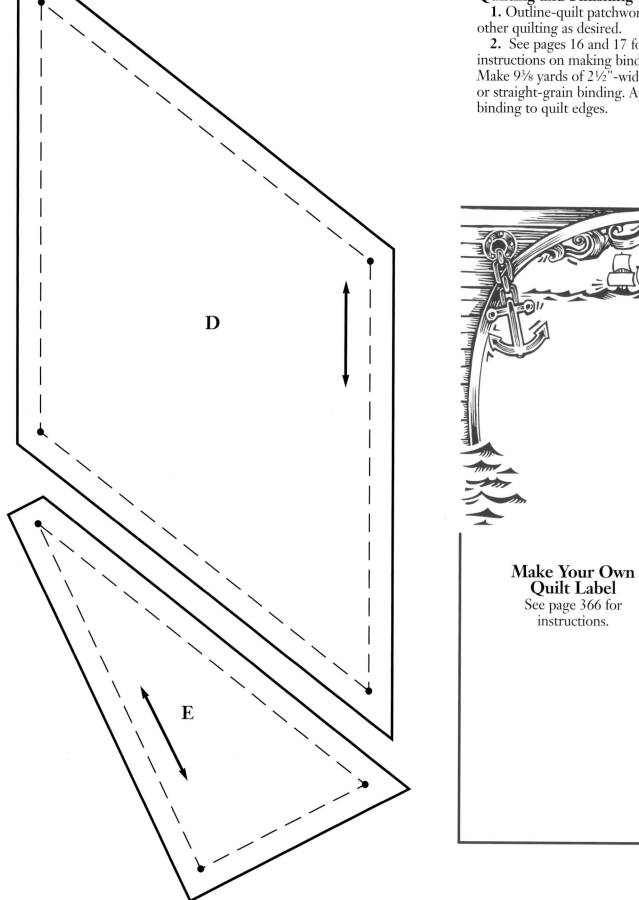

D

E

Quilting and Finishing
1. Outline-quilt patchwork. Add other quilting as desired.
2. See pages 16 and 17 for instructions on making binding. Make 9⅜ yards of 2½"-wide bias or straight-grain binding. Apply binding to quilt edges.

Make Your Own Quilt Label
See page 366 for instructions.

Sunbonnet Sue

Subonnet Sue and her friends have been loved by generations of quilters. They were born in the early 1900s when artist Bertha L. Corbett set out to convince friends that a faceless figure could express emotion. Corbett drew many Sunbonnet Babies, who later appeared in books, comic strips, and advertising motifs. The Babies were soon adopted as quilt designs and have been appliquéd in various poses ever since.

Quilt by Zelda Wheeler Fasciano
Greenville, North Carolina

Finished Quilt Size
78⅜" x 91½"

Number of Blocks and Finished Size
30 blocks   9¼" x 9¼"

Fabric Requirements
Green	4 yards*
Muslin	2¼ yards
Black or brown	scraps or ⅛ yard
Assorted prints	30 (7" x 9") pieces
Solids	30 (3") squares
Backing	6 yards

*Includes fabric for binding.

Other Materials
Assorted colors embroidery floss

Cutting
Make templates of patterns A–E on page 318. Cut all strips cross-grain.

From green
- 10 (9¾"-wide) strips. From these, cut 38 (9¾") setting squares and 4 (5" x 9¾") border rectangles.
- 1 (30") square for bias binding.
- 2 (5"-wide) strips. From these and scraps from previous steps, cut 22 (5") border squares.

From muslin
- 8 (9¾"-wide) strips. From these, cut 30 (9¾") squares for blocks.
- 15 *each* of Template D (arm) and Template D reversed.

From black
- 15 *each* of Template A (shoe) and Template A reversed.

From each print
- 1 of Template C (dress/bonnet) *or* Template C reversed.

From each solid
- 1 set of 1 Template B (pantaloons) and 1 Template E (sleeve) *or* 1 set of Template B reversed and Template E.

Setting Diagram

Quilt Top Assembly
1. Fold each muslin square in quarters diagonally; finger-press creases to make appliqué placement guidelines.

2. For 1 block, select 1 set of B and E pieces and 1 each of A, C, and D. Center and pin pieces on muslin square **(Appliqué Placement Diagram)**. Appliqué pieces in place in alphabetical order.

3. Using 3 strands of coordinating floss, embroider bonnet hatband in running stitch and bonnet ties in outline stitch as shown on pattern (see stitch diagram on page 182). Use 2 strands of contrasting floss to work small lazy daisy stitches on pantaloons and buttonhole stitches at bottom edges of

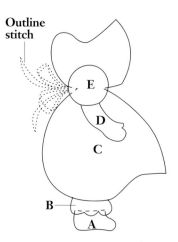

Outline stitch

Appliqué Placement Diagram

sleep and pantaloons (see stitch diagrams on page 318).

4. Make 30 blocks, half with girl turned to right and half to left using reversed pieces.

5. Lay out blocks in diagonal rows with green setting squares **(Setting Diagram)**. All girls face same direction in each diagonal row. Add 5" green squares to ends of rows. Note that center 2 rows have small squares at 1 end only. Join diagonal rows.

6. Join remaining 5" squares to ends of each 5" x 9¾" rectangle. Join 1 pieced unit to each corner of quilt top **(Setting Diagram)**.

Quilting and Finishing

1. Purchase a commercial stencil of a feathered wreath about 8" in diameter. Make a stencil of Heart Quilting Pattern below. Mark wreath in setting squares and heart on border setting squares.

2. Outline-quilt appliqué. Quilt marked designs. On quilt shown, remaining areas are quilted in a 1⅛" crosshatch pattern.

3. See pages 16 and 17 for instructions on making binding. Make 10 yards of 2"-wide bias or straight-grain binding. Apply binding to quilt edges, carefully mitering corners.

**Heart
Quilting
Pattern**

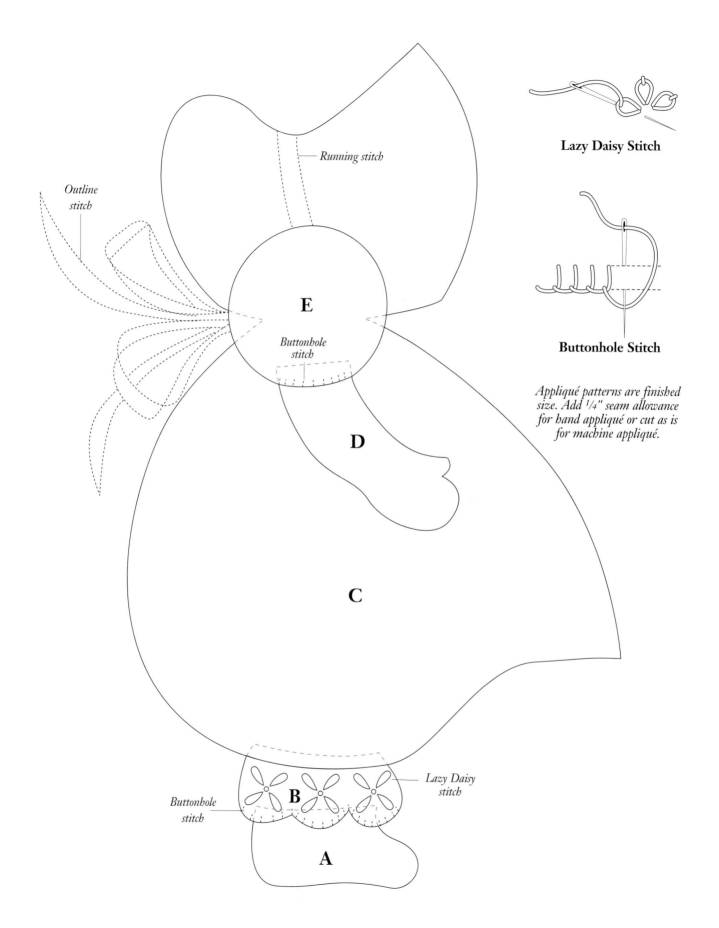

Lazy Daisy Stitch

Buttonhole Stitch

Appliqué patterns are finished size. Add ¹/₄" seam allowance for hand appliqué or cut as is for machine appliqué.

Running stitch

Outline stitch

E

Buttonhole stitch

D

C

Lazy Daisy stitch

B

Buttonhole stitch

A

Sunflower

If quilts could talk, *Sunflower* might tell us of being carefully
pieced by Mary Jo Coop Jackson's great-grandmother Virginia
Webb Coop in the early 1900s. In later years, *Sunflower* was passed
to Virginia's grandson Arthur Coop and then to Mary Jo. Now,
Sunflower rests contentedly among a multitude of family quilts.

Quilt owned by Mary Jo Coop Jackson and Leonard L. Jackson
Estill Springs, Tennessee

Finished Quilt Size
82" x 102"

Number of Blocks and Finished Size
27 blocks	11" x 11"
15 half blocks	
2 quarter blocks	

Fabric Requirements
Pumpkin	3½ yards
Green	3½ yards
Muslin	3¾ yards
Orange	⅞ yard*
Backing	6 yards

*Includes fabric for straight-grain binding.

Other Materials
½"-wide bias pressing bar

Cutting
Make templates of patterns A, E, G, J, and M on page 322. Remaining pieces can be rotary cut. Cut all strips cross-grain except as noted.

From pumpkin
- 2 (3¾" x 105") lengthwise border strips.
- 60 (1⅝" x 36") strips. From these, cut 840 of Template A.
- 4 (5⅞") squares. Cut each square in quarters diagonally to get 15 I triangles (and 1 extra).
- 1 (3¼") square. Cut square in half diagonally to get 2 L triangles.
- 3 (3¾"-wide) strips. From these, cut 27 (3¾") sashing squares.

From green
- 2 (2½" x 105") lengthwise border strips. Use 38"-wide strip left over for next 2 cuts.
- 24 (3¾" x 38") strips. From these, cut 70 (3¾" x 11½") sashing strips.
- 7 (2⅛" x 38") strips. From these, cut 35 of Template E and 35 of Template E reversed.
- 14 (1"-wide) strips. From these and scraps, cut 27 (1" x 10¾") H stems and 70 (1" x 4½") H stems.

From orange
- 9 (2½"-wide) strips for binding.
- 114 of Template J.

From muslin
- 24 (2⅛"-wide) strips. From these, cut 27 of Template G, 8 of Template M, 8 of Template M rev., and 402 (2⅛") B squares.
- 38 (3½"-wide") strips. From these, cut 114 (3½") squares. Cut each square in quarters diagonally to get 456 C triangles.
- 3 (6⅜"-wide) strips. From these, cut 14 (6⅜") squares. Cut each square in half diagonally to get 27 D triangles (and 1 extra).
- 1 (4⅛"-wide) strips. From this and scraps from previous steps, cut 14 (4⅛") squares. Cut each square in half diagonally to get 27 F triangles (and 1 extra).
- 8 (4¾") squares. Cut each square in half diagonally to get 16 K triangles.
- 8 (3¼") squares. Cut each square in half diagonally to get 16 L triangles.

Quilt Top Assembly
1. Join 8 A diamonds to make a sunflower, being careful to stitch all seams from seam line to seam line (**Sunflower Piecing Diagram**).

2. Set B squares and C triangles into openings between diamonds, leaving a small portion of 1 seam unstitched for insertion of stem (**Block Piecing Diagram**). (See page 10 for tips on sewing set-in seams.) Make 3 sunflower squares.

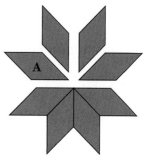

Sunflower Piecing Diagram

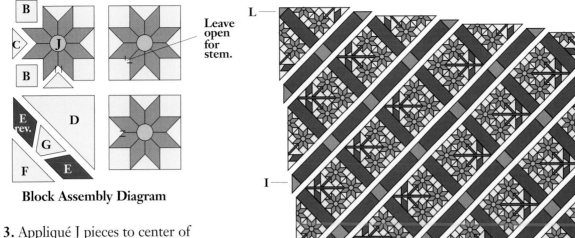

Block Assembly Diagram

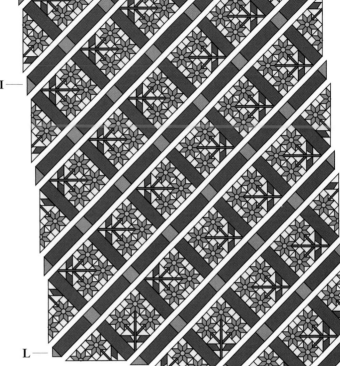

3. Appliqué J pieces to center of each sunflower.

4. Join D, E, E reversed, F, and G to make leaf unit (**Block Assembly Diagram**). Join leaf square and 3 sunflower squares.

5. Center 1 long stem piece on pressing bar and press ¼" on each long edge over bar. Repeat with 2 short stems. Appliqué short stems in place on block, inserting ends through unstitched openings in seam lines (**Appliqué Placement Diagram**). Appliqué long stem in place. Stitch block seams closed, catching stems.

6. Make 27 Sunflower blocks.

7. Make 1 flower quarter-block and 1 leaf quarter-block each as shown (**Quarter-Block Assembly Diagrams**). Appliqué stems and J centers to blocks. On half-flowers, trim Js even with seam allowance.

8. Make 8 half-blocks as shown (**Half-Block Assembly Diagram**). Then make 7 mirror-image half-blocks by switching positions of

Setting Diagram

half flower and leaf unit, using E rev. and M rev. pieces (**Setting Diagram**). Appliqué stems and Js on half-blocks. On half flowers, trim Js even with seam allowance.

9. Lay out blocks, half-blocks, and quarter-blocks in diagonal rows with sashing strips between

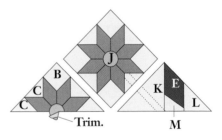

Half-Block Assembly Diagram

blocks (**Setting Diagram**). Decide if you want sunflowers pointing into center of quilt as shown or all pointing in same direction. Join units in each row. Press seam allowances toward sashing.

10. For each sashing row, alternate sashing squares and sashing strips as shown. Join I triangles or L triangles to ends of each sashing

continued

Appliqué Placement Diagram

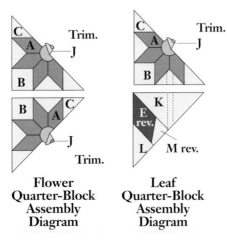

Flower Quarter-Block Assembly Diagram

Leaf Quarter-Block Assembly Diagram

Sunflower 321

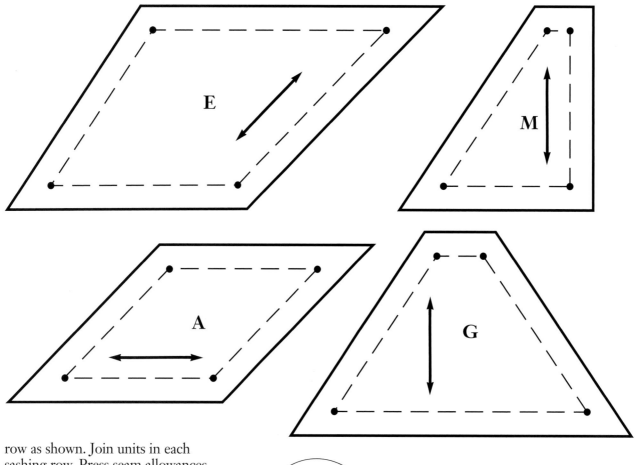

row as shown. Join units in each sashing row. Press seam allowances toward sashing.

11. Join block rows and sashing rows as shown **(Setting Diagram).**

12. Join green and pumpkin border strips to make a 2-strip border unit for each quilt side. Join borders to sides of quilt.

Appliqué Pattern J is finished size. Add ¹⁄₄" seam allowance for hand appliqué or cut as is for machine appliqué.

Quilting and Finishing

1. Outline-quilt all seam lines of blocks, half-blocks, and quarter-blocks. On sashing strips, quilt parallel diagonal lines, ½" apart. Outline-quilt triangles I and L. Quilt straight lines from corner to corner of sashing squares. Quilt parallel lines, ½" apart, lengthwise on green border strips and ³⁄₄" apart on orange border strips.

2. Stitch orange strips end-to-end to make 10³⁄₈ yards of continuous binding. See pages 16 and 17 for instructions on making binding. Apply binding to quilt edges.

Make Your Own Quilt Label
See page 366 for instructions.

Texas Star

This star pattern, one of many associated with the Lone Star State, was first published in 1928. The scrappy fabrics recall a time when quilts were made from necessity and not just for beauty and pleasure.

Quilt by Mable Azbill Webb
Jackson, Tennessee

Finished Quilt Size
95" x 96"

Number of Blocks and Finished Size
68 stars   11" x 11"
8 half-stars   5" x 11"

Fabric Requirements
10 print fabrics	½ yard each
7 solid fabrics	1 fat eighth each*
Blue print	1⅛ yards
Rose print	2¾ yards†
Muslin	3 yards
Backing	9 yards

* Fat eighth = 9" x 22".

† Includes fabric for straight-grain binding.

Cutting
Make templates of patterns A–H on pages 325 and 326. Cut strips cross-grain except as noted.

From print fabrics
- 40 (3¾"-wide) strips. From these, cut 360 of Template B (60 star sets of 6).
- 4 (3¾"-wide) strips. From these, cut 16 of Template B, 8 of Template C, and 8 of Template C reversed (8 half-star sets of 2 Bs, 1 Cs, and 1 C reversed).
- 14 of Template F.
- 2 of Template G and 2 of Template G reversed.

From solid fabrics
- 68 of Template A.
- 8 of Template D.

From blue print
- 8 (3½"-wide) strips for borders.
- 3 (3¾"-wide) strips. From these, cut 24 of Template B (4 star sets of 6).

From rose print
- 4 (3½" x 99") lengthwise strips for outer borders.
- 24 of Template B (4 star sets of 6).

From muslin
- 8 (2½"-wide) strips for border.
- 23 (3¼"-wide) strips. From these, cut 227 of Template E.
- 10 of Template H.

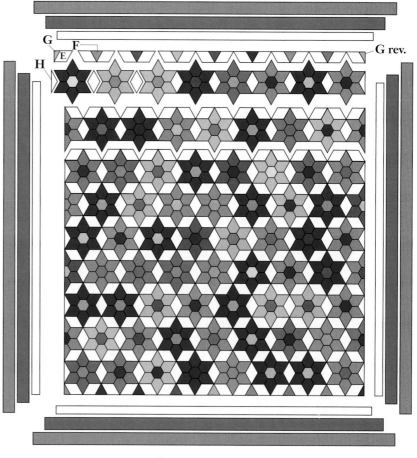

Setting Diagram

Quilt Top Assembly
See page 10 for instructions on sewing set-in seams.

1. Select 1 set of 6 B pieces and 1 A for each star. Sew bottom edge of each B to A, making sure not to sew into seam allowance **(Star Assembly Diagram)**. Join adjacent Bs, sewing from A to outside seam line. Be sure not to sew into seam allowance at outside edge to allow for setting in E and H pieces.

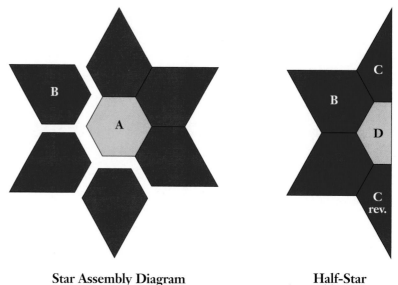

Star Assembly Diagram

Half-Star Assembly Diagram

2. Make 68 blocks.

3. For each half-star, select a set of 2Bs, 1 D, 1 C, and 1 C reversed. Join pieces in same manner as for whole blocks (**Half Star Assembly Diagram**). Make 8 half-stars.

4. Lay out stars and half-stars in 9 horizontal rows (**Setting Diagram**). Arrange blocks to get a nice balance of color. Fill in between blocks and at edges with E, F, G, and H pieces where indicated.

5. When satisfied with layout, join units in each row. Then join rows, setting each row into the next until all rows are joined.

6. Join 2 muslin border strips end-to-end to make a border for each side of quilt. Referring to instructions on page 14, trim 2 border strips to match measurement of quilt length. Join these to side edges of quilt. Measure, trim, and sew remaining muslin borders to top and bottom edges.

7. Join blue borders to quilt in same manner. Then add rose print borders.

Quilting and Finishing

1. Outline-quilt each piece or quilt as desired.

2. See pages 16 and 17 for instructions on making and applying binding. From remaining rose print, cut (2½"-wide) strips to make 10⅞ yards of straight-grain binding. Apply binding to quilt edges.

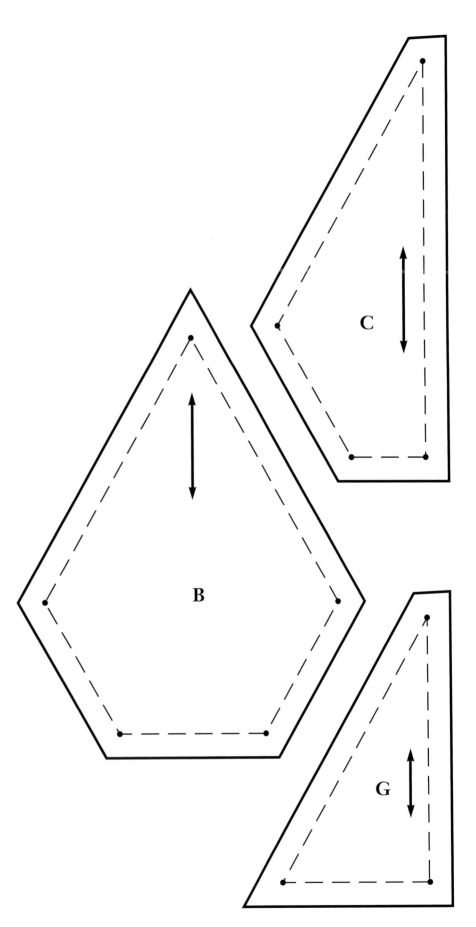

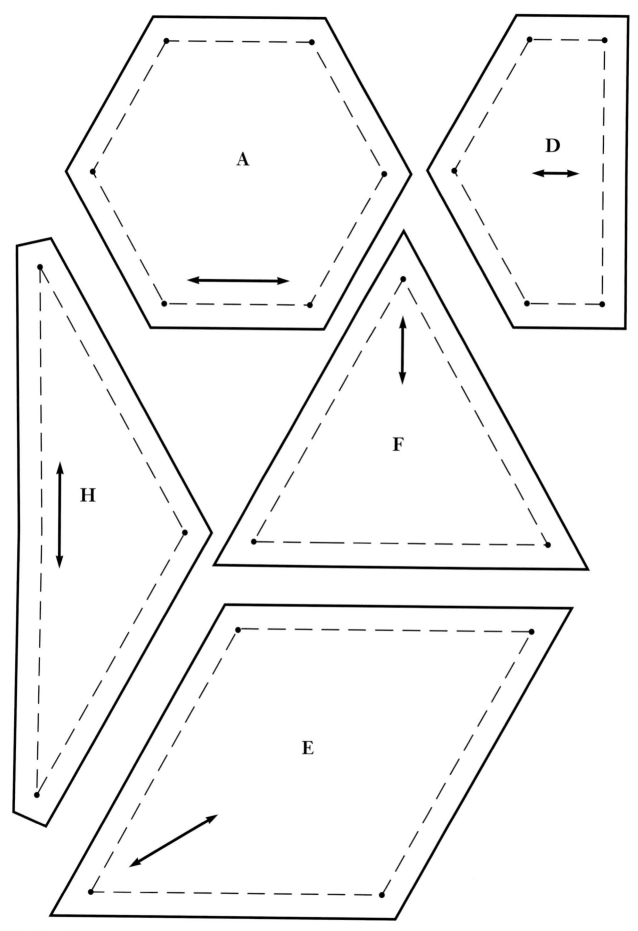

A

D

H

F

E

Tree of Life

Early quiltmakers gave patterns names from familiar sources, which is why so many blocks have biblical references. This pieced tree derives its name from Chapter 2 of Genesis: "And out of the ground made the Lord God to grow every tree that is pleasant to the sight and good for food; the tree of life also in the midst of the garden, and the tree of knowledge of good and evil."

Quilt owned by Laura Earnest Leatherwood
Birmingham, Alabama

Finished Quilt Size
68" x 68"

Number of Blocks and Finished Size
16 blocks   12" x 12"

Fabric Requirements*
Muslin   2½ yards
Red   ⅜ yard
10 brown prints   1 fat eighth each†
4 brown plaids
   or stripes   1 fat eighth each†
Pink   2¼ yards
Binding fabric   ⅞ yard
Backing   4¼ yards

* Yardage given for quilt as shown. If you want a larger quilt, you'll need 2¼ yards of a coordinating fabric from which to cut 4 (6" x 80") lengthwise border strips. Increase backing fabric to 4⅞ yards.
† Fat eighth = 9" x 22".

Cutting
Make a template of Pattern E on page 329. Other pieces are rotary cut. Cut all strips cross-grain.

From muslin
- 6 (6"-wide) strips. From these, cut 24 (6" x 11") pieces for quick piecing.
- 5 (4½"-wide) strips. From these, cut 16 of Template E and 16 of Template E reversed.
- 2 (5⅜"-wide) strips. From these, cut 16 (5⅜") squares. Cut each square in half diagonally to get 32 C triangles.
- 2 (2"-wide) strips. From these, cut 32 (2") B squares.
- 8 (4⅝") squares. Cut each square in half diagonally to get 16 G triangles.

From red
- 1 (6"-wide) strip. From this, cut 4 (6" x 11") pieces for quick piecing.
- 32 (2⅜") squares. Cut each square in half diagonally to get 64 A triangles.
- 16 (2") B squares.

From brown prints
- 20 (6" x 11") for quick piecing.
- 16 (2⅜") squares. Cut each square in half diagonally to get 32 A triangles.

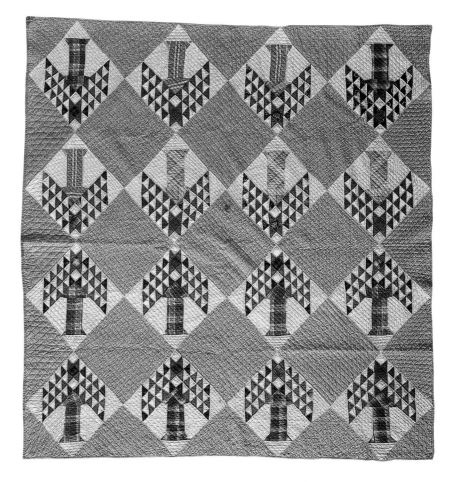

From brown plaids/stripes
- 8 (4½" x 22") strips. From each strip, cut 2 sets of tree trunk pieces as follows: 2 (3¼" x 6½") H pieces; 1 (3⅝") square cut in half diagonally to get 2 D triangles; and 2 (1⅞") squares cut in half diagonally to get 4 F triangles.

From pink
- 3 (12½"-wide) strips. From these, cut 9 (12½") setting squares.
- 2 (18¼"-wide) strips. From these, cut 3 (18¼") squares. Cut each square in quarters diagonally to get 12 side triangles.
- 2 (9⅜") squares. Cut each square in half diagonally to get 4 corner triangles.

Quick Piecing
See page 11 for tips on sewing quick-pieced triangle-squares.

1. On wrong side of each 6" x 11" muslin piece, mark a 2- x 4-square grid of 2⅜" squares **(Diagram 1).** Draw diagonal lines through squares as shown.

2. Match 1 muslin piece to a red piece, right sides facing. Machine-stitch ¼" from each side of all *diagonal* lines **(Diagram 2).** Cut on *all* grid lines to get 16 A triangle-squares. Press seam allowances toward red.

3. Repeat with remaining 6" x 11" pieces to get a total of 64

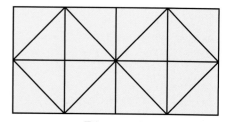

Diagram 1

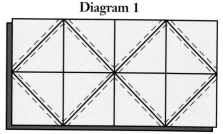

Diagram 2

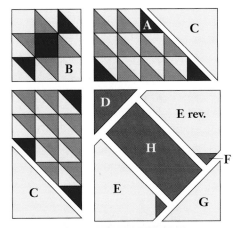

Block Assembly Diagram

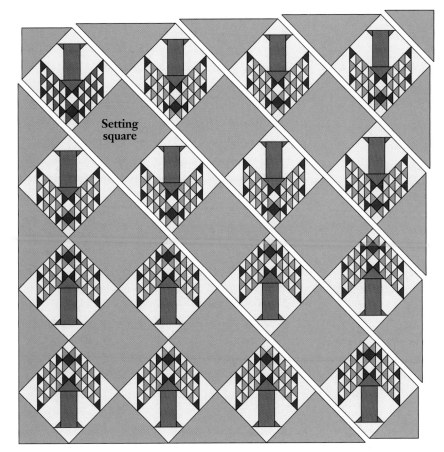

Setting Diagram

red/muslin triangle-squares and 320 brown/muslin triangle-squares.

Note: If you prefer traditional piecing, use 6" x 11" pieces of red, brown, and muslin to cut 2⅜" squares of each color; cut each square in half diagonally to get individual A triangles. Join pairs of triangles to make number of triangle-squares stated in Step 3.

Quilt Top Assembly

1. For each block, select 1 red B, 2 muslin Bs, 4 red/muslin triangle-squares, 20 brown/muslin triangle-squares, 4 red A triangles, 2 brown As, 2 Cs, 2 Fs, and 1 each of D, E, E reversed, G, and H.

2. For corner unit, join triangle-squares and B squares in rows; then join rows **(Block Assembly Diagram)**. For side units, join A triangles and triangle-squares in rows; then join rows and add C triangles to complete 2 side units.

3. For trunk unit, sew Fs to each E piece; then sew E/F to sides of H as shown. Add D and G triangles to complete unit.

4. Join units to complete block. Make 16 tree blocks.

5. Lay out blocks, setting squares, side triangles, and corner triangles in diagonal rows **(Setting Diagram)**. Join units in each row; press seam allowances toward setting squares and triangles. Join rows.

Quilting and Finishing

1. Outline-quilt seams. Add more quilting as desired.

2. See pages 16 and 17 for instructions on making binding. Make 8 yards of 2½"-wide straight-grain or bias binding. Apply binding to quilt edges.

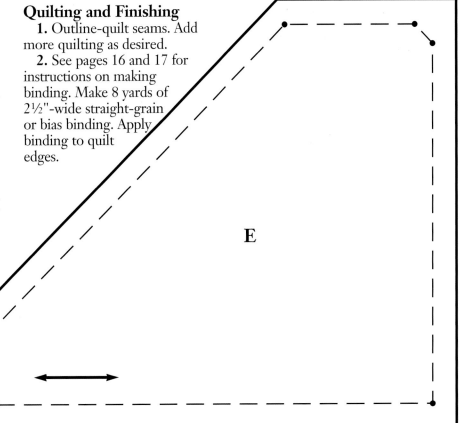

E

Triple Tulips

The tulip was once considered so valuable, its bulbs were used as currency. So it's no wonder that the tulip appears in many variations in the quiltmaker's lexicon. Mildred Smith's quilt is dramatic in strong hues, but you can make a garden in your own favorite colors. See page 332 for some other possible color schemes.

Quilt by Mildred E. Smith
Richmond, Indiana

Finished Quilt Size
79" x 99"

Number of Blocks and Finished Size
12 blocks   17½" x 17½"

Fabric Requirements
Pink   2½ yards
Dark pink   1⅞ yards
Aqua   3 yards
Black   6 yards
Backing   6 yards

Other Materials
¼"-wide bias pressing bar

Cutting
Make templates of patterns A–H on page 333. Cut all strips cross-grain except as noted.
From pink
- 2 (3" x 68") and 2 (3" x 88") lengthwise border strips.
- 2 (3" x 78") lengthwise strips for sashing.
- 9 (3" x 18") sashing strips.
- 48 of Template B.
- 96 of Template G.

From dark pink
- 8 (3"-wide) strips. From these, cut 48 of Template A and 48 of Template C.
- 8 (5"-wide) strips. From these, cut 96 of Template F.

From aqua
- 2 (4" x 95") and 2 (4" x 75") lengthwise border strips.
- 5 (4½" x 27") strips. From these, cut 48 of Template E and 48 of Template E reversed.
- 7 (2¾" x 27") strips. From these, cut 48 of Template D and 48 of Template D reversed.
- 7 (¾" x 27") strips. From these, cut 48 (¾" x 3½") stem pieces.
- 3 (10½" x 27") strips for H vines. See Step 1 for cutting vines.
- 53 (4") squares for prairie points from all remaining scraps.

From black
- 2 (5" x 84") and 2 (5" x 104") lengthwise border strips.
- 4 (18"-wide) strips. From these and scrap from previous step, cut 12 (18") squares.
- 9 (1½"-wide) strips for binding.
- 3 (5½"-wide) strips. From these and all remaining scraps, cut 56 (5½") squares for prairie points.

Quilt Top Assembly
1. On 1 corner of 1 (10½"-wide) aqua strip, measure and cut a 10½" triangle **(Bias Cutting Diagram).** Discard triangle. Measuring from cut edge, cut a ¾"-wide bias strips about 14¾"-long. Cut a total of 48 H bias vine pieces.

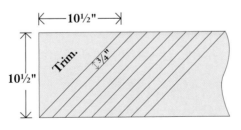

Bias Cutting Diagram

2. Center bias pressing bar on wrong side of each bias strip. Press edges of strip over pressing bar to get a folded strip about ¼" wide.

3. Fold 1 (18") black square in quarters diagonally, finger-pressing folds to make placement guidelines for appliqué.

4. Using H template as a guide for curve, position 4 H vines on black square and pin **(Appliqué Placement Diagram).** Refer to diagram to see how vines interlock at center of block. Pin F and G flowers at ends of each vine as shown. Pin 4 D leaves and 4 Ds reversed in place. Pin 4 short stems in place where vines cross, tucking ends under vines. Pin 1 E leaf and 1 E reversed on opposite sides of each stem; then pin A/B/C flowers at stem ends. When satisfied with placement of pieces, appliqué in place. Start with short stems; then stitch vines. Leaves and flowers can be stitched in any order.

5. Appliqué 12 blocks.

6. Lay out blocks in 3 vertical rows, with 4 blocks in each row with

continued

Appliqué Placement Diagram

Setting Diagram

Color Variations
These are some suggestions for other color schemes.

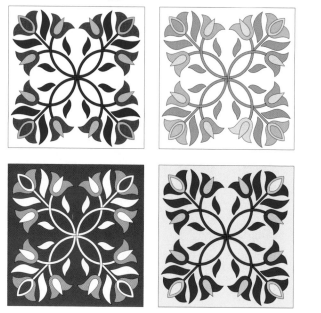

sashing strips between blocks as shown **(Setting Diagram).** Join blocks and sashing in each row. Press seam allowances toward sashing. Join rows with 78"-long sashing strips as shown.

7. Mark centers on edges of each border strip. Matching centers, join pink, aqua, and black border strips to make a 3-strip border unit for side of quilt. Mark centers on quilt edges. Sew borders to quilt edges and miter corners. (See page 14 for tips on mitering border corners.)

Quilting and Finishing
1. Outline-quilt appliqué. Quilt remaining areas as desired.

2. Fold each aqua square in half, wrong sides facing **(Prairie Points Diagram, Figure 1).** Fold top corners over to center bottom **(Figures 2 and 3).** Press. Fold black prairie points in same manner.

3. With right sides facing, pin 20 black points evenly along each side edge of quilt and 16 points at bottom edge. Pin aqua points between black points. (See photo on page 330.) Baste points in place.

4. Join 1½"-wide black strips end-to-end to make a length for each edge of quilt. Press under ½" on 1 long edge of each strip. With right sides facing and matching raw edges, stitch a strip to each side through all layers, including prairie points. Turn each strip to back of quilt and hand-stitch folded edge to backing.

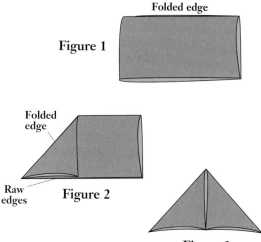

Folded edge

Figure 1

Folded edge

Raw edges   **Figure 2**

Figure 3
Prairie Points Diagram

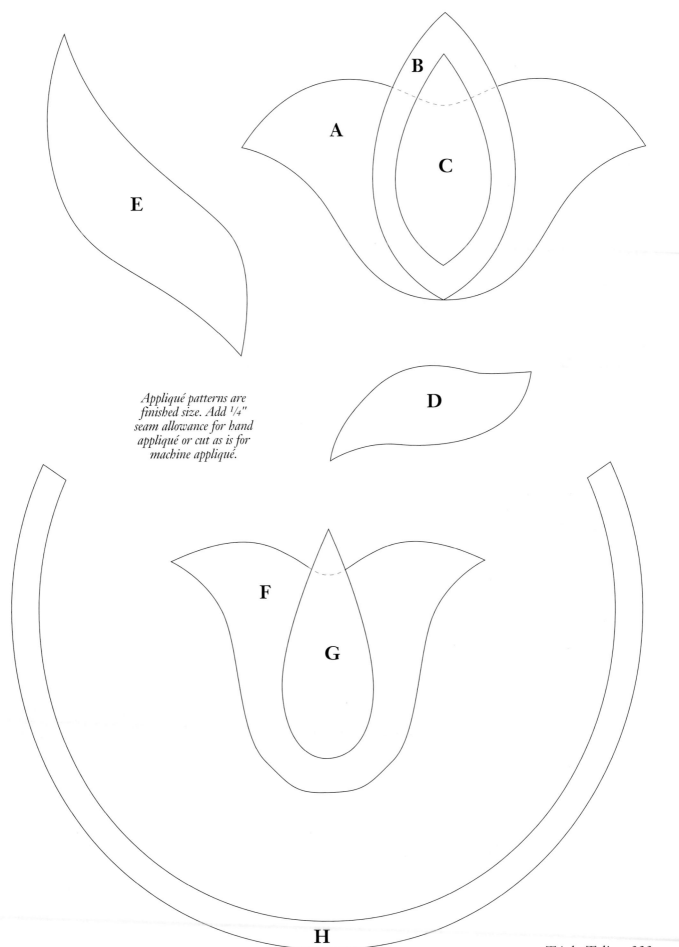

Appliqué patterns are finished size. Add ¹/₄" seam allowance for hand appliqué or cut as is for machine appliqué.

A

B

C

D

E

F

G

H

Tulip Treats

April showers bring May flowers, so spend a rainy day making rows of cheerful patchwork tulips. Multicolored pastel fabrics transform your bed into a festive field of spring flowers.

Quilt designed by Susan Ramey Cleveland, Leeds, Alabama
Made by Debra Baker Steinmann, Atlanta, Georgia

Finished Quilt Size
68" x 84"

Number of Blocks and Finished Size
45 blocks   6" x 10"

Fabric Requirements
Sky blue	1¾ yards
Green print	1 yard
5 light solids	¼ yard each
5 dark solids	⅛ yard each
Yellow print	2¼ yards
Floral print	2½ yards*
Backing	5 yards

*Includes fabric for binding.

Cutting
Make templates of patterns D and K. Remaining pieces are rotary cut. Cut all strips cross-grain except as noted.

From sky blue
- 6 (3¼"-wide) strips. From these, cut 23 of Template K, 23 of Template K reversed, and 23 (3¼") squares. Cut each square in quarters diagonally to get 90 C triangles (and 2 extra).
- 10 (1½"-wide) strips. From these, cut 22 of Template D, 22 of Template D reversed, and 46 (1½" x 4½") I pieces.
- 3 (6½"-wide) strips. From these, cut 22 (4½" x 6½") J pieces and 23 (1½" x 6½") H pieces.
- 22 (2⅝") squares. Cut each square in half diagonally to get 44 E triangles.

From green
- 5 (3⅞"-wide) strips. From these, cut 45 (3⅞") squares. Cut each square in half diagonally to get 90 G triangles. Cut remaining strip into 3 (1"-wide) strips for next step.
- 2 (1"-wide) strips. From these and strips from previous step, cut 22 (1" x 2½") F pieces and 23 (1" x 5½") L pieces.

From each light solid
- 7 (5¼") squares. Cut each square in quarters diagonally to get 27 A triangles (and 1 extra).

From each dark solid
- 9 (1⅞") B squares.

From yellow print
- 2 (2½" x 62") and 2 (2½" x 78") lengthwise strips for inner border.
- 4 (5½" x 55") lengthwise strips for sashing.

From floral print
- 2 (5" x 87") and 2 (5" x 72") lengthwise strips for outer borders.
continued

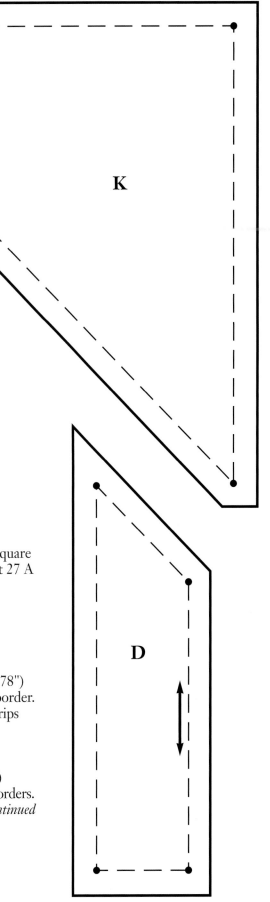

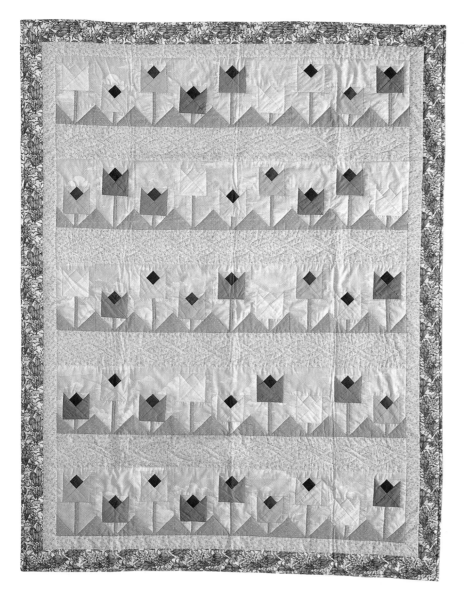

Quilt Top Assembly

1. For each tulip, select 3 A triangles of same fabric, 1 coordinating B square, and 2 C triangles.

2. Join Cs to 2 adjacent edges of B **(Block 1 Assembly Diagram).** Join 1 A to right edge of C/B/C unit.

3. Join 2 remaining A triangles as shown to form a triangle pair.

4. Join units to complete tulip. Make 9 tulips of each color.

5. For Block 1, join I pieces to side edges of tulip **(Block 1 Assembly Diagram).** Press seam allowances toward Is. Sew 1 H to top edge.

6. Aligning top edges of each piece, join K and K reversed to each side of 1 L. Press seam allowances toward Ks. Add G triangles to complete stem unit as shown.

7. Join tulip and stem units to complete block. Make 23 of Block 1.

8. For Block 2, join D and D reversed to side edges of tulip **(Block 2 Assembly Diagram).** Sew J to top edge.

9. Aligning top edges of each piece, join Es to sides of F.

10. Join tulip and stem units to complete block. Make 22 of Block 2.

11. Lay out blocks in 5 horizontal rows, with 9 blocks in each row. Alternate tall and short tulips in each row as shown. Add sashing strips between rows. Join rows and sashing strips. Press seam allowances toward sashing.

12. Mark centers on edges of each border strip. Matching centers, join yellow and floral borders in pairs to make a 2-strip border unit for each quilt edge. Matching centers of borders and quilt edges, sew borders to quilt and miter corners. (See page 14 for instructions on mitering border corners.)

Quilting and Finishing

1. Outline-quilt patchwork. Quilt sashing and borders as desired.

2. See pages 16 and 17 for instructions on making binding. Make 8¾ yards of 2½"-wide bias or straight-grain binding from remaining floral print. Apply binding to quilt edges.

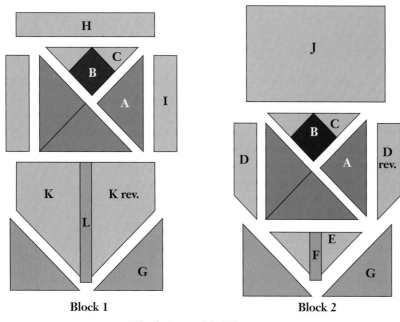

Block 1   Block 2

Block Assembly Diagrams

Tulip Vines

Marianne Fons and Liz Porter began their quilt-designing partnership in 1976 in a quilt class at a local college extension center. Their shared interest and talents have endured, and today Marianne and Liz teach quilting worldwide and star in the PBS television show, *Sew Many Quilts*. This classic quilt is one of Marianne's and Liz's early designs, quilted by Helen Martens.

Quilt by Marianne Fons and Liz Porter
Winterset, Iowa

Finished Quilt Size
82" x 98"

Fabric Requirements
Muslin	6 yards
Red print	¾ yard
Red solid	¾ yard
Green	1½ yards
Binding fabric	1 yard
Backing	2½ yards 108" wide

Other Materials
½"-wide bias pressing bar

Cutting
Make templates for patterns A, B, and C. Cut all strips cross-grain except as noted.

From muslin
- 3 (20½" x 108") lengthwise panels for quilt center.
- 2 (11½" x 108") lengthwise border panels.

From red print
- 3 (3½"-wide) strips. From these, cut 24 of Template A.
- 4 (2½"-wide) strips. From these, cut 46 of Template B.

From red solid
- 6 (3½"-wide) strips. From these, cut 46 of Template A.
- 2 (2½"-wide) strips. From these, cut 24 of Template B.

From green
- 3 (12"-wide) strips for bias vines.
- 10 (2"-wide) strips. From each of these, cut 12 of Template C.

Quilt Top Assembly
1. Fold each 20½"-wide panel into quarters and crease folds to make appliqué placement guidelines.
2. On 1 corner of a 12"-wide green strip, measure and cut a 12" triangle (**Bias Cutting Diagram**). Discard triangle. Measuring from cut edge, cut 1"-wide bias strips about 8"-long. Cut a total of 60 bias vine pieces.
3. Center bias pressing bar on wrong side of each bias strip. Press edges of strip over pressing bar to get a folded strip about ½" wide.

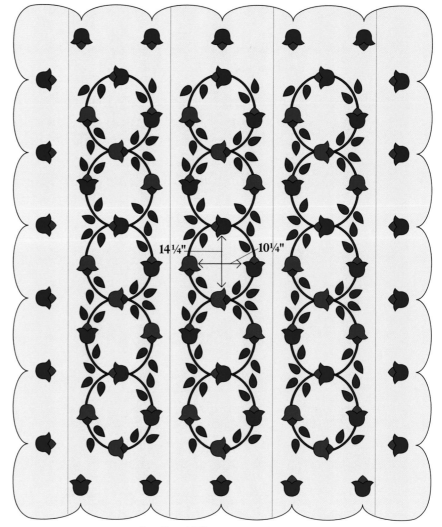

Appliqué Placement Diagram

14¼"   10¼"

4. Pin 20 bias strips on each panel (**Appliqué Placement Diagram**). Pin A and B pieces in place, using 1 solid and 1 print piece for each flower. (Set aside 22 red solid As and 22 print Bs for border.) When satisfied with placement, appliqué bias strips, flowers, and C leaves to each panel.
5. Join appliquéd panels. Sew border strips to sides.
6. Use a 12"- to 14"-diameter dinner plate as a guide to mark

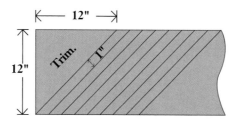

Bias Cutting Diagram

scallops around edges. *Do not cut* scallops yet. Pin A and B pieces in place around edge, 1½" from each scallop peak and appliqué in place.

Quilting and Finishing
1. Make a stencil of Tulip & Feathers quilting pattern. In center of each oval, mark just tulip and adjacent feathers. Mark whole design on each border scallop.
2. Outline-quilt appliqué. Quilt marked designs. Quilt remaining areas with 1" cross-hatch pattern.
3. See page 17 for instructions on continuous bias. Make 12 yards of 2"-wide continuous bias binding. Apply binding to quilt on marked lines, easing binding along curves and pivoting at corners.
4. Trim all layers to ¼" seam allowance. Fold binding to back and blindstitch in place.

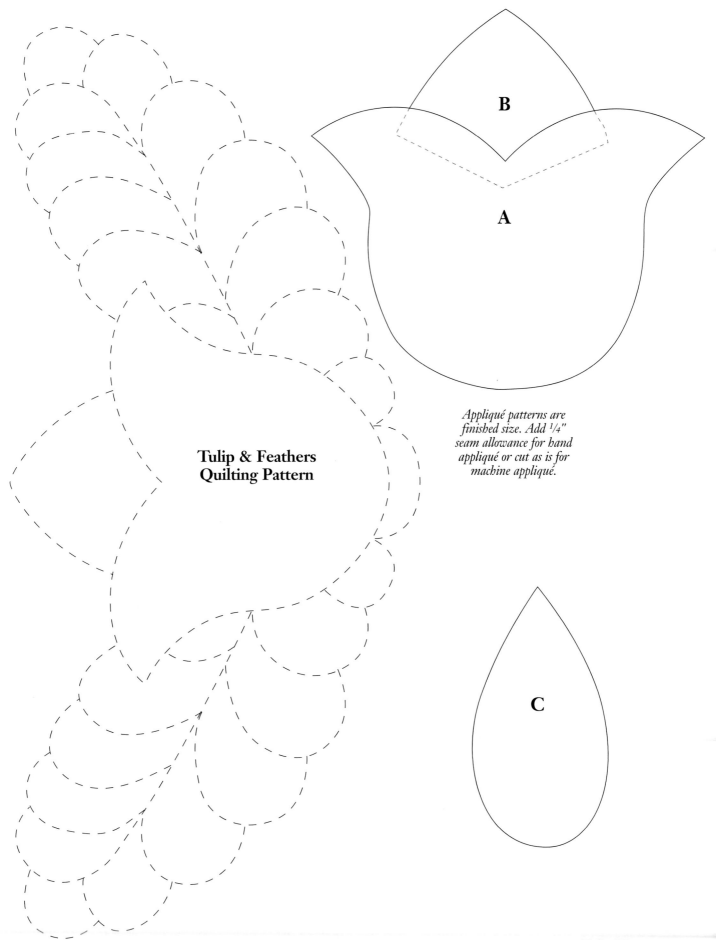

B

A

**Tulip & Feathers
Quilting Pattern**

*Appliqué patterns are
finished size. Add ¼"
seam allowance for hand
appliqué or cut as is for
machine appliqué.*

C

Tulips

During the first half of the nineteenth century, making red, white, and green appliquéd quilts was all the rage among the ladies of cities like Baltimore, New York, and Philadelphia. *Tulips* revisits that tradition, complete with the appliquéd swag border that is an age-old element of a finely made quilt.

Quilt by Penelope Wortman,
Candler, North Carolina

Finished Quilt Size
60" x 76"

Number of Blocks and Finished Size
12 blocks   16" x 16"

Fabric Requirements
Red   1 yard
Green   4¼ yards
White or muslin   4¼ yards
Binding fabric   1 yard
Backing   4½ yards

Cutting
Make templates of patterns A–F here and on pages 341–343. Cut all strips cross-grain except as noted.
From red
- 4 (5"-wide) strips. From these, cut 52 of Template A.
- 2 (5¼"-wide) strips. From these, cut 12 of Template E.
- 58 of Template C.

From green
- 13 (8¼"-wide) strips. From these, cut 52 of Template B and 58 of Template D.
- 2 (17¼"-wide) strips. From these, cut 14 of Template F.

From white
- 2 (6½" x 80") and 2 (6½" x 64") lengthwise strips for borders.
- 12 (16½") squares.

Quilt Top Assembly
1. Fold each white square horizontally, vertically, and diagonally; crease folds to make placement guidelines for appliqué.

2. For 1 block, select 1 E and 4 each of A, B, C, and D. Pin E at block center **(Placement Diagram)**. Pin As and Bs on diagonal guidelines and Cs and Ds on vertical and horizontal guidelines.

3. When satisfied with placement, appliqué pieces in alphabetical order.

4. Make 12 blocks.

5. Lay out blocks in 3 horizonal rows, with 4 blocks in each row. Join blocks in each row; join rows.
continued

6. Sew borders to quilt edges and

Placement Diagram

E

Appliqué patterns are finished size. Add ¹/₄" seam allowance for hand appliqué or cut as is for machine appliqué.

Place on fold.

½ **F**

Red and green is classic, but there are
so many other possibilities. Here are a few
suggestions for other varieties of tulips.

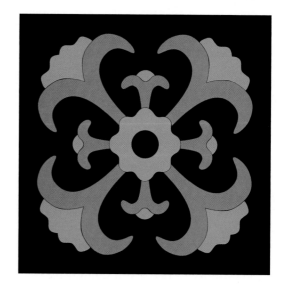

miter corners. (See page 14 for tips on sewing mitered corners.)

7. Pin 3 F swags each on top and bottom borders (see photo on page 340). Pin 4 swags on each side border. Pin A/B flowers on mitered seams and C/D flowers at junction of each pair of swags. When satisfied with placement of all pieces, appliqué swags in place; then appliqué flower pieces.

8. Use a large plate (or other round object) of approximately 14" diameter to mark scallops on border. Do not cut scallops yet.

Quilting and Finishing

1. Outline-quilt appliqué. Add more quilting as desired. (Quilt shown has lines of echo quilting rippling out from outline quilting, about 1" apart.)

2. See page 17 for instructions on continuous bias. Make 9½ yards of 2"-wide continuous bias binding. Apply binding to quilt on marked lines, easing binding along curves and pivoting at corners.

3. Trim all layers to ¼" seam allowance. Fold binding to back and blindstitch in place.

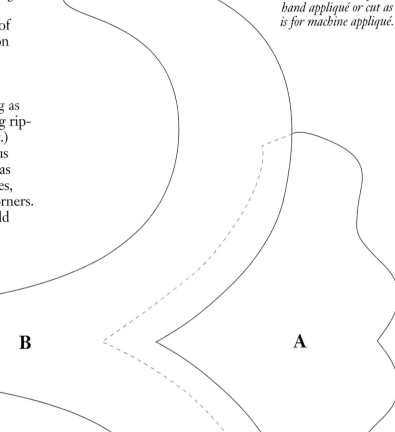

Appliqué patterns are finished size. Add ¼" seam allowance for hand appliqué or cut as is for machine appliqué.

B

A

C

D

Turtle Creek

If you're fond of the creekside variety, you'll love these box turtles in fabric. Strip piecing makes quick work of these snappy terrapins.

Quilt designed by Susan Ramey Cleveland, Leeds, Alabama
Made by Carol Tipton, Calera, Alabama

Finished Quilt Size
48" x 63"

Number of Blocks and Finished Size
12 blocks   12" x 12"

Fabric Requirements
Blue	1⅛ yards
Dark green print	1 yard
Light green print	½ yard
Brown	⅜ yard
Blue print	1¼ yards
Yellow print	¾ yard*
Backing	3 yards

*Includes fabric for straight-grain binding.

Other Materials
Yellow embroidery floss

Cutting
Make templates of patterns A–H on page 347. (Pieces C, D, and G are rotary cut.) Cut all strips cross-grain except as noted.

From blue
- 3 (2½"-wide) strips. From these, cut 24 (2½" x 5¼") C rectangles.
- 6 (2"-wide) strips . From these, cut 24 (2" x 9½") G rectangles.
- 2 (3¼"-wide) strips. From these, cut 24 (3¼") squares. Cut each square in quarters diagonally to get 96 D triangles.
- 4 (1½"-wide) strips. From these and remaining scraps, cut 12 of Template H, 12 of Template H reversed, 12 of Template B, and 12 of Template B reversed.

From dark green print
- 14 (2⅜"-wide) strips for strip piecing.

From light green print
- 7 (1⅞"-wide) strips for strip piecing.

From brown
- 1 (3¼"-wide) strip. From this, cut 3 (3¼") squares. Cut each square in quarters diagonally to get 12 D triangles. From remainder of strip, cut 12 of Template A.
- 48 of Template E.

From blue print
- 11 (3½"-wide) strips. From these, cut 31 (3½" x 12½") sashing strips.

From yellow print
- 2 (3½"-wide) strips. From these, cut 20 (3½") sashing squares.
- 6 (2½"-wide) strips for binding.

Strip Piecing
1. Join a dark green strip to both edges of each light green strip. Make 7 strip sets. Press seam allowances toward dark green.

2. From pattern on page 347, mark seam placement lines on Template F. Position template on 1 strip set, aligning seam placement lines with seam lines and top point of template with top edge of strip unit **(Cutting Diagram).** Mark and cut 1 F. Turn template, aligning top point of template with bottom edge of strip set and diagonal edge of template with cut edge. Mark and cut 1 F. Continue in this manner to cut a total of 48 Fs.

Quilt Top Assembly
1. For Top Section, join 1 B and 1 B reversed to diagonal edges of A **(Block Assembly Diagram).** Join 1 C to each side of A/B unit.

2. For Middle Section, join 1 blue D to each side of E. Make 4 D/E/D units. Join each unit to 1 F. Join 4 units as shown; then add 1 G to each side to complete section.

continued

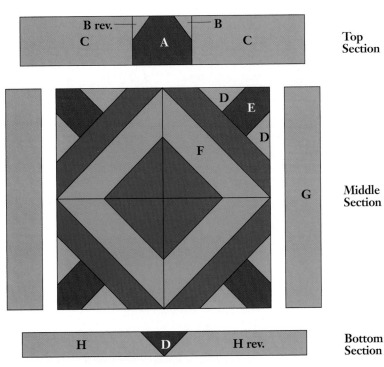

Block Assembly Diagram

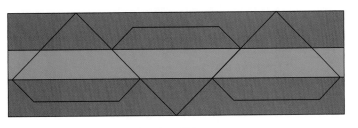

Cutting Diagram

Setting Diagram

3. For Bottom Section, join 1 H and 1 H reversed to 1 brown D.

4. Join sections to complete block. Make 12 turtle blocks.

5. Using 3 strands of embroidery floss, make French knots for turtles' eyes. (See stitch diagram on page 347.)

6. Lay out blocks in 4 horizontal rows, with 3 blocks in each row **(Setting Diagram)**. Turn blocks as shown or as desired to have turtles going in all directions, Place sashing strips between blocks and at row ends. When satisfied with placement of blocks, join blocks and sashing in each row. Press seam allowances toward sashing.

7. For each sashing row, join 4 sashing squares and 3 sashing strips as shown. Make 5 sashing rows. Press seam allowances toward sashing strips.

8. Join rows, alternating sashing rows with block rows as shown.

Quilting and Finishing

1. Outline-quilt patchwork. Quilt sashing as desired.

2. See pages 16 and 17 for instructions on making binding. Join yellow strips end-to-end to make 6½ yards of 2½"-wide straight-grain binding. Apply binding to quilt edges.

Make Your Own Quilt Label
See page 366 for instructions.

2002

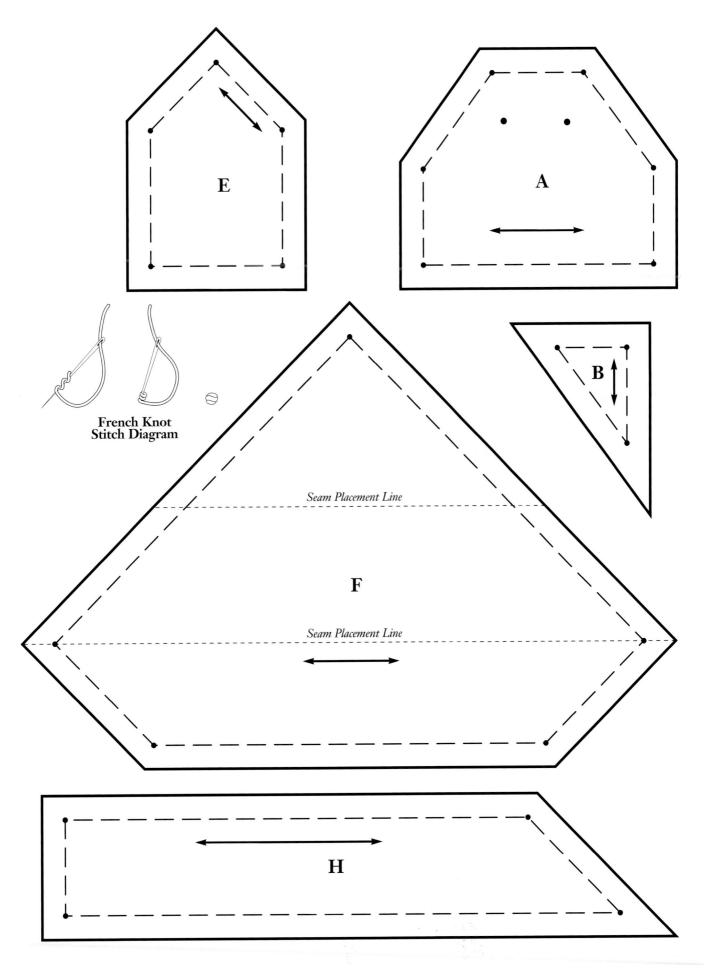

E

A

**French Knot
Stitch Diagram**

B

Seam Placement Line

F

Seam Placement Line

H

Umbrella Girl

This charming cousin of Sunbonnet Sue is typical of patterns that were popular in the 1920s and 1930s. Use your imagination and have fun embellishing the lady's ensemble with lace, buttons, beads, and other baubles.

Quilt owned by Annie Phillips
Hayden, Alabama

Finished Quilt Size
58¼" x 74"

Number of Blocks and Finished Size
30 blocks   9¼" x 10"

Fabric Requirements
Muslin   2¼ yards
30 assorted solids   1 (6" x 12") each
30 assorted prints   1 (8" x 14") each
Flesh   ⅜ yard
Yellow   2 yards
Binding fabric   1 yard
Backing   4½ yards

Other Materials
Assorted colors of embroidery floss

Cutting
Make templates of appliqué patterns A–K on page 350. Cut all strips cross-grain except as noted.

From muslin
- 8 (9¾"-wide) strips. From these, cut 30 (9¾" x 10½") blocks.

From each solid fabric
- 1 of Template A (bonnet).
- 1 of Template D (bodice).
- 1 of Template F (skirt).
- 1 of Template L (umbrella lining).
- 3 of Template J (flower).

From each print fabric
- 1 of Template B (bonnet brim).
- 1 of Template C (dress collar).
- 1 *each* of Template E (skirt) and Template E reversed.
- 1 of Template K (umbrella).

From flesh
- 3 (3"-wide) strips. From these, cut 30 *each* of templates G (right arm), H (left arm), and I (neck).

From yellow
- 6 (2½" x 72") lengthwise strips for vertical sashing and borders.
- 2 (2½" x 60") lengthwise strips for top and bottom borders.
- 25 (2½" x 9¾") sashing strips.

Quilt Top Assembly
1. Fold blocks in half horizontally and vertically; finger-press creases to make placement guidelines and mark center.

2. For each block, select 1 set of print appliqué pieces (B, C, E, E reversed, and K), 1 coordinating set of solid pieces (A, D, F, and L), 1 set of flesh pieces (G, H, and I), and any 3 flower pieces (J).

3. Pin D in place at block center. Pin remaining pieces in place as shown (**Appliqué Placement Diagram**). When satisfied with placement, appliqué flesh pieces (G, H, and I); then appliqué bodice (D), skirt (F, E, and E reversed), and collar (C), in that order. Appliqué bonnet brim (B) and then bonnet (A). Finally, appliqué umbrella pieces (L and K).

4. Use 3 strands of floss to embroider hatband, umbrella handle, shoes, flower stems, and flower details in outline stitch. (See stitch diagram on page 182). Work leaves in lazy daisy stitch. (See stitch diagram on page 318).

5. Make 30 blocks.

6. Lay out blocks in 5 vertical rows, with 6 blocks in each row. Place 5 short sashing strips between blocks. When satisfied with placement, join blocks and sashing in each row.

7. Join rows with sashing strips between rows and at both sides.

8. Join borders to top and bottom edges of quilt.

Quilting and Finishing
1. Outline-quilt appliqué. Add more quilting as desired.

2. See pages 16 and 17 for instructions on making binding. Make 10 yards of 2½"-wide bias or straight-grain binding. Apply binding to quilt edges.

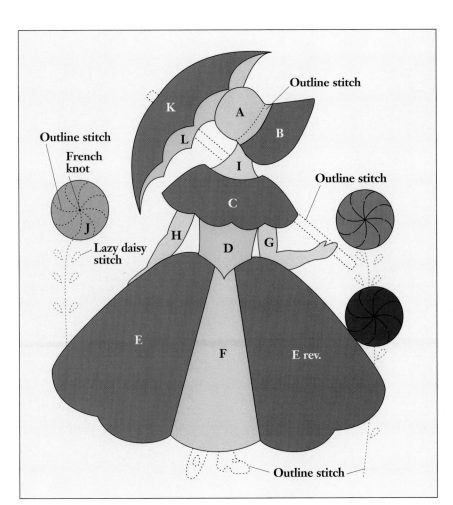

Appliqué Placement Diagram

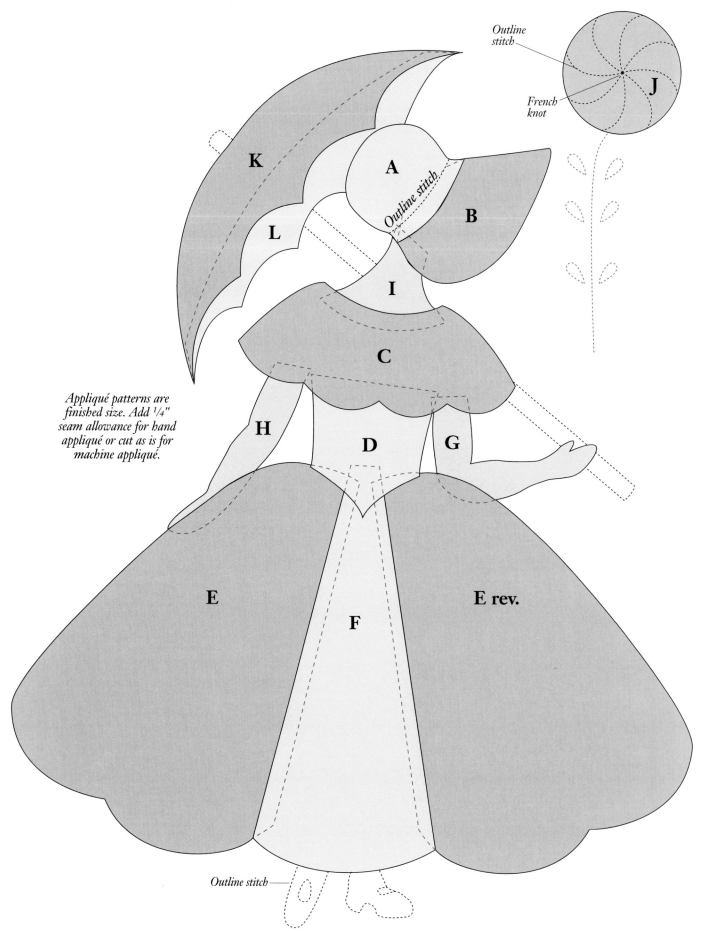

Outline stitch

French knot

J

A

Outline stitch

B

K

L

I

C

Appliqué patterns are finished size. Add ¼" seam allowance for hand appliqué or cut as is for machine appliqué.

H

D

G

E

F

E rev.

Outline stitch

350 Umbrella Girl

Utah Valley Basket

This striking quilt appears to have many fabrics, but there are only seven—black and six solids. The red-framed checkerboard differs in scale from the petite baskets, but color repetition keeps all the quilt's elements in harmony.

Quilt by Utah Valley Quilt Guild
Provo, Utah

Finished Quilt Size
71" x 91"

Fabric Requirements

Black	6½ yards
Red	1 yard
Purple	½ yard
Blue	½ yard
Light blue	½ yard
Green	½ yard
Yellow	½ yard
Binding fabric	1 yard
Backing	2¼ yards 104" wide

Cutting

Make templates for patterns A–D. Cut all strips cross-grain except as noted. Cut pieces in order listed to get best use of yardage.

From black
- 21 (1⅛"-wide) strips. From these, cut 85 (1⅛") G squares and 85 *each* of templates A and A reversed.
- 4 (3⅞"-wide) strips. From these, cut 43 (3⅞") squares. Cut each square in half diagonally to get 85 E triangles (and 1 extra).
- 13 (1½"-wde) strips. From these, cut 85 *each* of templates D and D reversed.
- 3 (2⅞"-wide) strips. From these, cut 43 (2⅞") squares. Cut each square in half diagonally to get 85 J triangles (and 1 extra).
- 5 (9¾"-wide) strips. From these, cut 19 (9¾") squares. Cut each square in quarters diagonally to get 75 K triangles (and 1 extra).
- 1 (8"-wide) strip. From this, cut 5 (8") squares. Cut each square in half diagonally to get 10 L triangles.
- 3 (5½"-wide) strips. From these, cut 80 (1½" x 5½") N pieces.
- 2 (4¾" x 62") and 2 (4½" x 75") lengthwise strips for first border.
- 5 (4½") squares. Cut each square in half diagonally to get 10 M triangles.
- 606 (1½") O squares.

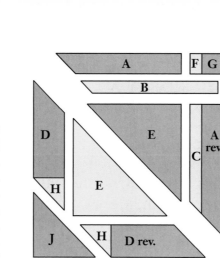

A F G
B
D   E   A rev.
C
H   E
J   H   D rev.

Block Assembly Diagram

From red
- 8 (⅞"-wide) strips. From these, cut 18 (⅞" x 1⅛") F pieces and 18 *each* of templates B and C.
- 1 (3⅞"-wide) strip. From this, cut 9 (3⅞") squares. Cut each square in half diagonally to get 18 E triangles.
- 1 (1⅞"-wide) strip. From this, cut 18 (1⅞") squares. Cut each square in half diagonally to get 36 H triangles.
- 15 (1"-wide) strips for borders.
- 101 (1½") O squares.

From purple and *blue*
- 3 (⅞"-wide) strips. From these, cut 12 (⅞" x 1⅛") F pieces and 12 *each* of templates B and C.
- 1 (3⅞"-wide) strip. From this, cut 6 (3⅞") squares. Cut each square in half diagonally to get 12 E triangles.
- 1 (1⅞"-wide) strip. From this, cut 12 (1⅞") squares. Cut each square in half diagonally to get 24 H triangles.
- 102 (1½") O squares.

From light blue and *green*
- 4 (⅞"-wide) strips. From these, cut 14 (⅞" x 1⅛") F pieces and 14 *each* of templates B and C.
- 1 (3⅞"-wide) strip. From this, cut 7 (3⅞") squares. Cut each square in half diagonally to get 12 E triangles. Cut remainder of strip into 2 (1⅞"-wide) strips. From these, cut 14 (1⅞") squares. Cut each square in half diagonally to get 28 H triangles.
- 102 (1½") O squares.

From yellow
- 4 (⅞"-wide) strips. From these, cut 15 (⅞" x 1⅛") F pieces and 15 *each* of templates B and C.
- 1 (1⅞"-wide) strips. From this, cut 15 (1⅞") squares. Cut each square in half diagonally to get 30 H triangles.
- 1 (3⅞"-wide) strip. From this, cut 8 (3⅞") squares. Cut each square in half diagonally to get 15 E triangles (and 1 extra).
- 102 (1½") O squares.

Quilt Top Assembly

1. For each basket, select 1 set of black pieces (A, A reversed, D, D reversed, E, G, and J). Also select 1 set of colored pieces (B, C, E, F, and 2 H).

2. For handle section, join A, F, and G pieces in a row (**Block Assembly Diagram**). Press seam allowances toward black. Add B to bottom of unit. Press seam allowances toward B. Set A/B unit aside. Then join A reversed, C, and black E in a row; press seam allowances toward black. Stitch A/B unit to top to complete handle section.

3. For basket section, sew H triangles to ends of D and D reversed as shown. Join these to adjacent sides of colored E; press seam allowances toward E. Add J to complete basket section.

4. Join handle and basket sections to complete block. Make 85 basket blocks: 18 red, 12 purple, 12 blue, 14 light blue, 14 green, and 15 yellow.

5. Lay out blocks in 5 vertical rows, with 17 blocks in each row (**Setting Diagram**). Place N strips between blocks as shown. Fill in at sides with 15 triangles and with L and M triangles at each end. Note different placement of blocks in rows 2 and 4, which are mirror-images of rows 1, 3, and 5. When satisfied with placement, join units in each row. Press seam allowances toward setting triangles.

6. Join 5 rows as shown.

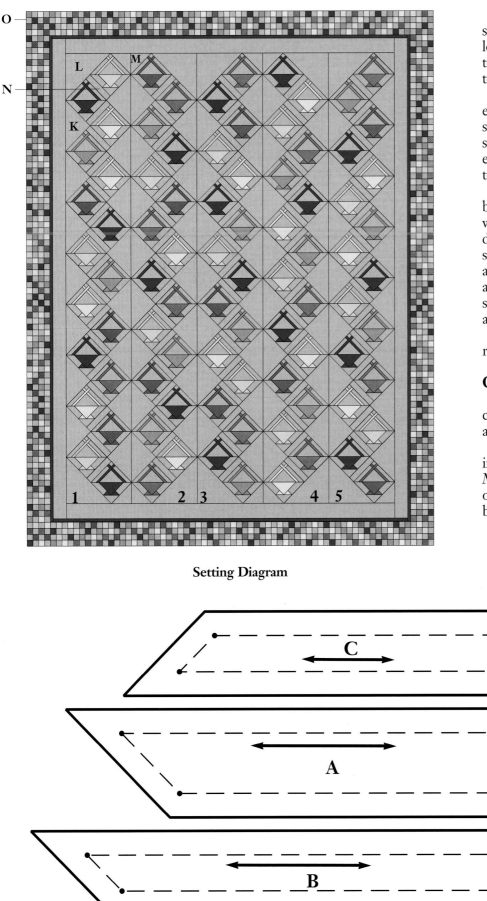

7. Sew 75"-long black border strips to quilt sides; then sew 62"-long black borders to top and bottom edges. Press seam allowances toward borders.

8. Join 1"-wide red strips end-to-end to make borders for each quilt side. Stitch 2 borders to sides; then sew 2 borders to top and bottom edges. Press seam allowances toward black.

9. To assemble checkerboard borders, alternate black O squares with colored squares. Make borders for top and bottom edges 4 squares deep and 62 squares long, and join these to quilt, easing to fit as needed. Make 2 side borders 4 squares wide and 90 squares long, and join these to quilt.

10. Repeat Step 8 to add outer red borders.

Quilting and Finishing

1. Outline-quilt baskets and checkerboards. Add other quilting as desired.

2. See pages 16 and 17 for instructions on making binding. Make 9¼ yards of 2½"-wide bias or straight-grain binding. Apply binding to quilt edges.

Setting Diagram

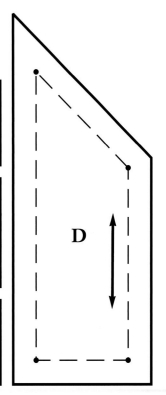

Virginia Wreath

This lovely variation of a traditional Bridal Wreath pattern is the first quilt Helen Jordan ever made. It offers good lessons in basic piecing and appliqué, as well as scalloped borders. A quilted swag design in the borders is a nice finishing touch.

Quilt by Helen Jordan
Norfolk, Virginia

Finished Quilt Size
84" x 104"

Number of Blocks and Finished Size
12 blocks   20" x 20"

Fabric Requirements
Red   1¾ yards*
Brown   ¾ yard
Beige print   ⅞ yard
5 green prints   1 fat quarter each**
2 yellow prints   1 fat eighth each**
Muslin or white   6½ yards
Red print   2½ yards
Backing   6½ yards
* Includes fabric for bias binding.
** Fat quarter = 18" x 22".
    Fat eighth = 9" x 22".

Other Materials
⅜"-wide bias pressing bar

Cutting
Make templates of patterns A, B, C, and D on pages 356 and 357. Cut all strips cross-grain except as noted.
From red
- 1 (34") square for bias binding.
- 3 (6"-wide) strips. From these and scrap from previous step, cut 48 of Template A.
- 12 of Template C.

From brown
- 24" square for wreath bias.

From beige print
- 4 (6"-wide) strips. From these, cut 48 of Template A.
- 24 of Template D.

From green and yellow prints
- 48 (2" x 22") strips. From these or scraps, cut 144 of Template B and 144 of Template B reversed.

From muslin
- 6 (20½"-wide) strips. From these, cut 12 (20½") squares.
- 2 (9½" x 90") and 2 (9½" x 108") lengthwise strips for border.

From red print
- 2 (3½" x 90") and 2 (3½" x 70"). lengthwise strips for border.
- 24 of Template D.

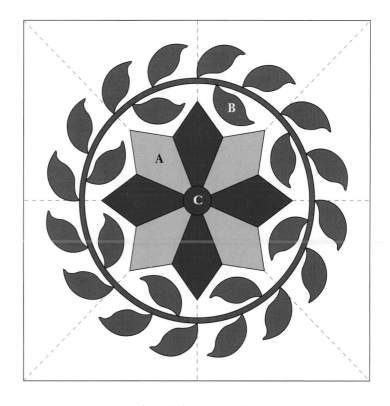

Appliqué Placement Diagram

Quilt Top Assembly
1. See page 17 for instructions on making continuous bias. From brown square, make 14 yards of ⅞"-wide continuous bias.

2. Center pressing bar on wrong side of bias strip and press edges over bar.

3. Fold 1 muslin square in half vertically, horizontally, and diagonally, creasing folds to make placement guidelines and to mark block center.

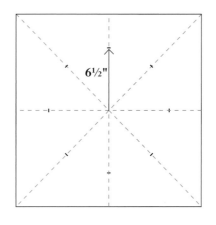

Circle Diagram

4. Starting at center, measure 6½" along each placement line and make a tiny pencil mark (**Circle Diagram**). Lightly connect marks to draw in a 13"-diameter circle.

5. Cut a 42" length of brown bias. Pin bias around inside edge of circle (**Appliqué Placement Diagram**). Select any 24 B leaves and pin in place. When satisfied with placement, appliqué wreath and leaves.

6. Select 4 red and 4 beige print A diamonds. Alternating colors, join diamonds to make a star. Press seam allowances open.

7. Turn under edges on outside edge of star. Center star on muslin square, aligning star points with placement lines. Appliqué star in place on square.

8. Appliqué C in place at center of star.

9. Make 12 blocks.

continued

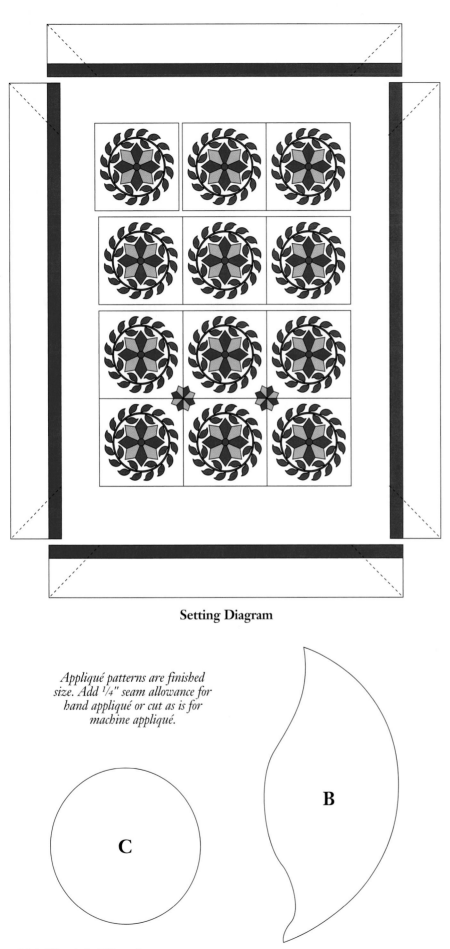

Setting Diagram

Appliqué patterns are finished size. Add ¼" seam allowance for hand appliqué or cut as is for machine appliqué.

C

B

10. Lay out blocks in 4 horizontal rows, with 3 blocks in each row (**Setting Diagram**). Join blocks in each row; then join rows.

11. Join 4 red print and 4 beige print D diamonds to make a star. Make 6 stars. Turn under edges for appliqué.

12. Center a star at each intersection of 4 blocks as shown and appliqué in place.

13. Matching centers, sew a 90"-long red print border strip to each 108" muslin border strip to make a single border unit for side edge of quilt. Repeat with remaining border strips for top and bottom edges. Matching centers of red strips with center of each quilt edge, sew borders to quilt and miter corners. (See page 14 for instructions on sewing mitered corners.) Do not cut scallops yet.

Quilting and Finishing

1. Make stencils of Scroll and Swag quilting patterns on page 358. Mark scroll design diagonally in corners of each block. Mark swag design on borders, centering 5 swags on top and bottom borders and 7 along each side, with bottom edge of swag about 1½" from edge of border. Adjust swag length to fit around corner. Mark additional designs as desired.

2. On quilt shown, stars are quilted in-the-ditch and both stars and appliqué are outline-quilted. Quilt blocks as desired. Quilt marked designs. In addition to swags, border on quilt shown has parallel lines, 2" apart, quilted from border seam to edge.

3. Use a large dinner plate and outline of quilted swags to lightly mark scallops around outside edge. Do not cut yet.

4. See page 17 for instructions on making continuous bias binding. Make 12 yards of 2"-wide bias binding. Apply binding to quilt on marked lines, easing binding along curves and pivoting at corners.

5. Trim all layers to ¼" seam allowance. Fold binding to back and blindstitch in place.

Color Variations

These are some suggestions for other color schemes.

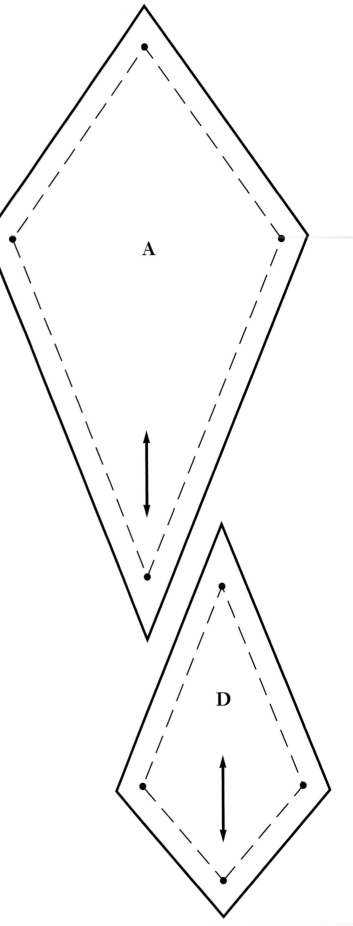

A

D

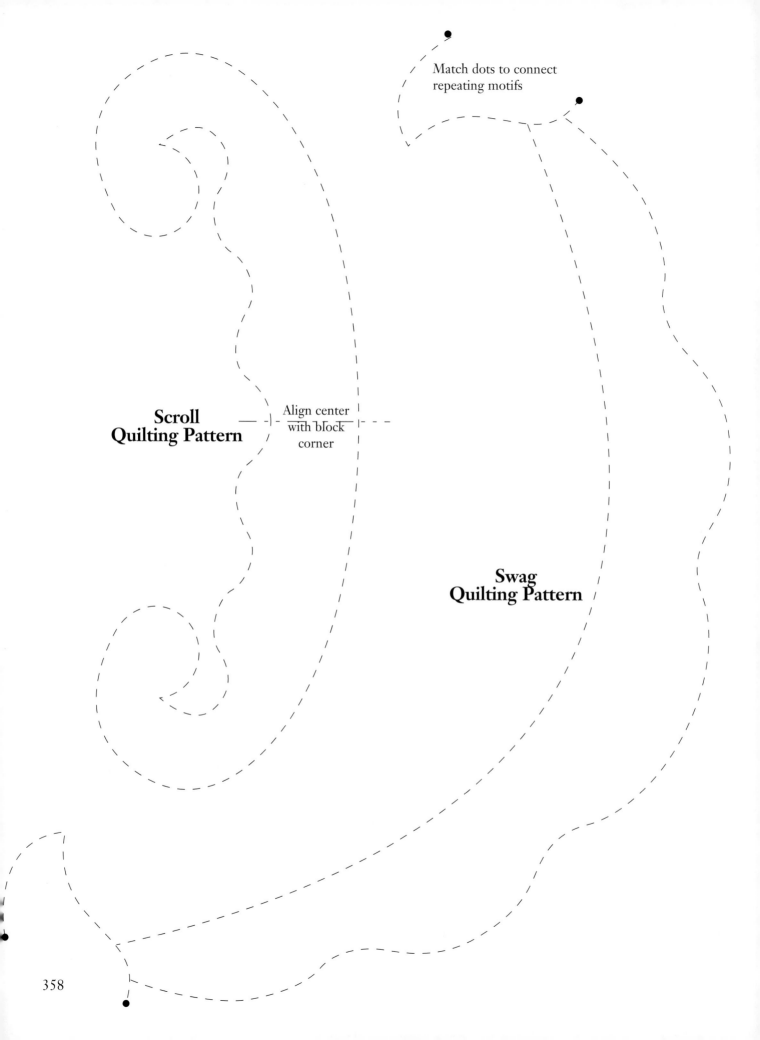

Match dots to connect
repeating motifs

**Scroll
Quilting Pattern**

Align center
with block
corner

**Swag
Quilting Pattern**

358

Wandering Star

Stars appear in more American quilts than any other design. Before the arrival of printed patterns, quilters made their own templates by folding squares of paper and then drawing diamonds on the fold lines. This challenging set, one of many eight-pointed star variations, requires numerous set-in seams.

Quilt by Ilse Perea
Greenville, South Carolina

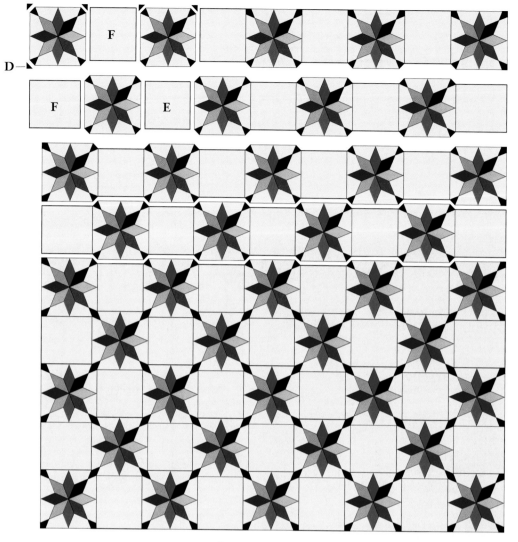

Setting Diagram

Finished Quilt Size
98" x 98"

Number of Blocks and Finished Size
41 blocks   10⅞" x 10⅞"

Fabric Requirements
Assorted prints   10 fat quarters*
Muslin or white   6¾ yards
Black print   1¼ yards**
Backing   3 yards 108" wide
* Fat quarter = 18" x 22".
** Includes 1 yard for binding.

Cutting
Make templates of patterns A, B, C, and D. (Template for D is optional, as it can be rotary cut.) Cut all strips cross-grain.

From print fat quarters
- 66 (2½" x 22") strips. From these, cut 328 of Template A.

From muslin
- 41 (3½"-wide) strips. From these, cut 164 of Template B and 164 of Template B reversed.
- 10 (9½"-wide) strips. From these, cut 24 (9½") E setting squares and 16 (9½" x 10½") F side rectangles.

From black print
- 19 (2⅝"-wide) strips. From these, cut 164 of Template C.
- 18 (1⅞") squares. Cut each square in half diagonally to get 36 D triangles. Or cut 36 of Template D.

Quilt Top Assembly
1. For each block, select 8 A diamonds. Join diamonds to make a star **(Block Assembly Diagram)**. Press seam allowances open.

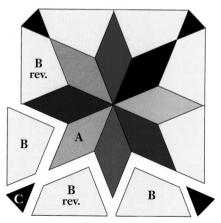

Block Assembly Diagram

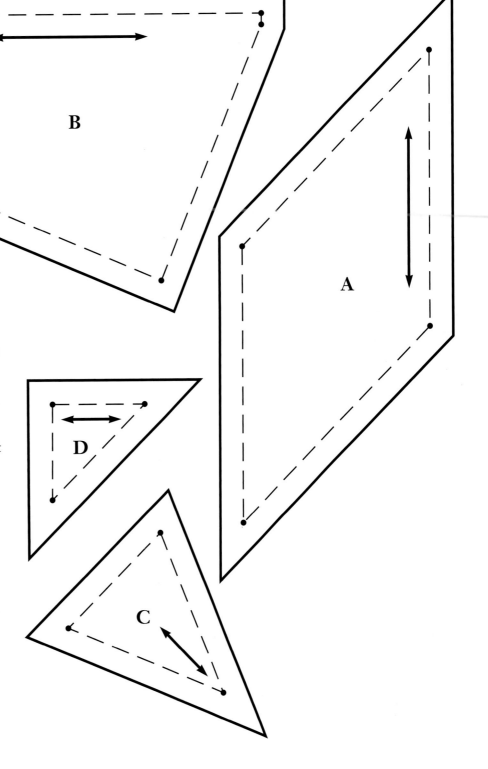

2. See page 10 for tips on sewing set-in seams. Set in 4 B reversed pieces as shown. Before adding 4 B pieces, sew a C triangle to short ends; then set in B/C units to complete block.

3. Make 41 star blocks.

4. Lay out blocks in 9 horizontal rows, alternating blocks and E setting squares as shown **(Setting Diagram)**. Use F setting squares at outside edges. Sew D triangles to blocks at outside edges as shown. When satisfied with placement, join blocks, setting squares, and side rectangles in each row. Press seam allowances toward setting squares and rectangles.

5. To join rows, stitch seams connecting blocks and setting square (or rectangle), being careful not to stitch into seam allowances. Then come back and stitch diagonal seams joining C triangles. Join all rows to complete quilt top.

Quilting and Finishing

1. Outline-quilt each block. Quilt shown also has a spider web design quilted in setting squares and side rectangles.

2. See pages 16 and 17 for instructions on making binding. Make 11⅛ yards of 2½"-wide bias or straight-grain binding from remaining black fabric. Apply binding to quilt edges.

Whig Rose

This quilt was made in 1865 by Barbara Middy Russell while she waited for the return of her husband, who served with the 51st Ohio Infantry during the Civil War. The sunny colors of the appliqué must have cheered Barbara's spirits during a troubled time. This is the only one of Barbara's quilts to have survived.

Quilt owned by David Sanders
Mobile, Alabama

Finished Quilt Size

81" x 81"

Number of Blocks and Finished Size

9 blocks   22" x 22"

Fabric Requirements

Muslin or white   5¾ yards*
Green   3¼ yards
Orange   2¼ yards
Pink print   1¼ yards
Binding fabric   1 yard
Backing   5 yards

* If muslin is a full 45" wide, it is possible to cut 2 (22½") squares from each width, in which case you'll need only 4½ yards.

Other Materials

⅜"-wide bias pressing bar

Cutting

Make templates of appliqué patterns A–F on pages 364 and 365. Cut all strips cross-grain except as noted.

From muslin
- 4 (4" x 90") lengthwise strips for outer borders.
- 9 (22½") squares.

From green
- 2 (13"-wide) strips for bias stems.
- 4 (2" x 80") lengthwise strips for borders.
- 36 of Template A.
- 144 of Template D.

From orange
- 4 (2" x 80") lengthwise strips for borders.
- 9 of Template C.
- 72 of Template E.

From pink print
- 2 (8½"-wide) strips. From these, cut 9 of Template B.
- 1 (4"-wide) strip. From this, cut 9 4" squares for block center.
- 2 (1¾"-wide) strips. From these and scraps from previous steps, cut 72 of Template F.
- 8 (1½"-wide) strips for borders.

Appliqué Placement Diagram

Quilt Top Assembly

1. On 1 corner of each 13"-wide green strip, measure and cut a 13" triangle (**Bias Cutting Diagram**). Discard triangles. Measuring from cut edge, cut 1"-wide bias strips. Cut 36 strips about 9"-long and 36 strips 4¼" long. (Use discarded triangles, if necessary, to cut enough short strips.)

2. Center bias pressing bar on wrong side of each bias strip. Press strip edges over pressing bar to get a folded strip about ⅜" wide.

3. Fold 1 muslin square in half vertically, horizontally, and diagonally and crease folds to make appliqué placement guidelines.

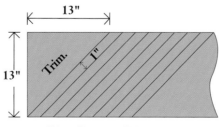

Bias Cutting Diagram

4. Pin a 4" pink square at center of muslin square.

5. Pin 4 A pieces in place, aligning center of each piece with horizontal and vertical placement lines and covering edges of center square (**Appliqué Placement Diagram**). Appliqué A pieces.

6. Pin B and C pieces in place as shown. Pin 4 (9"-long) stems in place on diagonal placement lines, tucking ends under B. Appliqué B and C.

7. Pin a short stem in place at right side of each long stem, hiding end under long stem. Pin E flowers at top of each stem. Pin 4 D leaves on each stem pair as shown. When satisfied with placement of pieces, appliqué stems, leaves, and flowers in place. Add Fs at center of each flower to complete block.

8. Make 9 blocks.

9. Lay out blocks in 3 horizontal rows, with 3 blocks in each row. Join blocks in each row. Join rows.

continued

10. Join 2 pink border strips end-to-end to make a border for each side of quilt.

11. Matching centers, join green, pink, orange, and muslin border strips to make a 4-strip border for each side of quilt. Matching centers of border with quilt edge, sew a border to each edge of quilt and miter corners. (See page 14 for tips on sewing mitered corners.)

Quilting and Finishing

1. Outline-quilt appliqué. Add more quilting as desired.

2. See pages 16 and 17 for instructions on making binding. Make 9⅜ yards of 2½"-wide bias or straight-grain binding. Apply binding to quilt edges.

Appliqué patterns are finished size. Add ¼" seam allowance for hand appliqué or cut as is for machine appliqué.

A

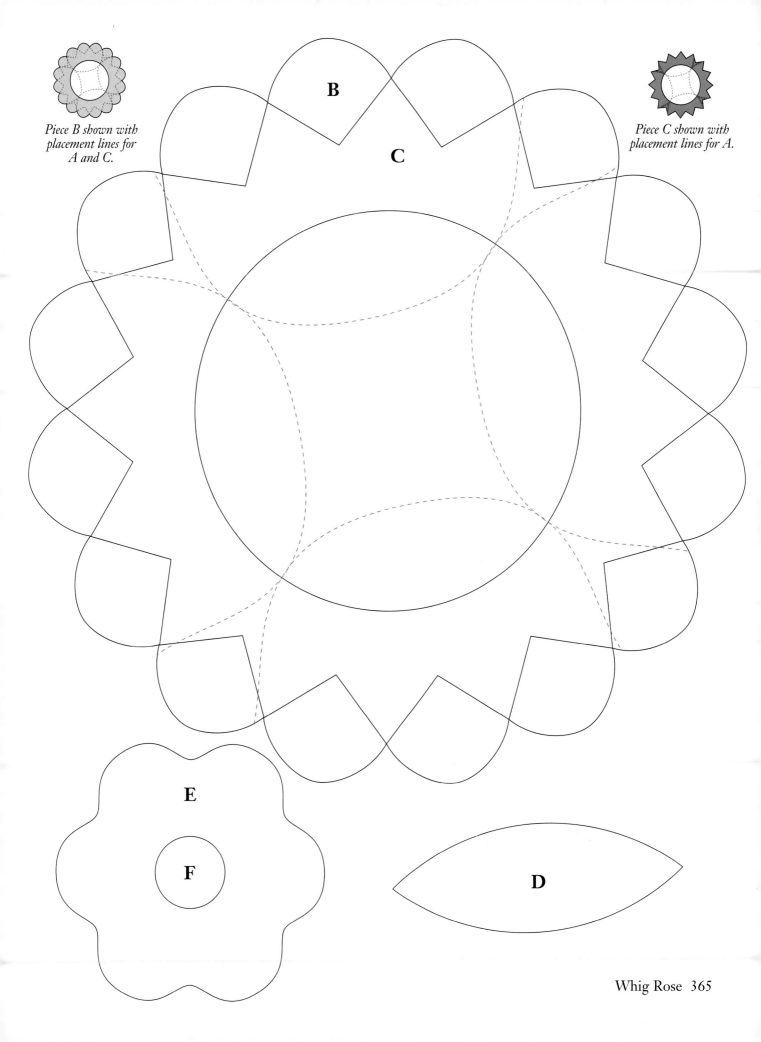

Piece B shown with placement lines for A and C.

B

C

Piece C shown with placement lines for A.

E

F

D

Whig Rose 365

Creative Quilt Labels

It is important to sign and date your quilt for posterity. Most antique quilts offer few clues about their origin, leaving empty pages where there could be history about women and family. A label on the back of a quilt gives future generations information about the quilt and its maker.

Incorporating a name or a date in the quilting is a time-honored method, as is embroidering these details on the quilt top or backing. A practical label is a piece of fabric, hemmed on all sides, on which you embroider or write the desired information. A label might include:

- the name of the quilt.
- the maker's name and place of residence.
- the recipient's name, if the quilt is a gift, and the occasion.
- the date on which the quilt was completed, and/or the date of presentation.
- instructions on how to wash and store the quilt.

In addition to the labels in this book, you can find design ideas in books, clip art, and on the internet. Of course, you can create your own original design so it coordinates with your quilt.

Materials

Use a light-colored fabric of prewashed 100% cotton and colorfast, fine-tipped markers such as Pigma Micron Permanent Pens. Pretest pens on a scrap before working on a label.

Scanning or Photocopying Labels

To duplicate printed labels, use photo transfer paper. This special paper is available for both ink-jet printers and color copiers, so be sure to get the type for the process you're using. Follow the directions on the package to reproduce a printed label.

Using Rubber Stamps

Stamping quilts, especially signature quilts, has been popular since the 1800s. To successfully stamp on fabric, the stamp design must be deeply etched into the rubber. Some stamps designed for paper stamping are not sufficiently etched and, as a result, make an unsatisfactory image.

Make sure the stamping ink is colorfast and fabric-safe, such as Fabrico™ ink. Practice stamping on scraps to determine how much ink you need and how much pressure to apply to get a good image. Let the ink dry before working with the label.

If desired, you can use colorfast markers to color in areas of the stamped design. If you use more than one color of pen, it's best to let each color dry before adding the next color.

Heat-set the completed label with a hot, dry iron on the back of the fabric.

Drawing or Tracing Labels by Hand

1. Cut a piece of freezer paper to the desired size of the label. Use a dark ink to trace the design on the nonwaxy side of the paper. (If design has letters or one-way motifs, reverse it and trace a mirror-image so it will appear correctly on completed label.)

2. Center the wax-coated side of the freezer paper on the wrong side of the label fabric. Press the paper in place.

3. Place the fabric on a light table so your drawing shows through the fabric. If you don't have a light table, tape the fabric to a brightly lit window.

4. Trace the design onto the fabric. If you're using more than one color of pen, it's best to let each color dry completely before adding the next color.

5. Once the label is traced, leave the freezer paper in place while you write in personal information. Remove freezer paper only when all ink is dry.

6. Turn under raw edges around the completed label. Stitch the label onto the back of quilt.

This quilt was made with love by

_____

for _____

Born _____

Height _____

Weight _____

Parents _____